RUCKS, MAULS & DIRTY BALLS

IRELAND'S JOURNEY TO THE TOP OF THE WORLD

BY JOHN D.T. WHITE

FOREWORD BY OLLIE CAMPBELL

PUBLISHED BY HERO BOOKS
LUCAN
CO. DUBLIN
IRELAND

First Published 2024
Copyright © John D.T. White 2024

Without limiting the rights under copyright reserved above,
no part of this publication may be reproduced, stored
in or introduced into a retrieval system, or transmitted
in any form or by any means (electronic, mechanical,
photocopying, recording or otherwise) without the prior
written permission of the publisher of this book.

A CIP record for this book is available from the British Library

DEDICATION

I am dedicating my book to my two sons, Marc and Paul.
I have loved you both from the moment you were born and I will never stop loving you.

Your Dad

CONTENTS

PREFACE	8
THOUGHTS FROM IRISH RUGBY LEGENDS	10
INTRODUCTION	13
FOREWORD	15

1940s

GRAND SLAM WINNERS FOR THE FIRST TIME	18
WHEN RUGBY WAS A FOREIGN SPORT	22
BLOODY FOUR FINGERS	29
JACK KYLE	35

1950s

NO MORE STANDING TO GOD SAVE THE QUEEN	43
THE FLANKER WHO BECAME A BATTER	46

1960s

MICK THE KICK – IRELAND'S ENGLISHMAN	61
IRELAND'S FIRST SUB	64
THE GREAT ESCAPE & TRUE GRIT	66

1970s

WILLIE JOHN MCBRIDE	73
MARLENE DIETRICH'S HAIRY LEGS	82

1980s

WHERE'S YOUR F*ING PRIDE?**	93
THE INAUGURAL RUGBY WORLD CUP	101
IRA BOMBS	103
THUNDERBIRDS ARE GO!	104
IRELAND'S WILLIE IS BIGGER THAN FRANCE'S CONDOM	107

CONTENTS

1990s

HEADLESS CHICKENS	110
RUGBY UNION'S PROFESSIONAL ERA	119
RUMPOLE OF THE BAILEY	124
THE IRISH OLYMPIAN WHO MADE RUGBY WORLD CUP HISTORY	125

2000s

LOOKING FOR A MARS BAR IN A BUCKET OF S**T	134
THE RED CARPET INCIDENT	155

2010s

KIDNEY FAILURE	170
A THIRD GRAND SLAM	192
2019 RUGBY WORLD CUP	194

2020s

THE BEST TEAM IN THE WORLD	197

THE HISTORY BOOKS: 1874-1947

THE BIRTH OF THE IRFU	227
COUNT DRACULA	231
WORLD WAR I HEROES	233
THE BRITISH AND IRISH LIONS	257

EPILOGUE	265
BIBLIOGRAPHY	268

Rucks, Mauls and Dirty Balls

ACKNOWLEDGEMENTS

I wish to say a 'Big Thanks' to Gerry and Geraldine McCollum from Bangor, County Down, who spent many hours reading and checking my work.
And, to Jo, for always being there.

John
August 2024

PREFACE

I grew up during *The Troubles* in the Short Strand, Belfast, Northern Ireland, a nationalist enclave in the heart of loyalist East Belfast. My mum was born and bred in the area, a Roman Catholic, and my dad came from the north of the city, a Protestant. I attended St Matthew's Primary School in my district and spent six years at Saint Augustine's Secondary School, Ravenhill Road, Belfast.

Football (soccer) was my sporting love and when I was growing up during my early years in the late 1960s and early 70s, and I knew exactly what I wanted to do in life. I was going to be the next George Best, my boyhood hero who played for Manchester United. Or so I thought. I underwent all of the preparation; my dad bought me a football that I kicked along the streets all of the way to St Matthew's (I lost count of how much my mum had to pay our neighbours for the many bottles of milk I knocked over and broke!), played football in the schoolyard at lunchtime, and practiced my dribbling skills and shooting after school against the wall of the factory at the end of my street, Harper Street. I went even further and had my mum cut out two large No.1's from a white bedsheet which she sewed on to the back of my red Manchester United shirt. Dad bought me a pair of white shorts and Mum knit me a pair of black socks with red and white stripes at the top of them. And, believe it or not, even though there was not a single garden in my area, or any type of field let alone a football pitch, my mum saved up enough money to buy me a pair of *Stylo* football boots, the same kind that Bestie wore. But I was nowhere as good as my fellow Belfast Boy and I blame it on the lifestyle I had at the time, particularly my diet. If Cookstown sausages were good enough for George and his family to eat then you can bet that I got mum to buy them and I ate a mountain of them!

I had never even heard of Mike Gibson or Willie John McBride until later in life. Rugby was a foreign sport to me as we played football, Gaelic football and hurling at school. Rugby was just an odd shaped ball that boys from the Protestant posh schools played. Indeed, the only prop I had heard off was the ones we used in our school plays, and as for a hooker, well I will leave that one to your own imagination.

I can still remember my first day at 'Big School' in early September 1974. St Augustine's was a few miles from my home and located in a Protestant area. I used to walk to St Matthew's, but going to 'Big School' meant a bus journey up the Ravenhill Road, the bottom of which was on the periphery of my area. My mates and I had heard awful stories about First Year pupils getting beaten up in kangaroo-style courts and having their head forced down a toilet bowl by older pupils who then pulled the chain to flush it (no fancy push buttons back then!) To avoid being on the receiving end of a beating, or getting my brand-new uniform soaking wet, presumably just with toilet water although my mind did wonder if the boys would provide some other form of soaking, I crawled through a hole in a wall located at the far end of the premises at St Augustine's. I found myself inside Ravenhill Rugby Ground. I had absolutely no idea that a team named Ulster played there, and the only Ulster I knew was the province which the Protestants held so sacrosanct as Proud Ulstermen. So, there I was gazing out at this luscious piece of grass surrounded by concrete stands, not knowing that just over a quarter of a century earlier, 13 March, 1948 to be precise, rugby union history was made when Ireland beat Wales 6-3 on the pitch which was before me to win the Grand Slam for the first time in their history.

So, there was myself and a few mates kicking a football about on the same pitch that The Boys of '48 had thrilled Irish fans up and down the country some 26 years before, until the groundsman chased us back through the hole in the wall.

However, I found rugby later in my life, although Manchester United still plays a big role in my life today. I can recall one event in 1973 that may have sparked my interest in rugby without me even realising it at the time, until I saw it again many years later in a documentary about Welsh rugby union stars. I saw a try being scored on our black and white television at home by a player wearing a black and white hooped shirt. I was transfixed at the beauty of the try and how the players weaved through the defence to score. It was of course Gareth Edwards' absolutely majestic try for the Barbarians against New Zealand at the Arms Park, Cardiff on 27 January, 1973. Seven men combined to create it - six Welshmen in Edwards, Phil Bennett, JPR Williams, John Dawes, Derek Quinnell and Tom David, plus one Englishman, hooker John Pullin. It was pure poetry in motion on a rugby pitch, totally mesmerising, with the Baa-Baas winning 23-21 in one of the greatest games of rugby ever seen. The closest thing I have seen to matching it on a football pitch was Diego Maradona's sublime goal for Argentina against England in the quarter-finals of the 1986 World Cup finals hosted by Mexico.

The game was 1-0 (the so called 'Hand of God' goal) to Argentina when Maradona collected a pass from a teammate in his own half of the pitch in the 55th minute. The diminutive genius dribbled past five England players and then rounded Peter Shilton in the England goal to slide the ball into the net with his left foot. His 11 touches of the ball in 11 seconds cemented his place as one of football's all-time greats. Argentina won the game 2-1 and went on to win the 1986 FIFA World Cup. I was a left-footer also, no surprise there as there was a popular joke in Belfast that Roman Catholics 'were all left-footers'. Well, I suppose I got that from my mum and, as I am right-handed, then that must be thanks to my dad, God Bless them both.

Fittingly, Edwards' try and Maradona's goal, both masterpieces in their own right, received the accolades they deserved being named as 'The Greatest Try of the 20th Century' and 'The Greatest Goal of the 20th Century'.

And so back to what this book is about, rugby union. Lansdowne Road may well be regarded by many as the ancestral home of Irish rugby but surely Ravenhill fully deserves to be known as its' spiritual home. It was where the 'Golden Age' of Irish rugby began with the Grand Slam winning team of 1948. As for me, Ravenhill was my home for six years (that hole in the wall was never filled in and the groundsman still chased us back through it every lunchtime) until I left St Augustine's in June 1980. And, who knows, if I had not tried to be like Georgie Best so much when I was a child and my dad had bought me a rugby ball instead of a football, I could have been the next Mike Gibson… the George Best of Irish Rugby, who was born 20 years before me. But wasn't Mike a right-footer? And maybe, just maybe, the groundsman may have let me and my mates play rugby at lunchtime.

John

THOUGHTS FROM IRISH RUGBY LEGENDS

'Ireland's journey to the 'Top of the World', being ranked the No.1 nation, has been a wonderful rugby odyssey which I am so very humbled and honoured to have been able to play a small part of. I loved playing for my country and I was also so very privileged to have been considered good enough to not only play for the British and Irish Lions, but to also captain the team on their 1974 Tour of South Africa. Halcyon days in 1974, when we returned to our homes in England, Scotland, Wales and Ireland as 'Invincibles'… undefeated, after our four magical performances in Test matches against the mighty Springboks. Games to remember. Days of our lives. And, so to John's book. Every now and then a wee treasure comes along and I have just found one in this book. Just glancing through it brings back so many wonderful memories for me personally… wearing the green jersey of my beloved country, and the historic red Lions' jersey… as I am sure it will for all of my former teammates.'

Willie John McBride
63 Ireland caps (1962-75)
17 caps for the British & Irish Lions

'I am sure that when John started writing this book he was hoping, like myself and all Ireland rugby fans, for a fairytale ending to it with Ireland winning the 2023 Rugby World Cup. Alas, we came up against a very good New Zealand side who ended our dreams of becoming World champions. Now, that would have been some ending to the book. However, what John has produced is the story of Irish rugby and how we became the No.1 ranked nation in the world.'

Willie Anderson
27 Ireland caps (1984-90)

'If you are looking for a 'Who? What? Where? When? Why?' book about the Ireland rugby team then here it is. What John has produced within the pages of this book has clearly been a labour of love. His research has been meticulous, the entries are informative and many of them tell stories I never knew before. What I like most about the book is that it is neither a history book nor a fact-book or a trivia book… indeed it is the Triple Crown of Ireland Rugby books as it encompasses all three.'

Ciaran Fitzgerald
25 Ireland caps (1979-86)
4 caps for the British and Irish Lions

'There are so many books available to fans of the Ireland rugby Uuion team, it is difficult to select one that will contain just about everything you would want to know. That was until now and John's book. Somehow, John, who has written two other rugby books, has managed to produce a book that not only covers the history of the national team, but also reveals many facts not too many fans will be aware of - including me - and has many interesting trivia entries. It is an incredible collection of work which has been put together magnificently. Once you open it, it is so hard to put it down.'

Michael Kiernan
43 Ireland caps (1982-91)
3 caps for the British and Irish Lions

'If you think you know all there is to know about the Ireland rugby team then it is time for you to think again. John's account of all things to do with Irish rugby is unequalled. His book is like entering Dr Who's Tardus, as he transports us on a journey packed full of highs, and often lows, as he weaves his way through the fabric of our history from its inception in 1879, to the Golden Boys of 1948, who claimed our first Grand Slam Championship title… and to our current team who held the distinction of being the No.1 ranked nation in the world. If you are a fan of Irish Rugby then you will love this book.'

Tony Ward
19 Ireland caps (1978-87)
1 cap for the British and Irish Lions

'Making your debut for Ireland is a memorable and emotional experience for any player. A moment to cherish. I was lucky to celebrate my first cap on the same day as Willie John won his 50th and led us out onto the Lansdowne Road pitch. Our opponents that day were England and it is remembered for the rapturous reception given to the English side who had honoured the fixture, unlike Scotland and Wales in the previous season. It was our opening game of the 1973 Five Nations Championship and we won 18-9. My experience was made all the more memorable by scoring a try in the first-half. John has captured the moment so wonderfully in his own unique writing style. For all sorts of reasons, my debut was very special and remains as vivid as ever to this day. Thanks for the memory, John, and recounting so many wonderful stories in this exceptional book which takes the reader on a history tour of Irish rugby like no book has done before.'

Richard Milliken
14 Ireland caps (1973-75)

'This is an eclectic journey through Irish rugby's history, delving into the game, its characters and this Island's history, which makes a fascinating and informative read. We are reminded of some of its great teams and players but are also provided with insights as to the character of the people involved. It illustrates well how rugby was able to manage the tensions at play over the years and deftly sidestep its way through, and by doing so maintain and build relationships while others were destroying them. As one Irish coach said to his players just before the match 'Spread out, but stick together!' Understanding gained from such as this book, equips us better to face the challenges of the future by recognising that teams of friends succeed, with an Irish-British identity that can accommodate all and build an ethos of interdependence that constantly strives to find ways diverse characters can work together constructively for the benefit of all. A great read and one you will constantly return to time and again. Thanks John.'

Trevor Ringland
34 Ireland caps (1981-88)
2 caps for the British and Irish Lions 1983

INTRODUCTION

Rugby is not a matter of life or death.

It is much more important than that.

Well, so one comedian thought when he told the following joke.

Rhys, a Welsh fan, was watching Wales play Ireland in a Six Nations Championship game at Lansdowne Road. In the packed stadium, there was only one empty seat and it was directly in front of him. Rhys tapped the man who was sitting beside the empty seat on the shoulder.

'Who does that seat belong to?' asked Rhys.

'I got the ticket for my wife,' replied the Irish fan.

'But why isn't she here?' asked Rhys.

'I'm afraid she died in an accident,' replied the Irish fan.

'So, you're keeping the seat vacant as a mark of respect,' said Rhys.

'No,' said the Irish fan, 'I offered it to all of my friends but none of them wanted it.'

'So why didn't they take it?' asked a puzzled Rhys.

'They've all gone to her funeral today,' replied the Irish fan.

This is a book about Ireland's Home Nations Championship wins, Five Nations Championship successes, Six Nations victories, four glorious Grand Slam wins and becoming the No.1 ranked rugby nation in the world, and all nicely mixed together with a few wooden spoons.

My book begins with the Boys of '48, Ireland's first Grand Slam-winning side which began a golden era for Irish rugby, and my international rugby odyssey ends with Ireland's participation at the 2023 Rugby World Cup. However, this is not to say that all that went before 1948 has been swept under the carpet and forgotten about. Nothing could be further from the truth. The history of Ireland's international rugby team is important to all Irish fans, indeed we are extremely proud of it, and so a chapter of the book takes us on a journey back in time when Ireland were a far cry from the winning machine they are today.

From the formation of the Irish Rugby Football Union in 1879 to a Wimbledon Lawn Tennis Champion and his family links to Count Dracula. A World champion high jumper to Irish Heroes of World War I. Historic Test series victories over Australia, South Africa and New Zealand to the dawning of the sport's professional era in 1995… and the making of Irish legends who toured with the British and Irish Lions. This book is a mixture of all things about Ireland's rugby union side.

Not every Irish player gets to answer Ireland's call. But the players who do always remember where they were when they first pulled on an Irish jersey and what they achieved wearing it. Ireland's historic four provinces have all provided us with many national heroes in a game that gets everyone talking. In the professional era Ireland have excelled, no more so than in 2023. Join me looking back at Ireland's rugby union journey, a long one which has seen them climb the Mount Everest of the sport to become the No.1 ranked team in the world. It has been a path tread for 144 years. A path which fans from generations of families all over Ireland, and those around the world born of Irish ancestry, have witnessed first-hand throughout the decades.

To paraphrase Al Pacino in the movie *Any Given Sunday*…

Life is like rugby... it is a game of inches.

In either game, life or rugby, the margin for error is small.

One half of a step too late or too early... and you don't quite make it. A half of a second, too slow, too fast... you don't quite catch it.

Either we heal as a team, or we're going to crumble... inch by inch, play by play, until we're finished.

The Ireland players fight for that inch.

They tear themselves and everyone else around them to pieces for that inch.

They claw with their fingernails for that inch... because they know that all of those inches are added up... that's going to make the f***ing difference between winning and losing... between living and dying.

I'll tell you this... in any fight, it's the guy who's willing to die, who's going to win that inch.

And every Irish player knows that if he is going to have any life anymore, it's because he is still willing to fight and die for that inch... because that's what playing for Ireland demands... the six inches in front of his face.

Now a coach can't make him do it...

He has to look at the teammate next to him, and look deep into his eyes.

What he will see is a teammate who is willing to go that inch with him.

He is going to see a teammate who is willing to sacrifice himself for the team... because he knows when it comes down to it... you're going to do the same for him.

That's a team, gentlemen.

And either the Irish players heal as a team or they will die as individuals.

That's rugby, guys... that's all it is.

Now, what are you going to do?'

I know what we, the Irish fans, are going to do so, because one thread runs seamlessly through us all and that is that we are prepared to stand shoulder to shoulder with one another, and when we are called upon... ***WE ARE READY TO ANSWER IRELAND'S CALL***.

John, an Ireland Fan

FOREWORD

Books are the quietest and most constant of friends, the most accessible and wisest of counsellors and the most patient of teachers.'
Charles W Eliot

Rucks, Mauls and Dirty Balls, Ireland's Journey to the Top of the World is very different to other Irish rugby books because of John's unique writing style. But this is not John's first book. Indeed, it is not even his first rugby book. An author of more than 50 books, mainly sport, makes John one of those unique authors who can be asked to write a book about a particular subject and then command it, making it his own with his creative style of writing. When it comes to writing sports books, John is the literary equal to a Decathlete, as he has penned titles covering Gaelic Football, Hurling, Formula 1, Six Nations Championship, Manchester United, Horse Racing, Golf, Tennis, Cricket and Darts.

So, it came as no surprise to me to discover that he has also written a book about the Rugby World Cup and the Olympic Games, but what did surprise me was that he could switch codes as it were and wrote *The RMS Titanic Miscellany* and even *The Only Fools and Horses Quiz Book* too! John has divided his book into chapters covering each decade from the 1940s to the 2020s but also delves deep into the history of Irish rugby in a separate chapter from the foundation of the Irish Rugby Football Union in 1879 up to Ireland's first golden age when we won the Grand Slam in Ravenhill in 1948, a game both my parents attended even though they didn't know each other at the time. Within each chapter John takes you on a 10-year journey and in each he recounts every Home/Five/Six Nations Championship campaign, Rugby World Cup participations since the inaugural tournament in 1987, players' debuts, coaches, captains and stories of many players - who, like me, are honoured to have had the privilege of pulling on the famous green jersey of Ireland - and includes Championship victories, Triple Crown successes, four truly memorable Grand Slams and one too many wooden spoons. There is even a chapter about Ireland's Lions.

Saturday 7 December 1963 was the defining day of my life. It was the day Ireland played Wilson Whinerary's All Blacks in Lansdowne Road… 'The oldest international rugby ground in the World' as my dad always reminded me. Thanks to him, a passionate rugby man, I was there for the first time. I was nine years of age and although Ireland lost 6-5, I was mesmerised by the whole occasion and have been hooked on rugby ever since. So, on a personal level, I was naturally delighted to discover that John had included that particular game in this book, and my whole life flashed before me while I read it, as I am sure yours will too as you weave your way through the living history in the pages ahead.

Rugby is like having an international passport and an international language. It should be fun and an adventure too, not all about winning, but how the game is played, and how it is remembered as well.

If you share this view, you have an enjoyable and enriching adventure in store as you relive Ireland's colourful, fascinating and wonderful rugby odyssey in the capable hands and mind of John White.

Work Hard. Play Hard. Love Rugby.

Ollie Campbell
Ireland 22 caps (1976-84)

1940s

GRAND SLAM WINNERS FOR THE FIRST TIME

THE BEGINNING OF A GOLDEN ERA FOR IRISH RUGBY

WHEN RUGBY WAS A FOREIGN SPORT

BLOODY FOUR FINGERS

JACK KYLE

'Alone we can do so little; together we can do so much.'
Helen Keller, Activist

GRAND SLAM WINNERS 1948

In 1948, Ireland were crowned Five Nations Grand Slam champions for the first time in the country's history in the tournament which began as the Home Nations Championship in 1883. It was the 19th edition of the tournament since France were admitted in 1910, and the 54th northern hemisphere Rugby Union Championship.

Ireland kicked off the 1948 tournament with a 13-6 win over France at Stade Olympique de Colombes on 1 January 1948. It was a fantastic New Year's Day for the Irish players in the French capital. Queen's scrum-half Ernest Strathdee, who was a Minister at Newtownbreda Presbyterian Church, Belfast, and was given the captaincy. Ireland's previous game had been a 16–3 defeat to Australia on 6 December 1947 at Lansdowne Road before 50,000 fans. Australia were on a 1947-48 Tour of Great Britain, Ireland, France and North America.

Next up for Ireland was a trip to Twickenham Stadium and they edged England out 11-10 on 14 February 1948. The captaincy had been passed to 21-year-old medical student Karl Mullen prior to the game, with Strathdee dropped. Two weeks later Ireland welcomed Scotland to Lansdowne Road and defeated their Celtic rivals 6-0. The victory meant Ireland had clinched the 1948 Five Nations Championship (their fifth title) with only Wales standing in their way of being crowned Grand Slam winners for the first time and Triple Crown winners for the third time. It was also the first time Ireland had won the championship at Lansdowne Road. On 13 March 1948, 33,000 fans poured into Ravenhill Stadium, although reports at the time suggested 100,000 fans would have been inside the ground had it been big enough to accommodate the demand for a match ticket. Ireland won the encounter 6-3. It was a historic day for the Irish team, and for the Irish fans, a feat they would not emulate again until 2009.

In the week Ireland were crowned Grand Slam champions, the first primate was blasted into space… Albert, the rhesus monkey in a jumpsuit. The term 'Grand Slam' had not yet been coined; an anonymous rugby correspondent working for *The Times* newspaper is credited with first using 'Grand Slam' when writing about England's Five Nations victories over France, Ireland, Scotland and Wales in 1957.

The Boys of '48 were captained by Karl Daniel Mullen. A jubilant captain summed up Ireland's Triple Crown and Grand Slam success: 'Ireland had not won a Triple Crown since the end of the last century and Wales had denied us on the final day on eight previous occasions'. Just 12 months earlier the Principality beat the Irish 6-0 in Swansea, making it six times in the last 12 Five Nations Championships that the Welsh had burst Ireland's balloon. Bleddyn Williams, the magnificent Welsh centre and captain said: 'I suppose it had become the norm. The Irish would turn up with all the talk about the Triple Crown. And they'd go away with this awful sense of anti-climax'. On this particular occasion the men in green did not let the men in red rain on their parade.

Mullen, aged 21, was one of five medical students in the squad who were studying at the College of Surgeons in Dublin. One sportswriter expertly summed up Mullen: *Mullen brought a tactician's mind and a motivator's heart to the role. Critically, there was also an inner confidence to trample over the nerves'*. After Ireland's historic achievement, Mullen, a future British Lions captain, said: 'The extraordinary thing was the feeling I had that we couldn't lose that day, that the guys we had were so good. I told them that if we played to our best, we would win'.

When the final whistle was blown there was pandemonium inside Ravenhill and loose head prop John 'Jack' Daly' had his green jersey ripped off his back as he was carried shoulder high off the pitch (according to some, upside-down). Rumour has it that his shirt was cut up into 100 pieces and auctioned off in Dublin. Daly, born in Cobh, Cork, was a telephone lineman working in London at the time of the game and during World War II he lugged wireless equipment across northern Italy. It has been claimed Daly spotted a girl wearing a piece of his shirt sewn into her jacket on a night out in Dublin and the two of them disappeared for a week, resulting in Daly losing his job.

It was Ireland's only Grand Slam win in the 20th Century, they had not won the Triple Crown since 1899 and it was only the second season after rugby union had resumed following the Second World War.

There were six Ulster men on their home pitch to clinch Ireland's first Grand Slam: Jack Kyle, Albert McConnell, Bill McKay, Des McKee, Jimmy Nelson and Ernie Strathdee.

In 1948, the movie, *The Snake Pit*, was popular with cinemagoers, whilst one of the most played songs on the radio was *I Can Dream, Can't I?* sung by The Andrews Sisters and Gordon Jenkins. Going into a scrum with the Irish pack in 1948, was like entering a snake-pit and at the end of the 1948 Five Nations Championship, all of Ireland's dreams came true when the country won the Grand Slam for the first time.

Ireland's 1948 team are known as the 'Golden Generation' and won two more Five Nations Championships, in 1949 (Triple Crown winners also) and 1951, but it would be 61 years before Ireland's second Grand Slam success.

1948 will forever be remembered as the year which defined Irish rugby.

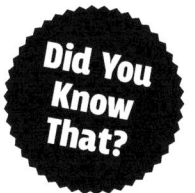

Stade Olympique de Colombes was built for the 1924 Olympic Games hosted by Paris. It was the main stadium used in the Summer Games. On 19 June 1938, the stadium was the venue for the FIFA World Cup final which saw Italy beat Hungary 4-2 in a thrilling final.

In His Own Words

'*This is it boys… boot, bollock and bite.*'
Ireland captain Karl Mullen giving his now legendary battle cry as Ireland lined-up to leave the dressing-room at Ravenhill on 13 March 1948. Ireland beat Wales 6-3 to claim their first ever Grand Slam.

THE HOME NATIONS CHAMPIONSHIP

The 1939 Home Nations Championship was the 52nd edition of the tournament (including those years when it was known as the Five Nations Championship). It was also the last edition of the tournament which did not feature France who had been expelled from participation after the 1931 Five Nations Championship following allegations over administrative deficiencies and professionalism by paying players.

No tournament was held from 1940-46. The 1947 tournament welcomed France back to the fold, making it the 18th Five Nations Championship. Wales were crowned champions despite losing their opening game 9-6 against England at the Arms Park, Cardiff. Ireland ended the campaign third in the table, losing 12-8 to France at Lansdowne Road, trouncing England 22-0 in Dublin, winning 3-0 versus Scotland at Murrayfield, and going down 6-0 to Wales in Cardiff.

In 1948, Ireland were the dominant force in northern hemisphere rugby and beat all before them to win the Five Nations Championship and the Grand Slam.

The following year, Ireland were denied successive Grand Slams losing only one game, their opener in the tournament resulting in a 16-9 defeat by France at Lansdowne Road.

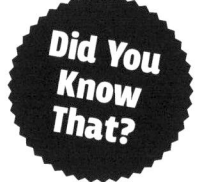

The 1939 Calcutta Cup match was the last international game before World War II. England defeated Scotland 9-6 at Murrayfield on 18 March 1939. Six players who took part in the game lost their lives during the war, while only seven would return to international rugby after the hostilities ended in 1945.

IRELAND'S THREE MUSKETEERS

In 1948, *The Three Musketeers* was a huge success in movie theatres in Ireland. It is an adventure film adaptation of the classic 1844 novel of the same name written by Alexandre Dumas. That same year, Ireland were crowned Grand Slam champions for the first time and the Irish side had their own Three Musketeers - the back row combination of Dolphin's James McCarthy, along with Old Belvedere's Des O'Brien and Queen's University's Bill McKay. The trio are among the finest in Irish rugby history.

 **Dolphin Rugby Football Club was founded in 1902 by members of Dolphin Swimming Club who wanted a new sport to participate in during the winter months. Michael Kiernan is the club's most capped international player with 43 appearances. Along with James McCarthy, Terry Kingston**

also played for Dolphin and captained Ireland. Kingston famously captained the Munster team that beat Australia (1991 Rugby World Cup winners) 13-6 at Thomond Park on 21 October 1992. Another, former player, Tomás O'Leary, was the scrum-half in Ireland's 2009 Grand Slam-winning side. James Coughlan is the club's all-time leading try scorer in the AIB League and Cup with 37. Declan Kidney, Ireland coach 2008-13, played for the club in the 1980s and early 90s.

In His Own Words

'Well, it would be close. However, half our team are over 80 and the other half are dead."
Jack Kyle, a Grand Slam winner with Ireland in 1948, after being asked how the team he played in would compare with the 2009 Grand Slam winning Ireland team captained by Brian O'Driscoll.

SPIRIT IN THE SKY

Ernest Strathdee was born on 26 May 1921 in Belfast. He attended Belfast High School and Queen's University where he won an Ulster Senior Cup medal in 1947. During his career he also played at scrum-half for Ulster, the Barbarians and Ireland. After impressing in two post-war unofficial victory internationals in 1946, he was handed his debut for Ireland on 8 February 1947 - Ireland defeated England 22-0 at Lansdowne Road in the 1947 Five Nations Championship. Strathdee was still at nuiversity at the time.

On 6 December 1947, he captained Ireland for the first time, a 16-3 loss to a touring Australia side. His second appearance as captain came in Ireland's opening game of the 1948 Five Nations Championship, a 13-6 victory against France in Paris. Surprisingly he was dropped for the games versus England (Ireland won 11-10) and Scotland (Ireland won 6-0) and lost the captaincy to hooker, Karl Mullen. However, he was recalled for Ireland's 6-3 win over Wales at Ravenhill which saw them claim the coveted Grand Slam for the first time. Ernie missed Ireland's opening game in the 1949 Five Nations Championship, a 16-9 loss to the French in Dublin but played in their wins over England (14-5), Scotland (13-3) and Wales (5-0) to help Ireland win successive Triple Crowns and Five Nations Championship titles. In total he was capped nine times for Ireland (won 7, lost 2) and was regarded as a very astute player who was a shrewd kicker from a scrum and a very accurate long-range passer. He played alongside the legendary Irish captain and fly-half, Jack Kyle at club, provincial and international level.

In tandem with his studies and rugby, Strathdee was a licensed Minister at Newtownbreda Presbyterian Church in Belfast. However, he left the Ministry without receiving ordination and took up a career as Belfast Health Education Officer and later had employment with a medical firm as a representative. But his passion was for sport and he got a job with Ulster Television as a sports commentator. On 17 July 1971, he was one of three persons who lost their lives in a fire that gutted the top floor of the Regency Hotel, Lower Crescent, Belfast.

Did You Know That? In 1971, whilst working for Ulster Television, Ernie Strathdee hosted a historic discussion on The Troubles in Northern Ireland which featured the leaders of the four main Churches in Northern Ireland.

WHEN RUGBY WAS A FOREIGN SPORT IN IRELAND

When Ireland won their first Grand Slam title in 1948, sport in Ireland was 'controlled' by the Gaelic Athletic Association (GAA). Rugby Union was the country's fourth most popular sport and lagged a long way behind Gaelic football, hurling and football (soccer), the latter very much considered to be a foreign sport invented by the English. Rule 27 of the GAA's Official Guide banned its' members from playing foreign sports which included football, cricket, hockey and of course, rugby, a sport considered to be an English private schoolboys' sport. Indeed, the country's ruling body for sport went a step further and also banned their members from watching any '*foreign sport*'.

Jack Lynch, generally considered by many to be one of the greatest dual Gaelic games players ever and who went on to become Taoiseach from 1977-79, was handed a ban by the GAA after a member of the GAA's Vigilance Committee reported him for watching his brother play in a provincial rugby final. During his time as President of Ireland, Douglas Hyde, then a patron of the GAA, attended a soccer match involving Ireland and Poland at Dalymount Park on 13 November 1938 and was removed from his patron's role. Éamon de Valera was also at the game in his role as Taoiseach and was a big fan of rugby. However, he decided not to attend any rugby matches after 1913 as a direct result of the GAA's intolerant attitude toward '*foreign games*'. Ireland won the game 3-2.

These foreign sports were also referred to by the GAA as '*Garrison Games*' in reference to Ireland being subjected to British Rule up until the country's independence.

The GAA (*Cumann Lúthchleas Gael*) was founded on 1 November 1884 in Thurles, Tipperary, as an Irish international amateur sporting and cultural association. The organisation's raison d'être was to promote indigenous Gaelic games and Irish pastimes, which included the traditional Irish sports of camogie, Gaelic football, handball, hurling and rounders. The association was also a big promoter and advocate of Irish dance and Irish music and the Irish language.

Rule 4 of the GAA's Official Guide states:

'*The Association shall actively support the Irish Language, Traditional Irish Dancing, Music, Song, and other aspects Of Irish Culture. It shall foster an awareness and love of the national ideals in the people of Ireland, and assist in promoting a community spirit through its clubs.*'

Since its' formation in the Billiard Room of Hayes' Hotel, when a group of Irishmen met to formulate a plan to establish an organisation to preserve and promote the athletic pastimes and games of Ireland, the GAA has been linked with Irish nationalism.

Rule 42 of the GAA's Official Guide states that GAA property may only be used for the purpose or in connection with the playing of games controlled by the association. Sports not considered *'in conflict'* with the GAA have been permitted. On 16 April 2005 the GAA's Congress voted to temporarily relax Rule 42 and allow international soccer and rugby to be played in Croke Park while Lansdowne Road was closed for redevelopment.

BROTHERS IN ARMS

Kevin Patrick O'Flanagan (10 June 1919-26 May 2006) was an Irish sportsman, physician and sports administrator. He was an outstanding sportsman: an excellent sprinter (Irish sprint champion at 60 and 100 yards) and the country's No.1 long jumper, who played for Dublin's minor team as a GAA footballer. He missed out on representing Ireland at the Olympic Games because of the suspension during World War II. In his spare time he enjoyed playing golf.

On 26 January 1946, he played in Ireland's 4-3 loss to France at Lansdowne Road in a rugby union friendly and a week later he played football for a Football Association of Ireland XI against Scotland. Between 1942-47 he played rugby for Ireland on three occasions (he never scored any points) and he played football for Bohemians (1936-45), Arsenal (1945-47) and Brentford (1949-50), as well as representing the Irish Football Association and the League of Ireland. O'Flanagan played rugby for University College Dublin, Lansdowne, London-Irish and Leinster.

When O'Flanagan began his international football career in 1937 there were two Ireland teams, which were selected by two different associations, the Irish Football Association (IFA) in Northern Ireland and the Football Association of Ireland (FAI) in the Republic of Ireland. Anyone born in either country could play for both international teams. He won 10 caps and scored three goals for the Republic of Ireland, including a goal in 3-3 draw versus Norway in a qualifying game for the 1938 FIFA World Cup finals, and two goals in a 2-2 draw away to Hungary on 18 May 1939. He also played twice for Northern Ireland and represented a League of Ireland XI side on two occasions without scoring.

His younger brother, Mick (29 September 1922–13 September 2015) was also a notable sportsman and represented Ireland at rugby union and football. On 30 September 1946 both brothers played together for the FAI XI versus England.

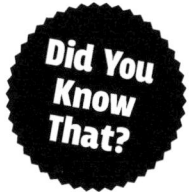

Billiards is an English sport which was invented in 1800, some 84 years before the GAA was formed in a Billiards Room in Thurles.

In His Own Words

'In our day, we were trying to avoid the opposition. Nowadays, they're deliberately running into people. It's a much tougher game... you need to be able to take the knocks.'
Jack Kyle, 1948 Grand Slam winner

Mick played football for Bohemians from 1939-49 and was the League of Ireland's top goal-scorer in season 1940-41 with 19 goals (he scored a total of 31 goals in 31 games that season). He was capped by the Republic of Ireland football team once, playing in the same international as Kevin, a 1-0 loss to England at Dalymount Park, Dublin on 30 September 1946.

On the day of the game, which kicked off at 5.30pm, Mick was working in his pub at 88 Marlborough Street, Dublin when he received a telephone call at 2.30pm from one of the selectors of the Republic of Ireland team who asked him to play in place of the injured Davy Walsh. Mick later recalled the moment: '*I went home to Terenure for a bite to eat, had a short rest and then headed off to Dalymount. It was not really sufficient notice as, only the previous evening, I had brought a party of English journalists to Templeogue Tennis Club and I hadn't got home until nearly two in the morning*'. Today the pub is known as The Confession Box, because of its' proximity to St Mary's Church which is located on Marlborough Street in the city centre.

Mick began playing rugby in 1947 when he joined Lansdowne and a year later, 26 February 1948, he played for Ireland in the Five Nations Championship, a 6-0 win over Scotland at Lansdowne Road. The win helped Ireland win the Triple Crown, the Grand Slam and the 1948 Five Nations Championship. It was the only cap he won. During the summer of 1949, Mick guested for Belfast Celtic on their tour of North America.

A third brother, Charlie, also played for Bohemians.

THE IDES OF MARCH

When Ireland beat Wales 6-3 at Ravenhill on 13 March 1948, to claim the Grand Slam for the first time, a book written by Thornton Wilder, an American author, was about to top the list of best-selling books (non-fiction) of 1948 by *The New York Times* newspaper. The novel was entitled *The Ides of March*, a fantasia on certain events and persons of the last days of the Roman Republic. There was no fantasia about Ireland's historic triumph and whilst the famous American tabloid never reported Ireland's achievement, the world of rugby soon knew their name.

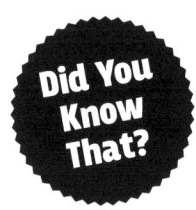

Did You Know That?

Kevin Patrick O'Flanagan was a member of the International Olympic Committee (IOC) from 1976-94, and when he died in 2006 aged 86, the IOC made him an Honorary Lifetime Member.

In His Own Words

'None of us had a motor car... we either walked or cycled. It gave us a natural fitness.'
Des O'Brien, No. 8 in the 1948 Grand Slam winning team

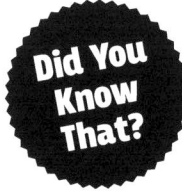

Did You Know That?

At the 1948 Academy Awards ceremony, held on 20 March 1948, a week after Ireland's triumph, the Oscar for Best Picture went to the movie Gentleman's Agreement.

A RECORD TALLY OF INDIVIDUAL POINTS

When Ireland won the 1949 Five Nations Championship, George Norton scored 26 of his country's total of 41 points, a record for an Irish player in the history of a single tournament. Dickie Lloyd scored 25 points for Ireland in the 1913 Five Nations Championship. Norton played in all four Five Nations Championship matches in 1950 and scored a further 15 points. In 1950, he toured Australia and New Zealand with the British Lions but his tour ended early after he broke an arm playing for The Lions against Southland, New Zealand in their fifth match. The following year, 1951, he was once again Ireland's full-back and helped the side to lift their third Five Nations Championship title in four years. Norton was capped 11 times at full-back between 1949 and 1951 and scored 41 points. He would have won a greater number of caps had an injury not resulted in a premature end to a career.

> 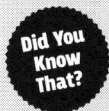 In 1973, Barry McGann scored 28 points in four appearances for Ireland, including six points in Ireland's 10-10 draw with New Zealand at Lansdowne Road on 20 January 1973.

SWITCHING CODES DURING THE WAR

Prior to World War II, Rugby Union players were not permitted to play in a Rugby League game without losing their Union membership and given a lifetime ban. The same rule applied to Rugby League players who played in a Rugby Union match. However, during the war, 1939-45, the armed forces were exempt and players could switch codes without any punishment being handed down to them.

> On 23 January 1943 and 24 April 1944, opposing teams made up of Rugby League and Rugby Union players played against each other twice under Rugby Union rules. The first match was played at Headingley, Leeds, between a Northern Command Rugby Union XV and a Northern Command Rugby League XV. The second game took place at Odsal Stadium, Bradford, when the Combined Services Rugby Union XV met the Combined Services Rugby League XV. Both matches were won by the teams of Rugby League players (18-11 and 15-10 respectively) which, despite the inclusion of a handful of former Welsh Rugby Union internationals, were mostly made up of players who had little or no experience of Rugby Union's 15 players a side game.

In His Own Words

'Ireland changing rooms are pretty eclectic places and priests are very much part of everyday life in Ireland. They certainly didn't tone the language down on my account.'

Thomas Gavin, the only Priest to play for Ireland, recalling the two international caps he won for his country in the 1949 Five Nations Championship, stating that his teammates were unfazed by his Roman collar.

MIGHTY QUINN

Kevin Joseph Quinn was born on 14 March 1923 in Gort, Galway. He attended Belvedere College in Dublin and went on to study medicine at the Royal College of Surgeons, Dublin. Whilst studying medicine he played rugby for Old Belvedere. He was capped five times by Ireland, making his debut on 25 January 1947 in a 12-8 loss to France at Lansdowne Road in the 1947 Five Nations Championship. On 6 December 1947, he played against Australia when The Wallabies were touring Great Britain, Ireland, France and North America. Australia won the game 16-3 at Lansdowne Road. In the 1953 Five Nations Championship he represented Ireland three times versus France (won 16-3 in Belfast), England (drew 9-9 in Dublin) and Scotland, his last appearance, in a memorable 26-8 victory at Murrayfield.

Quinn was also known for his cricket ability and in 1957 he made his debut in first class cricket for Ireland versus Scotland at College Park, Dublin. He made two further First-Class appearances for Ireland, in 1958 against Scotland at Alloway, Ayr, Sotland and a game against Leicestershire County Cricket Club during Ireland's 1959 Cricket Tour of England. In total, he scored 43 first class runs, with a highest innings of 25.

PIRATE WHO SWITCHED RUGBY CODES

John 'Jack' Christopher Daly was born in Cobh, Cork on 12 December 1917. He played his club rugby for Cobh Pirates RFC, Cork Institution and London Irish. Daly also played for Munster, The Barbarians and Ireland. He won sevcen caps for Ireland: in 1947 against France, England, Scotland and Wales, and in 1948 against England, Scotland and Wales. During World War II, he served as a signaller with the London Irish Rifles in North Africa

Did You Know That?

Two of Kevin Quinn's brothers, Frank and Gerry, both played cricket for Ireland. Gerry also played international rugby union for Ireland, making two appearances for his country in the 1946 Victory International matches. Gerry died aged 51 on 20 November 1968, while playing tennis in Dublin with Michael Dargan and Karl Mullen.

and Italy and fought in the Battle of Monte Cassino to help the Allies break through the German's and Italian's 'Winter Line' to facilitate a march on Rome. The battle comprised four different military assaults from 17 January 1944 to 18 May 1944.

After he was transferred to Huddersfield, England in 1948, he switched rugby codes and played Rugby League. Daly played for Huddersfield from 1948-51 and was then transferred to Featherstone Rovers. He also played for Other Nationalities, a team which was made up of Rugby League players from Ireland, Scotland and the southern hemisphere, against France twice in 1950, versus England and Wales in 1951, in 1952 against England and France and versus Wales in 1953. In 1949, he represented the British Empire XIII Rugby League side that played France.

In His Own Words

'Jack Kyle is to Irish rugby what Pele was and continues still to be to football in Brazil.'
Tony Ward, 19 caps for Ireland

IRELAND'S INSURANCE MAN

Colm Patrick Callan was born on 6 January 1923 in Port, County Louth and was educated at Castleknock College, Dublin. He was a member of the Ireland team that won the Grand Slam in 1948 and retained the Five Nations Championship the following year, including the Triple Crown. An insurance man by profession, he played as a second row for Lansdowne Football Club. He won 10 caps for Ireland, making his debut on 25 January 1947, in a 12-8 loss against France at Lansdowne Road in the 1947 Five Nations Championship. His last appearance in the green shirt came on 12 February 1949, against England, a 14–5 victory, also played in Dublin. However, before rugby was restored after the Second World War, he played for Ireland against France, England, Scotland and Wales in the unofficial internationals of 1946.

> **Did You Know That?**
> When Jack Daly ran onto the pitch, he performed a double somersault, unless it was an international match for Ireland when he did a double back-somersault to show the opposition just how fit he was. On 25 March 2004, he was inducted into Rugby League Ireland's inaugural Hall of Fame.

> **Did You Know That?**
> When he made his debut for Ireland, Colm Callan was one of 14 new caps in the game which included his future Grand Slam winning teammate, Jack Kyle.

A GOLDEN BAND OF BROTHERS

Ireland's 1948 Grand Slam winning side were more than just a team, they were a unique Band of Brothers who were friends off the pitch as well as on it. They enjoyed each other's company. When the squad was in Belfast, they would all call round to the home of Jack Kyle's parents. In Dublin, Karl Mullen played host to his teammates in the Dundrum area of the city and if the squad were training in Cork, then it was over to Jim McCarthy's place. Matches at Thomond Park were preceded with a night's entertainment at the home of Tom Clifford who lived close to the ground. Recalling that wonderful golden era of Irish Rugby, Karl Mullen once remarked: *'That was the greatest thing we had. The closeness and friendship. I think today's team have it as well'*.

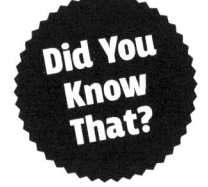

Prior to Ireland's trip to play England at Twickenham Stadium in the 1948 Five Nations Championship, the Irish Rugby Football Union (IRFU) decided to replace Ernest Strathdee as team captain and hand it to a 21-year-old medical student, Karl Mullen. Upon his elevation to the captaincy, Mullen received a curt letter from the IRFU about the upcoming Test match versus England, which read: 'Please bring your own shorts and socks and ensure they are well laundered.'.

 When the team were at Karl Mullen's home, his wife, Doreen, would sing the songs of the day.

IRELAND'S SCARLET PIMPERNEL

Jack Kyle has been likened to *The Scarlet Pimpernel* and the following quote describing him, is paraphrased from *The Scarlet Pimpernel* which was the first novel in a series of historical fiction written by Baroness Orczy and first published in 1905.

They seek him here, they seek him there,
Those Frenchies seek him everywhere,
That paragon of pace and guile,
The damned elusive Jackie Kyle.

PULLING PINTS OFF THE PITCH

Des O'Brien, Ireland's No.8 in their 1948 Grand Slam winning team, worked full-time for Guinness and later became a dedicated piano tuner before obtaining a Master's in Architectural History.

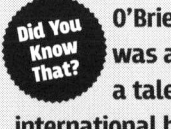 O'Brien was also a talented international hockey and squash player.

BLOODY FOUR FINGERS

When Ireland prepared to face Wales at Ravenhill on 13 March 1948, they did not have a coach to advise them how to handle the biggest game of their lives. A victory on home soil would see Ireland crowned Triple Crown winners, Five Nations Champions and Grand Slam winners. Ireland had never won a Grand Slam before so the pressure on their captain, Karl Mullen, a medical student aged 21, was enormous. Indeed, the squad had only met up on the previous day for lunch. But Mullen was a master tactician and probably the reason why the IRFU appointed him captain. Speaking many years after Ireland beat Wales 6-3 that day to win their first Grand Slam, Mullen said that he based his strategy for the game on the advice he was given by a Jesuit priest who taught him at Belvedere School. Father John Mary O'Connor, nicknamed *Bloody Four Fingers* (he lost a finger in an accident), used coins on a table to highlight plays in a game with each coin representing a player.

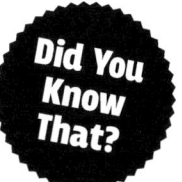

It has often been said that Mullen, who was a gynaecologist, delivered enough babies in his career to fill Ravenhill that day when 32,000 fans celebrated Ireland's inaugural Grand Slam victory.

HOMECOMING

When Ireland won their first Grand Slam in 1948, the movie *Homecoming* was a popular one to see in the local cinema ohuses all over Ireland.

 **Homecoming was devised by writer Sidney Kingsley as a story in 1944, called The Homecoming of Ulysses.**

In His Own Words

'When we got to Paris somebody gave me a little note asking if we wanted to go to the Folies Bergeres. Of course, we went. We stayed there till the wee hours.'
Jack Kyle recalling arriving in Paris with his Ireland teammates before they played France in the opening game of the 1948 Five Nations Championship

LAST MAN STANDING

When Ireland faced France at Lansdowne Road on 25 January 1947 the Ireland team had 14 debutants in their side. France won the opening game of the 1947 Five Nations Championship 12-8. It was Ireland's first competitive game since the outbreak of World War II on 1 September 1939, and the only surviving pre-war international was Cornelius Joseph 'Con' Murphy. Not surprisingly, Murphy was made captain for the game having already made his debut in the green of Ireland on 11 February 1939, a 5-0 victory versus England at Twickenham Stadium in the 1939 Home Nations Championship. France had been expelled from the tournament in 1931 and permitted back in again in 1947.

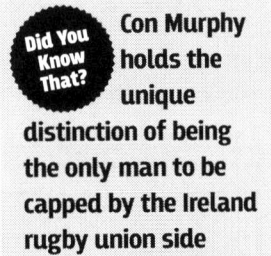

Did You Know That? Con Murphy holds the unique distinction of being the only man to be capped by the Ireland rugby union side before and after the Second World War.

Ireland's 14 new players were: Robert Agar, Colm Callan, Ray Carroll, John Daly, John Harper, Donal Hingerty, Ernie Keeffe, Jack Kyle, William McKay, Barney Mullan, Karl Mullen, Matthew Neely, Brendan Quinn and Kevin Quinn.

Ireland won two of their games but the following year, they were crowned Grand Slam winners for the first time. Con Murphy was not part of the all-conquering side having played his fifth and last game for his country on 8 February 1947, a 22-0 victory over England at Lansdowne Road.

IRELAND'S COUNCIL OF WAR

It has been reported that when Ireland played Wales at Ravenhill on 13 March 1948, Karl Mullen, the Ireland captain, conducted a *Council of War* in the Home dressing-room during the half-time break. Wales came to Belfast with only one thing on their minds, to prevent Ireland from winning the coveted Grand Slam for the first time in their history. The Welsh had denied Ireland the Championship and/or Triple Crown on multiple occasions in the past and at Ravenhill they were not just going to let the home side roll all over them and then go and celebrate a clean sweep of victories over all four nations having already beaten France 13-6 in Paris, England 11-10 at Twickenham Stadium and Scotland 6-0 at Lansdowne Road. Mullen stood in the centre of the changing room and addressed his troops, fixated on his every word.

Did You Know That? Ireland's 6-3 victory over Wales meant that they won the Triple Crown for the first time in 50 years.

He asked his players to listen to the sound they could hear echoing from the stands to their dressing-room. The Irish fans, all 32,000 of them, were hysterical. They had come to see their heroes, they had come to see a game of rugby, but they had also come to be a part of Irish Rugby Union history. Ireland won the match 6-3 and history makers were born.

'HE ASKED HIS PLAYERS TO LISTEN TO THE SOUND THEY COULD HEAR ECHOING FROM THE STANDS TO THEIR DRESSING-ROOM. THE IRISH FANS, ALL 32,000 OF THEM, WERE HYSTERICAL. THEY HAD COME TO SEE THEIR HEROES, THEY HAD COME TO SEE A GAME OF RUGBY, BUT THEY HAD ALSO COME TO BE A PART OF IRISH RUGBY UNION HISTORY. IRELAND WON THE MATCH 6-3 AND HISTORY MAKERS WERE BORN.'

In His Own Words

On 4 February 1967, Dr Karl Mullen was interviewed by Jimmy Magee for RTE Sport and their programme entitled *Where Are They Now?*

'*Much has been written, and read and heard about the 1948 and 1949 teams that won the Triple Crown. I wonder how much of it is this case of age-lending enchantment? Were they really that good of a team?*'

Jimmy Magee, RTE

'*Well, I am sure, as you say, age does lend enchantment, but the great thing about the sides then was that they were winners. And as you know, in any sport, golf or Gaelic football or rugby, that most of the winning is in the mind and this side felt they were capable of going out to win. As a team we were together for four years and we won a total of 14 out of 16 matches. So, I feel that we were a great winning team.*'

Karl Mullen, Ireland's captain when they won the Grand Slam in 1948 and Triple Crown in 1949

IRELAND'S ONLY CAPPED PRIEST

Thomas Joseph Gavin was born on 28 March 1922, in Coventry, England. On 29 January 1949, he won the first of his two international caps at centre for Ireland in their 16-9 loss to France in the 1949 Five Nations Championship at Lansdowne Road. His debut meant that he was the only Priest to have played international rugby after being ordained. However, it was not the start the Irish wanted in defence of their Five Nations Championship title, Grand Slam winners in 1948. But Gavin impressed the Ireland selection committee and retained his place in the side for the visit of England to Dublin on 12 February 1949. On this occasion, Ireland won 14-5 and went on to retain the Five Nations Championship and Triple Crown but Gavin never wore the green of Ireland again. 'My fly-half in my two tests, Jack Kyle, was an absolute rugby genius, a star in any era. He was worth the admission price alone.'

Some of his fellow clerics had misgivings as to whether playing international rugby was compatible with being a Priest, but Gavin had an admirer of his rugby skills with Cardinal Bernard Griffin, the Archbishop of Westminster giving the 26-year-old Irish centre

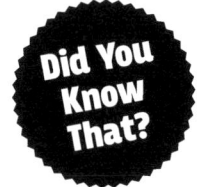

In 1998, Thomas Joseph Gavin and his Irish teammates were reunited for a celebration of the 50th anniversary of their 1949 Triple Crown triumph.

his unequivocal support. He studied for the Priesthood at St Mary's College, Oscott, Sutton Coldfield, West Midlands and was ordained in 1946. He then read classics at Christ's College, Cambridge, graduating in 1949. He taught for a year at Ampleforth College, North Yorkshire, England where he met the future Cardinal Basil Hume, who became a lifelong friend. Gavin loved his rugby and played for Moseley Rugby Football Club in Birmingham and for London Irish. Monsignor Tom Gavin served as the Parish Priest of St Thomas More, Coventry from 1978-2004, and organised the open-air Mass of Pope John Paul II at Baginton Airfield, Coventry on Pentecost Sunday, 30 May 1982, which was attended by 350,000 pilgrims.

BACK-TO-BACK CHAMPIONS

When Ireland won back-to-back Five Nations Championship titles in 1948 and 1949, it was the only the fifth time in history a team had successfully defended its' crown. England were the first nation to do it winning the Home Nations Championship in 1883 and 1884, then Wales did it in 1908 and 1909 followed by England in 1913 & 1914 and again by England in 1923 & 1924 (Five Nations Championship).

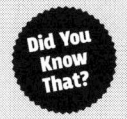

> **Did You Know That?** The 1883 Home Nations Championship was the inaugural tournament between the home four nations at the time – England, Ireland, Scotland and Wales.

In His Own Words

'When you have tried too hard for something and finally you get it, the immediate after-effect is one of anti-climax. Afterwards, of course, it sank in and was really marvellous.'
James McCarthy speaking about winning the Grand Slam with Ireland in 1948

THE FORGOTTEN 12 IRELAND CAPS

From Ireland's inaugural international game in 1875 to 1986, more than 111 years of international Home Nations Championship games, Five Nations Championship games and Tours by the national side, the IRFU adopted a policy of only awarding caps to players who made appearances in Test matches against the established *original* international rugby nations of Australia, England, France, New Zealand, Scotland, South Africa and Wales, meaning many played for Ireland without actually winning caps. One of those players was Brian O'Driscoll's father, Frank, who played two Test matches for Ireland in 1970 against Argentina, but without winning a cap for either match.

In June 2014, Brian took to social media to express his feelings about Ireland's uncapped heroes and with hundreds of thousands of Irish fans supporting his call to honour these players, his father included. At the time Brian said: 'Congrats to all the new caps on tour. In 1970, Ireland toured Argentina with one Frank O'Driscoll. 2 Tests, no cap. IRFU need to put it right'. Nine years later, the IRFU buckled under the pressure and in April 2023, they issued a statement to announce that they would be awarding international Test caps to 12 players

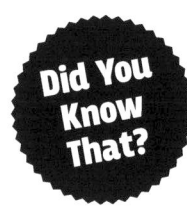

Did You Know That?

The Ireland Tour party to New Zealand in 1970 was:
Backs: Barry Bresnihan (London Irish), William Brown (Malone), Alan Duggan (Lansdowne), Tom Grace (University College Dublin), Liam Hall (Garryowen), Tom Kiernan, Captain (Cork Constitution), Barry McGann (Cork Constitution), John Moloney (St Mary's College), Henry Murphy (University College Dublin), Barry O'Driscoll (Manchester), Frank O'Driscoll (University College Dublin)
Forwards: John Birch (Ballymena), James Buckley (Sunday's Well), Padraig Cassidy (Corinthians), Mick Hipwell (Terenure College), Ronnie Lamont (Instonians), Sean Lynch (St Mary's College), Willie John McBride (Ballymena), Paddy Madigan (Old Belvedere), Syd Millar (Ballymena), Mick Molloy (London Irish), Terry Moore (Highfield), Phil O'Callaghan (Dolphin)

who had previously gone unrecognised in the famous Irish green jersey which they all wore with pride for their country. Including one Frank O'Driscoll.

Brian could not hide his delight and took to Twitter: *9 years on from this request & 53 from the Test debut itself Frank O'Driscoll is finally getting his Test cap awarded to him. It means a hell of a lot to him. Thank you IRFU for getting there.*

Ireland toured Argentina in August 1952, playing two non-capped games at the Gymnastics and Fencing Arena in Buenos Aries, drawing 3-3 in the First Test before winning 6-0 in the Second Test. In 1970, Ireland returned to Argentina, losing both non-capped matches at the Ferro Carril Oeste, 8-3, then 6-3, when Frank O'Driscoll lined out at centre alongside the British and Irish Lions representative, Barry Bresnihan. Incidentally, Argentina's first visit to Ireland (Lansdowne Road) came in November 1973 but, again, it wasn't recognised by the IRFU as a full international. Captained by the talismanic, Willie John McBride, Ireland won 21-8.

The 12 players were honoured and presented with their caps in a pre-match ceremony at Ireland's World Cup warm-up game versus against England at the Aviva Stadium on 19 August 2023. Added to the list of Irish international players was international No.1,149 Frank O'Driscoll, 53 years after he made his first appearance for Ireland and 24 years after his son first pulled on the green jersey for Ireland, versus Australia on 12 June 1999.

The 12 players who received their long overdue Test cap and recognition from the IRFU were:

#1142 - **Jack Delton** (Old Belvedere) – 1946
#1143 - **Hugh Dolan** (UCD) – 1946
#1144 - **Hugh Greer** (NIFC) – 1946
#1145 - **Jack Guiney** (Bective Rangers) – 1946
#1146 - **Des Thorpe** (Old Belvedere) – 1946
#1147 - **Paul Traynor** (Clontarf) – 1952
#1148 - **John Birch** (Ballymena) – 1970
#1149 - **Frank O'Driscoll** (UCD) – 1970
#1150 - **Leo Galvin** (Athlone) – 1973
#1151 - **Emmet O'Rafferty** (Wanderers) – 1976
#1152 - **Rab Brady** (Ballymena) – 1985
#1153 - **Paul Clinch** (Lansdowne) - 1989

JACK KYLE – FLYING WITHOUT WINGS

Who is the Greatest Ever player in the history of Irish Rugby?

That is a question which has transcended generations of Irish fans and there are, according to the various fans' polls conducted, several contenders for the mantle. Mike Gibson, Willie John McBride, Brian O'Driscoll, Ronan O'Gara and Johnny Sexton are, to quote the title of the 1995 classic movie, *The Usual Suspects* names which come to the fore. But again, it comes down to a generational thing as these polls are a recent topic of discussion in the pubs of Belfast, Dublin and every crack, nook and cranny of the Emerald Isle.

To ask an Ireland rugby fan today to name the Top 5 players in the famous green jersey without having seen all of the leading contenders play for their country, is a bit like asking a Manchester United fan to name an equivalent Quintet. Manchester United's *Usual Suspects* rarely change when fans are polled, but one Ireland rugby union star was his country's *Sirius*. He is the equivalent to *The Usual Suspects'* main character portrayed by Kevin Spacey, Keyser Söze, and that player is John 'Jack' Kyle.

John Wilson Kyle was born in Belfast on 10 February 1926, and was educated at Belfast Royal Academy. He was one of five children who were born to John and Elizabeth, nee Warren, Kyle. His father was an only child born to a Master Baker from Derry, and he worked as a manager for the Edinburgh-based North British Rubber Company. Jack's dad was in charge of the company's operations in Ireland. Rugby was not part of the Kyle or Warren family history until Jack's older brother, Eric played for Ulster and was given a trial by Ireland. At school the young boy from Belfast was inspired to play rugby by his headmaster, Alexander Roulston Foster, who captained Ireland winning 17 caps between 1910 and 1921, and who was also capped twice by the British Isles (later became the British and Irish Lions) on their Tour of South Africa in 1910. The pupil hung on his teacher's every word. Kyle played for the Ulster Schools at full-back but it was on entering Queen's University Belfast to read medicine in October 1944 that he came to senior prominence after a rival for the out-half position, Derek Monteith, broke a leg.

He played for Queen's University First XV, North of Ireland Rugby Football Club and his home Province, Ulster. His first appearance for Ireland came during the Second World War in a friendly versus a British Army XV, but no caps were awarded to the men in green for this game. In 1947, post the aftermath of the war, the Five Nations Championship was resurrected. Despite his young age, 20, Kyle was given his Test debut by the IRFU's Selection Committee. Twenty years of age was very young for a rugby union player in 1947, today's equivalent would probably be 17. He was one of 14 debutants for Ireland in the game, with captain, Con Murphy, the only player in the side to have played an international before the onset of war in Europe, which then spread to other parts of the world. But it was not the start the Belfast born Kyle had dreamed of, as Ireland lost 12-8 to France at Lansdowne Road. But, someone at the IRFU was orbiting the same planet as Jack, because he was selected to play in all of Ireland's three games in the 1947 Five Nations Championship.

'*I Think I Have Found You A Genius.*' These immortal words were sent on a telegram by Manchester United's Chief Scout in Northern Ireland, Bob Bishop, to Matt Busby, the Manchester United manager, after Bishop had stood on the sidelines watching a 15-year-old

Belfast boy named George Best weave his magic on the pitch, scoring twice for Cregagh Boys Under-16 team in a 4-2 win against the much bigger and stronger boys from Boyland Football Club. In Jack Kyle, the IRFU had found their very own genius.

On 6 December 1947, Ireland welcomed Australia to Dublin for an international friendly. Kyle was naturally selected at fly-half in a team that comprised Bill McKay, Karl Mullen and the captain, Ernest Strathdee. However, the IRFU tinkered with the side that had played in the 1947 Five Nations Championship, and awarded eight new caps: Jimmy Corcoran, Albert McConnell, Desmond McCourt, William McKee, Jimmy Nelson, Kevin O'Flanagan, Paddy Reid and Richard Wilkinson. Perhaps the IRFU selection committee had one eye on the forthcoming Five Nations Championship campaign because Ireland were no match for the experienced Wallabies - their XV did not contain any debutants - winning the encounter with relative ease, 16-3.

Ireland won the 1948 Five Nations Championship and with it, the Triple Crown and their first ever Grand Slam title. It was the beginning of a Golden Age for Irish rugby and Kyle, who scored a try in the wins over England and Scotland, would go on to play a significant role in this renaissance period for the Boys in Green. Kyle, McKay, Mullen (captain) et al helped Ireland defend their title by winning the 1949 Five Nations Championship, only a loss versus France in their opening game in Dublin deprived Ireland of winning back-to-back Grand Slams. Kyle may not have scored during the championship but he was pivotal in the three games Ireland won, forever looking to receive the ball, slaloming his way through defences and passing the ball to a teammate who was in a better scoring position than he was with pinpoint accuracy.

Mullen may well have been Ireland's leader on the pitch, a superb tactician, but it was Kyle who masterminded Ireland's successes. He was surgical and explosive on the field, forever making an exquisite nuisance of himself, sucking defenders towards a final spiral as he flew himself forward refusing to look back over his shoulder, knowing that he possessed the nerve and nous to escape a tackle. When Kyle had the ball in his arms it was as though the players before him were moving in slow motion as he navigated his way through opposing defences, seeing everything unravel before him in ultra high definition.

In 1950, after Ireland finished joint-third in the Five Nations Championship, Jackie was selected to tour Australia and New Zealand with the British and Irish Lions. His name, and that of his fellow doctor and Ireland teammate, Karl Mullen were among the first placed on the squad list made up by the Lions' selection committee and coach Leslie B. Osborne. Mullen captained the side. Kyle was playing for Queen's University at the time of his selection and postponed his medical studies to go on the four month-long tour to the southern hemisphere, much to the annoyance of his parents.

'It was a huge honour getting picked, of course. But it wasn't without its difficulties. I was studying medicine at University in Belfast and going on Tour by ship for months meant postponing my exams for a long time. My father certainly wasn't happy about me going. I just had to reassure him that I would study extra hard on the ship. The joy of those Tours was the time you got to spend making friends with players from all over the British Isles you had never met on a personal level and reaching places you had only read about in the encyclopaedia.'

The Tour involved six Test matches, two versus the Wallabies and four against the All

Blacks. Kyle was only one of four players to play in all six Test matches, the others were Roy John (Lock, Neath & Wales), Bill McKay (Flanker, Queen's University & Ireland) and Jack Matthews (Centre, Cardiff & Wales). In total he played in 20 of the Lions' 29 Tour matches, the highlight of which saw him score a try in the First Test, a 9-9 draw with New Zealand at Carisbrook, Dunedin. Kyle was the Man of the Match also setting up a try for Ken Jones (Wing, Newport & Wales) and winning a penalty which was scored by John Robins (Prop, Birkenhead Park & Wales). The Lions lost their tour series 3-0 to the All Blacks but defeated the Wallabies 2-0, with Kyle scoring a try in the Second Test, a 24-3 win at the Sydney Cricket Ground. He also scored a hat-trick of tries versus Buller (a 24-9 win in Westport) and against West Coast (a 32-3 victory in Greymouth). He remains the only Irish fly-half in Lions' history to score a double hat-trick of tries. Indeed, his performances on the tour were so good he was named one of the six players of the year by the *New Zealand Rugby Almanac*. High praise for the boy from Belfast.

'If your actions inspire others to dream more, learn more, do more, and become more, you are a leader.' - John Quincy Adams

Jack Kyle inspired everyone around him by setting a standard his teammates followed. He made them better players. Kyle may not have captained Ireland in every match he played for his country, but there is no question that he was the leader. And, no matter who he played for - club, country or the British and Irish Lions - his performances never dropped below outstanding. And, in 1951, Kyle once again inspired Ireland to greatness when they won their third Five Nations Championship in just four seasons. To say that Kyle was magnificent in all four games barely pays tribute to the great man. Ireland beat France 9-8 in Dublin, then England 3-0 at Lansdowne Road, Scotland 6-5 at Murrayfield Stadium, and only Wales prevented them from claiming a fifth Triple Crown and a second Grand Slam, when the pair drew 3-3 at Arms Park on Matchday 4. With his magnetic energy and mesmeric ability, Kyle was a sea of chaos to opposing teams. He made history and art at the same time.

He graduated from Queen's University, Belfast in 1951 and went into practice as a General Practitioner in the city.

In 1955, he should have been an automatic choice for the British and Irish Lions Tour of South Africa, but for some inexplicable reason the Lions' took the decision not to select him or any player who was aged 30 or over. Kyle was 29 at the time.

On 1 March 1958, there was barely a dry eye inside Lansdowne Road when Jackie played his 46th, and final ever game, in the green jersey of Ireland. Quite fittingly, he got the send-off he so richly deserved for the service he gave his country on a rugby field. Ireland defeated Scotland 12-6 in their 1958 Five Nations Championship match. Kyle scored 24 points, including seven tries, for his country. He was only 32-years old when he called time on his international career, relatively young for a player today to hang-up his boots when you consider that Johnny Sexton was 38 years old when he retired. But, then again Kyle and Sexton played in eras that were so very different.

Some rugby players today have their own personal trainers, a dietician to advise them on how best to fuel their body to prepare for a game, their own physiotherapist, an agent and a manager. When Jackie Kyle made his international debut, professionalism in the sport was 40 years away, he trained at night on his own after long hours working as a doctor during the day, he had nobody to advise him as to what to eat to maximise his performances and if he received an injury that needed treatment by a physio, then he would have to take his place in the queue after a game as Ireland only had one physiotherapist to look after the entire first team squad.

It is extremely difficult to compare players of different generations, even more so when you compare these legends of the amateur and professional eras. Jack Kyle would have been the David Beckham of rugby union with sponsors knocking on his door (because a sports agent was anathema when Jack played for his country) to get him to endorse their products ranging from Brylcreem for your hair to an aftershave product. Kyle was more into his rugby than his public profile, much to the benefit of his club and country.

When he retired, his 52 international caps (46 for Ireland and six for the British and Irish Lions) was a world record at the time. But he continued playing the game he loved and was a regular for the North of Ireland Rugby Football Club, Belfast. Fans who paid to see him play clutched their match tickets as if it was a winning ticket in a National Lottery Rollover, just to have the proof that they saw him play, watching him glide over the grass beneath his magical feet like Torvill and Dean skating over the ice on their way to winning a gold medal in the Figure Skating Pairs discipline at the 1984 Winter Olympic Games hosted by Sarajevo, Yugoslavia.

Kyle made eight appearances for Barbarian Football Club between 1948 and 1954, scoring three points in total.

'He was so beautifully balanced and had this gift of lulling opposition into a false sense of security. You'd think he was doing nothing, and yet in an instant he'd pull the ball back, and there he was in a position to score or make a try.' Cliff Morgan, the legendary Wales and Lions out-half, and a playing contemporary of Jackie's speaking after one of the games Kyle starred in for the Baa-Bas.

Jack Kyle was awarded an OBE in 1959, and in 1962 he went to work on a humanitarian project in Indonesia. He then returned home but could not resist helping others less fortunate than himself, and in 1966, he moved to Chingola, Zambia, where he worked as a doctor until his retirement from the medical profession in 2000. His work in Zambia was honoured with an honorary doctorate from Queen's University in 1991, and a lifetime achievement award by the Irish Journal of Medical Science and the Royal Academy of Medicine of Ireland.

'I was not a great tackler. If I'd had to play rugby as a forward, I would have never played the game! Our back row of Jim McCarthy, Bill McKay and Des O'Brien was so strong that I didn't have to bother too much with the normal defensive duties of a fly-half.'

In 2002 he was voted the Greatest Ever Irish Player in a poll by the IRFU, and in 2008, he was inducted into the International Rugby Board Hall of Fame. In 2009, when Ireland ended a 61-year drought of winning a second Grand Slam, Jackie was in Cardiff to watch the game and was the first person to congratulate Brian O'Driscoll, the Ireland captain, on the team's achievement. At long last, Jackie was able to pass on the torch of greatness to a future Irish Legend of the sport.

Kyle's other highlights in the Ireland jersey included his outstanding individual try against

'JACK KYLE INSPIRED EVERYONE AROUND HIM BY SETTING A STANDARD HIS TEAMMATES FOLLOWED. HE MADE THEM BETTER PLAYERS. KYLE MAY NOT HAVE CAPTAINED IRELAND IN EVERY MATCH HE PLAYED FOR HIS COUNTRY, BUT THERE IS NO QUESTION THAT HE WAS THE LEADER.'

France in the 1953 Five Nations Championship, a game Ireland won 16-3 at Ravenhill; his drop goal from the touchline to beat Wales 11-3 in Dublin in the 1956 Five Nations Championship; and his tactical kicking was vital in the 9-6 defeat of Australia at Lansdowne Road on 18 January 1958. Apart from his attacking prowess, Kyle was a shield to his team as a defender at a time when the laws of the game permitted the flanker to stand very close to the opposing No.10. Kyle could read a game like a child could read a comic book story, as he persistently covered cross-field towards the corner flag and made many of the last-ditch tackles that today's game rarely sees anyone other than the full-back commit to. In many ways, Jackie Kyle, was over courageous, but as far as the Irish fans were concerned, he was brave to a fault.

And, on a windy day in the Irish capital on 11 January 1958, Australia were in the ascendency and sought to blow away Ireland who were fighting the wind in the second-half. But, up stepped the unflappable Kyle to make courageous marks into touch to deny the Wallabies using the wind factor to their advantage as Ireland blew them away 9-6.

'They couldn't touch him. He'd play games and he wouldn't need his shorts laundered afterwards. Jack was just the best.' - Jim McCarthy, an Ireland teammate of Kyle's, 1948-55

In 1964, Cassius Clay Jr. (he later changed his name to Muhammad Ali) was 22 years old when he fought Sonny Liston for the World Heavyweight Boxing Championship. Liston was the reigning World Champion having won the belt two years previously. Just before he entered the ring Clay was asked how he would cope with the onslaught that Liston was about to offload on him. Clay smiled and said: '*I am going to float like a butterfly and sting like a bee. The hands can't hit what the eyes can't see*'. Clay won the contest by technical knockout. The young man from Louisville, Kentucky, must have seen footage of Kyle playing for Ireland because, for 11 years Jackie Kyle floated around a rugby pitch and stung his opponents with his ability to shift his bodyweight from one leg to the other, torturously twisting and turning his opponents, leaving them standing like a human corkscrew as he weaved his way up-field cutting through hapless defences like a hot knife going through butter. Little wonder then that he enjoyed two quite apt nicknames… *Ghost* and *Scarlet Pimpernel*. Sadly, Jackie passed away aged 88 on 28 November 2014. And, quite possibly the greatest ever tribute paid to Jackie was paid to him by another Irish legend, the greatest ever Lion, Willie John McBride, who said this of Jackie: 'We talk about gentleman, I could not sum that word up any better than saying - give me Jack Kyle.'

Without question we will never see his like again. If the Ireland fans had been asked to place one word on his tombstone, it would have been… 'Immortal.'

The one thing that stood out about him more than anything else was his humility. Speaking about himself, he once said: 'When you think of models, they have to look a certain way. They will be 6ft tall and beautiful. With rugby, it's the same. I just happened to be born with something that meant I could go for a gap and just hope for the best'.

In 1948 and 1949, Humphrey Bogart had massive box office appeal, starring in *The Treasure of the Sierra Madre* and *Tokyo Joe*. Movie-goers flocked to their local cinema to see him. Jack Kyle did his acting on a rugby pitch and thousands paid into Rugby stadia in Cardiff, Dublin, Edinburgh, London and Paris to see him play.

In the Pantheon of Irish Sporting Legends, regardless of the sport, Jack Kyle unquestionably occupies the top step. In 1520, Robert Whittington wrote *Vulagria*, which contains the following line… '*A Man For All Seasons*'. John Wilson 'Jack' Kyle was Ireland's main man for 11 seasons.

> **Did You Know That?** Interestingly, in the year of Jack Kyle's birth the following all occurred: The Great Miami Hurricane, Winnie The Pooh was published by author A. A. Milne, John Logie Baird conducted the first public demonstration of a television, and Hirohito was crowned Emperor of Japan. Jack Kyle was a whirlwind in a green jersey but his was not a story of fiction, he was Ireland's Rugby Emperor, he was made for TV audiences to enjoy.

1950s

NO MORE STANDING TO GOD SAVE THE QUEEN

THE FLANKER WHO BECAME A BATTER

A FIRST TEST SERIES WIN OVER AUSTRALIA

'It is the long history of humankind (and animal kind, too) that those who learned to collaborate and improvise most effectively have prevailed.'
Charles Darwin

NO MORE STANDING TO GOD SAVE THE QUEEN

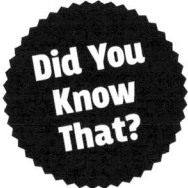

On 24 August 2007, Ireland played a warm-up match for the 2007 Rugby World Cup finals at Ravenhill, defeating Italy 23-20. This match remains the last time Ireland played a Test match at Ravenhill.

In 1954, Ireland were captained by Munster's James Stephen McCarthy, a member of Ireland's 1948 Grand Slam winning side. McCarthy was born in Cork on 30 June 1924 and aged 22 he made his debut at wing forward for Ireland in their opening game of the 1948 Five Nations Championship and celebrated the occasion with a try in their 13-6 win against France in Paris. After finishing fourth in the 1954 Five Nations Championship, McCarthy, who was the Ireland captain at the time, informed a senior official at the IRFU that several of the team would no longer be standing for the playing of the national anthem, *God Save The Queen*, prior to an international match at Ravenhill. On 27 February 1954, Ireland beat Scotland 6-0 at Ravenhill, which was the last occasion they played a Test match in Belfast for more than half a century. Since 1956, Ireland have played the vast majority of their home games in Dublin.

McCarthy was one of the sport's great characters, instantly recognisable on the pitch with his flowing red hair. He joined Dolphin Rugby Club from Christian Brothers College (CBC), Cork. In 1941, he was captain of the CBC side that lost to Mungret College in the final of the Munster Schools Junior Cup. However, two years later he lifted the Munster Senior Cup with CBC, beating Rockwell in the final. In 1944, he helped Dolphin defeat Garryowen in the Munster Senior Cup final. He was only 19 years old and the following year Dolphin retained the trophy, with two of his teammates going on to become distinguished internationals for Ireland, Bertie O'Hanlon and Dave O'Loughlin.

On 13 February 1954, he became the first Munster man to captain Ireland, a 14-13 loss to England at Twickenham in the 1954 Five Nations Championship. In 1950, he was a member of the British and Irish Lions side that toured Australia and New Zealand and was one of the most popular of the tourists, during

which he made 13 appearances. He was a prodigious try scorer, scoring eight in the 28 caps he won for his country between 1948 and 1955.

His most famous try helped Ireland win back-to-back Triple Crowns. On 12 March 1949, Ireland faced Wales at Saint Helens, Swansea and McCarthy scored a try in Ireland's 5-0 victory which crowned them Five Nations champions, in addition to winning the Triple Crown. Only their 16-9 loss at home to France prevented this golden age of Irish players from winning successive Grand Slams. Many years later, McCarthy recalled the try in an interview with the *Examiner*: '*A lineout was followed by a ruck around the Welsh 25. We won the ball and Jack Kyle went left to the blind side before kicking inwards. Frank Trott, the Welsh full-back, was under it but I came racing up, launched myself into the air, caught the ball and my momentum carried me over the line with three or four Welshmen hanging on to me. George Norton converted and from then on, we were on top*'.

When he was asked about the secret to his success as a flanker he simply replied: '*Wherever the ball is, you be there. When I was playing for Ireland, the best place to be was two feet behind Jackie Kyle*'.

Following his retirement after the 1955 Five Nations Championship he concentrated on his second love in sport, golf, and participated in the Irish Senior Cup with Cork Golf Club.

THE 1950 FIVE NATIONS CHAMPIONSHIP – KISSING THE TITLE GOODBYE

Ireland went into the tournament as the holders having defended the Crown they won in 1948 as Grand Slam champions and in 1949, when they narrowly missed out on winning back-to-back Grand Slam titles. The 1950 tournament was a disappointing campaign for Ireland, captained by Karl Mullen, winning just one of their four games, drawing one and tasting defeat in two. They finished third in the table. Ireland's only victory came against Scotland, a 21-0 mauling of the visitors at Lansdowne Road. They lost 3-0 to England at Twickenham and 6-3 to Wales at Ravenhill. The draw (3-3) was versus France at Stade Olympique de Colombes.

One of the biggest movies of the year was *Kiss Tomorrow Goodbye* starring James Cagney. In 1950, Ireland kissed the Five Nations trophy goodbye when it was won by Wales.

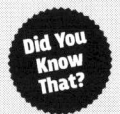 **Wales won the Grand Slam in 1950 with other wins over England (15-11 at Twickenham Stadium), France (21-0 at the Arms Park) and Scotland (12-0 at the Arms Park). It was Wales' 11th title, 8th Triple Crown and their fourth Grand Slam following their previous successes in 1908, 1909 and 1911.**

THE SPRINGBOKS HOP INTO DUBLIN AND SKIP OUT OF EUROPE

In season 1951-52, South Africa were on a Tour of Europe and on 8 December 1951, the Springboks were in the Irish capital. It was the sixteenth game of their Tour, having won 14 and losing just one and it was the fourth occasion they had faced Ireland. The solitary defeat came against an invitational London Counties team on 10 November 1951, losing 11-9 at Twickenham. The Springboks beat Ireland 17-5 at Lansdowne Road to maintain a 100% winning record versus Ireland. South Africa won 30 of their 31 games on their Tour, including wins over England (8-3 at Twickenham), France (25-3 at Stade Olympique de Colombes), Scotland (44-0 at Murrayfield) and Wales (6-3 at the Arms Park) and a 17-3 win over the Barbarians at the Arms Park.

Did You Know That? The Tour marked the Springboks first ever game against the Barbarians.

South Africa completed their third Grand Slam by winning all four Tests against the Home Nations sides. It was their sixth Tour and their fourth in the Northern Hemisphere.

Ireland: John Murphy, William McKee, Noel Henderson, Antony Browne, Mick Lane, Jack Kyle, John O'Meara, Tom Clifford, Karl Mullen, John Hartley Smith, Patrick Lawlor, Robin Thompson, William McKay, Jim McCarthy and the captain, Des O'Brien

THE 1951 FIVE NATIONS CHAMPIONSHIP – A PLACE IN THE SUN

Ireland put their disappointments behind them from the previous tournament when they could only manage a third place finish in the table. It was supposed to be the Golden Age of Irish rugby and so, the players who had been selected to represent their country had a point to prove to those who doubted them. Pride is very important to any sportsman or sportswoman, and, in 1951, the Ireland squad wore their pride on their green jersey.

Ireland defeated France 9-8 at Lansdowne Road in their opening game, a talisman hopefully to stir the *Spirit of 48* when they beat the French in the opening game of their 1948 Grand Slam winning campaign. Game two produced a 3-0 win against England at Lansdowne Road. Ireland's next match took them to Edinburgh, and a tough game versus Scotland at Murrayfield, but Ireland won the Battle of the Celts 6-5. On 10 March 1951, only Wales stood in Ireland's way of being crowned Five Nations champions of 1951. The game was played at the Arms Park in the heart of the Welsh capital. But it was not a game for the feint hearted with the outcome of the result meaning so much to the army of Irish fans who had invaded Cardiff, the eleventh largest city in the United Kingdom, in support of their team. The Welsh Dragon failed to breathe any fire as the contest ended in a dull 3-3 draw, meaning Ireland missed out on winning a second Grand Slam. But Ireland won their seventh Home/Five Nations Championship. Their captain was Karl Mullen.

In season 1951-52, the laws of the game were changed to standardise the scrum's front row

to have three players. Law 15c.

A Place In The Sun, starring Elizabeth Taylor, was one of biggest grossing movies of the year. In the 1951 Five Nations Championship, it was Ireland who were bathing in glory.

 **Despite his famous three B's remark 'Boot, Bollock and Bite' to his players before Ireland beat Wales to win the Grand Slam in 1948, Karl Mullen's teammate, wing forward Jim McCarthy, described his captain as: 'A quiet sort of man.'**

THE FLANKER WHO BECAME A BATTER

During the 1952 Five Nations Championship, Michael James Dargan (born in Dublin on 9 October 1928) played in two of Ireland's games as a flanker. He made his debut on 23 February 1952 in a 12-8 win over Scotland at Lansdowne Road and played his second and last game for Ireland in their 14-3 home defeat to Wales on 8 March 1952. Ireland finished fourth in the table with two wins and two defeats. In September 1954, Dargan made a solitary appearance for the Ireland cricket team in a first-class match versus the Marylebone Cricket Club (MCC) scoring 10 runs. He was a right-handed batsman.

THE 1952 FIVE NATIONS CHAMPIONSHIP – NO FAIRYTALE ENDING

Ireland were the holders of the Five Nations Championship and were determined to hold on to their crown as the best team in the Northern Hemisphere having won the championship in three of the previous four years, including a memorable Grand Slam victory in 1948. Only Wales and their famous Grand Slam-winning side of 1950 stood in their way of winning their fourth title in five years. Ireland kicked off in defence of the title with an 11-8 win over France at Stade Olympique de Colombes. Scotland were the visitors to Lansdowne Road on 23 February 1952 and were sent packing back across the North Channel on the end of a 12-8 defeat.

Ireland's third game was against Wales, who were starting

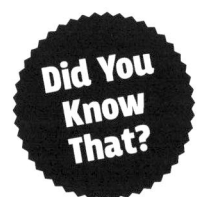

Marylebone Cricket Club was formed in 1787 and the following year the club took responsibility for the Laws of Cricket, issuing a revised version that year. Changes to the Laws of Cricket are now made by the International Cricket Board (ICB), but the copyright is still owned by MCC.

to become their nemesis, and the rivals met in Dublin on 8 March 1952. Like Ireland, the Welsh were also on course for the Triple Crown and Grand Slam having beaten England 8-6 at Twickenham and Scotland 11-0 at the Arms Park. On the day Wales were just too sharp for the Irish backline, winning the match 14-3. Wales wrapped up the Championship and Grand Slam by defeating France 9-5 at St Helen's Rugby and Cricket Ground, Swansea on 22 March 1952. England's 3-0 win over Ireland at Twickenham meant it was they and not Ireland who finished runners-up to Wales.

It was Wales' 12th title, 9th Triple Crown and their fifth Grand Slam (their second in three years).

In 1952, Hans Christian Anderson, a musical, was one of the most watched movies of the year but for Ireland on the rugby pitch, there was no fairytale ending as their crown slipped from their grasp into the arms of Wales.

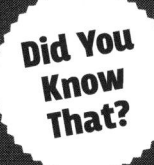

Did You Know That?

The Ireland versus Wales game was their first meeting at Lansdowne Road since 1927, as all of the matches in the intervening period had taken place at Ravenhill. It also marked Wales' first win at Lansdowne Road since 1910.

NOEL JOSEPH HENDERSON

Noel Joseph Henderson was capped 40 times by Ireland (1949-59) and was a member of the British and Irish Lions side that toured Australia and New Zealand in 1950, winning one cap. He played his club rugby for North of Ireland FC and won his first cap for Ireland when he was just 20 years old. His debut came in the 1949 Five Nations Championship when Ireland were the reigning champions and Grand Slam holders. On 26 February 1949, he played in Ireland's 13-3 win over Scotland at Murrayfield which helped Ireland retain the Triple Crown and the Five Nations Championship title. In 1951 he won the Five Nations Championship, playing in all four games and in 1956 he was appointed captain of the team. On 19 April 1958 he captained Ireland for the last time, an 11-6 loss to France in Paris in the 1958 Five Nations Championship. For the game he switched position from centre to full-back and played at full-back in all four games in the 1959 Five Nations Championship. He was elected president of the IRFU for the 1990-91 season.

Did You Know That? Ronnie Dawson succeeded Henderson as the Ireland captain.

1953 FIVE NATIONS CHAMPIONSHIP – THE BAD AND THE BEAUTIFUL

The tournament commenced on 10 January 1953 and after 10 games were played, it concluded on 28 March 1953. Including the previous incarnations as the Home Nations Championship and Five Nations Championship, this was the fifty-ninth series of the northern hemisphere rugby union championship.

Wales, Grand Slam winners the previous year, were red hot favourites to retain the title and win back-to back-Grand Slams. But their campaign got off to a bad start, losing 8-3 at the Arms Park to their biggest rivals, England. Ireland beat France 18-3 at Ravenhill in their opening fixture, an impressive victory as the French had defeated Scotland 11-5 at Stade Olympique de Colombes in their first game. Round 2 saw England visit the Irish capital where they drew 9-9 at Lansdowne Road. Ireland's next game was versus Scotland at Murrayfield which proved to be an easy day out, winning 26-8. Wales against Ireland at St Helen's, Swansea resulted in a 5-3 victory for the host nation. England beat Scotland 26-8 at Twickenham which saw them crowned 1953 Five Nations Champions.

Did You Know That? It was England's 14th Championship title.

The Bad and the Beautiful starring Kirk Douglas was a major box office attraction in 1953. In Ireland's victories over France and Scotland, they played some of the most beautiful rugby Irish fans had not witnessed since the Golden Boys of 1948 won the Grand Slam.

LANSDOWNE ROAD'S HOUSEWARMING PARTY

On 31 December 1955, an Ireland and Scotland XV played an England and Wales XV at Lansdowne Road to celebrate the opening of a new stand in the stadium. The specially commissioned match programme described the game as a 'Housewarming Party' as it was being played on New Year's Eve, Hogmanay in Scotland.

Eight Irish players made-up the Celtic alliance:

Scotland and Ireland: R. W. T. Chisholm (Melrose, Scotland); A. R. Smith (Cambridge University, Scotland), A. J. F. O'Reilly (Old Belvedere, Ireland), A. C. Pedlow (Queen's University, Belfast, Ireland), J. S. Swan (Coventry, Scotland); J. W. Kyle (N.I.F.C, Ireland, captain), A. F. Dorward (Gala, Scotland); H. F. McLeod (Hawick, Scotland), R. Roe (Richmond, Ireland), P. J. O'Donoghue (Bective Rangers, Ireland), J. R. Brady (C.I.Y.M.S., Ireland), P. J. Lawlor (Clontarf, Ireland), J. T. Greenwood (Dunfermline, Scotland), T. E. Reid (London Irish, Ireland), A. Robson (Hawick, Scotland). Scorers

The opposition turned party poopers by beating the Ireland and Scotland XV (18-15). The 'home' side's try scorers were O'Reilly (2), Greenwood and Smith, with Smith also scoring a penalty.

> **Did You Know That?** Lansdowne Road was named after the nearby road, which in turn was named after William Petty-Fitzmaurice, 1st Marquess of Lansdowne. He was also the Earl of Shelburne with the nearby Shelbourne Road also named after him.

ENGLAND VERSUS IRELAND MATCH CALLED OFF FOLLOWING THE DEATH OF KING GEORGE VI

The England versus Ireland Five Nations Championship match scheduled to be played at Twickenham on Saturday 9 February 1952, was postponed following the death of King George VI on 6 February 1952. The game was played on 29 March 1952, with England winning 3-0.

1954 FIVE NATIONS CHAMPIONSHIP – A STAR IS BORN

The 1954 Five Nations Championship ended in a three-way share of the title, but Ireland could only manage a fourth-place finish leaving winless Scotland with the wooden spoon. England, France and Wales won three of their four games. Ireland lost 8-0 to France at Stade Olympique de Colombes followed by a 14-3 defeat to England at Twickenham. On 27 February 1954, Ireland beat Scotland 6-0 at Ravenhill and Wales then beat Ireland 12-9 at Lansdowne Road.

It was the first title won by France, who stopped England from claiming the Grand Slam by winning 11-3 in Paris, although England did win the Calcutta Cup (they beat Scotland 13-3 at Murrayfield) and the Triple Crown (they also beat Wales 9-6 at Twickenham).

In 1954, the musical drama *A Star is Born*, starring Judy Garland, was one of the top movies in Hollywood. On 8 October 1954, a true star was born, Anthony Ward who went on to play for Ireland.

> **Did You Know That?** Prince Charles was the Prince of Wales in 1952 when they won the Grand Slam and 50 years later he became the King of the United Kingdom & Other Commonwealth States on 8 September 2022, following the death of his Mother, Queen Elizabeth II.

> **Did You Know That?** The match at Ravenhill was the last time Ireland played an international at the Belfast ground until 2007. Ireland's Republic of Ireland born players threatened not to line out for the United Kingdom national anthem unless the Irish national anthem, A Soldier's Song, was also played and the Irish Tricolour was flown along with the Union Jack. After the game the IRFU announced that all future home matches would be played at Lansdowne Road. In 2007, Ravenhill was used for an Ireland Test match once again as Lansdowne Road was under reconstruction where the Aviva Stadium was being built on the same site.

FIVE STAR SCHOOL REPORT

On 25 February 1956, Noel Henderson was handed the captaincy of Ireland for the first time. He inspired Ireland to a 14-10 victory at Lansdowne Road in the 1956 Five Nations Championship. Henderson was born in Drumahoe, Derry and attended Foyle College, Derry. But some nine years before the men who selected the Ireland team recognised the 27-year-old Henderson's leadership abilities, the editor of the Foyle College magazine was in no doubt that his 18-year-old student was destined for greatness. The editor wrote the following in the 1947 edition of the magazine:

'Of Noel Henderson the captain and right centre, I find it difficult to speak with sufficient restraint. He has everything that a centre needs: weight, great strength, almost incredible stamina, determination, speed, safe hands, a powerful kick, unselfish. A sportsman to his last inch and ounce, and the best schoolboy captain I have yet seen. I have never said anything like those last three sentences of any boy before. I could better have imagined myself writing anything of the sort for an obituary notice rather than for a report like this and it may be years before I do so again. But let the doubter speak to any member of Henderson's team and he will find that I do not exaggerate. His magnificent covering of the whole back line, his wise captaincy, his quiet, modest personality, added 50 percent to the efficiency of every one of his teammates. I have known no other such player in 11 years of Foyle teams.'

> **Did You Know That?** Noel Henderson was the captain of Ireland when they recorded their first ever victory over a team from the southern hemisphere. On 18 January 1958, Ireland beat Australia at Lansdowne Road during The Wallabies' Tour of Europe. With the scores level at 6-6, Henderson picked the ball up on the halfway line, evaded two tacklers and scored the try to give Ireland victory by 9 points to 6. The try has gone down in Irish sporting folklore and the commentator on the British Pathe news footage eulogised it perfectly, saying: 'Watch this run, it will be talked about as long as Irishmen play rugger'.

'THE BIGGEST MOVIE OF THE YEAR WAS A FRENCH FILM ENTITLED DIABOLIQUE, MEANING DIABOLICAL. THERE WAS NO QUESTION ABOUT IT, THAT IN THE 1955 FIVE NATIONS CHAMPIONSHIP, FRANCE WERE MAGNIFIQUE BUT IRELAND WERE DIABOLIQUE.'

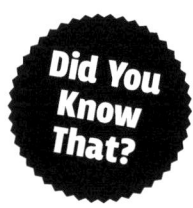

Jim McCarthy was a member of Ireland's 1948 Grand Slam winning side and was capped 28 times for Ireland between 1948-55, scoring 24 points. He also played 13 times for the British and Irish Lions on their 1950 Tour of Australia and New Zealand but did not play in any of the team's six Test matches on the tour.

1955 FIVE NATIONS CHAMPIONSHIP – A DIABOLICAL CAMPAIGN

This was the 26th edition of the Five Nations Championship, and the 61st edition of the northern hemisphere's rugby union championship. It was a disastrous one for Ireland who finished it rooted to the foot of the table, winners of the wooden spoon. Ireland had two captains during the tournament, Jim McCarthy and Robin Thompson.

On 22 January 1955, Ireland lost 5-3 to France at Lansdowne Road in their opening game. Three weeks later, England and Ireland drew 6-6 in Dublin. Ireland's first of two consecutive away games resulted in a 12-3 loss to Scotland at Murrayfield which was followed-up with a 21-3 defeat to Wales at the Arms Park.

France and Wales were crowned joint champions, with France missing out on winning the championship outright, and claiming a first ever Grand Slam, by losing 16-11 to Wales at Stade Olympique de Colombes in their final game.

The biggest movie of the year was a French film entitled *Diabolique*, meaning Diabolical. There was no question about it, that in the 1955 Five Nations Championship, France were Magnifique but Ireland were Diabolique.

AS CLEAR AS GLASS

Dion Caldwell Glass was born in Belfast, Northern Ireland on 15 May 1934. He won four caps for Ireland, making his debut versus France at Stade Olympique de Colombes on 19 April 1958. Ireland lost the 1958 Five Nations Championship game 11-8. His last appearance in the green jersey was a 24-8 defeat to South Africa at Newlands Stadium, Cape Town on 13 May 1961.

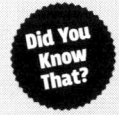 **Eric Brown and Syd Millar also made their debuts for Ireland in the loss to France.**

In His Own Words

'The game was a bit dull and I found myself with the ball with a chance to drop-kick-it was my first cap but I decided to go for it. I hit it. Bang. It sliced to the right wing miles away. It was very embarrassing but it ended up at the touchline corner-flag and we scored. I was extremely lucky as I got picked again.'

Alexander Cecil Pedlow after making his debut for Ireland in a 5-3 loss to Wales at St. Helen's Swansea in the 1953 Five Nations Championship

1952 TOUR OF SOUTH AMERICA

Fifty-three years after embarking on their very first Tour, to Canada in 1899, Ireland undertook their second Tour. This time they travelled to South America to play eight matches in Argentina and one game in Chile. Ireland departed on their journey on 20 July 1952, and on 9 August 1952, they kicked off their Tour with a game against Chile, a game they won 30-0 in Santiago, the capital city. However, the Tour was almost cancelled as Eva Peron, the wife of the Argentina President, Juan Peron, died on 26 July 1952, plunging the entire country into a period of mourning.

The squad then set off for the Argentine capital, Buenos Aires, for their remaining eight encounters. On 12 August 1952 they beat Capital 12-6, followed by an 11-6 loss to Club Pucura three days later. A 6-6 draw with Provincia on 17 August 1952, preceded a 19-3 victory over an Argentina A side on 21 August 1952.

The first Test of the Tour was played on 24 August 1952 at Estadio Gimnasia y Esgrima, Buenos Aires. The game ended in a 3-3 draw and ironically the referee was called Glasgow, but came from Ireland, Ossie Glasgow. It was the first time the two nations had faced one another in a Test match. Four days later Ireland hammered an Argentina B side 25-3 and then faced the home nation for the Second Test Ireland won the game 6-0 thanks to two penalties scored by Michael Dargan and Mick Hilary. In their final game, played on 3 September 1952, Ireland beat Club Universitario de Buenos Aires, commonly known as CUBA, 19-11 at Estadio Gimnasia y Esgrima, the venue for all eight of their matches in the country.

No caps were awarded for the two Tests against Argentina.

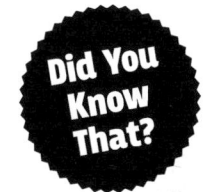

Did You Know That?

Michael Dargan won two caps for Ireland, both in the 1952 Five Nations Championship (versus Scotland & Wales) and was also capped once by the Ireland international cricket team. His solitary First-Class cricket match was versus Marylebone Cricket Club in September 1954. He was a right-handed batsman.

1956 FIVE NATIONS CHAMPIONSHIP – THE SEARCHERS

After winning the same number of games as England and France – two - Ireland finished in a three-way tie for second place in the table (points scored in games difference was not applicable). Ireland's first two games were away from Dublin and they tasted defeat in both, losing 14-8 against France at Stade Olympique de Colombes and 20-0 at Twickenham Stadium to England who finished the tournament in runners-up spot. On 25 February 1955, Ireland beat Scotland 14-10 at Lansdowne Road and two weeks later Wales came to Dublin for Game No.4. Ireland won the match 11-3. Wales' final game saw them crowned champions after beating France 5-3 at the Arms Park, meaning that their loss to Ireland deprived them of winning the Triple Crown and another Grand Slam.

The Searchers, starring John Wayne, was the second biggest grossing movie of the year. Ireland ended their 1956 Five Nations campaign still searching for their first title win since 1951.

> **Did You Know That?** In 1956, Wales were captained by one of the greatest Welsh players of all time, Cliff Morgan. He won his first cap for Wales against Ireland in the 1951 Five Nations Championship, playing opposite his hero, Jack Kyle. Cliff was a member of Wales' 1952 Grand Slam winning team and in 1953, he inspired both Cardiff and Wales to historic victories over the touring All Blacks. He was capped 29 times by his country (1951-58), scoring nine points and won four caps (scored three points) for the British and Irish Lions on their 1955 Tour of South Africa.

POETRY ON A RUGBY PITCH

'Life is divided into three terms – that which was, which is, and which will be. Let us learn from the past to profit by the present, and from the present, to live better in the future.'
William Wordsworth, English romantic poet (7 April 1770-23 April 1850)

Jack Kyle (Ireland 1946-58, 46 caps, 24 points) was pure poetry in motion on a rugby pitch. When he decided his time on a rugby pitch was up, he packed his bags and travelled to Zambia, Southern Africa where he worked as a doctor for 35 years. Just like he did when he travelled with the Ireland team, he took volumes of poetry by William Wordsworth on his journey with him.

>  **Did You Know That?** Cardiff Arms Park was demolished in 1997 to make way for the Millennium Stadium. Poet, Marc Harris, wrote a poem in memory of the famous ground which had played host to some wonderful Wales versus Ireland games.

1957 FIVE NATIONS CHAMPIONSHIP – A SEARCH FOR PARADISE

For the second season in a row, Ireland finished in a three-way tie for second place in the 1957 Five Nations Championship after winning two of their four games. Once again, the number of points scored in a game by a team was not applicable in determining placings. Ireland beat France 11-6 in their opener at Lansdowne Road and then lost 6-0 in their second game to England in Dublin. Game No.3 resulted in a 5-3 defeat at Murrayfield to Scotland before narrowly losing their final game, 6-5 to Wales at the Arms Park.

France lost all four of their games and received the wooden spoon. England won their 13th Triple Crown, the championship for a fifteenth time and a seventh Grand Slam after beating Wales 3-0 at the Arms Park, France 9-5 at Twickenham Stadium and Scotland 16-3, also played at Twickenham Stadium.

Search For Paradise was a big success in the cinema houses in 1957 but it was Ireland who were left searching for the form that would see them crowned champions once again.

> **Did You Know That?** Niall Henry Brophy made his debut for Ireland in the 11-6 victory versus France and scored a try. He attended Blackrock College and in 1954 he was Leinster Schools athletic champion over 100 yards and 220 yards, and he also won the same two titles in the Irish Schools Athletics Championship. On Saint Patrick's Day 1954, he captained Blackrock College to success in the Leinster Schools Senior Cup with a win over Belvedere in the final. His future Ireland teammate, Anthony O'Reilly captained Belvedere in the final. Brophy also represented University College Dublin and the Irish Universities Athletics Association in athletics.

THY SHALL NOT PASS

Noel Henderson was not a one position player. As well as his favoured centre role, he was equally comfortable at full-back and on the wing. He earned a reputation as being a very strong runner who was fearless and hard-hitting in the tackle which earned him the moniker: 'Thy shall not pass'.

> **Did You Know That?** Henderson was travelling with Jack Kyle from Belfast to Dublin to attend an Ireland training camp and met a girl named Betty in the restaurant on the train. Betty was an international hockey player and was also attending a training camp. Incredibly, they were both on the same train home and when they arrived back in Belfast, Noel gave his kitbag to Jack and took Betty to the cinema. The couple married in 1953.

1958 FIVE NATIONS CHAMPIONSHIP – THE WORLD'S GREATEST FLY-HALF

Ireland finished bottom of the table in the 1958 Five Nations Championship with one win and three losses. It was a dismal campaign for the Irish side, losing 6-0 at Twickenham to England, 9-6 to Wales at Lansdowne Road, and suffered an 11-6 reversal to France at Stade Olympique de Colombes. Their solitary victory was a 12-6 win over Scotland in the Irish capital. So, once again they ended up with the wooden spoon. England claimed their 16th title.

In 1958, the movie *The Fly* entertained the movie-goers. But, at the end of the 1958 Five Nations Championship perhaps the greatest fly-half of all time, Ireland's Jack Kyle, brought the curtain down on his international career.

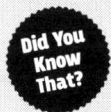 Alexander Cecil Pedlow scored a try for Ireland against Scotland in the 12-6 win. Pedlow was an exceptional sportsman and also represented Ireland at squash and controversially missed out on representing Ireland in the Davis Cup in tennis. However, he did go on to represent Irish tennis at veteran and vintage representative levels and won numerous titles all over Ireland. Pedlow had already played tennis for Ireland at junior level, playing in the Junior Wimbledon tournament at the All England Lawn Tennis Club, after winning the Under-18 title at the 1952 All-Ireland Tennis Championships at Fitzwilliam Tennis Club, aged 17. During his schooldays he displayed some early promise at cricket and hockey. He won 30 caps for Ireland and scored 31 points.

SEVENTH HEAVEN

David Hewitt was aged just 18 years and 131 days when he made his debut at centre for Ireland on 18 January 1958. And, what a historic game it was to play in as Ireland defeated Australia 9-6 at Lansdowne Road during The Wallabies' Tour of Europe. It was the first time Ireland had beaten a team from the southern hemisphere. Hewitt became the seventh youngest player to play for Ireland.

 Hewitt was capped 18 times by Ireland, scoring 32 points, and won six British and Irish Lions caps (16 points).

1959 FIVE NATIONS CHAMPIONSHIP – IN THE SHADOWS

In 1959, France finally got their hands on the Five Nations Championship trophy as outright winners for the first time, following shared championship wins in 1954 and 1955. Despite defeating France, Ireland finished joint runners-up in the table along with England and

Wales. Meanwhile, Scotland took home the wooden spoon. On 14 February 1959, Ireland lost their opening fixture 3-0 to England at Lansdowne Road. Ireland's next two games were away from Dublin, winning 8-3 versus Scotland at Murrayfield and losing 8-6 at the Arms Park to Wales. France met Ireland in Dublin on 18 April 1959, with the French already crowned champions having beaten Scotland 9-0 at home, drawing 3-3 away to England and an 11-3 victory in Paris versus Wales. Ireland defeated France 9-5.

In 1959, the movie *Shadows* was very popular and it summed up the state of Irish rugby at the end of the decade, as they were still living in the shadow of the Ireland team that had last won the tournament in 1951.

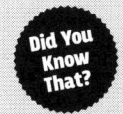

In 1959, Ronnie Dawson was the captain of Ireland and in 1969, became the first ever coach of the Ireland team.

1960s

MICK THE KICK
IRELAND'S ENGLISHMAN
IRELAND APPOINT THEIR FIRST HEAD COACH
IRELAND'S FIRST SUB
THE GREAT ESCAPE & TRUE GRIT

'The ultimate measure of a man is not where he stands in moments of comfort, but where he stands at times of challenge and controversy.'
Martin Luther King Jr.

IRELAND HEAD COACHES

The Irish Rugby Football Union did not appoint its first coach of the national team until 1969. The following men have also held the honour of managing Ireland's Rugby Union side.

Ronnie Dawson	1969-72
Syd Millar	1973-75
Roly Meates	1975-77
Noel Murphy	1977-80
Tom Kiernan	1980-83
Willie John McBride	1983-84
Mick Doyl	1984-87
Jim Davidson	1987-90
Ciaran Fitzgerald	1990-92
Gerry Murphy	1993-95
Murray Kidd	1995-97
Brian Ashton	1997-98
Warren Gatland	1998-2001
Eddie O'Sullivan	2001-08
Michael Bradley	2008 (Interim Coach)
Declan Kidney	2008-13
Les Kiss	2013 (Interim Coach)
Joe Schmidt	2013-19
Andy Farrell	2019-

Did You Know That? Graham Henry is the greatest coach in the history of Rugby Union. He managed New Zealand from 2004-2011 in a period when they dominated the international rugby scene. Some cynics will say that managing the All Blacks is an easy job with success guaranteed. It is true to say that Henry took over a team that comprised the country's most talented players, including upcoming stars, but he gelled them into a winning machine. Henry possessed the ability of harnessing the raw individual strength and talent of his squad and then turning them into a winning machine, a group of players who were so methodically disciplined which was coupled with their ease in scoring try after try regardless of the opposition. Sir Graham Henry (he was Knighted in 2012) coached the All Blacks in 103 Tests, winning 88 and losing 25, a staggering winning ratio of 85.4%. The pinnacle of his reign was New Zealand's 8-7 victory over France in the 2011 Rugby World Cup final which was achieved on home soil. The final was played at Eden Park, Auckland.

1960 FIVE NATIONS CHAMPIONSHIP – FEELING LONELY

Having finished runners-up to France the previous year, Ireland's hopes of a title success were high in 1960. Although the decade would see the dawn of Ireland appointing a coach for the first time in their history, the 1960 campaign kicked-off with the Ireland captain in charge of tactics. Or in this case, two captains, as Andy Mulligan and Ronnie Dawson would share the duties for the tournament.

Ireland lost their opening game to England at Twickenham when they succumbed 8-5. But the loss was a blessing in disguise for the Irish because a young man from Cork won his first cap in the match and impressed the Irish selectors. Tom Kiernan, aged 21, was that player and he went on to have a very distinguished career in the green jersey. Walter Bornemann and Barton McCallan also ran out for the senior side for their maiden Test that day. Ireland then had back-to-back home games at Lansdowne Road. Next up was Scotland, who left the Emerald Isle with a 6-5 victory on 27 February 1960, followed with another loss for Ireland by a single point, 10-9 versus Wales on 12 March 1960. Jerry Walsh made his debut in the Scotland match and Locky Butler wore the Irish jersey for the first, and only, time in the defeat to the Welsh.

On 9 April 1960, the Ireland team were in the French capital to take on the reigning champions. A win for the home side would see them share the title with England, who had won three games (versus Ireland, Scotland & Wales) and a 3-3 draw against France at Stade Olympique de Colombes. France had already defeated Scotland and Wales. But, visiting the tourist sights of the French capital, including the Arc de Triomphe, Eiffel Tower, Montmarte, Mont Saint-Michel, Palace of Versailles and Palais des Papes, was not on the Ireland players' itinerary. A win for Ireland would see them finish fourth in the table and condemn the Scots to the bashfulness of taking the wooden spoon back to Murrayfield for the second year in a row. Ireland were beaten 23-6, but despite their lack lustre performances at a snail's pace in all four matches, at least the players were spared the indignity of having to eat a French delicacy, *Escargot* (snails), in the after match dinner. France's victory meant England and France shared the 1960 Six Nations Championship title, whilst Ireland had something to stir Irish stew with. England secured their 14th Triple Crown. Had the match points scored difference been in place, France would have been crowned outright winners with +27 score to England's +20. Pat Costello won his first and only cap for Ireland in Paris.

In 1960, Roy Orbison had his first UK No.1 hit single with *Only The Lonely*. Ireland were feeling very lonely at the foot of the Five Nations Championship table.

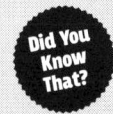 England would not win another Triple Crown for 20 years, 1980 whilst Dawson went on to become Ireland's first ever coach.

MICK THE KICK – IRELAND'S ENGLISHMAN

Michael Anthony Francis English was born in Limerick on 2 June 1933. He was educated at Rockwell College, Cashel, Tipperary and was a member of Bohemian Rugby Football Club (Limerick), winning Munster Senior Cups in 1958, 1959 and 1962. Mick then moved to Dublin and joined Lansdowne Football Club where he won a Leinster Senior Cup in 1965. He later became club President in 1989/90. English played out-half for Ireland from 1958 to 1963, his career sandwiched between two of the greatest ever players to wear a green jersey, Jack Kyle and Mike Gibson. Nicknamed 'Mick the Kick,' English won 16 caps and scored nine points (all from drop goals). When he made his Irish debut on 15 March 1958, he replaced Kyle in the team. Ireland lost the game 9-6 to Wales at Lansdowne Road in the 1958 Five Nations Championship. In 1959, he was a member of the British and Irish Lions side that toured Australia and New Zealand, playing twice before he had to go home early through injury. He played in the 39-11 victory against Queensland, and the 23-14 win over Poverty Bay/East Coast.

TOM AND JERRY

Jeremiah Charles 'Jerry' Walsh was born on 3 November 1938 in Cork. He played club rugby for University College Cork RFU and Sunday's Well and won 26 caps for Ireland from 1960-67. In 1961, he toured South Africa with Ireland and in 1966 he was selected for the British and Irish Lions Tour of Australia and New Zealand. However, he had to fly home early from the Tour down under without winning a Lions' cap as his father was seriously ill. The following year he was a member of the Irish squad that toured Australia. On 13 May 1967, he turned out for Ireland for the last ever time when they beat Australia 11-5 at Sydney Cricket Ground on their 1967 Tour of the country. It was only the fourth time Ireland had played The Wallabies in a Test match since their first encounter in 1927, when Ireland lost 5-3 at Lansdowne Road. Amazingly, Walsh brought the final curtain down on his international career by scoring his first ever try for Ireland in the 11-5 victory. When he retired from the sport aged just 29, he pursued a career as a doctor. Jerry's captain in the game and for the 1967 Tour of Australia was Tom Kiernan.

> **Did You Know That?**
>
> In recognition of his contributions to Irish rugby, the Rugby Writers of Ireland inducted Mick English into the Hall of Fame in 2008.

> **Did You Know That?**
>
> Paul O'Connell, 108 Ireland caps from 2002-15, scoring 40 points, has the middle name Jeremiah.

BORN IN INDIA
PLAYED FOR IRELAND
DIED IN THE USA

Along with Ronnie Dawson, Andy Mulligan captained Ireland in the 1960 Five Nations Championship. Andrew Armstrong Mulligan was born on 4 February 1936 in Kasauli, India. He attended Gresham's School, Holt, Norfolk, from 1945-54 and captained the School's First XV rugby team in 1953-54. His rugby coach considered him to be a gifted scrum-half with an abundance of leadership qualities. At university he played varsity rugby for Cambridge and captained London Irish. On 28 January 1956, he was awarded the first of his 22 caps, a 14-8 loss to France at Stade Olympique de Colombes in the 1956 Five Nations Championship. In 1961, he was selected to tour Australia and New Zealand with the British and Irish Lions and captained the side on 11 August 1961, a 26-6 victory against Manawatu/Horowheuna played at Palmerston North, New Zealand.

His last game for Ireland was against South Africa on 13 May 1961, a 24-8 loss at Olen Park, Cape Town. Ireland toured South Africa in the summer of 1961, played four matches, winning three of them, but only one of the games was against The Springboks.

When he retired from international rugby, having captained Ireland three times, Andy moved to France where he began a career in journalism. In the beginning he got a job writing sports articles for *The Observer* newspaper before writing news articles for both the *Observer* and *The Daily Telegraph*. The *Observer* appointed him Bureau Chief of their Paris office. Later he worked in television for ITN's *News At Ten* and the BBC's *Panorama* shows.

Andy passed away on 24 February 2001, in Medford, Oregon, USA.

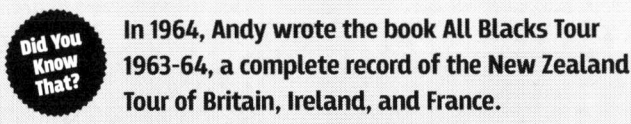

In 1964, Andy wrote the book All Blacks Tour 1963-64, a complete record of the New Zealand Tour of Britain, Ireland, and France.

1961 FIVE NATIONS CHAMPIONSHIP
– A TEAM OF WOODEN HEARTS

Wooden spoon winners the previous year, 25 points scored on the pitch and 47 conceded, surely things could not get any worse in the 1961 Five Nations Championship for Ireland, or could they?

Ronnie Dawson led the Ireland team out of the tunnel at Lansdowne Road for their opening game. Their opponents were England, co-winners with France in 1960, and it was a winning start for the Boys in Green, 11-8. The ghost of 1960 was a distant memory for the Irish fans who went home happy and optimistic for the remaining three games. Ron McCarten and Jonathan Moffat made their debuts for Ireland in the match which saw Ronnie Kavanagh's try converted by Moffett, who also kicked two penalties. Scotland burst Ireland's bubble on Matchday 2, winning 16-8 at Murrayfield which was followed by a 9-0 loss to Wales at the

Arms Park.

Ireland's last game saw two new caps awarded, Tom Nesdale and Dennis Scott pulling on the green jersey. France won the encounter 15-3 and were crowned Five Nations champions for a second time, with three victories and a draw, 5-5 with England.

When France defeated Ireland, Elvis Presley was enjoying his seventh UK No.1 hit song with *Wooden Heart*. How appropriate the song title was in rugby terms as Ireland propped up the Five Nations Championship table once again and added another wooden spoon to their kitchenware.

THE BISH'S FLYING MACHINE

Eamonn McGuire was born in Galway on 28 June 1939, but lived for more than 45 years in Dundalk. He began playing rugby at St Joseph's Patrician College (The Bish) in Galway where he was selected for the Connacht Schools team and was a member of their side which won a Connacht Junior Cup in 1957. When he left The Bish he studied engineering at University College Galway (UCG), where he won several Connacht Senior League and Cup titles. McGuire was a natural athlete; his sprinting ability helped him to become a prolific try scorer. His performances in the UCG shirt attracted the attention of the selectors of a Combined Universities team to play a touring South Africa side in 1965. On 6 April 1965, a Combined Universities team caused one of the biggest ever upsets in rugby union when they beat The Springboks 12-10 at Thomond Park, with McGuire playing a star role in the win.

Aged 23, Eamonn won his first international cap when he was chosen to play in the back-row alongside No. 8 Ian Dick and Matthew Kiely for the 1963 Five Nations Championship match against England at Lansdowne Road on 9 February 1963. Amazingly, the game ended 0-0 and Eamonn impressed the Irish selectors and retained his place in the team, playing alongside stars such as Mike Gibson, Jerry Walsh, Pat Casey, Niall Brophy, Mick English, Syd Millar, Ronnie Dawson, Noel Murphy, Bill McBride, Tom Kiernan and Bill Mulcahy (captain).

His greatest performance in a green jersey was unquestionably against New Zealand at Lansdowne Road on 7 December 1963. According to many sportswriters at the time not only did he

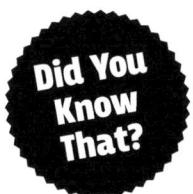

Charles John 'Ian' Dick made his Ireland debut in the Welsh capital when Ireland were defeated 9-0.

When Eamonn moved to Dundalk he played with Lansdowne, Bective and then Dundalk RFC. He won a Leinster Towns Cup final in 1970 with Dundalk and also coached Dundalk the next time they were to win that cup in 1987.

outshine the legendary All Black, Mac Herewini, but Ireland should have won the game. The result was an agonising one for Ireland, losing 6-5, but to this day the game will forever be remembered for the try that never was. McGuire crossed over the New Zealand try line with the ball in his arms but the referee, HB Keenan (England), didn't see him ground it and consequently did not award the try. It would have been a first ever win for Ireland over the All Blacks.

On 8 February 1964, he was part of the Ireland team that recorded a famous victory by beating England for the first time in 16 years, 18-5 at Twickenham Stadium in the 1964 Five Nations Championship.

McGuire won eight caps for Ireland from 1963-64, until a broken leg cut short his career. During his career he also won three Provincial Championship sprinting medals and medals for rowing, and played Gaelic football with Claddagh Gaels in Galway. In 2012, he received the Connacht Rugby Hall of Fame award.

IRELAND V SCOTLAND – HOME AND AWAY

Since their first meeting on 19 February 1877, Ireland and Scotland have played each other 142 times with both nations using different stadiums to host the games.

Ireland at Home	Scotland at Home
Ormeau Cricket Ground, Belfast	Hamilton Crescent, Glasgow
Lansdowne Road	Raeburn Place, Edinburgh
Balmoral Showgrounds, Belfast	Powderhall Stadium, Edinburgh
Croke Park, Dublin	Inverleith, Glasgow
Aviva Stadium, Dublin	Murrayfield Stadium

Murrayfield Stadium's record attendance of 104,000 was set on 1 March 1975 when Scotland beat Wales 12-10 in the 1975 Five Nations Championship. This attendance stood as a world record until 28 August 1999, when 107,042 spectators watched Australia beat New Zealand 28-7 at Stadium Australia, but the 104,000 remains a European record. On 15 July 2000, a new world record was achieved when New Zealand defeated Australia 39-35 at Stadium Australia in front of 109,874 fans. The stadium's capacity at the time was 110,000.

FIRST IRISH SUB

On 25 January 1969, Michael Hipwell became the first substitute to be used by Ireland in an international match (excluding official trial games and international representative matches). Ireland beat France 17-9 at Lansdowne Road in their opening game of the 1969 Five Nations Championship. Hipwell came on for an injured Noel Murphy.

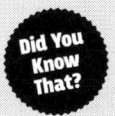 **Mick Hipwell's brother, David, played for the Zimbabwe national rugby union side and when he moved to Rhodesia, he served in the British South Africa Police Force.**

NINE IRELAND DEBUTANTS IN ONE TEST

Laurence Perot Farrar 'Larry' L'Estrange won his first and only cap for Ireland versus England on 10 February 1962, at Twickenham. Ireland lost the game 16-0, which saw eight other debutants in a green jersey: Jimmy Dick, Francis Gilpin, Michael Hipwell, William Raymond Hunter, Raymond McLoughlin, Jimmy Quirke, Noel Turley and a 21-year old Lock from Ballymena Rugby Football Club, William James McBride.

 **Larry L'Estrange undertook National Service and was deployed as part of the Parachute Regiment during the 1956 Suez crisis. Post his military career, he started to play rugby for London Irish where he was awarded the 1963–64 Backs Honours tie.**

In His Own Words

Mick English, 16 caps for Ireland 1958-63, was a popular speaker at rugby dinners and had a tremendous sense of humour. One of his best lines was a description of what happened in a game against England when he went to tackle his opposite number Phil Horrocks-Taylor:
'Horrocks went one way, Taylor went the other and I was left holding the bloody hyphen!'

THE 1962 FIVE NATIONS CHAMPIONSHIP – NO LIGHT AT THE END OF THE TUNNEL

In 1962, Ireland were headed for a unique, but very much unwanted *Treble*. For the previous two seasons they were the strongest side in the Five Nations Championship; well, they propped up all of the other nations by finishing bottom to claim the wooden spoon. In 1959, Ireland finished runners-up to champions France in the table but with only one victory in the next two campaigns in the tournament they got what they deserved, a wooden spoon on each occasion.

Things got off to a really bad start on Matchday 1 when they were completely outclassed by England, thrashed 16-0 at Twickenham on 10 February 1962. Ireland still did not have a coach at the time and were led by their captain, Bill Mulcahy, who was given nine debutants by the Irish selection committee. One of the players wearing the green jersey for the maiden time in the game was a player who would go on to firmly cement his place in the history of not only

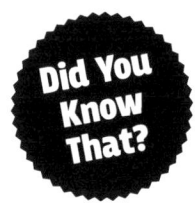

Did You Know That?

Raymond Hunter won 10 caps for Ireland from 1962-66, and played for the British and Irish Lions on their tour of South Africa in 1962, but he was an accomplished cricketer before he played rugby union for Ireland. He played 28 times for the Ireland cricket team between 1957 and 1967, including 111 First-Class matches. For Ireland he scored 800 runs at an average of 21.05 per innings, scoring three half-centuries, and he took 33 wickets at a bowling average (a player's bowling average is the number of runs they have conceded per wicket taken) of 29.97 runs, claiming five wickets in an innings twice. His First-Class career saw him rack-up 202 runs at an average of 11.22 per innings and he took 19 wickets at a bowling average of 23.42 runs. He took five wickets in an innings once. Hunter was a right-arm batsman and a right-arm medium bowler.

Irish rugby but become immortal in the history of the British and Irish Lions, Willie John McBride. No doubt, Mulcahy was thanking the wisdom of the selectors when he trudged off the pitch, head bowed in defeat.

Two weeks later Scotland hammered Ireland 20-6 at Lansdowne Road, with Raymond Hunter scoring a try and a penalty for Ireland. Gerald Hardy made his Irish debut in the game. On 14 April 1962, France defeated Ireland 11-0 at Stade Olympique de Colombes which saw yet another two players winning their first Irish caps, Noel Byrne and James Kelly. Ireland's final game was not played until 17 November 1962 in the 'Hangover Game'. However, the name given to the match had nothing whatsoever to do with the players' going on a drinking binge. A smallpox epidemic broke out in South Wales in March 1962 and April 1962, which caused the postponement of Ireland's home Five Nations Championship game against Wales originally scheduled to be played on 17 March 1962. Nineteen people lost their lives and 900,000 people were vaccinated after a tourist from Pakistan arrived in Cardiff in January 1962 and was diagnosed with the disease.

France had already been crowned 1962 Five Nations champions before the Ireland versus Wales match as they had won three of their four games, whereas Ireland had lost their first three and Wales had won one and lost the other two. The 3-3 draw in Dublin on 17 November 1962, did nothing to console the Irish fans with the selectors tinkering once again with the side by introducing Patrick Dwyer, Matthew Kiely and Michael O'Callaghan into the huge bowl of gruel the fans were fed. Mick English scored a drop goal for Ireland who ended up with the unwanted *Treble*.

In the 1962 Five Nations Championship, Ireland scored just nine match points and conceded 50 to end the competition with a -41 match points difference. They found themselves in a very dark tunnel which did not have any light at the end of it.

1963 FIVE NATIONS CHAMPIONSHIP – THE GREAT ESCAPE

Ireland's Five Nations losing hangover continued into the 1963 Five Nations Championship, losing their opening fixture 25-5 to France at Lansdowne Road. Patrick Casey and John Murray made their debuts for Ireland in the game. Scotland then defeated Ireland 3-0 at Murrayfield before Ireland and England played out a 0-0 draw in Dublin, the first scoreless game between the pair since 1910.

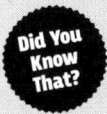

Did You Know That? When Ireland faced Scotland, they were captained by Bill Mulcahy, whilst the Scottish captain was called Ken Scotland.

Wayward Wind, sung by Frank Ifield, was at No.1 in the UK singles charts during the tournament which saw too many of the Irish players throw too many wayward passes in the wind. In their final game Ireland beat Wales 14-6 at the Arms Park, a much welcomed victory that kept them from being presented with four wooden spoons on the bounce. At last, a chink of light appeared at the end of the tunnel.

Wales occupied last place when they lost their last match to France at Stade Olympique de Colombes. But Ireland had performed a feat to mirror what was the biggest grossing movie in 1963, appropriately named *The Great Escape*. Ireland had performed their own Great Escape - ironically, the movie included three tunnels being dug to help allied prisoners of war escape a German Prisoner of War camp. The tunnels were affectionately named *Tom*, *Dick* and *Harry*. Ireland's 1963 Five Nations Championship included a *Tom* (Tom Kiernan) and a *Dick* (Ian Dick), but no Harry appeared.

1964 FIVE NATIONS CHAMPIONSHIP – NEEDLES AND PINS

The 1960s are known as the *Swinging Sixties* in music terms but for Ireland Rugby team they were proving to be a decade to forget.

IRELAND'S RESULTS
England 5 v Ireland 18 – Twickenham
Ireland 3 v Scotland 6 – Lansdowne Road
Ireland 6 v Wales 15 – Lansdowne Road
France 27 Ireland 6 - Stade Olympique de Colombes

Ireland were awarded the wooden spoon again. To liken Ireland's performances to a song enjoyed by the Ireland fans at the time: they were riddled with needles and pins in search of their heroes in green jerseys taking way their pain. Searchers had a No.1 hit song entitled *Needles and Pins*.

Did You Know That? Paddy Lane won his first and only cap for Ireland in the game against Wales. But the question on the lips of all Irish fans, lips that had tasted wood for the fourth time in five years, was what lane would Ireland be travelling down in 1965?

'IN THE 1962 FIVE NATIONS CHAMPIONSHIP, IRELAND SCORED JUST NINE MATCH POINTS AND CONCEDED 50 TO END THE COMPETITION WITH A -41 MATCH POINTS DIFFERENCE. THEY FOUND THEMSELVES IN A VERY DARK TUNNEL WHICH DID NOT HAVE ANY LIGHT AT THE END OF IT.'

1965 FIVE NATIONS CHAMPIONSHIP – REVOLVING DOORS

The *Swinging Sixties* were more like the decade of *Revolving Doors* for Ireland as their form, and the performances of their players, hit highs and lows, as they ebbed and flowed their way through international matches. The Ireland team appeared to be sleepwalking their way through matches.

IRELAND'S RESULTS:
Ireland 3 v France 3 – Lansdowne Road
Ireland 5 v England 0 – Lansdowne Road
Scotland 6 v Ireland 16 – Murrayfield
Wales 14 v Ireland 8 – Arms Park

Ireland finished joint second with France, Wales won the Championship. Two of the No.1 songs in the UK charts during the tournament were:
 4 February 1965 - *You've Lost That Loving Feeling* - The Righteous Brothers
 11 March 1965 – *It's Not Unusual* - Tom Jones
 The Irish fans loving feeling towards the team was most definitely waning, in fact, it was sitting on a sheet of thin ice; and it wasn't really that unusual for Ireland to be beaten by Wales as the dragons had beaten Ireland 11 times already since rugby recommenced in 1947 after World War II had ended.

> **Did You Know That?** Five players made their debuts for Ireland in the draw with France: Mick Doyle, Ken Kennedy, Sean MacHale, Ronnie Lamont and Roger Young.

1966 FIVE NATIONS CHAMPIONSHIP THE GOOD THE BAD AND THE UGLY

One of the biggest Box Office attractions in the Cinemas across Ireland in 1966, was a spaghetti western starring Clint Eastwood entitled *The Good, The Bad and The Ugly*. Ireland's performances on the pitch during the 1966 Five Nations Championship, were occasionally good, by defeating Wales in Dublin, bad losing to France in Paris... and ugly when Scotland beat Ireland 11-3 at Lansdowne Road.

IRELAND'S RESULTS
France 11 v Ireland 6 - Stade Olympique de Colombes
England 6 v Ireland 6 – Twickenham Stadium
Ireland 3 v Scotland 11 – Lansdowne Road
Ireland 9 v Wales 6 – Lansdowne Road
Ireland finished the campaign fourth in the table.

> **Did You Know That?** Mick Molloy made his debut versus France, and Barry Bresnihan made his debut versus England.

1967 FIVE NATIONS CHAMPIONSHIP – IRELAND'S GRADUATE

The top movie in 1967 was *The Graduate,* and *I'm a Believer* by the Monkees was the No 1 song in the music charts from 19 January 1967 to 16 February 1967.

Ireland had their own 'graduate'. Ken Goodall made his debut versus Australia on 21 January 1967, a 15-8 victory at Lansdowne Road. He went on to play another 18 times for his country, all 19 games played in succession, including all four of Ireland's games in the 1967 Five Nations Championship.

IRELAND'S RESULTS
Ireland 3 v England 8 – Lansdowne Road
Scotland 3 v Ireland 5 - Murrayfield
Wales 0 v Ireland 3 – Arms Park
Ireland 6 v France 11 - – Lansdowne Road

Ireland finished joint second with England, France were champions and Wales were awarded the wooden spoon. At long last the Irish fans were believers again.

> **Did You Know That?** In 1970, Ken Goodall switched codes to join the rugby league side, Workington Town in England, playing 82 games, scoring 25 tries.

1968 FIVE NATIONS CHAMPIONSHIP – THE GREEN BERETS

It was only towards the end of the decade when Ireland's fortunes on the rugby pitch took a turn for the better. After practically waddling their way through the decade in a daze, they hit the ground running in the 1968 Five Nations Championship. Ireland won three of their four games to finish runners-up in the table, with their only loss coming against France in Paris on Matchday 1. France were the dominant force in northern hemisphere rugby at the time and won their fifth Championship that year and with it, their first Grand Slam title.

IRELAND'S RESULTS
France 16 v Ireland 6 - Stade Olympique de Colombes
England 9 v Ireland 11 - Twickenham Stadium
Ireland 14 v Scotland 6 – Lansdowne Road
Ireland 9 v Wales 6 – Lansdowne Road

Later in the year (10 April 1968), Cliff Richard had a huge hit with the song *Congratulations*, which seemed a nice follow-up to how Ireland had performed in their four games whilst one of the big movies of the year was *The Green Berets*, directed by and starring John Wayne. Tom Kiernan was the Ireland captain and led his men in the green jersey from the front.

1969 FIVE NATIONS CHAMPIONSHIP - TRUE GRIT

There was something in the air in the last two years of the 1960s and it wasn't just the No.1 song in the charts entitled *Something In The Air* by Thunderclap Newman. The previous year Ireland claimed a runners-up spot in the Five Nations Championship, their highest position in the table of the decade, a decade which saw the Ireland players eat quite regularly with a wooden spoon. In the 1969 Five Nations Championship, Ireland kept up their good run of results and for the second championship in a row they won three games and lost one to finish runners-up for the second year on the trot.

IRELAND'S RESULTS
Ireland 17 v France 9 – Lansdowne Road
Ireland 17 v England 15 – Lansdowne Road
Scotland 0 v Ireland 16 – Murrayfield
Wales 24 v Ireland 11 – Arms Park

Wales won the 1969 Five Nations Championship, having won three and drawn one of their four matches in the tournament.

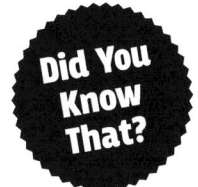

Brian O'Brien made his debut in the loss to France, thereby becoming Shannon Rugby Football Club's first ever international. O'Brien spent over 14 years playing at senior level with Shannon RFC, before going on to coach them to consecutive Munster Senior Cup titles in 1977 and 1978.

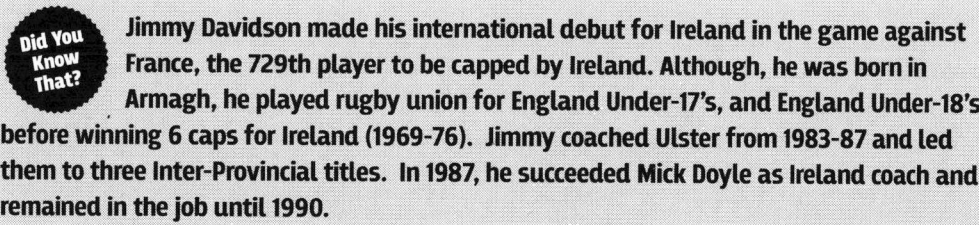

Jimmy Davidson made his international debut for Ireland in the game against France, the 729th player to be capped by Ireland. Although, he was born in Armagh, he played rugby union for England Under-17's, and England Under-18's before winning 6 caps for Ireland (1969-76). Jimmy coached Ulster from 1983-87 and led them to three Inter-Provincial titles. In 1987, he succeeded Mick Doyle as Ireland coach and remained in the job until 1990.

1970s

WILLIE JOHN MCBRIDE
THE INVINCIBLES
BLOODY SUNDAY
MARLENE DIETRICH'S HAIRY LEGS

'My job is not to be easy on people. My job is to take these great people we have and to push them and make them even better.'
Steve Jobs

WILLIE JOHN MCBRIDE – THE GREATEST EVER LION

'This patch of grass. This blood-stained ground. This cauldron of noise. This maker of Kings. This sanctuary. A fortress built to enthral. Forged to stand against adversaries. Apprentices, testers, against true competitors and those who merely come to compete. This Lion's den. This Lansdowne Road. A world on its own. This journey of ours. Dark nights. Endless dawns. Blood, sweat and tears. Serving as refuge, home and shelter. This arena. This theatre. This battleground. This conquest. Hand me my robe. Put on my crown. I have eternal longings to be King.'

William James McBride was born in Toomebridge, County Antrim, Northern Ireland on 6 June 1940. Aged just four he lost his father and spent most of his childhood helping out on the family farm. There was no rugby history in the McBride family until he attended Ballymena Academy, County Antrim. Aged 17, a house match at his school would change that and his life forever. 'They came to me and said, you're a big guy. If you play, we'll have 15. I hadn't a clue about this game, but I was big and it wasn't a problem to me, I could shake people off. Next week I was picked for the school 3rd XV, and the following week the 2nd XV... then the following week the school's first XV,' recalled Willie about the time the rugby coaches at Ballymena Academy asked him to play for their team.

On 10 February 1962, at 6'4" and weighing 16 stones and one pound, 21-year-old McBride won his first cap for Ireland. But it was a debut to forget as Ireland lost 16-0 to England at Twickenham in the Five Nations Championship, losing three and drawing one (3-3 with Wales in Dublin) of their four games to end up with the unwanted wooden ppoon. Later that same year he was selected by the British and Irish Lions for their Tour of South Africa. On 10 April 1965, Willie was a member of the Irish side that defeated The Springboks for the first time in their history, winning 9-6 at Lansdowne Road. Two years later, 13 May 1967, WJ helped Ireland record their first ever win in Australia when they beat the Wallabies 11-5 at Sydney Cricket Ground. It was the first time a Home Nations side had beaten a major southern hemisphere team in their own country. In 1966 (New Zealand) and 1968 (South Africa) he toured with the Lions again.

In the much feted, glorious and illustrious history of Ireland's and the British & Irish Lions rugby union odyssey, one man, Willie John McBride, stands majestically high above all others, as … *King of Kings*. He was a 'Leader of Men', a rugby 'Demigod', his teammates happy to be subservient to his every call to arms. Willie is the undisputed Lion King and he donned his red King's Robe 17 times, a record number of Test caps won by a British and Irish Lion. He was the man who conquered rugby's Mount Everest when he helped the Lions to a first ever Test series win over New Zealand in 1971. Despite being considered by some rugby commentators to be 'Over the hill' in 1971 aged 31, Willie was made 'Leader of the Pack' on that historic

1971 Tour to the southern hemisphere. One of the lines from the song *Leader of the Pack*, written by George 'Shadow' Morton, Jeff Barry, and Ellie Greenwich, a No.1 pop hit in the USA Billboard Charts in 1964 for the American girl group The Shangri-Las, is *'I'll never forget him, the leader of the pack'*.

When the Lions toured South Africa in 1974, their manager, Syd Millar, who was also the head coach of Ireland (1973-75) knew only too well who he wanted as his captain. And he did not have to look too far from the Emerald Isle, appointing Big WJ captain of his Lions, which included a few uncapped cubs in the squad. The Lions' 1974 Tour of South Africa was marred by some of the most brutal and violent international matches ever played. But the Ulsterman led his men from the front and attacked The Springboks like an Irish wolfhound, ordering his troops never to take a step backwards. He instigated a policy of 'One In, All In' … meaning that when one Lion retaliated against an opponent, his 14 teammates were required to join in the melee or pick a fight with the closest Springbok to him. The plan was known as the '99' (as opposed to the '999' a person telephoned for an emergency) and it worked to great effect as the referee was left bewildered as to which player had actually started the violence that had unfolded on the pitch. The lack of cameras at games at the time meant that the referee was left powerless in terms of handing out punishment to any single instigator and no Lion was sent off during the Tour. The '99' was used a few times on the tour and most memorably in the Third Test at Port Elizabeth when the legendary Wales full-back, JPR Williams, ran half the length of the pitch to knock out Springbok second-row, Johnnes van Heerden.

Willie John led the Lions to a historic, and first Test series win over South Africa, winning 21 of the 22 matches they played, including a clean sweep with a 3-0 Test series victory. The Lions were held to a draw in the fourth Test, 13-13 at Ellis Park, Johannesburg in controversial circumstances. In the dying minutes of the game, Irish flanker Fergus Slattery broke through the South African line and appeared to successfully ground the ball, only for the referee to adjudge it was held up. The referee was South African (Max Baise). With the Lions just two metres from the Springboks' line in the 76th minute of the game, Baise, a schoolmaster, blew for the final whistle. It denied the tourists a whitewash in South Africa, at a time when apartheid was a cancer in the country, but it granted the 1974 British and Irish Lions the legendary moniker of 'The Invincibles'. When he was asked about the decision afterward, Baise is said to have replied: 'Look boys, I have to live here'.

On 1 March 1975, McBride pulled on the Irish jersey for the 62nd and penultimate time and led his men across the white chalk line at Willie's spiritual home, Lansdowne Road as their captain for the 10th time. Ireland's opponents were France in a Five Nations Championship game. That day he could do no wrong and the big 34-year-old lock not only led his side to a comfortable 25-6 victory but he even managed to score a try himself, his only score for his beloved Ireland. At the final whistle every man, woman and child in the 50,000 audience stood up and applauded as Big Willie John walked off the hallowed Dublin turf, McBride's Tara - like Conn Cétchathach, also known as Conn of the Hundred Battles, a semi-legendary High King of Ireland (*Ard-Rí na hÉireann*) - leaving a battlefield, majestic in victory. Two weeks later, 15 March 1975, he played for and captained Ireland for the last time in an illustrious career, a 32-4 loss to Wales in Cardiff in the 1975 Five Nations Championship.

After retiring from playing the game, he coached the Irish team from 1983-84 and managed the British and Irish Lions on their 1983 Tour of New Zealand. In 1997 he was an inaugural inductee into the International Rugby Board Hall of Fame; in 2004 he was named by *Rugby World* magazine as '*Rugby Personality of the Century*', and he was awarded an MBE in 1971 and a CBE in 2019.

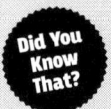 **Willie John McBride is a leading supporter of the Wooden Spoon Society, a charity which does so much wonderful work for children and young people with disabilities.**

BLACK OR WHITE

The IRFU's decision to play a Test match against South Africa at Lansdowne Road on 10 January 1970, was met with huge controversy by many across Ireland as a result of South Africa's racist apartheid policy. During the early 1960s anti-apartheid protestors could be regularly seen in O'Connell Street, Dublin holding signs that called for the boycott of South African goods. The IRFU found itself in a tight corner and announced that: '*Cultural and sporting relations were the last links that should be broken with a country whose laws and policies incurred condemnation*'. The Springboks actually visited Ireland a few years prior to 1970, winning 9-6 in Dublin on 10 April 1965.

Prior to the arrival in Dublin of the all-white South African squad, *The Irish Times* front page read: '*SPRINGBOKS' HOTEL TO BE 'BLACKED'* - *P.O. union will ban mail, phone service.*'

An official from Post Office Union told a reporter: 'If the Springboks' headquarters hotel was known, all telephone and mail services to it would be withdrawn. When we find out the hotel, we will give the telephone number to all exchanges and see that it is not serviced. Similarly, no mail will be delivered to the hotel. All other guests will be affected. The ban will last for the Springboks' stay'. Added to this, the Trade Union responsible for staff working for RTE issued a statement to the effect that none of their members would work on televising the match for the broadcaster. All across the Republic of Ireland Trade Unions voiced their disapproval of the game. Students at Trinity College, Dublin voiced their anger too and voted not to allow the tourists to train on-campus with the headline in their student paper, *Trinity News*, reading: '*NO RACISTS HERE*'. Indeed, the groundswell of opposition to the game resulted in some heated debates inside the Dáil with Fine Gael TD Patrick Donegan making his views clearly known on the matter:

'We have heard a great deal about the Springboks' tour. We all deplore the fact that there is discrimination in South Africa, but I have come to the conclusion that 15 men on one side and 15 men on the other, all young, rolling around in the mud, have nothing on their minds but where they are going to get the prettiest girl and take her out for a meal as soon as the match is over, and I am afraid that is not political. If I am not at the Springboks match, I shall be out hunting and anyone who wants to protest about either can protest away'.

The debates unfolded a wide divergence in opinion of South Africa which cascaded its' way into public opinion on the issue of whether the game should go ahead or not. There were those who recognised the historical relationship between Irish nationalists and the Boers, who both

'With the Lions just two metres from the Springboks' line in the 76th minute of the game, Baise, a schoolmaster, blew for the final whistle. It denied the tourists a whitewash in South Africa, at a time when apartheid was a cancer in the country, but it granted the 1974 British and Irish Lions the legendary moniker of 'The Invincibles'. When he was asked about the decision afterward, Baise is said to have replied: 'Look boys, I have to live here'.'

fought British rule of their country. Some other South African sympathisers cited that politics had no place in sport. The Irish Revolutionary Youth Movement totally opposed the visit. In late December 1969, an unsuccessful attempt was made by some protestors to set fire to the press box at Lansdowne Road, whilst veiled threats from the Irish Republican Army had also raised an ugly head.

When the team finally arrived at Dublin Airport on 7 January 1970, they were greeted by dozens of anti-Apartheid activists in the airport itself carrying *BOKS GO HOME* and *NO RACIALISM IN SPORT* signs. And, when their coach left the airport, it was pelted with eggs … white ones of course. The team was booked into the Royal Starlight Hotel in Bray, Wicklow by the IRFU, incidentally a non-union hotel at the time, where once again protestors had gathered to voice their opinions. Protestors held homemade placards aloft which read: *BLACK AND WHITES UNITE'* and *SPRINGBOKS' GAME, IRELAND'S SHAME*. However, not everyone outside the hotel was opposing the visit as a few hundred local schoolchildren, young Irish rugby fans, cheered the arrival of the Springboks.

One of the most popular songs being played on the radio was *Bad Moon Rising* by Creedence Clearwater Revival. On the afternoon of the game there was a mini-rising in the Irish capital when a crowd of 10,000 protestors marched in solidarity from Parnell Square to the ground in opposition to the fixture. One of the marchers was a young man named Charlie Bird, who would go on to have a successful career at RTE. Writing about the event in his memoirs some years later he said:

'*My spare time was increasingly taken up with political involvement. There was an upsurge in left-wing activism in Dublin. It was the same all over Western Europe. I got involved in the Labour Party and with the Young Socialists. These were exciting times… In January 1970, the all-white South African rugby team arrived in Dublin. The Springboks' were touring Britain and Ireland and the opening match of the tour was scheduled for Lansdowne Road. I was one of those on the picket outside the Royal Starlight Hotel in Bray where the Springboks were staying. There was a huge march outside the stadium on the afternoon of the match: 10,000 protestors marched from the city centre to Lansdowne Road. I helped to carry a Labour Party banner. Despite the size of the crowd, the demonstration passed off without any serious incidents*'.

The South African team was taken to Lansdowne Road

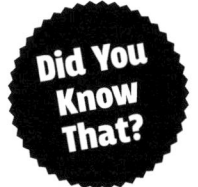

South Africa were also due to play Ulster at Ravenhill during their visit to Ireland but the game was cancelled on the advice of the Royal Ulster Constabulary. At the time the Natal Mercury, an English language newspaper published in Durban, South Africa was quick to comment that because of the recent violence in the north of Ireland, 'the battlefield was already booked'. All across Belfast barbed-wire was on daily display wrapped around wooden structures by the British Army in the form of temporary road blocks.

by a non-union coach company, again arranged by the IRFU, and the game went ahead on 10 January 1970, before a relatively small crowd for a home international. The match ended 8-8; Alan Duggan scored a try which was converted by captain Tom Kiernan who also kicked over a penalty. Landsdowne Road, normally crammed to the rafters for the visit of an opposing nation, was more like a ghost town in parts with no fans behind the goals. Barbed-wire fencing surrounded the pitch to prevent any of the protestors from hunting down a Springbok.

President Éamon de Valera declined an invitation from the IRFU to attend the game.

Four days later the tourists beat Munster 25-9 at Thomond Park, with another heavy Gardai presence in attendance. However, The Springboks were given a warm welcome to Limerick by a local organisation called *The National Movement*. The Movement's members visited the hotel where the South African entourage were staying and delivered a welcoming letter to the team. Some carried placards which read: *We Support White Christian South Africa* and *Boks Yes, Reds No*.

In November 1991, Michael Jackson had a hit single entitled *Black or White*. Some 21 years earlier, Ireland had its' version of the song title played out on the pitch at Lansdowne Road. And that day there was not only no winner in the game, there was no winner on or off the terraces either.

1970 FIVE NATIONS CHAMPIONSHIP – FROM SECOND TO THIRD

Ireland ended the 1960s with a runners-up place to Wales in the 1969 Five Nations Championship. In 1970, Ronnie Dawson was still in charge of the team and Tom Kiernan was still his first choice as captain. In their opening game Ireland lost 8-0 to France, Five Nations champions in 1967 and Grand Slam winners in 1968, at Stade Olympique de Colombes. The match was played on 24 January 1970, 14 days after the opening fixture in the tournament (France beat Scotland 11-9 at Murrayfield) because Ireland played South Africa on 10 January 1970.

In Game No.2, Ireland lost 9-3 to England at Twickenham and then beat Scotland 16-11 in Dublin. On 14 March 1970, the team nicknamed 'The Team of all the Talents', Wales, arrived in Dublin in search of back-to-back Triple Crowns. Wales, the reigning champions, had already seen off the challenges of Scotland, 18-9 in Cardiff, and England, 17-13 in London. The odds were stacked against the Irish but on the day, they outplayed and out-ran the Welsh, backed-up with an impregnable defence. No one inside Lansdowne Road could quite believe it and nor did they ever envisage such a comfortable win, 14-0.

France and Wales shared the title with Ireland two points behind them to finish third.

> **Did You Know That?** Rugby Union history was made in the England versus Wales match at Twickenham. The match referee, Robert Calmet (France), had to leave the field at half-time and was replaced by Johnny Johnson of England. Twenty minutes from time, Gareth Edwards had to leave the field of play with an injury and was replaced by Ray 'Chico' Hopkins. It was the first and only time that Edwards failed to finish a game in his 63-cap career (53 for Wales and 10 for the British and Irish Lions). Chico then helped create the piece of history by scoring a try, the first try scored by a replacement player, to be awarded by a replacement referee at international level. It was Hopkins' only ever appearance for Wales but will forever be remembered by all Welsh fans.

1971 FIVE NATIONS CHAMPIONSHIP – THIRD PLACE AGAIN

The 1971 Five Nations Championship is one many Ireland fans will wish to forget, winning just a single game, drawing one and losing two. Ireland began their campaign with a 9-9 draw versus France at Lansdowne Road. Edwin Grant scored a try and Barry O'Driscoll converted two penalties. England then beat Ireland 9-6 in Dublin, with Grant scoring another try, along with a try from Alan Duggan. Tom Kiernan was the Ireland captain in the first fixture but Mike Gibson took over the captaincy from Game No.2 onwards. Ireland's solitary victory came at Murrayfield when they defeated Scotland 17-5, thanks to tries from Duggan (2) and Grant, with Gibson scoring one conversion and two penalties. Wales battered Ireland 23-9 at the Arms Park, with Gibson scoring all of the visitors' points from three penalties. In their final game, Wales beat France 9-5 at Stade Olympique de Colombes meaning they won the 1971 Five Nations Championship for the seventeenth time, won their twelfth Triple Crown and landed a sixth Grand Slam which was their first since 1952.

For the second year in a row, Ireland finished third in the table, France ended runners-up.

> **Did You Know That?** Alan Duggan (25 caps, 11 tries) made his debut for Ireland against New Zealand at Lansdowne Road on 7 December 1963 aged 19 years old. The game will forever be remembered for a bad refereeing decision made when Ireland were leading 5-3. In the final 20 minutes of the match, Pat Casey, the University College Dublin centre, put in a high crossfield kick. Eamon Maguire, the University College Galway flanker, was the first player to react and leaped into the air and caught it in the corner to score a try. But the referee, Mr H Keenan from England, ruled out the try for offside.
> Ireland's Bill Mulcahy who played in the match later recalled the moment: 'Eamon, God rest him, was very fast out of the traps. He tore up and jumped in the air, caught it Gaelic fashion, if you like. I think the referee probably decided he couldn't possibly be onside because he was so fast out of the traps'.

1972 FIVE NATIONS CHAMPIONSHIP – AN ESCALATOR TO HELL

This was the first Home Nations/Four Nations/Five Nations Championship in which a try was worth four points.

In 1972, the Five Nations Championship was not completed for the first time since the Second World War. Scotland and Wales refused to travel to Dublin as a result of the unsettling political tension in Ireland with The Troubles raging in Northern Ireland and following the wake of 'Bloody Sunday'. On 2 February 1972, the British Embassy in Merrion Square, Dublin was attacked with petrol bombs. The Dublin Fire Brigade were unable to reach the Embassy and the building was gutted.

On 29 January 1972, Ireland beat France 14-9 at Stade Olympique de Colombes and a fortnight later they defeated England 16-12 at Twickenham. Although the remaining fixtures of the schedule were fulfilled, as both Ireland and Wales won all their matches (Wales beat England 12-3 away, France 20-6 and Scotland 35-12, both games were played at the Arms Park), neither nation were awarded the championship title.

Ireland, coached by Syd Millar, and captained by Tom Kiernan, would surely have won the 1972 title given the home advantage they would have had over Scotland and Wales had they not pulled out of travelling to the Irish capital. The Ireland squad was not merely a good group of Irish players, they were an elite crew that can rival any in the country's proud history. The team included the immensely talented Barry McGann and John Moloney, the modern-day Johnny Sexton and Conor Murray, as well as Kevin Flynn and Tom Grace. The squad had seven Ireland captains, Kiernan becoming the seventh among them. Added to the mix, Ireland could also field seven British and Irish Lions: Mike Gibson, Ken Kennedy, Sean Lynch, Stewart McKinney, Ray McLoughlin, Fergus Slattery and the Lion King himself, Willie John McBride.

This wasn't only an excellent group of Irish players, they were a hugely talented squad that were denied that Grand Slam opportunity for reasons best known to the Welsh Rugby Union (WRU) and the Scottish Rugby Union (SRU) when dealing with issues way beyond sport. Bear in mind also that it was the first time since Ireland won the Grand Slam in 1948, that they had beaten France and England away from home in the same Five Nations Championship campaign. Naturally, beating the Scots and the Welsh in Dublin would not have been a formality, but the least this Galácticos of Irish rugby deserved was a shot at emulating Ireland's Golden Boys from 1948.

Almost every radio station in the world was playing the same songs when the championship matches were being played, including the person in the announcer's booth at Lansdowne Road whose job it was to entertain the fans by playing songs that were popular in the charts at the time. Songs played before games in Cardiff, Dublin, Edinburgh and London included: *I'd Like To Teach The World To Sing (In Perfect Harmony)* by The New Seekers, *Jeepster* by Tyrannosaurus-Rex, *Is This The Way To Amarillo* by Tony Christie, '*Coz I Luv You*' by Slade ... and the Irish fans' favourite, *Stairway To Heaven* by Led Zeppelin. Terrorism had disrupted the 1972 Five Nations Championship and later that same year, five Israeli athletes and six Israeli coaches were killed in cold blood by the Palestinian militant organisation, The Black September, at the 1972 Olympic Games in what became known as 'The Munich Massacre'. Sporting events around the world stood on a precipice looking at an escalator to hell.

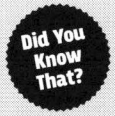 **The 1972 Five Nations Championship marked the last time France used Stade Olympique de Colombes as their home venue for international matches. In the summer of 1972, the rebuilt Parc des Princes was reopened, meaning France moving its Five Nations Championship matches to it.**

1973 FIVE NATIONS CHAMPIONSHIP – FIVE WAY CHAMPIONSHIP TIE THANKS TO A MONSTER KICK

Ireland won the 1973 Five Nations Championship but so too did England, France, Scotland and Wales. It was the first and only time in the competition's history the championship was shared by all of the nations that had participated. Each country won two games at home and lost two games away. There were no bonus points on offer back then or deciding the winners on a points difference basis. If the points difference system had been in operation at the time, Wales would have been crowned champions as they had a points difference of +10 (France +2, Ireland +2, Scotland -4 and England -10). Wales were the reigning champions as the 1972 edition of the tournament had been abandoned. Going into the 1973 competition the Welsh were the firm favourites to win the title and in their opening game they thrashed England 25-9 at the Arms Park. The Welsh side was full of legends: Phil Bennett, Gerald Davies, Mervyn Davies, Gareth Edward, Derek Quinnell and the quite majestic, JPR Williams.

In their opening match Ireland beat England 18-9 (the famous game when the Irish fans cheered the English players out on to the pitch) at Lansdowne Road. Dick Milliken from Bangor, County Down made his debut in the green jersey and the 22-year-old celebrated it with a try. Two defeats then followed on the road: 19-14 to Scotland at Murrayfield and a 16-12 defeat by Wales at the Arms Park. It all came down to the final game when France visited Dublin on 14 April 1973. A draw or win would see France crowned champions as they already had four points from their three games played, as had England, Scotland and Wales who had all played four matches. Ireland were on two points. Lansdowne Road was packed out, a crowd of 50,000 holding their breath to see if Ireland could secure a win which would see all five nations share the title of 1973 Five Nations Champions.

Syd Millar, the Ireland coach, recalled Mick Molloy to partner Willie John McBride in the heart of the Irish defence. Millar's tactic worked as the Irish stifled the French attacks by dominating set piece plays. Jean-Pierre Romeu, top points scorer in the 1973 tournament with 26 to his name, scored a try for the visitors who missed four kicks at goal, three penalties and a conversion. Ireland for their part scored two penalties, one from Mike Gibson and the other from Anthony Howard 'Tony' Ensor which is considered to be one of the greatest ever scores in the competition's long and illustrious history.

It was a very windy day at Lansdowne Road when Ireland won a free kick about five yards inside their own half. Ensor approached the referee and told him that he wanted to kick for

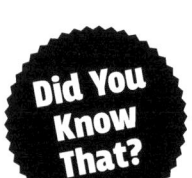

Did You Know That?

During the post-match dinner following Ireland's 18-9 win over England, John Pullin, the England captain, delivered a quip summing up how his side had played: 'Well we might not be any good but at least we turned up'. which was received with a loud applause.

goal. The TV cameras showed Tony studding the ground quite forcefully with the heel of his right boot despite the fact that it was already well torn up. Ensor had the wind at his back and wanted to make sure that the ball would not blow over. Kicking tees were non-existent in rugby in 1973. Ensor ran at the ball and booted it with his right foot, giving it everything he had … and the crowd exploded into cheers when it crossed over the bar for three points. It was a monster of a kick and one that will be remembered forever by those who witnessed it that day with Ireland winning 6-4.

Tony made his international debut for Ireland in the 1973 Five Nations Championship, playing in the loss to Wales. He was capped 22 times for Ireland, scoring 36 points including a solitary try versus France in 1975 in a 25-6 win for the Irish at Lansdowne Road. On 18 March 1975, he won his last cap against England, a 15-9 loss at Twickenham.

MARLENE DIETRICH AND HAIRY LEGS

'Tony Ward is the most important rugby player in Ireland. His legs are far more important to his country than even those of Marlene Dietrich were to the film industry. A little hairier, maybe, but a pair of absolute winners.'

Mike Gibson writing about Tony Ward, the Ireland fly-half and goal kicker, in a match programme during the 1979 Five Nations Championship. Ward scored in all four of Ireland's games in the tournament.

IN HIS OWN WORDS

'He was one of the finest players of his generation, one of the finest players ever to represent Ireland and the British & Irish Lions, and a man who epitomised the very ethos of the game and its values.'

Syd Millar speaking about his former teammate, Mike Gibson, after Gibson was inducted to the IRB Hall of Fame in May 2011

1974 FIVE NATIONS CHAMPIONSHIP – CHAMPIONS

The 1974 Five Nations Championship was a very close affair and was not settled until the final weekend of games when the outcome of the Scotland versus France and England against Wales matches had been decided.

Ireland began the 1974 Five Nations Championship, the 45th edition of the tournament with France included, and the 80th edition of the northern hemisphere rugby union championship involving England, Ireland, Scotland and Wales, with a 9-6 defeat to France at their new home, Parc des Princes. Tony Ensor scored two penalties for Ireland in the match. The legendary Moss Keane made his debut for Ireland in the game aged 25. In Game 2, Ireland drew 9-9 with Wales at Lansdowne Road, with the reliable Ensor kicking three penalties for the home side. Two legendary players scored the Welsh points that day: J.J. Williams scored a try and Phil Bennett converted it and then kicked a penalty.

Game 3 meant a trip to the English capital for the Boys in Green. The Irish fans poured into Twickenham in Richmond, London to watch their heroes play, many of them living closer to London than their native Dublin. It was a good night in London for the Irish fans who celebrated a 26-21 win. Ireland's last game was against Scotland in Dublin on 2 March 1974. A victory for Ireland could not give them the Triple Crown or a Grand Slam, but depending on the results of the other four nations in their final game, could see Ireland crowned champions. Dick Milliken scored a try for the home side, converted by Mike Gibson, and Stewart McKinney added a penalty to give Ireland a 9-6 win.

Gibson's Zodiac birth sign is Sagittarius, the half-human and half-horse, the learned healer whose higher intelligence forms a bridge between Earth and Heaven. Also known as the 'Archer', Sagittarius is represented by the symbol of a bow and arrow. Gibson wasn't permitted to take a bow and arrow on to the pitch with him, nor a catapult, but he did not need either as his right foot was both. He would have put William Tell to shame.

Ireland topped the table with two wins, one draw and one loss, meaning they had five points.

Scotland defeated France 19-6 at Murrayfield to finish on four points (they also beat England 16-14 in the Scottish

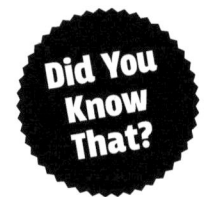

Did You Know That?

Max Boyce, a Welsh comedian, entertainer and singer, and a huge fan of Wales, often carried a giant inflatable leek on stage to his concerts, composed a song after his country's loss to England about 'blind Irish referees'.

*I am an entertainer,
and I sing for charity.
For Oxfam and for Shelter,
for those worse off than me.
Bangladesh,
Barnardos Homes,
and though I don't get paid,
It does one good to
do some work
for things like Christan aid.
But of all the concerts that
I've done
for the homeless overseas,
The one I did that pleased
me most
was not for refugees.
Was for a home in Ireland
that stands amongst
the trees –
The Sunshine Home
in Dublin
for blind Irish referees!*

capital) whilst England saw of the challenge of Wales with a 16-12 victory on home turf. Amazingly, it was England's only win the 1974 Five Nations Championship (wooden spoon winners), but one which had Irish eyes smiling, because it meant Ireland won their eighth title outright (seven other titles had been shared with other teams). But it could so easily have gone in favour of Wales when winger JJ Williams appeared to score a winning try late in their game against England, but it was disallowed by the referee John West, who just so happened to be Irish, born in Cork on 27 July 1939.

Ireland won their first title in 24 years whilst Mike Gibson, David Duckham (England) and Williams (Wales) were the leading try scorers with three apiece.

IRELAND V WALES – HOME AND AWAY

Since their first meeting on 28 January 1882, Ireland and Wales have played each other 134 times with both nations using different stadiums to host the games.

IRELAND AT HOME
Lansdowne Road
Ulster Cricket Ground, Belfast
Thomond Park
Balmoral Showgrounds, Belfast
Ravenhill
Croke Park
Aviva Stadium

WALES AT HOME
National Stadium/Arms Park, Cardiff
Birkenhead Park, Birkenhead, England
St Helen's, Swansea
Stradey Park, Llanelli
Wembley Stadium, London
Millennium Stadium, Cardiff

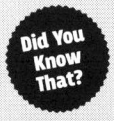

Did You Know That? During the 1999 Five Nations Championship, Wales used Wembley to host their home matches as the Millennium Stadium was still being built. Ireland beat Wales 29-23 in London and Wales then played England in their final game of the tournament. Wales were the 'home' side and an 'away' win for England would see them crowned Five Nations champions, Triple Crown winners and Grand Slam winners. England led 31-25 and were on course for all three titles until a superb last-gasp try from Scott Gibbs, followed by a conversion from Neil Jenkins, broke the hearts of the England fans inside the stadium. And, to add salt to the wound, Scotland won the last ever edition of the Five Nations Championship with a superior points scored difference to that of England's, +41 to +25.

1975 FIVE NATIONS CHAMPIONSHIP – NOT GOOD ENOUGH

The 1975 Five Nations Championship resulted in a disappointing third place finish in the table for Ireland, the reigning champions, despite being captained by the iconic and legendary, Willie John McBride. The champions started soundly with a 12-9 victory over England at Lansdowne Road on 18 January 1975. Mike Gibson kept up his good try scoring form with another try whilst William 'Billy' McMachan McCombe also scored a try and successfully converted his and Gibson's. But, in their next outing, Scotland clipped Ireland's wings with a 20-13 win at Murrayfield. However, the ever-resilient Ireland rose from the ashes and defeated France 25-6 in Dublin to get back in the race to retain their title. Alas, it was a false dawn because Wales taught Ireland a rugby lesson in Cardiff, winning the match 32-4 at the Arms Park. The victory gave the Welsh their 18th title whilst McCombe was the top points scorer notching-up an impressive 26.

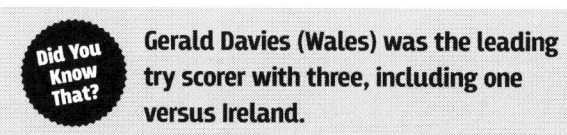

Did You Know That? Gerald Davies (Wales) was the leading try scorer with three, including one versus Ireland.

IRELAND AND THE HAKA

Ask any sports fan what they consider to be sport's greatest and most iconic pre-match ritual and most will respond *'The Haka'*. New Zealand perform their ceremonial Haka before every international, and is feared and respected by opponents and loved by fans of all rugby nations. Ireland have faced the Haka on many occasions. However, the Haka is not just a rugby war dance, it is any form of Maori ceremonial dancing which includes a celebration or a welcome to guests. It is a ritual which is embedded in Maori culture and mythology, and is believed to have originated from Tane-rore, the son of the Sun God, Tama-nui-te-ra, and his second wife, Hine-raumati, the Summer maid. The trembling hand action performed during the Haka is a physical representation of the shimmering air referred to in *Te haka a Tanerore*. The Maoris believe that when the land is very hot, the air shimmers. The current Haka, *Kapa o Pango*, (meaning *Team in Black*) was specifically written in 2005 for the All Blacks and its composer pointed out that it has nothing whatsoever to do with war. 'It's ceremonial. It's about building your physical, spiritual and intellectual capacity prior to doing something very important. This is not a war dance. It's about building the confidence inwardly. It's a preparation,' said its composer Professor Derek Lardelli, who is an expert in Maori customs and cultural advisor to the national team. Lardelli's Haka includes references to the symbol of New Zealand rugby, the Silver Fern, and calls on the players to dominate and show their supremacy.

The Haka was first witnessed in rugby in Australia in 1884 and came to prominence four years later when a team of Maori players toured England, Ireland, Wales, Australia and New Zealand in 1888-89. However, it was not a regular feature of All Blacks rugby over the following

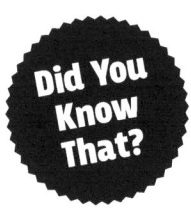

Did You Know That?

On 18 November 1989, Willie Anderson, the Ireland captain, led his men into the All Blacks' half in defiance of the Haka. The crowd at Lansdowne Road gave him a standing ovation but his team lost the game 23-6. Then, exactly 19 years later, 18 November 2008, the Munster team, led by their New Zealand quarter of Doug Howlett Lifeimi Mafi, Rua Tipoki and the replacement Jeremy Manning, performed their own version of the Haka before the All Blacks began their own. Howlett was the most capped All Black on the field, having won 62 caps, scoring a record 49 tries, before jumping ship after the 2007 Rugby World Cup to sign for Munster. Despite throwing down the gauntlet, Munster narrowly lost the match 18-16 at Thomond Park.

100 years particularly when the team did not contain several Maori players. In 1905, it was performed before most games played outside New Zealand but was not a constant until 1987 when it became a pre-match ritual in New Zealand. When the All Blacks toured the United Kingdom and Ireland in 1974, the Haka was only performed once in the 26 games they played. The Haka is usually led by a player with Maori heritage but this is not always the case. The *Kapa o Pango* was led by Tana Umaga in 2005 - he was born in New Zealand and is of Samoan descent, and more recently by TJ Perenara, who was born in New Zealand. Graham Henry, the coach of the All Blacks from 2004-11, said the *Kapa o Pango* represented modern New Zealand with its Maori, Pacific nations (Fiji, Samoa & Tonga) and European heritage saying: 'We felt it was a great representation of the unity of the group'. The most famous Haka is called the *Ka Mate*, and was written circa 1820 by the head of the Ngati Toa Rangatira tribe and was first performed before an All Blacks' game in 1906. Over the next 99 years it was the most-used Haka, although other versions were composed for particular tours. New Zealand is not the only nation to perform a ceremonial dance before a match. Fiji first performed their own dance, the *Cibi*, on a tour to New Zealand in 1939. In 2012, Fiji adopted a new war cry, the *Bole*. Meanwhile, Samoa performs the *Siva Tau*, and Tonga perform the *Sipi Tau*.

In His Own Words

'Willie John McBride will always be synonymous with the great game of rugby and in particular with the British and Irish Lions. It's been a pleasure to have played alongside him, it's been a great pleasure to have known him. Without question, he's not only a fine rugby player, he's a great gentleman.;
Gareth Edwards (Wales) who was a teammate of Willie on the 1971 (New Zealand) & 1974 (South Africa) British & Irish Lions Tours.

1976 FIVE NATIONS CHAMPIONSHIP – MIKE GIBSON APPOINTED CAPTAIN

Following the retirement of Willie John McBride the previous year, Mike Gibson was Roly Meates' new choice as captain of Ireland. Ireland had a dismal campaign winning only once and losing the other three matches. Ireland tasted defeat in their opening fixture going down heavily in Paris. France won their encounter 26-3 at Parc des Princes, with John Robbie scoring a penalty. Ireland suffered a second successive heavy defeat when Wales ran all over them at Lansdowne Road to record a 34-9 victory. The Welsh were in scintillating form with three of their superstars scoring in the win: Phil Bennett scored a try, converted three tries and kicked three successful penalties; Gerald Davies scored two tries, and Gareth Edwards also grabbed a try for the Welsh Dragons. Allan Martin also scored a penalty for the fire-breathing men in red.

Game 3 finally gave the Irish fans something to cheer about when Ireland defeated England 13-12 at Twickenham. In their final game, Ireland lost 15-6 to Scotland in Dublin. England finished rock bottom of the table with four losses to win the wooden spoon. Wales retained their title, their 19th, won their 13th Triple Crown and claimed their seventh Grand Slam.

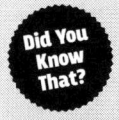 John Robbie was awarded his first cap for Ireland against Australia at Lansdowne Road on 17 January 1976, a 20-10 defeat, and went on to win a further eight caps. In 1980, he toured South Africa with the British and Irish Lions and played in one Test. In 1981, he moved to South Africa and when he was playing for Transvaal in the Gateung region of the country, he was selected twice for The Springboks but was never capped by South Africa.

CROAK PARK - DON'T STEP ON THE FROGS

In early June 1976, Ireland stopped off in Fiji on their way home from a tour to New Zealand where they had played seven games, including one Test match which the All Blacks won 11-3. When they arrived in Suva, the Fijian capital, most of the senior Fiji team were in Australia on tour. A scheduling mistake was to blame, according to a Fiji Rugby Union spokesperson. However, the home nation gathered a side together to face Ireland at Buckhurst Park, Suva on 9 June 1976. Despite the home side missing their key players the game was a sell out with 15,000 fans turning up to watch it - in a tight little ground with the try-line very close to the dead ball line. Indeed, at one point during the game, Ireland's Tony Ensor crossed both at the same time. It was a stifling hot evening and as well as the humid conditions the players had to cope with a pitch invasion which saw hundreds of frogs leap all over the pitch as they tried to make their way to a nearby marsh area. Ireland won the game 8-0, with no caps awarded to the Irish players.

 On 9 November 1970, NASA sent two bullfrogs into space to study weightlessness, in a satellite named The Orbiting Frog Otolith (OFO).

'THE HAKA IS NOT JUST A RUGBY WAR DANCE, IT IS ANY FORM OF MAORI CEREMONIAL DANCING WHICH INCLUDES A CELEBRATION OR A WELCOME TO GUESTS. IT IS A RITUAL WHICH IS EMBEDDED IN MAORI CULTURE AND MYTHOLOGY'

1977 FIVE NATIONS CHAMPIONSHIP – WOODEN SPOON WINNERS

Wales, Grand Slam winners the previous year, were scorching hot favourites to win back-to-back Slams. Tom Grace took over the Ireland captaincy from Mike Gibson, whilst Roly Meates was still head coach.

First up for Ireland was a trip to the Principality where they lost 25-9 to the defending Champions at the Arms Park. Gibson scored all nine points for Ireland from three penalties. On 5 February 1977, Ireland and England played out an uneventful match at Lansdowne Road with the two sides separated by a single try scored in the game which went to England for a 4-0 win. Ireland then lost Game 3, a slender 21-18 loss to Scotland at Murrayfield. Gibson scored a try which he converted, plus two penalties, with Mick Quinn scoring a drop goal and a penalty.

Game 4 saw Ireland entertain France in the Irish capital. France had already defeated Wales 16-9 in Paris, England 4-3 in London and Scotland 23-3 at Parc des Princes. Ireland lost 15-6, a penalty each scored by Gibson and Quinn, meaning France were Champions for the sixth time and secured their second Grand Slam title. Wales retained the Triple Crown, equalling England's record of 14 Triple Crown wins, and they were the first Triple Crown winners to finish runners-up in the tournament. Ireland took the wooden spoon.

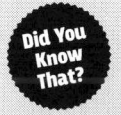

France won the 1977 Grand Slam using the same fifteen players in all four of their games, a unique achievement for a Grand Slam winning side, and they never conceded a try. England are the only other nation to win a Grand Slam without allowing a try to be scored against them, achieving this in 1913. Wales' match versus France was the subject of the 1978 movie Grand Slam. However, when they lost the game, some of the final scenes had to be rewritten including one scene where two of the main characters contemplated the 1978 Five Nations Championship clash between Wales and France at Arms Park. Wales won the 1978 encounter 16-7 and won an eighth Grand Slam.

1978 FIVE NATIONS CHAMPIONSHIP – A NEW COACH AND A NEW CAPTAIN

The 1978 Five Nations Championship brought with it three things for Ireland. It brought a sense of optimism having taken the unwanted wooden spoon home from the biggest dinner table in rugby union in the northern hemisphere the previous year. Secondly, Ireland had a new coach, Noel Murphy, who as a player was capped 41 times by Ireland from 1958-69 (scored 15 points from his flanker position) and was capped eight times by the British and Irish Lions (scored three points). Irish rugby was in his DNA. And, with a new coach, came a new captain, in the shape of John Moloney.

Ireland got off to a good start winning their opening fixture, 12-9 against Scotland at

Lansdowne Road. Stewart McKinney scored a try, whilst the new protégé for Irish rugby, Tony Ward, made his debut in the game and converted the try as well as scoring two penalties. A point was the difference in the scores when Ireland met France at Parc des Princes but, unfortunately, it was in the home side's favour as they won a close contest 10-9. Ward kicked three successful penalties. Ireland lost to Wales in Game 3, going down 20-16 in Dublin with the new Golden Boy of Irish rugby, Ward, scoring 12 of Ireland's points tally, three penalties and a drop goal, whilst the Irish captain scored a try. England beat Ireland 15-9 in their final game of the 1978 Five Nations Championship at Twickenham Stadium.

The Welsh exacted revenge over the French from the previous year when they beat them 16-7 at the Arms Park on 18 March 1978, in a match which was a straight shootout for the Grand Slam. Wales were crowned champions for the 20th time, claimed a 15th Triple Crown and landed an 8th Grand Slam.

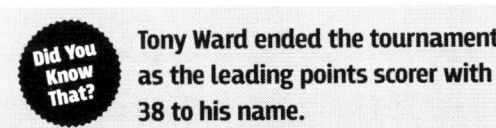

Did You Know That? Tony Ward ended the tournament as the leading points scorer with 38 to his name.

1979 FIVE NATIONS CHAMPIONSHIP – SLATTERY BECOMES THE NEW CAPTAIN

Noel Murphy was still in charge of the national team for the 1979 Five Nations Championship but he appointed a new captain, Fergus Slattery.

The new captain was a seasoned campaigner in an Ireland shirt having made his debut versus South Africa at Lansdowne Road on 10 January 1970, in an 8-8 draw. He was a flying flanker who played club rugby for Blackrock College and University College Dublin. Slattery went on tour with the British and Lions in 1971 but did not start any of the Test matches as the tourists collected their first, and only, series win in New Zealand. With the back-row berths claimed by John Taylor, Peter Dixon and Mervyn Davies, and Slattery still a newcomer at international level, he would have to wait until the Lions' 1974 for his chance to play in a Test match wearing the famous Lions' jersey. He was capped 61 times by Ireland and four times by the British and Irish Lions.

Game 1 produced a 9-9 draw against France at Lansdowne Road. Tony Ward scored three penalties to maintain his excellent scoring form in the green jersey. The reigning Champions and Grand Slam holders, Wales, just about edged out Ireland at the Arms Park, winning the battle 24-21. Ireland bounced back in Game 3 by defeating England 12-7 in Dublin thanks to a try from Freddie McLennan and points from who else but the prolific Ward, kicking a conversion, scoring a penalty and landing a drop goal. In their last game, Ireland met Scotland at Murrayfield where the two closely matched sides drew 11-11.

Wales retained the title and the Triple Crown but were denied back-to-back Slams by France who beat them 14-13 at Parc des Princes.

> **Did You Know That?** Slattery captained Ireland's hugely successful Tour of Australia in 1979 when they won seven of eight matches in Australia including the two Tests in Brisbane and Sydney. In 1982, he started all four games of Ireland's Triple Crown winning season, being denied the Grand Slam by France in the final game of the tournament that year.

THE ALL-IRELAND CHAMPION HURLER

Edward Michael Joseph 'Ned' Byrne was born in Kilkenny on 14 September 1948. The young Ned attended Kilkenny Christian Brothers School where he enjoyed a keen interest in hurling. Later he went to Cistercian College, Roscrea where he played both hurling and rugby union. However, this was frowned upon at the time by the GAA whose members were not permitted to play non-Gaelic sports. Ned was banned from being a member of the college's hurling team in his fifth year there and so took the decision to leave the college rugby team to concentrate on a career in hurling.

Byrne joined his local club, St Canice's, and played Hurling and Gaelic football for them, earning a county minor winners' medal in both sports in 1964. Not long afterwards, the club folded and he joined James Stephens where he won a senior county hurling title in 1969, followed by a second victory in 1975. In 1971, he made his debut for Kilkenny in the National Hurling League winning a Leinster title in his first season before losing the 1971 All-Ireland Senior Hurling Championship to Tipperary, 5-17 to 5-14. A year later he claimed a second Leinster title winners' medal and once again Kilkenny reached the All-Ireland Senior Hurling Championship final. Kilkenny beat their arch-rivals, Cork, 3-24 to 5-11, at Croke Park with Byrne playing in the game.

Within a few days of winning an All-Ireland medal, Byrne signed for Blackrock Rugby Football Club and was soon a regular choice in the Leinster team when they played Representative Matches. He was capped six times by Ireland, making his debut on 19 February 1977, a 21-18 loss to Scotland at Murrayfield in the 1977 Five Nations Championship. Ned played alongside his cousin, Willie Duggan, in all six internationals.

>  **Did You Know That?** Kilkenny have won more All-Ireland Senior Hurling Championship titles than any other county, 36, with Cork second in the list of most wins on 30.

1980s

WHERE'S YOUR F***ING PRIDE?

IRELAND'S WILLIE IS BIGGER THAN FRANCE'S CONDOM

THE INAUGURAL RUGBY WORLD CUP

IRA BOMBS

THUNDERBIRDS ARE GO!

'A leader is like a shepherd. He stays behind the flock, letting the most nimble go out ahead, whereupon the others follow, not realising that all along they are being directed from behind.'
Nelson Mandela

CIARAN FITZGERALD - WHERE'S YOUR F***ING PRIDE?

First up for Ireland in the 1985 Five Nations Championship was a trip to the Scottish capital, Edinburgh, where they defeated Scotland 18-15 at Murrayfield. According to most rugby pundits at the time, Ireland had no chance of winning the game against the reigning Champions. It was more a case of by how many points would Ireland lose the match. In their second game of the 1985 tournament, Ireland drew 15-15 with France at Lansdowne Road but the championship title and the Triple Crown was still on. Game 3 took Ireland to the *Land of my Fathers*, where they beat Wales 21-9 at the Arms Park. On 30 March 1985, Ireland welcomed England to Lansdowne Road for their final game - the Triple Crown was at stake as was the outcome of the Five Nations Championship.

On the day the Irish players delivered, they stepped up to the mark, and won the game 13-10. But they needed a little encouragement from their captain, Ciaran Fitzgerald. With 10 minutes of the game remaining Ireland were trailing 10-7 (Brendan Mullin scored a try and Michael Kiernan scored a penalty) and many of them looked down and out, a quagmire of a pitch having sapped their energy. Fitzgerald walked up to his forwards and although the television microphone nearby could not pick up what he said, everyone could read his lips as he uttered: 'Where's your f*****g pride?' Many of the fans standing in the decrepit old stands at Lansdowne Road heard their captain's 'Call to arms' and the forwards answered. Michael Kiernan scored a penalty to level the scores before Rob Andrew saw his third penalty attempt sail wide, which would have given England a three-point advantage once again (Rory Underwood scored a try with Andrew stroking two penalties between the posts).

Cometh the Hour, Cometh the Man and that man was Kiernan who scored a deftly taken drop goal to seal victory for Ireland, win the Triple Crown and claim the 1985 Five Nations Championship. You could have forgiven Kiernan, the Cork-born centre, if he had said 'Pride F***ing Restored' after winning the match for Ireland but alas he held his emotions well and truly in check. Coach Mick Doyle had a smile on his face wider than the pitch itself.

Ciaran Fitzgerald was a true champion, a soldier and a fighter on and off the field, and every time he pulled on a green jersey he showed his *F***ing Pride*.

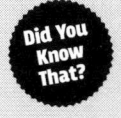 **When Captain Ciaran Fitzgerald retired from the army in 1986, the soldiers at his barracks held a whip round and bought him a Hi-Fi system as a going away present.**

1980 FIVE NATIONS CHAMPIONSHIP – WHAT'S ANOTHER YEAR?

Having finished in third place in the championship table a year earlier, Ireland went one step further in the 1980 edition of the tournament, by claiming runners-up spot to England. Noel Murphy was no longer in charge of the team; Tom Kiernan, an Ireland Legend was the new coach whilst Fergus Slattery was still the captain of the side. Ireland started the campaign slowly, losing 24-9 to England at Twickenham. The reliable Ollie Campbell kicked three penalties, Jim Glennon and Kevin O'Brien made their debuts in the game. Game 2 was a home game which saw Ireland defeat Scotland 22-15 at Lansdowne Road - Terry Kennedy and Moss Keane scored a try each, Ollie scored a conversion, a drop goal and three penalties. Next up for Ireland was a trip to Paris where they lost an extremely close and tense match, 19-18, to France at Parc des Princes. Freddie McLennan scored Ireland's solitary try which Mr Reliable, Mr Campbell, successfully converted as well as kicking three penalties and landing a drop goal. It was a bitter pill to swallow.

Ireland's final match brought the reigning Champions and Triple Crown winners, Wales to Dublin. England beat Scotland 30-18 at Murrayfield to win the Championship for the 18th time, a 15th Triple Crown and an 8th Grand Slam. It was a shootout for the Irish and Welsh to determine which one would be second best in the table - Ireland won out 21-7 thanks to tries scored by Ciaran Fitzgerald, David Irwin and John O'Driscoll, with Campbell converting all three in addition to scoring a penalty. It was only Irwin's second international having made his debut in Paris. Johnny Logan won the 1980 Eurovision Song Contest for Ireland with What's Another Year? 1980 was just another year for the Ireland fans to add to the previous five they had endured without a Five Nations Championship success.

 John O'Driscoll is the uncle of the legendary Brian O'Driscoll and won 26 caps for Ireland from 1978-84, plus six British and Irish Lions caps (1980-83). John's older brother, Barry, was capped four times by Ireland in 1971, but they are not related to another O'Driscoll, who won 23 caps (2001-11) for Ireland, Mick.

1981 FIVE NATIONS CHAMPIONSHIP – JUST IMAGINE

Imagine by the former Beatle, John Lennon, was the No.1 song in the charts when the 1981 Five Nations Championship commenced on 17 January 1981. In the minds of all Ireland fans they imagined their team could produce good enough performances on the pitch to win their first title since 1974. But, it was more a case of dreaming than imagining as Ireland lost all four of their matches, two of them by the slenderest of margins, a single point.

IRELAND'S RESULTS
Ireland 13 v France 19 - Lansdowne Road
Wales 9 v Ireland 8 – Arms Park
Ireland 6 v England 10 - Lansdowne Road
Scotland 10 v Ireland 9 - Murrayfield

Ireland took the wooden spoon whilst France won their seventh crown and third Grand Slam.

> **Did You Know That?** Hugo MacNeill made his debut in the loss to France, scoring a try in the game. He also scored a try in Ireland's losses to Wales and England.

1982 FIVE NATIONS CHAMPIONSHIP – THE LAND OF MAKE BELIEVE

Wooden spoon winners 12 months earlier, not even the most diehard of Ireland fans held out much hope of their side being crowned Five Nations champions in 1982. Ireland faced Wales at Lansdowne Road in Game 1. The game was played on 23 January 1982; Tom Kiernan was still the Ireland coach, but the captaincy had switched to Ciaran Fitzgerald and Willie Duggan. Prior to the game the Irish fans were listening to songs being played on the loudspeaker system all around the ground, including the No.1 hit at the time, *The Land of Make Believe,* by Bucks Fizz. When the game ended it was the Ireland fans who found themselves in the 'Land of Make Believe' after defeating Wales 19-12. Quite a few bottles of Bucks Fizz were popped in the bars in and around Lansdowne Road in celebrating a long-awaited victory. Michael Kiernan, a nephew of the Ireland coach, made his international bow for Ireland in the win against Wales.

 **Did You Know That?** The Ireland versus Wales game was delayed by a week due to a frozen pitch in Dublin.

In their second game, Ireland eked past England at Twickenham, winning their encounter 19-18. On 20 February 1982 Ireland welcomed Scotland to Dublin - a win for the home side would guarantee a first Triple Crown success since 1949 and, cometh the hour, cometh the man, with Ollie Campbell putting in a virtuoso performance in the No.10 jersey. Ireland claimed a 19-12 victory with Campbell, Ireland's Trump Card, scoring six penalties and a delightfully taken drop goal.

Only France stood in the way of Ireland claiming a first Grand Slam since 1948. The venue was Parc des Princes on 20 March 1982. It was one hurdle too far for the boys in green, going down 22-9 but there was a silver lining for Ireland in the shape of a 9th championship success (excluding seven shared) and a 5th Triple Crown. Not surprisingly, Ollie scored all nine of Ireland's points and ended the 1982 Five Nations Championship as the top points scorer with 46. When he played it was as though he was wearing golden boots every time he stepped on to the field.

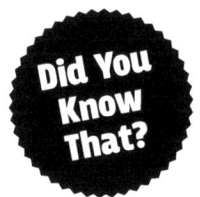

Did You Know That?

France's Patrick Esteve finished the campaign as the leading try scorer with five, and remarkably he scored against all four nations, the first time since 1925 that such a feat had been achieved. Scotland's Johnnie Wallace scored a try against England, France, Ireland and Wales in 1925, to match the feat of England's Carston Catcheside who scored a try against the other four nations in the 1924 Five Nations Championship.

1983 FIVE NATIONS CHAMPIONSHIP – JOINT WINNERS

Tom Kiernan was still Ireland coach for the 1983 Five Nations Championship and Ciaran Fitzgerald was his leader on the pitch. Fitzgerald combined his amateur playing career with a career in the Irish Army, serving as an aide-de-camp to the President of Ireland, Dr Patrick Hillery. Having won the title the previous season, Ireland went into the 1983 edition of the tournament as firm favourites.

First up for Ireland was Scotland at Murrayfield which the visitors won 15-13; Michael Kiernan scored a try, Ollie Campbell scored Ireland's other 11 points (a conversion and three penalties). Ireland then bossed France about for 80 minutes winning their match 22-16 at Lansdowne Road. Moss Finn scored two tries and no guessing who grabbed the remaining 18 – Campbell, of course. Game 3 threw a spanner in the works when they lost 23-9 at the Arms Park. However, the title was still up for grabs when England arrived in Dublin to coincide with Wales' visit to Paris to face France. Ireland and England had two victories each and the one loss, but a points' for and against ratio was not in place at the time to decide the outcome of the championship. France beat Wales 16-9 at Parc des Princes and Ireland defeated England 25-15 at Lansdowne Road, meaning France and Ireland shared the 1983 Five Nations Championship. For the second year in a row, Campbell's golden boots kicked him into top place in the points scored charts with 52.

1984 FIVE NATIONS CHAMPIONSHIP – WILLIE'S WIMPS

The 1984 championship saw a change of coach for Ireland. In September 1983, Tom Kiernan stepped aside as coach to be succeeded by Willie John McBride. Willie opted for a joint captaincy of Ciaran Fitzgerald and Willie Duggan. Having shared the title with France the previous year, and been crowned champions in 1982, McBride had a hard act to follow as coach of the national side. A warrior on the pitch, home and abroad, Willie knew what he wanted from his players; total dedication

to the team cause, bravery in the tackle, concentration in possession, loyalty, respect for your teammates and your opponents, all out aggression and most importantly of all, heads held high with pride as victors or as losers in the green jersey he wore himself for 14 years, 1962-75.

Footloose starring Kevin Bacon was a massive movie in the cinemas in 1984. Ireland were more foot tied than footloose on the rugby field as the form they showed in the 1983 tournament nosedived like a peregrine falcon swooping down on its' prey. Willie's Warriors had unexpectedly morphed into Willie's Wimps, losing all four of their matches.

IRELAND'S RESULTS
France 25 v Ireland 12 - Parc des Princes
Ireland 9 v Wales 18 - Lansdowne Road
England 12 v Ireland 9 - Twickenham
Ireland 9 v Scotland 32 - Lansdowne Road

Ireland went from runners-up the previous season to wooden spoon winners in 1984.

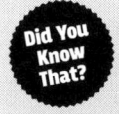

Scotland won the championship outright for the first time since 1938. It was their twelfth outright championship, excluding a further seven shared titles. Their four wins gave them the Grand Slam for the first time since 1925, their second, and the Triple Crown, their ninth and first since 1938.

1985 FIVE NATIONS CHAMPIONSHIP - AGAINST ALL ODDS

Mick Doyle replaced the legendary Willie John McBride as the Ireland coach for the 1985 Five Nations Championship - Ciaran Fitzgerald retained the captaincy. Despite the humiliation of losing all four games in 1984 (wooden spoon winners), when the IRFU placed the match tickets on sale for Ireland's two home games in the 1985 Five Nations Championship, the Ireland fans remained loyal to their team and snapped-up every ticket available.

In Doyle, the IRFU had a seasoned professional both in a green jersey and in a tracksuit having won 30 caps for Ireland (1965-68) and a British and Irish Lions' cap in 1967. He moved into coaching after his flanker days were behind him, guiding Leinster to Inter-Provincial Championship success five times between 1979 and 1983.

But, the difference between Interprovincial rugby and International Test match rugby was as different as night and day.

First up in the 1985 Five Nations Championship for Ireland was a trip to Edinburgh to play the reigning Grand Slam holders, Scotland. The Scots had given the Irish a Rugby masterclass 12 months earlier, winning 32-9 in Dublin. The fans wearing green inside the stadium were probably hoping not to be too embarrassed and leave the Scottish capital on the end of a narrow defeat. Who knows what Doyler (his nickname) said to his players in the dressing-room before kick-off but it worked because Ireland shocked the rugby fraternity by defeating the champs 18-15 in their own backyard. Trevor Ringland scored two tries which were converted by Mike

Kiernan, who also scored a drop goal and a penalty. England, France and Wales suddenly looked at their forthcoming encounters against Ireland through a different lens.

Game 2 ended in a draw for Ireland, 15-15 versus France before a sold-out Lansdowne Road. Kiernan kicked five penalties over the bar for Ireland. On 16 March 1985, the Principality was more a sea of green than the red of a dragon's den when Ireland met Wales at the Arms Park - Ireland extinguished the fiery hostility pouring down on them from the home fans by scoring two tries (Keith Crossan and Ringland) which were converted by Kiernan and a hat-trick of penalties from the laser right boot of Kiernan, to claim a 21-9 victory. The band Dead or Alive had the top selling music single at the time with their song *You Spin Me Round (Like A Record)*. Doyler had spun Ireland's fortunes around with his fast-moving attacking style of play.

Did You Know That? Scotland went from ecstasy to agony, ending the 1985 Five Nations Championship as wooden spoon winners having lost all four of their matches.

A fortnight later, 30 March 1985, Ireland met England in Dublin with the championship and Triple Crown within their grasp. England were there to spoil a countrywide party, as it would be a tenth title (excluding eight other shared titles) and a sixth Triple Crown for the players wearing green. The 15 players in white gave all they had as they could still land the Triple Crown, and were still in the race for the championship, with a trip to Cardiff still to come. But Ireland stayed focused, and with a steely determination beat England 13-10 thanks to a Brendan Mullin try along with a Kiernan drop goal and two penalties.

Not only did Ireland win the 1985 Five Nations Championship and Triple Crown, but Ringland was the leading try scorer in the tournament with three and Mr Consistency himself, Mike Kiernan, the top points scorer with a mammoth 42.

In March 1985, the movie *Against All Odds*, was released for cinema-goers to enjoy. Mick Doyle's Ireland beat all odds to land the 1985 Five Nations Championship and come within a single point of claiming the country's first Grand Slam since the halcyon days of Irish rugby in the late 1940s when Ireland won the Grand Slam for the first time in 1948.

1986 FIVE NATIONS CHAMPIONSHIP – BIG TROUBLE IN IRELAND

The Mick Doyle-Ciaran Fitzgerald combination of coach and captain of Ireland continued into the 1986 Five Nations Championship. As far as the IRFU was concerned it was a case of 'Why fix something that wasn't broken?' Ireland went into the 1986 edition of the tournament as the reigning champions and many rugby fans' favourites to retain their crown. But as it transpired a turnaround in fortunes saw the champs become *Chumpions*, losing all four games, whereas Scotland, wooden spoon winners a year before, shared the title with France.

IRELAND'S RESULTS
France 29 v Ireland 9 – Parc des Princes
Ireland 12 v Wales 19 – Lansdowne Road
England 25 v Ireland 20 – Twickenham
Ireland 9 v Scotland 10 - Lansdowne Road

The Ireland fans who tuned in to their TV sets to watch Ireland's opening game versus France were less than impressed with how their players underperformed and unlike the No.1 song in the charts at the time, *The Sun Always Shines On TV*, by A-Ha, there was a dark cloud hanging over television sets throughout Ireland. And, it lasted for more than the two weeks the Norwegian group spent at the Top of the UK Charts.

One of the most popular movies the Ireland fans went to see in 1986 was *Big Trouble in Little China*. After the 1986 Five Nations Championship, there was Big Trouble in Ireland.

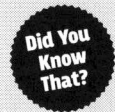

Did You Know That? Ralph Keyes, aged 24, made his debut for Ireland in the game versus England. He won eight caps from 1986-92, playing in all four of Ireland's games at the 1991 Rugby World Cup.

1987 FIVE NATIONS CHAMPIONSHIP - IRELAND'S MARADONA

Ireland got their 1987 Five Nations Championship campaign off to a perfect start, defeating England 17-0 in Dublin. But two losses then followed versus Scotland and France respectively, book ended with a win over Wales in the Principality.

IRELAND'S RESULTS
Ireland 17 v England 0 - Lansdowne Road
Scotland 16 v Ireland 12 - Murrayfield
Ireland 13 v France 19 - Lansdowne Road
Wales 11 v Ireland 15 - Arms Park

The romantic comedy, *Mannequin,* was a huge success when it was released in the cinemas during the tournament. There were times, especially in the game against France, when the Irish players resembled 15 Mannequins on the pitch. When France beat Ireland, they were crowned champions for the eighth time, with a fourth Grand Slam to boot. Ireland finished in runners-up place. Had it not been for Mike Kiernan's kicking ability, Ireland would have finished as wooden spoon winners, which actually went to a very poor England team. A year earlier Diego Maradona inspired Argentina to FIFA World Cup glory when he captained them in their 3-2 win against West Germany in the final played at Estadio Azteca, Mexico City. The 1986 FIFA World Cup finals will forever be remembered for Maradona's 'Hand of God' goal during their 2-1 win over England. The little Argentinian jumped for the ball with Peter

Shilton in the England net and hit the ball into the back of the net with a glance of his left hand. Kiernan did not possess the dribbling skills of Maradona. He didn't need them; a sidestep or shimmy was all he needed in his repertoire. Maradona could pass the ball with unrivalled accuracy to the foot of a teammate. Kiernan could find touch deep into enemy territory with nonchalant ease. Both men shared the same God-given quality in that they were natural scorers. Diego hit 34 goals in 91 international appearances for Argentina; Mike scored 308 points in 43 Tests for Ireland. And, both players possessed the ability to drive their side forward and win games. When Ireland defeated England 17-0, Kiernan contributed nine of the points by scoring a try, which his right boot converted, and a penalty. The hit single from the movie was called *Nothing's Gonna Stop Us Now*. Who was even capable of trying to stop the march of Les Bleus. Napoleon never made it as far as Dublin, but the French National rugby team conquered every opponent in their path in 1987, with the exception of New Zealand who beat them 29-9 in the inaugural Rugby World Cup final later that year. The final was played at Eden Park, Auckland.

Did You Know That? Donal Lenihan was appointed the captain of Ireland in 1987 by Mick Doyle.

IRELAND'S FIRST RUGBY WORLD CUP COACH

Mick Doyle was Ireland's coach from 1984-87 and guided them to the Five Nations Championship and Triple Crown in 1985. Only a draw with France, 15-15 at Lansdowne Road, prevented his side from emulating *The Boys of '48* and clinching the Holy Grail of northern hemisphere ruby, the Grand Slam.

Doyle was born in Castleisland, County Kerry on 13 October 1941, and began his rugby playing career with Newbridge College, County Kildare. When he left college he played rugby for University College Dublin, where he studied veterinary science. On 23 January 1965, he made his Ireland debut, a 3-3 draw versus France at Lansdowne Road in the 1965 Five Nations Championship, scoring Ireland's solitary try in the game. Whilst playing for Ireland he also studied at Cambridge University and won a 'Blue' in the Varsity match against Oxford. A 'Blue' is the highest honour that may be bestowed on a Cambridge athlete, and is a much coveted and prestigious prize. Incredibly, Doyle also went to Edinburgh University and played for Edinburgh Wanderers. A gifted flanker, he played 20 times for Ireland (scored two tries), all consecutive games without missing any through injury or being dropped from the team.

In 1967 he toured Australia with Ireland and in 1968 he was a member of the British and Irish Lions touring party to South Africa, winning one cap. His last game for Ireland as a player was against Australia on 26 October 1968 - a 10-3 victory at Lansdowne Road when he lined out alongside his brother, Tommy

He coached Leinster from 1979-83 and led them to Interprovincial Championship success five times before he succeeded Willie John McBride as Ireland coach during the 1984–85 season. In 1987, he coached Ireland at the inaugural Rugby World Cup which was co-hosted by Australia and New Zealand. At the tournament's 'Welcoming Dinner' he suffered a suspected heart attack but recovered in time for Ireland's opening game. Nicknamed 'Doyler' he had a long battle with illness and he wrote about his recovery from a brain problem in his book *0.16*.

After retiring from coaching, he became a TV pundit on RTE and was a regular guest on their *Rugby After Dark* Sunday night highlights programme, until having to retire due to ill-health in the late 1990s.

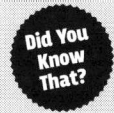

Did You Know That? In 1854, Trinity College, the sole constituent college of the University of Dublin, founded Old Rugbeians, the first rugby club in Ireland.

1987 RUGBY WORLD CUP

New Zealand went into the 1987 tournament as the overwhelming favourites to be crowned the first ever Rugby World Cup winners. The All Blacks won all three of their Pool 3 games racking-up 130 points, conceding just 34 points and scored 30 tries. In the quarter-finals they saw off Scotland with a 30-3 victory and in the semi-finals, they cruised to a 49-6 victory over Wales. Their opponents in the final, France, were the best side in the Northern Hemisphere having won the Five Nations Grand Slam two months prior to their encounter with the All Blacks which included away wins over England and Ireland. However, Les Bleus just pipped Scotland to winning their Pool by scoring 25 tries to the Scots' 20. The pair drew their Pool 4 encounter 20-20. In the quarter-finals the French beat Fiji 31-16 and then defeated Australia 30-24 in the semi-finals in one of the greatest ever games in the history of the competition. However, when it came to the final France just seemed to have run out of steam as New Zealand dominated the game from start to finish to run out 29-9 winners before a home partisan crowd at Eden Park. Grant Fox scored 17 points for the All Blacks in the final and ended the tournament as the leading points scorer with 126. His teammates, Craig Green and John Kirwan, were the leading try scorers with 6 each.

IRELAND'S RESULTS:
Pool 2
Ireland 6 Wales 13 – Athletic Park, Wellington
Canada 19 Ireland 46 – Carisbrook, Dunedin
Ireland 32 Tonga 9 – Ballymore, Brisbane
(Ireland finished Pool 2 runners-up to Wales)
Knockout Stage
Australia 33 Ireland 15 – Concord Oval, Sydney

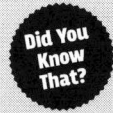

Did You Know That? New Zealand full-back, John Gallagher was back on his policeman's beat the morning after he won a Rugby World Cup winners' medal.

UNUSUAL NATIONAL ANTHEMS

Ireland's first ever game at a Rugby World Cup was played on 25 May 1987 at Athletic Park, Wellington, New Zealand. Wales won the encounter 13-6 with Michael Kiernan scoring two penalties for Ireland, thereby becoming the first Irish player to score in the tournament. The game was noteworthy for the national anthems. The Welsh team listened to a rendition of *Land of our Fathers* sung by the massed Welsh Choirs which was recorded at the Arms Park. When it came to the Irish national anthem the team lined-up to hear a recording of *The Rose of Tralee* by James Last and his Orchestra from a concert held at Austin Stack Park, Tralee.

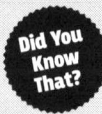

Did You Know That? The Ireland squad flew to New Zealand 10 days before their game versus Wales, a 34-hour flight with refuelling stop-offs in Los Angeles and Hawaii, and an unscheduled diversion to Wellington.

1988 FIVE NATIONS CHAMPIONSHIP - I THINK WE'RE ALONE NOW

When Ireland beat Scotland 22-18 at Lansdowne Road in their opening fixture of the 1988 Five Nations Championship, you could forgive the Irish fans for believing that maybe this was their year to land a Grand Slam for the first time in 40 years. After all, Ireland had finished joint second only a year earlier.

Young Guns was a big movie hit in 1988, and Ireland had a young side - Philip Danaher aged 22, Denis McBride aged 23, Brendan Mullin aged 24 and Michael Bradley aged 25. With their youth, the Irish squad was not short of experience with Willie Anderson, Mike Gibson, Michael Kiernan and captain Donal Lenihan in their squad. Jimmy Davidson was the Ireland coach; he won six caps in the green jersey from 1969 to 1976 and coached Ulster from 1983-87, before replacing Mick Doyle as the Ireland coach.

Bu, they were derailed by France in Paris, going down heavy with a 25-6 defeat. Game 3 brought Wales to the Irish capital and they edged out a 12-9 victory. In their final game they were humiliated, losing 35-3 away to England. Ireland's Young Guns were no match for seasoned gunslingers, including the dynamic French duo of Serge Blanco and Philippe Sella, and Scotland's one-man point scoring machine, Gavin Hastings, who was the tournament's top points scorer with 41, scoring 10 against Ireland.

IRELAND'S RESULTS
Ireland 22 v Scotland 18 - Lansdowne Road
France 25 v Ireland 6 - Parc des Princes
Ireland 9 v Wales 12 - Lansdowne Road
England 35 v Ireland 3 - Twickenham

During the tournament, Tiffany enjoyed her only No.1 hit single with *I Think We're Alone Now* which spent three weeks at the Top of the Hit Parade. When the tournament ended, Ireland found themselves alone, rock bottom of the table with the wooden spoon to add to their growing collection of timber.

> **Did You Know That?** During England's game against Ireland, the English fans inside Twickenham burst into song with Swing Low, Sweet Chariot, after Chris Oti (only the second black player, and the first for 80 years, to be capped by England) scored a hat-trick of tries. The song later was adopted as the unofficial rugby anthem for the England Rugby Union team.

1989 FIVE NATIONS CHAMPIONSHIP – WHERE IS BATMAN?

Jimmy Davidson was still the coach of Ireland when they began their 1989 Five Nations Championship campaign, with a new captain in charge, Philip Matthews. After their debacle the previous year, finished bottom of the table, to quote the title of a popular song at the time by *Yazoo and the Plastic Population*, as far as the Ireland fans were concerned, *The Only Way Is Up*. Alas, the title of a song means nothing when it comes down to a confrontation between two teams in the Five Nations Championship.

> **Did You Know That?** Michael Kiernan was the top points scorer in the 1989 Five Nations Championship with 37.

Ireland lost 26-21 to France at Lansdowne Road in Game 1. They then caused a surprise when they beat Wales 19-13 at the Arms Park, a result which later proved to be very significant. But Ireland flattered to deceive and lost 16-3 to England in Dublin. In their final game, the Irish forwards would have been better off tossing cabers than throwing a rugby ball, losing 37-21 to Scotland at Murrayfield.

Batman was the biggest grossing movie of the year. When the Mayor of Gotham City needed help to solve crimes, he pressed the Bat Signal on a searchlight which appeared in the sky above Gotham City as a means to summon the Marvel Comics' Superhero. If only Jimmy Davidson had a Bat Light at his disposal to ignite the Dublin skyline.

Ireland ended the competition in joint bottom place with Wales.

Back to Life by Soul II Soul was a massive hit song during the year, but not even Batman was capable of bringing this Ireland side back to life.

IRA BOMB ENDS PROMISING CAREER

Nigel Carr was born on 27 July 1959 in Belfast. He played flanker for Regent House School and Queen's University. Carr was awarded Under-23 and B caps for Ireland in 1979 and won further B caps in 1980, 1982 and 1984, although injury plagued him. Finally, on 2 February 1985, he won his first senior cap when Ireland beat Scotland 18-15 at Murrayfield in the Five Nations

Did You Know That?

Nigel Carr never toured with the British and Irish Lions but he did play in a Test for them in 1986, against a World XV to celebrate the centenary of the IRB and he also represented The Barbarians.

Championship. Ireland won the 1985 championship and Triple Crown with only France stopping them from winning their first Grand Slam since 1948. France and Ireland drew 15-15 at Lansdowne Road with Carr unquestionably the key player in coach Mick Doyle's squad. In 1985, Carr toured Japan with Ireland and was selected for the Irish squad which would play in the inaugural Rugby World Cup co-hosted by Australia and New Zealand in 1987.

On 25 April 1987, Carr and two of his teammates, David Irwin and Philip Rainey, were in a car travelling from Belfast to Dublin for a pre-World up training camp. Unknown to the three players, the Provisional Irish Republican Army (IRA) were planning to kill Lord Justice Sir Maurice Gibson who was travelling back from a holiday with his wife. A 500lb bomb was detonated at Killean, County Armagh on the border with the Republic of Ireland. The three internationals were driving on the same road when an explosion killed Lord and Lady Gibson. All three players somehow managed to escape serious injury, although Carr's injuries brought an early and abrupt end to his promising career, winning just 11 caps. Irwin, a medical doctor, treated the injured at the scene. 'I pulled him so hard I actually pulled him out of his trainers. I thought he was going to miss the World Cup,' said Irwin.

THUNDERBIRDS ARE GO!

Ireland embarked on a Tour of North America and played four games, two of which were Test matches. On 30 August 1989, Ireland kicked off their tour with a game versus British Colombia who they beat 21-18 at Thunderbird Stadium, British Colombia, Canada. Three days later Ireland defeated Canada 24-21 at Royal Athletic Park, Victoria. The third match of their tour took them to Northfield, Minnesota where they beat a Midwest XV side 58-6. The second Test was a game against the USA played at Randall's Island Stadium, New York. Ireland won the game 32-7. Willie Anderson captained the Ireland team for the tour.

Thunderbird Stadium was opened on 7 October 1967 and features twelve 80-foot-high concrete support towers, all topped with a concrete Thunderbird statue.

>  **Thunderbirds** is a British science-fiction television series created by Gerry and Sylvia Anderson which was made between 1964 and 1966 using a form of electronic marionette puppetry (dubbed 'Supermarionation'). It is about the Tracy family, Jeff a retired astronaut, and his five sons who all pilot a vehicle for International Rescue. Thunderbird 2 is a huge green supersonic aircraft carrier that transports various supporting rescue vehicles and equipment in detachable capsules called 'Pods'. International Rescue kicked into action with the words 'Thunderbirds Are Go!'

NAME ON THE SHIRT

In 1982, the IRFU agreed a contract with O'Neills, an Irish sports manufacturing company, to make the Ireland kit. The deal lasted until 1985 when Adidas took over. Since then, the following companies have had the honour of making the famous green jersey:

1991-93: Umbro
1994-2000: Nike
2000-09: Canterbury
2009-14: Puma
2014-Present: Canterbury

In 1996, Irish Permanent became the first company to have their name emblazoned on the front of the Irish jersey. *O2* took over the privilege in 2009, followed by *3* from 2014-16, then the current sponsors Vodafone.

>  A shamrock has been incorporated into the emblem on the shirt since the side played in their first Test match against England in 1875.

RTE SPORTS PERSON OF THE YEAR AWARD

The RTÉ Sports Person of the Year Award is an annual event which was first held in 1985 and is similar to the BBC's Sports Personality of the Year Award which was first awarded in 1954. The winner of the RTÉ Sports Person of the Year Award was originally selected by a special panel of RTÉ journalists and editorial staff, but in 2016 the format changed and since then the winner has been chosen by the general public by way of a vote from a pre determined shortlist of Irish sports personalities. Barry McGuigan was the recipient of the inaugural award after he defeated Panama's Eusebio Pedroza on 8 June 1985 to win the World Boxing Association Featherweight Championship of the World. McGuigan, who was born in Clones, County Monaghan, also won the 1985 BBC Sports Personality of the Year Award thereby becoming the first person who was not born in the United Kingdom to win the coveted award. No Irish sports star has won it since or even been named in the Top 3.

Only four Ireland Rugby Union players have been named RTÉ Sports Person of the Year.

1991: Ralph Keyes
2009: Brian O'Driscoll
2004: Ronan O'Gara
2018: Johnny Sexton

Did You Know That? Sonia O'Sullivan (athletics) has won the most number of RTÉ Sports Person of the Year Awards, claiming five (1993, 1994, 1995, 1998 and 2000). Only one Irish sports star has won the BBC's Overseas Sports Personality World Sport of the Year Award, Rachel Blackmore. In 2021, Rachel Blackmore became the first female to be the leading jockey at the Cheltenham Festival riding six winners, including triumph in the Champion Hurdle on Honeysuckle. On 10 April 2021, she rode Minella Times to victory in the Grand National, the first female jockey to win the most famous horserace in the world in the 182-year history of the race.

IRELAND'S BAMBI

In 1942, Walt Disney's *Bambi* movie hit the silver screen. In the movie, Bambi was a white-tailed deer who famously found it difficult to stand and walk when he was born. Some 40 years later, Barry John Murphy was born on 28 November 1982 in Limerick. He was capped four times by his country from 2007-09 and scored one try. He was given the nickname Bambi' by his Munster (2003-11) teammates.

Did You Know That? He was forced to retire aged just 28. Murphy announced himself on the Munster scene in the 2005-06 season and scored a very memorable try against Sale Sharks at Thomond Park in the Pool Stages of the Heineken Cup. The Limerick born boy forged an effective centre partnership with Trevor Halstead (South Africa) that year, but unfortunately, he did not play in his province's historic European Champions Cup (Heineken Cup) 29-13 victory over Biarritz (France) at the Millennium Stadium on 20 May 2006, after injuring his ankle playing against Ulster.

IRELAND V ENGLAND – HOME AND AWAY

Since their first meeting on 15 February 1875, Ireland and England have played each other 142 times with both nations using different stadiums to host the games.

IRELAND AT HOME	ENGLAND AT HOME
Rathmines	The Oval, London
Lansdowne Road	Whalley Range, Manchester
Mardyke, Cork	Rectory Field, Blackheath
Ravenhill, Belfast	Meanwood Road, Leeds
Croke Park	Athletic Ground, Richmond
Aviva Stadium	Welford Road, Leicester
	Twickenham

> **Did You Know That?** Rectory Field was the unofficial home of the England National Rugby Union team prior to the construction of Twickenham. The ground was also used for First-Class cricket matches by Kent County Cricket Club from 1887 to 1972. The ground is named after the Charlton Rectory that once stood at the site. It is used today by Blackheath Sports Club for cricket, rugby, squash and tennis.

A TALE OF TWO NATIONS

Ireland have met Western Samoa/Samoa on seven occasions, winning six and losing one of their encounters. Western Samoa missed out on the inaugural Rugby World Cup in 1987 but have qualified for every tournament since, including the 2023 edition. Western Samoa became Samoa in 1997.

29 October 1988 – Tour Match: Ireland 49 Western Samoa 22, Lansdowne Road
12 November 1996 – Tour Match: Ireland 25 Western Samoa 40, Lansdowne Road
11 November 2001 – Autumn Test: Ireland 35 Samoa 8, Lansdowne Road
20 June 2003 – Summer Tour: Samoa 14 Ireland 40, Apia Park, Apia, Samoa
13 November 2010 – Guinness Series: Ireland 20 Samoa 10, Aviva Stadium
9 November 2013 – Guinness Series: Ireland 40 Samoa 9, Aviva Stadium
12 October 2019 – 2019 Rugby World Cup: Ireland 47 Samoa 5, Fukuoka International Stadium, Fukuoka, Japan

> **Did You Know That?** The Samoa national rugby union team are also known as 'Manu Samoa'. The name Manu Samoa is in honour of a famous Samoan warrior.

IRELAND'S WILLIE IS BIGGER THAN FRANCE'S CONDOM!

William 'Willie' Anderson was born on 3 April 1955, in Sixmilecross, County Tyrone, and attended Omagh Academy. Willie made his international bow on 10 November 1984, a 16-9 loss at Lansdowne Road to Australia who were touring Great Britain and Ireland.

On 2 March 1985, Ireland played France at Lansdowne Road in the Five Nations Championship, a match that ended 15-15 which prevented Ireland from claiming the Grand Slam for only the second time in the nation's history. The TV cameras spanned the crowd and spotted a banner which an Irish fan had made for the game. The banner read: *Our Willie's bigger than your Condom!* Jean Condom played in the game and won 61 caps for France from 1982-90. Willie was capped 27 times by Ireland between 1984 and 1990.

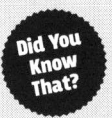

Did You Know That? Willie is the father of the fashion designer, Jonathan Anderson, who designed the outfit worn by Rhianna at the Superbowl on 12 February 2023. Beyonce also wore one of his outfit designs on her 2023 World Tour.

In His Own Words

'I do not think that players today practice individual skills. Perhaps skills come naturally, but you can improve these things. I used to practise sidestepping past a line of flagpoles. Likewise, I could never kick with my left foot until an accident to my right ankle made me use the left foot all the time. By the time my right ankle had recovered, I was a better kicker with my left foot than with my right.'

Michael English, nicknamed '*Mick the Kick*' won 16 caps for Ireland at fly-half from 1958-63, scoring 9 points (speaking in January 1981)

IRELAND V ITALY – HOME AND AWAY

Since their first meeting on 31 December 1988, Ireland and Italy have played each other 37 times with both nations using different stadiums to host the games.

IRELAND AT HOME	ITALY AT HOME
Lansdowne Road	Stadio Comunale di Monigo, Monigo
Thomond Park	Stadio Renato Dall'Ara, Bologna
Ravenhill	Stadio Flaminio, Rome
Croke Park	Stadio Olimpico, Rome
Aviva Stadium	

Did You Know That? On 2 October 2011, the two countries met in the Rugby World Cup in a Pool C match played at Otago Stadium, Dunedin. Ireland were the victors, 36-6. Four years later they faced each other again in a Rugby World Cup encounter at the Olympic Stadium, London. Italy lost the Pool D game 16-9.

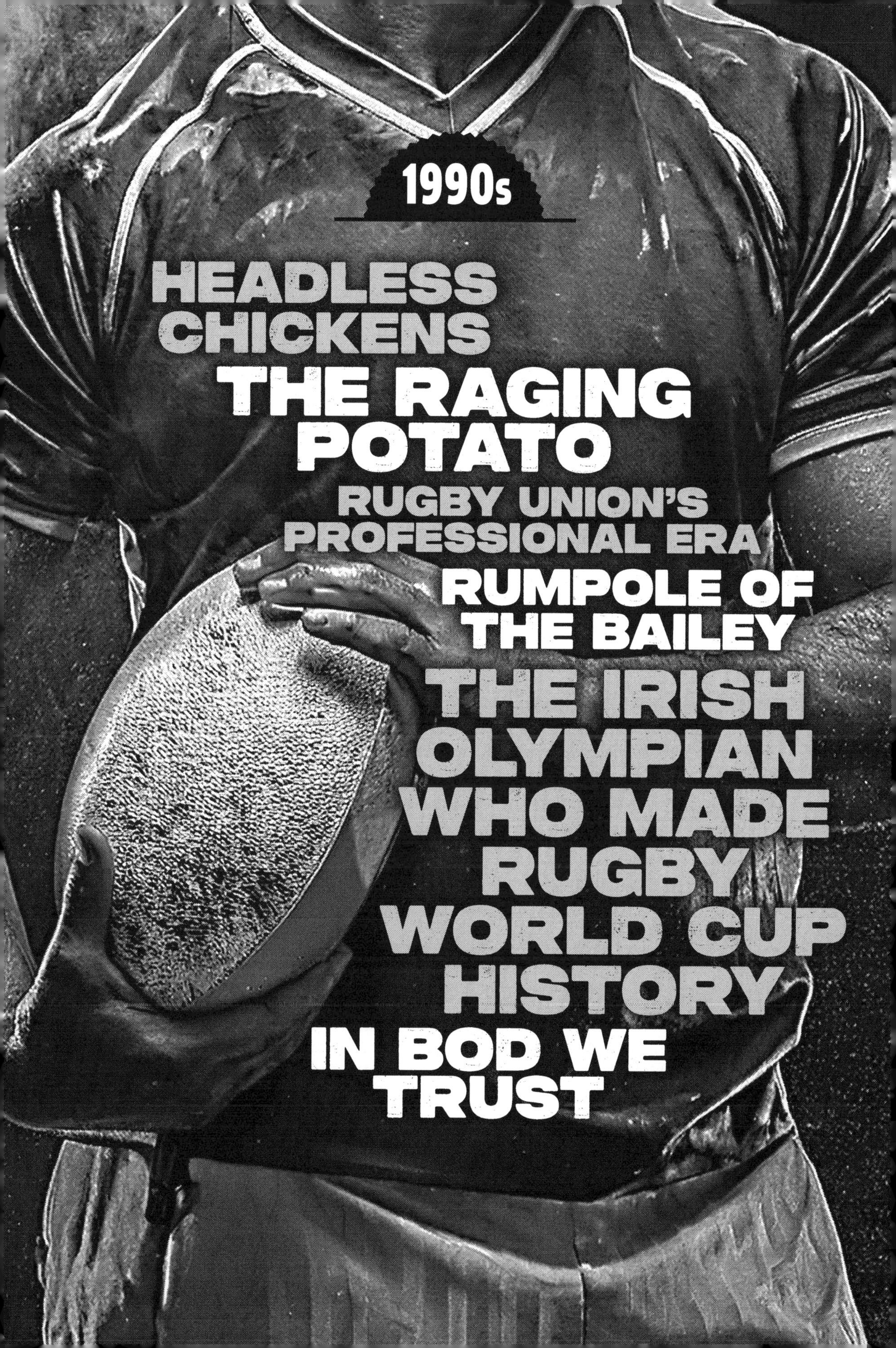

1990s

HEADLESS CHICKENS

THE RAGING POTATO

RUGBY UNION'S PROFESSIONAL ERA

RUMPOLE OF THE BAILEY

THE IRISH OLYMPIAN WHO MADE RUGBY WORLD CUP HISTORY

IN BOD WE TRUST

'He who doesn't want to face his challenges shall always face challenges!'
Ernest Agyemang Yeboah

HEADLESS CHICKENS

'I don't know whose game plan that was out there but it wasn't mine.'

Ireland coach Brian Ashton replying to journalists' questions about Ireland's tactics in a 17-16 loss to Scotland at Lansdowne Road on 7 February 1998 in the first game of the 1998 Five Nations Championship. The journalists were inferring that the Irish players were running around like headless chickens. Ashton resigned on 20 February 1998, and was replaced by Warren Gatland four days later.

1990 FIVE NATIONS CHAMPIONSHIP – DAYS OF THUNDER

The decade did not get off to a dream start for Ireland as they finished one place above the wooden spoon winners, Wales in the table. Ciaran Fitzgerald had replaced Jimmy Davidson as Ireland coach and Fitzgerald replaced Philip Matthews as captain with Willie Anderson and Donal Lenihan.

Ireland were beaten heavily by England at Twickenham in their opening game, losing 23-0. Next up was an impressive Scotland side who left the Irish capital with a victory after winning 13-10 at Lansdowne Road. Ireland then went down 31-12 to France at Parc des Princes, but beat Wales 14-8 in Dublin in their final game, a result which doomed the Welsh to finish bottom of the table.

Days of Thunder starring Tom Cruise was a big box office film of the year but it was Ireland who were under the weather having failed to move themselves away from the bottom half of the table for the third year in a row, after finishing joint-bottom in 1988 and 1989.

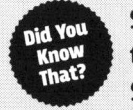

Scotland won the 1990 Five Nations Championship, their thirteenth title, a tenth Triple Crown and they also claimed a third Grand Slam victory. This was Scotland's final Grand Slam success in the Five Nations Championship and a penultimate overall victory, as they went on to win the last ever edition of the tournament in 1999 on points difference over England, +41 to +25. Scotland have not won a Grand Slam since Italy joined what became the Six Nations Championship in 2000.

1991 FIVE NATIONS CHAMPIONSHIP - IRELAND LEFT NEEDING A HOOK

Ireland had a truly awful experience in the 1991 Five Nations Championship, winless and only a draw to their name.

IRELAND'S RESULTS
Ireland 13 v France 21 - Lansdowne Road
Wales 21 v Ireland 21 – Arms Park
Ireland 7 v England 16 - Lansdowne Road
Scotland 28 v Ireland 25 - Murrayfield

England won the 1991 Five Nations Championship, the Triple Crown and a ninth Grand Slam. Ireland finished joint bottom along with Wales.

Hook, starring Dustin Hoffman as Captain Hook, Julia Roberts as Tinkerbell and Robin Williams as Peter Pan, was a massive movie in 1991, and at the end of the 1991 Five Nations Championship it was Ireland who was left looking for some form of a hook to pin their hopes on of bringing back the glory days of Irish rugby. They found one in the shape of Simon Geoghegan who made his debut against France and scored two tries in the tournament.

1991 RUGBY WORLD CUP

The second Rugby World Cup finals was co-hosted by five countries - England, France, Ireland, Scotland and Wales - and once again 16 teams participated. Unlike the inaugural tournament, the IRB invited all member unions to enter qualifying rounds. The eight quarter-finalists in 1987 (Australia, England, Fiji, France Ireland, New Zealand, Scotland and Wales) were automatically guaranteed berths. The remaining eight slots were contested by 25 countries with South Africa still banned from the tournament because of its apartheid system. Four regional qualifying competitions were held which resulted in the following eight nations progressing to the 1991 Rugby World Cup finals: Africa – Zimbabwe; Americas – Argentina; Canada and United States, Asia & Oceania – Japan and Western Samoa; Europe – Italy and Romania. This meant that 15 of the

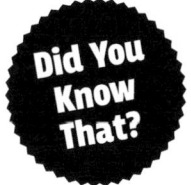

Did You Know That?

In the final game England and France met at Twickenham with both teams going for the Grand Slam. England won a very close contest 21-19, and the try scored by France's Philippe Saint-Andre was later voted as 'Twickenham's Try of the Century'.

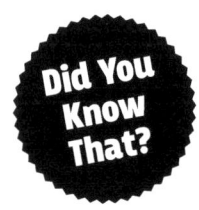

Did You Know That?

Ireland's Ralph Keyes was the top points scorer at the 1991 Rugby World Cup finals with 68. He made his international Test debut at the age of 24 on 1 March 1986 in a 25-20 loss to England at Twickenham in the Five Nations Championships. Amazingly, Keyes was not selected again by Ireland until he was named in their 1991 Rugby World Cup finals squad. He played in all four of Ireland's 1991 Rugby World Cup finals games and only pulled on the Irish jersey three more times, winning his 8th and last cap on 15 February 1992, an 18-10 defeat to Scotland at Lansdowne Road in the Five Nations Championship.

16 teams which competed in 1987 also competed in 1991 along with Western Samoa who qualified ahead of Tonga.

The All Blacks won Pool 1 with England runners-up whilst Scotland and Ireland dominated Pool 2 (Scotland won it and Ireland finished second). Newcomers Western Samoa finished runners-up to Australia in Pool 3 with impressive victories against Wales and Argentina. Fiji had a disappointing tournament finishing bottom of Pool 4 after losing all three of their games: Canada 13-3 (Pool runners-up), France 33-9 (Pool winners) and Romania 17-15. The quarter-finals did not produce any shocks with all four favoured teams reaching the semi-finals: England 19-18 France (Parc des Princes), Scotland 28-6 Western Samoa (Murrayfield), Australia 19-18 Ireland (Lansdowne Road) and New Zealand 29-13 Canada (Stadium Lille-Métropole, Villeneuve-d'Ascq, France).

The semi-finals paired the two northern hemisphere teams together and the two southern hemisphere teams together. England beat Scotland 9-3 in a scrappy affair at Murrayfield whilst the Wallabies defeated the defending World champions, the All Blacks, 16-6 at Lansdowne Road. A new name would be inscribed on the Webb Ellis Cup. Four days before the final, New Zealand beat Scotland 13-6 in the Third Place Play-Off at the Arms Park. The final took place at Twickenham on 2 November 1991 with the home nation hoping to see off the power of Australia. Throughout the tournament England had relied on their forwards and the trustworthy boot of Jonathan Webb (four conversions, seven penalties and a try in the Pool games; one conversion and three penalties in the quarter-finals, and two penalties in the semi-finals). The Wallabies' David Campese, who won the Player of the Tournament award, criticised England's style of play in the press. When it came to the final, England altered their game plan and decided to run at the Wallabies' defence. It backfired and Australia won the game 12-6 thanks to a converted try which was scored by Tony Daly and converted by Michael Lynagh who also scored two penalties. Webb scored two penalties for England and the Webb Ellis Cup was presented to the Australian captain, Nick Farr-Jones.

IRELAND'S RESULTS:
POOL 2
Ireland 55 Zimbabwe 11 – Lansdowne Road
Ireland 32 Japan 16 – Lansdowne Road
Ireland 15 Scotland 24 – Murrayfield
Ireland finished Pool 2 runners-up to Scotland.
Knockout Stage
Australia 19 Ireland 18 – Lansdowne Road

1992 FIVE NATIONS CHAMPIONSHIP – END OF THE ROAD

Ciaran Fitzgerald was still the Ireland coach with Phillip Matthews and Phil Danaher sharing the captaincy.

England were like a Rolls Royce in the 1992 Five Nations Championship, winning all four of their games to win back-to-back Grand Slam titles. Ireland were like an old tractor struggling to make its' way across a muddy field losing all four of their matches. But it could have all been so different for Ireland.

On 18 January 1992, Ireland welcomed Wales to Dublin and it was the team wearing red that won a game 16-15 that ebbed and flowed for the full 80 minutes of play. And when England blew Ireland away on Matchday 2, winning 38-9 at Twickenham, the tractor's engine packed in.

Ireland were beaten 18-10 by Scotland at Lansdowne Road and if they were blown away in London, a hurricane hit them in Paris when France steamrollered them at Parc des Princes with a 44-12 victory.

Boyz II Men had their only UK No.1 hit during the year with *End of the Road*. As it turned out the IRFU decided it was the end of the road for coach Ciaran Fitzgerald, who was succeeded by Gerry Murphy.

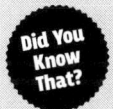 England set a new tournament record for most tries scored with 15, six of them came in the win against Ireland. England conceded just four tries compared to the 16 Ireland's tractor gave up for a dismal points difference of minus 70.

THE CLAW

Peter Clohessy, was born on 22 March 1966 in Limerick and played rugby union for Munster, Queensland Reds (Australia) and Ireland. Nicknamed 'The Claw', he played most of his career (1987-2002) at tight-head prop before switching to loose-head. He made his debut for Ireland versus France on 20 February 1993, a 21-6 loss at Lansdowne Road in the Five Nations Championship. In June 1994, he scored the first of his four international tries but missed out on selection for the Ireland squad which took part in the 1995 Rugby World Cup hosted and won by South Africa. However, four years later he was part of the Irish squad which went to the 1999 Rugby World Cup hosted by Wales and won by Australia. Clohessy never represented the British and Irish Lions, he was not selected for their 1993 Tour on New Zealand and had to withdraw from the 1997 Tour of South Africa through injury. On 6 April 2002, he pulled on the Irish jersey for the 54th and final time, a 44-5 defeat to France at Stade de France in the 2002 Six Nations Championship.

> **Did You Know That?** Clohessy formerly owned a pub in Limerick called 'Clohessy's' and an adjoining night club called 'The Sin Bin'.

1993 FIVE NATIONS CHAMPIONSHIP - RELIGHTING THE FIRE

Gerry Murphy was the new man charged with reversing Ireland's fortunes on the field having taken over as coach from Ciaran Fitzgerald. Murphy handed the captaincy of the side to the Munster scrum-half, Michael Bradley. Some fans thought that the appointment of Murphy by the IRFU was the equivalent of an American Football coach instructing his quarterback to throw a 'Hail Mary' pass in the dying seconds of a game. Murphy had played for Dublin University and Wanderers but was never capped by Ireland. Prior to the IRFU's leap of faith, he had coached Wanderers. Bradley on the other hand was a seasoned campaigner, a regular for his club since 1980 and he made his Ireland debut in 1984.

Surely Murphy's team could not do any worse than the previous year's embarrassing Five Nations Championship when opponents scored tries against them with ease, resulting in Ireland being awarded the wooden spoon. First up for the new coach and captain was Scotland at Murrayfield where it was a case of the 'same old, same old' as Ireland lost 15-3. Not quite the start the men in blazers at IRFU Headquarters had hoped for.

Game 2 was a contest versus France at Lansdowne Road. It was time for Murphy to show the IRFU, and more importantly the Ireland fans, that he was the right man to lead his country forward with a Rugby World Cup finals only two years away. The men in green rarely got out of second gear losing 21-6 to the visitors. Ireland were on a slippery path to back-to-back wooden spoons.

However, the Rugby Gods took pity on them in Game 3 when Ireland ripped up the form book and defeated Wales 19-14 at the Arms Park. A chink of light had just appeared of what had previously been a very dark passageway after Ireland had lost nine and drawn one of their previous 10 matches in the tournament. Ironically the draw was against Wales, who were also the last nation Ireland had beaten, doing so on the final day of the 1990 campaign when they won 14-8 in Dublin.

In their fourth and final game Ireland's new coach and his players sent the fans home happy following a 17-3 victory over England at Lansdowne Road. Mick Galwey scored a try, whilst Eric Elwood kicked two penalties and landed two drop goals. The IRFU recorded a much-improved performance insertion on their pupil's report card.

The boyband, Take That, had three No.1 hits in the UK charts during the year with *Pray*, *Relight My Fire* (with Lulu) and *Babe*. The Ireland fans' prayers appeared to have been answered as Murphy had relit the fire on the pitch.

 The 1993 Five Nations Championship was the first year the tournament champions, on this occasion France, were presented with a winners' trophy.

ALL-IRELAND GAELIC FOOTBALL AND RUGBY UNION WINNER

Michael Joseph Galwey was born in Currow, Kerry on 8 October 1966 and won the first of his 41 caps for Ireland (four times as captain, scored 15 points) in a 21-13 loss to France at Lansdowne Road on 2 February 1991 in a Five Nations Championship game. Between 1987 and 2003, he played 130 times for Munster (85 as captain), scoring 85 points. Prior to commencing his rugby union career, he won an All-Ireland Senior Football Championship title with Kerry in 1986. He was only 19 years old when The Kingdom beat Tyrone, who were playing in their first final, 2-15 to 1-10 at Croke Park. He also holds County Championship medals in Senior, Junior and Minor grades.

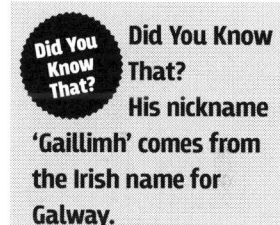 Did You Know That? His nickname 'Gaillimh' comes from the Irish name for Galway.

Galwey was a key figure in Shannon Rugby Football Club's team during the 1990s when they won four AIB Championship titles in a row - 1995, 1996, 1997 & 1998. Therefore, he is the only winner of an 'All-Ireland' in both Gaelic football and rugby union.

In 1993, he was a member of the British and Irish Lions touring party of New Zealand. With Munster he won a Celtic League title whilst as a Shannon RFC player he lifted 10 Munster Senior Cups and six All-Ireland Leagues. In total, he played 113 games for Shannon in the All-Ireland League, scoring 28 tries, and went on to coach the side to two All-Ireland League victories and two Munster Senior Cups.

1994 FIVE NATIONS CHAMPIONSHIP - THINGS CAN ONLY GET BETTER

The 1994 Five Nations Championship was the 100th Northern Hemisphere rugby union championship. The Gerry Murphy and Michael Bradley combination of coach and captain continued into the 1994 Five Nations Championship for Ireland. The pair hoped to improve on the two wins Ireland achieved the previous season when they finished one place above the wooden spoon winners, Wales. Alas, their hopes vanished into thin air because they actually fared worse, winning just a single match, losing two and drawing with Scotland in Dublin.

'NOT ONLY WERE IRELAND LEAKING POINTS LIKE A HOSE WHICH A GARDENER HAD JUST PUT A PITCHFORK THROUGH, FIVE TRIES CONCEDED AND 13 PENALTIES SCORED AGAINST THEM, THEY ONLY MANAGED ONE TRY IN THEIR FOUR GAMES.'

Amazingly the win came against England at Twickenham Stadium which most definitely was not foreseen on any Fortune Teller's tarot cards.

Not only were Ireland leaking points like a hose which a gardener had just put a pitchfork through, five tries conceded and 13 penalties scored against them, they only managed one try in their four games. Simon Geoghegan crossed the white line in the win over England. *Frankenstein* was a popular movie in the cinemas in 1994, but Irish rugby fans had already seen two horror shows by their team during the 1994 Five Nations Championship. And, had it not been for the accurate right boot of Eric Elwood, who scored all of Ireland's other 44 points from 14 penalties and a conversion, Ireland would surely have ended up as wooden spoon winners. Thankfully, for Murphy and Bradley, Scotland took that unwanted piece of kitchen equipment home to Edinburgh.

Meanwhile Wales turned their form around 360 degrees by winning the championship and were denied a Grand Slam victory by England, losing 15-8 at Twickenham on the last day.

IRELAND'S RESULTS
France 35 Ireland 15 - Stade de France
Ireland 15 Wales 17 - Lansdowne Road
England 12 Ireland 13 - Twickenham
Ireland 6 Scotland 6 - Lansdowne Road

On 22 January 1994, D-Ream went to No.1 in the UK charts with *Things Can Only Get Better*. As far as Irish rugby fans were concerned, they most certainly hoped so.

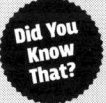

Did You Know That? Simon Patrick Geoghegan was born in Knebworth, Hertfordshire, England and qualified to play for Ireland through his father, who was born in Galway. His grandfather played for Galway in the 1929 All-Ireland Senior Hurling Championship final, losing 4-9 to 1-3 to Cork.

1995 FIVE NATIONS CHAMPIONSHIP - IRELAND'S APOLLO 13 MISSION

Well D-Ream hadn't a clue what they were singing about the year before, because in the 1995 Five Nations Championship things did not get better for Ireland. Once again, Ireland finished in fourth place in the table, this time recording only one victory. Wales went from champs to chumps in 12 months by losing all four of their games to take home the wooden spoon. The Welsh kitchen was more used to silverware than wooden utensils.

Gerry Murphy was still at the helm of the ship as coach but he brought a new captain onboard, Brendan Mullin. In Game 1, England avenged their home loss to Ireland a year earlier by winning 20-8 at Lansdowne Road. Anthony Foley scored a try and Paul Burke kicked over a penalty. Game 2 meant Scotland at Murrayfield. The poster advertising the 1995 Edinburgh

Fringe Festival featured a clown made up like a Court Jester. On 4 February 1995, the Ireland team were made to look like clowns following an inept performance, hardly brought on by stage fright, losing 26-13 to Scotland. Craig Joiner scored a try for the home side whilst Gavin Hastings successfully kicked two conversions and four penalties. The game was not quite a re-enactment of the Battle of Hastings (1066) but Ireland urgently required a joiner to build a new door for their defence. In keeping with the Court Jester theme, France ran Ireland a merry dance at Lansdowne Road winning 25-7. In their final game Ireland met the defending champions at the Arms Park. The game would decide the outcome of a 'trophy' but it wasn't a Triple Crown decider. Ireland won the encounter 16-12 to condemn Wales to something a joiner could carve, a wooden spoon.

Apollo 13 was one of the must-see movies in 1995, starring Kevin Bacon and Tom Hanks. Apollo 13 (11-17 April 1970) was the seventh crewed mission in the Apollo Space Programme and the third one which was meant to land on the Moon. However, the craft which was launched from Kennedy Space Center did not reach its intended destination. The lunar landing was aborted after an oxygen tank in the Service Module failed two days into the mission. The crew instead looped around the Moon in a circumlunar trajectory and returned safely to Earth.

Ireland's 1995 Five Nations Championship campaign was their Apollo 13, not quite reaching their destination of clinching the title they had ironically lifted 13 years previously.

> **Did You Know That?** During the 1995 Five Nations Championship, the 'Lansdowne Road Football Riot' occurred during what was supposed to be an international football friendly match between the Republic of Ireland and England. On 15 February 1995, the Republic of Ireland played England at the home of Irish rugby which also doubled up as the home of the country's international football team. Ireland took the lead in the 22nd minute through a David Kelly goal, but after a goal scored by David Platt four minutes later was disallowed for offside, some of the English fans began throwing debris down into the lower stands, including parts of benches which they had ripped out earlier in the match. The referee took the two teams off the pitch and as the Republic of Ireland manager was walking off the pitch, he was subjected to cries of 'Judas, Judas'. Clearly, these individuals did not know their football history as Jack Charlton was a member of the England team which won the FIFA World Cup in 1966. The fans in the lower stands then spilled out onto the pitch to escape the missiles which were thrown by the English fans. Some Irish fans had mistakenly been put into the area where the English fans were when the Football Association returned a number of tickets to the Football Association of Ireland. The decision to abandon the match was subsequently taken as the rioting escalated.

THE PROFESSIONALS

The IRB opened the sport to professionals in August 1995, after the completion of the 1995 Rugby World Cup finals held in South Africa. In 1886, Ireland, Scotland and Wales formed the International Rugby Football Board (IRFB) after unsuccessful attempts to unify and formalise rugby's rules. The new organisation introduced a points structure of three points for a goal and one for a try. The three member nations of the IRFB agreed not to play England until they joined the IRFB. England eventually became a member in 1890.

> **Did You Know That?** In 1930, the four member nations agreed that they would play all future rugby matches under the laws of the IRFB. In 1998, the IRFB changed its name to the International Rugby Board (IRB) and then in 2014, it changed its name again to World Rugby (WR).

RUGBY WORLD CUP HOSTS

Ireland has never played host to a Rugby World Cup but it has played host to three Pool games in the competition as well as a quarter-final and semi-final match. In 1991, England, Ireland, Scotland, Wales and France were co-hosts of rugby union's most prized tournament. Ireland hosted three Pool 2 games: Ireland 55 Zimbabwe 11 at Lansdowne Road; Ireland 32 Japan 16 at Lansdowne Road, and Japan 52 Zimbabwe 18 at Ravenhill. On 20 October 1991, Australia beat the Irish 19-18 with a last-gasp try from fly-half Michael Lynagh when Ireland were leading 18–15. A week later the Wallabies beat the reigning Rugby World Cup holders, New Zealand, 16-6 in Dublin to reach the final. Australia defeated England 12-6 in the 1991 Rugby World Cup final which was played at Twickenham on 2 November 1991.

Wales were the official hosts of the 1999 Rugby World Cup even though most of the matches were played outside the country with England, Ireland, Scotland and France hosting. On this occasion three Irish venues were used: Lansdowne Road, Ravenhill and Thomond Park. On 24 October 1999, France defeated Argentina 47-26 in the quarter-finals in Dublin. Australia beat France 35-12 in the final at the Millennium Stadium. Ireland were invited to host some games for the 2007 Rugby World Cup but due to a delay in the construction of the Aviva Stadium the IRFU eventually had to advise the IRB that it was not in a position to host any of the tournament's matches. France were the host nation in 2007 although four games were played at the Millennium Stadium and two at Murrayfield.

> **Did You Know That?** Zimbabwe participated in the inaugural Rugby World Cup in 1987. Zimbabwe's national rugby team was invited as the African entrant. No other African countries were invited, as South Africa was banned from competing in the tournament due to a sporting boycott adopted by the international community in response to apartheid. World Cup Rugby, the tournament's organisers, had no time for the system of institutionalised racial segregation which was prevalent in South Africa and South West Africa from 1948 to 1990. On 21 March 1990, South West Africa gained independence from South Africa and became Namibia.

1995 RUGBY WORLD CUP

The eight quarter-finalists from the 1991 Rugby World Cup final all received automatic entry for the 1995 tournament along with the host nation, South Africa: Australia, Canada, England, France, Ireland, New Zealand, Scotland and Western Samoa. The remaining seven slots went to the winners of the regional qualifying competitions: Argentina (the Americas), Cote d'Ivoire (Africa), Japan (Asia), Tonga (Oceania) and the three European qualifiers, Italy, Romania and the nation which finished third at the inaugural Rugby World Cup finals in 1987, Wales.

This was the first Rugby World Cup to be hosted by one nation and the last before the professional era. A total of nine stadiums were used, with the majority being given upgrades prior to the tournament to ensure they were up to the required standard. The largest four - Loftus Versfeld, Newlands, King's Park Stadium and Ellis Park - were used for the knockout games. There were games originally scheduled to have been played in Brakpan, Germiston, Pietermaritzburg and Witbank, but these games were reallocated to other venues. The organisers said the changes made had to do with facilities for both the press and spectators, as well as for security reasons.

VENUES WERE PAIRED:
Pool 1: Cape Town, Port Elizabeth and Stellenbosch
Pool 2: Durban and East London
Pool 3: Johannesburg and Bloemfontein
Pool 4: Pretoria and Rustenburg

Pool A was won by the South Africa with the defending World champions, Australia taking the runners-up position. The opening game brought these sides together with The Springboks defeating the Wallabies 27-18 at Newlands, Cape Town. England won Pool B which saw Western Samoa pip Italy (third) and Argentina (fourth) to a quarter-finals place. New Zealand claimed top spot in Pool C which was the most difficult Pool, whilst Ireland finished second ahead of Wales and Japan. Pool D was won by France, with Scotland also qualifying for the quarter-finals. South Africa had the easiest route to the semi-finals after being draw to play Western Samoa who they beat 42-14 at Ellis Park, Johannesburg. France beat Ireland 36-12 at Kings Park Stadium, Durban, England won a tight match against Australia (25-22 at Newlands) and the All Blacks eased into the semi-finals with a 48-30 win over Scotland at

Loftus Versfeld, Pretoria. South Africa found it tough going against a powerful France side in the semi-finals but progressed to a home final with a 19-15 victory at King's Park Stadium. The All Blacks prevented England from becoming the first country to play in back-to-back finals when they defeated them 45-29 at Newlands. France, runners-up in the inaugural tournament in 1987, won the Third-Place play-off match against England, 19-9 at Loftus Versfeld.

The final between New Zealand and South Africa saw the best attack come up against the best defence. The All Blacks went into the showpiece game having scored 315 points in the tournament, with the home nation only conceding 55. Without a try scored in the opening 80 minutes they went into extra-time locked at 9-9. Both sides scored penalties during the first half of extra-time but it was Joel Stransky's drop goal which secured South Africa the Rugby World Cup in front of a sell-out fanatical crowd at Ellis Park. When the final whistle was blown the entire crowd stood to its feet as all of South Africa celebrated as one. Two skydivers flew into the stadium with signs which read *Congratulations South Africa* and *See You In Wales 1999*. An emotional South Africa captain, Francois Pienaar, who inspired his team on the field and his country off it, gathered his teammates together in a huddle and went down on one knee saying a prayer. This game showed that in times like this the pain is so great for one and the ecstasy is so great for the other. Plenty of games had been played without a try being scored, dull affairs, but this one was a thriller. The image of President Nelson Mandela wearing a No.6 Springbok jersey and baseball cap, handing over the Webb Ellis Cup to Pienaar, is still one of the most memorable in sporting history. Madiba raised his fists in celebration, as the crowd chanted his name.

The Rainbow Nation had triumphed.

In a post-match TV interview Pienaar was asked what it was like to have 62,000 fans supporting his team. He responded: 'There were not 62,000 people supporting us today. There were 43 million'. And when he was asked what it was like to receive the Webb Ellis Cup from President Mandela, he said: 'What happened was Nelson Mandela said "thank you very much for what you've done for South Africa" but I said "thank you for what you've done". I almost felt like hugging him but it wasn't appropriate, I guess. Then I lifted the trophy which was unbelievable. I can't describe the feeling as I wouldn't do it justice.'

IRELAND'S RESULTS:
Pool C
Ireland 19 New Zealand 43 – Ellis Park
Ireland 50 Japan 28 – Free State Stadium, Bloemfontein
Ireland 24 Wales 23 – Ellis Park
Ireland finished Pool 2 runners-up to New Zealand.
KNOCKOUT STAGE
France 36 Ireland 12 – Kings Park Stadium

> **Did You Know That?** The term 'Rainbow Nation' was first heard a year before South Africa hosted the Rugby World Cup finals in 1995. In 1994, the African National Congress won South Africa's first free democratic election by a landslide margin. Archbishop Desmond Tutu coined the phrase 'Rainbow People of God', to describe the population of South Africa shortly after the 1994 election Tutu was the Archbishop of Cape Town (1986-96) at the time, the first indigenous black African to hold the position, and he regularly referred to 'the Rainbow People of God' during his sermons. The word rainbow alludes to the Book of Genesis and the Biblical story of Noah's flood, God's decision to return the earth to its watery pre-creation state and then remake it in a reversal of creation, an ensuing rainbow of peace. The word has significant meaning in the African Xhosa culture where 'umnayama' means hope and a bright future. In political terms, the word symbolises the coming together as one of the South Africa people, a unity of many diverse cultures. Within weeks of becoming the President of South Africa (10 May 1994 – 14 June 1999), President Nelson Mandela used the term in a speech to the nation: 'Each of us is as intimately attached to the soil of this beautiful country as are the famous jacaranda trees of Pretoria and the mimosa trees of the bushveld – a rainbow nation at peace with itself and the world'.
>
> South Africa has 11 official languages; Afrikaans, English, Ndebele, Northern Sotho, Sesotho, Swati, Tsonga, Tswana, Venda, Xhosa and Zulu. South African Sign Language is also used.

1996 SIX NATIONS CHAMPIONSHIP - MISSION IMPOSSIBLE

Gerry Murphy made way as coach for the 1996 Five Nations Championship and was replaced by Murray Kidd, and following the retirement of Brendan Mullin, Kidd chose co-captains in Niall Hogan and Jim Staples. Following the professionalism of the sport after the 1995 Rugby World Cup finals, Kidd became Ireland's first coach in the professional era.

One of the top selling singles of the year, a No.1 hit in the UK charts, was *Killing Me Softly*, by The Fugees. Ireland's squad for the 1996 Five Nations Championship was slowly killing the Irish fans with their inept performances, slow style of play and overall general lack of inventiveness. When Ireland went behind in a game, which they did all too often, Kidd had no Plan B to switch to whilst neither Hogan or Staples provided the necessary leadership qualities needed by an Ireland captain during matches when things simply were just not going to plan.

IRELAND'S RESULTS
Ireland 10 v Scotland 16 - Lansdowne Road
France 45 v Ireland 10 - Stade de France
Ireland 30 v Wales 17 - Lansdowne Road
England 28 v Ireland 15 - Twickenham

England were crowned champions but Scotland missed out on a fourth Grand Slam by losing 18-9 to England at Murrayfield. England and Scotland both won three games and lost one (France beat England 15-12 in Paris), but the title went to England on a points scored and points conceded difference - England +25 to Scotland's +4. It was the second successive season Scotland lost out on claiming the Grand Slam to their deadly enemies, following their 24-12 loss at Twickenham Stadium 12 months earlier.

Ireland scored 65 points across their four matches during the tournament but left their back door open too many times for unwanted visitors who racked up 106 points, a points difference of -41.

In 1996, *Mission Impossible* was one of the biggest movies of the year but not even Ethan Hunt (Tom Cruise) and the Impossible Missions Force (IMF) could have saved Ireland from claiming the wooden spoon in the 1996 Five Nations Championship.

> **Did You Know That?** France actually went into the final weekend of games just needing a victory against Wales to win the 1996 Five Nations Championship thanks to their superior points difference, but lost their encounter at the Arms Park by a single point, 16-15. The result meant that Wales not only avoided a whitewash but climbed above Ireland on points difference, -21.

AXEL FOLEY

Anthony Gerard Foley was born in Limerick on 30 October 1973. He began his rugby career in 1992 with his local club, Shannon and then joined Munster in 1995. The No.8 won his first cap for Ireland in the 1995 Five Nations Championship, scoring a try in Ireland's 20-8 loss at Lansdowne Road. At the 1995 Rugby World Cup finals in South Africa he played in one Pool game as a replacement when the Irish beat Japan 50-28 at Free State Stadium, Bloemfonteim. He missed the 1999 Rugby World Cup finals in Wales but was back for the 2003 competition when Australia were the host nation. Foley, who was affectionately nicknamed 'Axel' by his teammates, featured in two of Ireland's Pool games in Australia (a 45-17 win over Romania and a narrow 17-16 loss to The Wallabies).

Detective Axel Foley is a fictional character who was portrayed by Eddie Murphy in the *Beverly Hills Cop* series of movies. Anthony Foley captained Ireland on three occasions: in 2001 v Samoa and twice in 2002 v Romania and Georgia. His 62nd and last cap for his country came against Wales in the 2005 Six Nations Championship, Ireland going down 33-20 in the Millennium Stadium. In total, he scored five international tries; against England in 1995, Romania in 2001, Fiji in 2002, France in 2004 and Wales in 2004. In 2014, he was made Head Coach of Munster.

His father, Brendan, and his sister, Rosie, also played rugby for Ireland. Sadly, he passed away in his sleep on 16 October 2016 aged just 42. He was staying in a hotel in Paris with the Munster squad where the Irish side were due to play Racing 92 in their opening game of the

2016-17 European Rugby Champions Cup. An autopsy revealed that he died of heart disease which had caused an acute pulmonary edema.

> **Did You Know That?** To honour Anthony Foley's memory and contribution to European rugby, European Professional Club Rugby (EPCR) announced that the 2016–17 European Player of the Year would receive the Anthony Foley Memorial Trophy. Owen Farrell from Saracens was the inaugural winner of the newly named trophy. Prior to 2017, a trophy was awarded to the European Professional Club Rugby Player of the Year and was first presented in 2010 to Munster's Ronan O'Gara. Other Irish winners of the award are: 2011 – Sean O'Brien (Leinster), 2012 – Rob Kearney (Leinster) and in 2022 when Leinster's Josh van der Flier scooped the award which was presented to him by Anthony's wife, Olive, and their two sons, Dan and Tony.

FRED THE RED MEETS RUMPOLE OF THE BAILEY

Fred Howard (England) refereed the Ireland versus Wales match on 18 January 1992 at Lansdowne Road. It was both team's opening game of the 1992 Five Nations Championship. Howard was a no-nonsense referee who had sent more international players off in European Rugby than any other official, hence his nickname 'Fred the Red'. However, to the amazement of the fans inside the stadium and those watching on television, Howard allowed Tony Copsey, who was making his Welsh debut, to stay on the field despite the fact that the 6' 7" lock landed a punch on the left cheekbone of Ireland's Neil Francis, that Mike Tyson would have been proud of. As one journalist put it: 'Francis was seeing more stars than what Sir Patrick Moore had seen in all of the episodes of *The Sky at Night* TV show he appeared in'.

Copsey owed a lot to his captain Ieuan Evans that day for not possibly having the shortest career in international rugby. Copsey told *Wales Online*: 'Fred Howard is still on my Christmas-card list. And Ieuan is still my defence lawyer. Seriously, I think Fred took into account it was my first cap and that a few other things had been going on. He knew I was fired up and a bit hot-headed. But it didn't look great for me at the time. If it had happened today, there is no question that I would be off. It could have been the shortest Test career on record.' Wales won the game 16-15.

> **Did You Know That?** Going into the Ireland game, Wales had only won one of their previous 13 matches in the Five Nations Championship. BBC Wales celebrated the victory by showing clips of the game to the Thin Lizzy song, The Boys are Back in Town. The ITV show, Rumpole of the Bailey, was popular at the time of the game and was about a barrister who defended underdog clients at the Old Bailey Courthouse, London.

THE IRISH OLYMPIAN WHO MADE RUGBY WORLD CUP HISTORY

Victor Carton Patrick Costello was born on 23 October 1970 in Stepaside, Dublin. On 6 January 1996, he won the first of his 39 caps for Ireland in a 25-18 win over the United States of America. The match was played at LIFE Clinic, Atlanta and was part of Ireland's Tour of North America. The hard running No.8's final appearance in the Irish jersey was a 37-16 victory against Scotland at Lansdowne Road on 27 March 2004 in the 2004 Six Nations Championship. Costello played three matches at the 2003 Rugby World Cup and scored a try in a 45-17 win over Romania in a Pool A game. By scoring the try he made history becoming the first Olympian to score a try at a Rugby World Cup. He scored a total of four tries for Ireland. But rugby was not Costello's first love. He won his first national shot-put title at the age of just 16 and won five Irish titles between 1987 and 1991. He represented Ireland at the 1992 Summer Olympic Games in Barcelona, and finished in 11th place in the Qualifying Round in the shot-put. After the Olympiad, he retired from athletics and turned his attention to playing rugby for Connacht and Leinster.

Looking back on his achievements he said: 'Barcelona was an incredible experience. Many good Irish athletes never got to the Olympics, but fortunately the timing worked well for me. In the back of my mind, I thought it was the end of my athletics career, rather than the start. I always knew I wanted to play rugby. I felt that the team mentality was much more rewarding and fulfilling than the selfish, singular mentality of field events. The decision to leave athletics and play rugby was hard to justify to the Irish Athletics Board at 21 years of age, but rugby was better funded in Ireland and had better structures in place.'

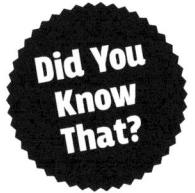

Victor's father, Paul Joseph Costello, was also an Irish national shot-put champion and won one cap for Ireland at second-row. His sole appearance in an Irish rugby union jersey came on 9 April 1960, a 23-6 loss to France at Stade Olympique de Colombes in the 1960 Five Nations Championship.

1997 FIVE NATIONS CHAMPIONSHIP - A TIME TO SCREAM

Murray Kidd was named coach of Ireland on 13 October 1995, succeeding Gerry Murphy and held the office for a year, until resigning following Ireland's appalling displays in the 1996 Five Nations Championship. In his nine games in charge of the

national team, they won three and lost six. The team needed new blood and the players needed a new direction on their style of play to avoid another wooden spoon in the 1997 Five Nations Championship.

The IRFU decided to dispense with tradition and appointed their first 'foreign' coach when they persuaded Brian Ashton to leave Bath Rugby Club's Recreation Ground for Lansdowne Road. The men in blazers at IRFU Headquarters either thought that Ashton, who had hardly set the rugby world alight in his previous posts, including assistant coach to England's coach in 1985, Dick Greenwood, or he was the one-man revolution required to turn around Ireland's fortunes. In 1985, Ireland won the Five Nations Championship and Triple Crown, Dick's England finished second from bottom of the table. Amazingly, the IRFU gave Ashton a six-year contract and also appointed Pat Whelan as team manager.

The new look Ireland under Ashton's stewardship kicked off their 1997 Five Nations Championship campaign with a home game versus France. Lansdowne Road was packed, turning out to see if an Englishman could give an Ireland team the same lift that Jack Charlton gave the Republic of Ireland football team over the previous 10 years, 1986-96, when the England World Cup winner in 1966 helped lift a nation off their knees in world football rankings to rise up, like a Phoenix from the ashes, with their exploits in Europe and at the FIFA World Cup finals.

In 1997, cinema-goers in Ireland were spoilt for choice with movies such as *Titanic, Batman and Robin, The Devil's Advocate, Con Air, The Game, Hercules, Face/Off, Scream 2, Lost Highway* and *As Good As It Gets* all available to see. Under Ashton, Ireland's performances could envelope all of these movie titles into one massive box office flop for Ireland fans. Ireland did not feature in the rugby Oscars as they lost three of their four games and won one, a 26-25 win over Wales at the Arms Park, a horror picture for the residents of the Principality.

Like Titanic, Ireland's performances were a tragic disaster: Batman and Robin got on well together but Ashton and Whelan had too many arguments and disagreements, more like the cartoon characters *Tom & Jerry* than the Dynamic Duo; the IRFU failed to play the role of Devil's Advocate between coach and manager; the Irish fans had been conned into thinking their team had turned a corner in terms of performances; Ireland had no A or B game; if Hercules had worn a green jersey not even his famous strength would have stopped Ireland's opponents from rampaging through their straw wall of a defence; Ashton and Whelan had too many Face/Offs that were all too frequently aired in public; Screams were frequently heard from the Irish fans when Ireland's defence melted like a Choc Pop lolly sitting on a table in the midday sun; Ireland had no path to follow under Ashton, they were on AC/DC's *Highway To Hell* and unfortunately for Ireland rugby fans, their team's performances were as good as it got.

IRELAND'S RESULTS
Ireland 15 v France 32 - Lansdowne Road
Wales 25 v Ireland 26 - National Stadium
Ireland 6 v England 46 - Lansdowne Road
Scotland 38 v Ireland 10 - Murrayfield

'LANSDOWNE ROAD WAS PACKED, TURNING OUT TO SEE IF AN ENGLISHMAN COULD GIVE AN IRELAND TEAM THE SAME LIFT THAT JACK CHARLTON GAVE THE REPUBLIC OF IRELAND FOOTBALL TEAM OVER THE PREVIOUS 10 YEARS'

Ashton did inject new blood into the side by giving four players their debuts during the campaign: Paul Flavin, Denis Hickie, Ross Nesdale and Brian O'Meara. But it was more of an intravenous drip than a full transfusion. Ashton resigned a year into his contract and was replaced by Warren Gatland, born in New Zealand.

In 1997, Puff Daddy and Faith Evans went to No.1 in the UK charts with *I'll Be Missing You*. The Spice Girls had the 1997 Christmas No.1 hit song, their sixth No.1 hit, with *Too Much*. The Ireland fans would not be missing Ashton as they had endured too much of his negative style of rugby.

> **Did You Know That?** Jack Charlton was born in Ashington, Northumberland, England on 8 May 1935.

IRELAND V FRANCE – HOME AND AWAY

Since their first meeting on 20 March 1909, Ireland and France have played each other 103 times with both nations using different stadiums to host the games.

IRELAND AT HOME	FRANCE AT HOME
Lansdowne Road	Parc des Princes
Mardyke	Stade Olympique de Colombes
Ravenhill	Stade de France
Croke Park	Stade Chaban-Delmas
Aviva Stadium	

> **Did You Know That?** On 10 June 1995, France beat Ireland 36-12 at King's Park Stadium, Durban in the 1995 Rugby World Cup. Eight years later, 9 November 2003, Ireland lost 43-21 to France at Telstar Dome, Melbourne, in the 2003 Rugby World Cup. France completed a Rugby World Cup hat-trick over Ireland at the 2007 Rugby World Cup, winning 25-3 on home soil, at Stade de France. After three successive losses in the most famous rugby tournament in the world, Ireland finally recorded a victory over the French on 11 October 2015. They met one another in a Pool D game at the Millennium Stadium which Ireland won 24-9.

1998 FIVE NATIONS CHAMPIONSHIP – GREAT EXPECTATIONS

Ireland's 1998 Five Nations Championship began with Brian Ashton as coach and Keith Wood, The Raging Potato (also known as Uncle Fester because of his striking bald head), as the new captain of the side. Ireland's drunken stoop from the previous year showed its' ugly head once again in the opening game of the competition, a theme which permeated the team in all four of their matches.

Game 1 was played on 7 February 1998 with Scotland the visitors to Lansdowne Road. Ireland lost a tight encounter 17-16 and less than a fortnight later, 20 February 1998, Ashton resigned. At the time he walked away from Lansdowne Road, Aqua were at No.1 in the Music charts with *Doctor Jones*. Ireland's players certainly needed some form of help, perhaps a brain surgeon as opposed to a General Practitioner.

Warren Gatland, born in Hamilton, New Zealand, was appointed the new coach of Ireland on 24 February 1998. He had played hooker for Waikato University winning 140 caps from 1986-94, a record number of caps. He also won 18 caps for the All Blacks between 1998-91 but more importantly he knew Irish rugby as he left his job as the Director of Rugby at Connacht to answer the IRFU's call to take charge of Ireland.

Gatland was thrown right into the thick of action as Ireland faced France in their next match at Stade de France. France were the in-form team having already played two games which they won and scored an impressive 75 points in the process. France defeated England 24-16 in the French capital and had a field day at Murrayfield where they beat Scotland 51-18. A new look Ireland lost 18-16 in Paris. However, Gatland was not able to stop the rot of results for Ireland as they lost 30-21 to Wales in Dublin and were defeated 35-17 by England at Twickenham Stadium. The quick fix the IRFU had hoped for did not happen. In 1998, a modernisation of the Charles Dickens' classic novel, *Great Expectations*, was released in the cinemas. The IRFU had great expectations for the Ireland team following their appointment of Gatland. However, with four defeats from four, 70 points scored and 100 points conceded, Ireland got exactly what was coming to them, another wooden spoon.

LA BAJADA OUT DANCES THE IRISH JIG

On 20 October 1999, Ireland met Argentina in the quarter-final play-off stages of the 1999 Rugby World Cup at Stade Bollaert-Delelis, Lens. The winners would face France in the quarter-finals at Lansdowne Road which, like Stade Bollaert-Delelis, was one of the grounds used for the 1999 tournament although the official host nation was Wales. Ireland were favourites to win having finished runners-up in their Pool to Australia whilst The Pumas had finished third in their Pool behind winners Wales

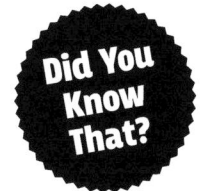

Warren Gatland guided Wasps Rugby Football Club to three Premiership titles and one Heineken Cup during his time as coach of the club, 2002-05. He was the head coach of the British and Irish Lions squad that secured a 2-1 Test Series victory over Australia in 2013.

and second placed Samoa. In what was only the third ever meeting between the two nations, Argentina outwitted Ireland to win the game 28-24.

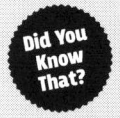 Dr Francisco Ocampo pioneered the unorthodox scrum technique back in the 1960s in Argentina. His twin loves of physics and scrummaging combined to devastating effect to create the Bajada, Argentina's classic set-piece counter-drive. The locks bind round the props' hips with their outside arms, rather than through the legs as standard. Pinning the props inwards towards the hooker, all the power shoots through the centre of the front row.

1999 FIVE NATIONS CHAMPIONSHIP – WHEN THE GOING GETS TOUGH

The 1999 Five Nations Championship was the 70th and final edition of the tournament before Italy joined the elite five in 2000, when it became the Six Nations Championship. Including previous incarnations of the tournament, the 1999 edition was the 105th northern hemisphere rugby competition.

Warren Gatland was still in charge of the team and Keith Wood was still the captain of his country. During the 1999 Five Nations Championship, Boyzone were enjoying their fifth UK No.1 single with the old Billy Ocean song *When the Going Gets Tough*. The going got tough for the Ireland players but their tough guys, including Wood, just never got out of first gear, apart from one afternoon in London.

IRELAND'S RESULTS
Ireland 9 v France 10 - Lansdowne Road
Wales 23 v Ireland 29 - Wembley Stadium
Ireland 15 v England 27 - Lansdowne Road
Scotland 30 v Ireland 13 - Murrayfield

When Ireland beat Wales 29-23 away on 20 February 1999, the Irish fans did not celebrate the victory on the streets of Cardiff. Instead, they partied in London as the game was played at Wembley Stadium because the Arms Park had been demolished to make way for a new home to Welsh rugby, the Millennium Stadium.

Scotland won the 1999 Five Nations Championship on a dramatic last day and in the final minutes of a match. England were the bookies' favourites to beat Wales at Wembley and claim both the title and a Grand Slam. England led the game by six points as it entered injury time. Scott Gibbs, the Wales centre, managed to evade a number of tackles to score a try from 20 metres out. Up stepped Neil Jenkins who scored the conversion to give Wales a 32-31 *home* victory in a match played on English soil. With Scotland having beaten France, the reigning Grand Slam holders, 32-16 at Stade de France the previous day, the 1999 Five Nations Championship, Triple crown and Grand Slam title went to Scotland. Indeed,

Scotland performed heroics scoring five first-half tries to beat France in Paris for only the second time in thirty years. Ireland finished one place above France in the table and gladly passed on the wooden spoon to a team who were unbeatable in the competition just a year earlier, but who on this occasion could only manage one win, their victory against Ireland in Dublin.

In 1999, Irish cinema-goers flocked to movie houses all over the country to see *The Boondock Saints*, a film about two Irish Catholic brothers who become vigilantes and wipe out Boston's criminal underground in the name of God. How the Irish fans could have done with the pair wearing a green jersey in 1999.

1999 RUGBY WORLD CUP

Wales were the official host nation of the 1999 Rugby World Cup although some of the matches were also played in England, France, Ireland and Scotland.

On 6 November 1999, Australia faced France in the first professional Rugby World Cup final at the Millennium Stadium. Australia won all three of their Pool E games, 57-9 versus Romania, 23-3 versus Ireland and a 55-19 win over the USA, scoring 135 points and conceding just 31. Meanwhile France also dominated Pool C, winning all three games, 33-20 versus Canada, 47-13 versus Namibia and a 28-19 victory over Fiji, scoring 108 points whilst conceding 52. The quarter-finals draw pitched The Wallabies against the host nation whilst France were drawn to play Argentina.

Australia progressed to the semi-finals after defeating Wales 24-9 with France beating the Pumas 47-26. In the semi-finals, The Wallabies won a dramatic and tight encounter against the defending World champions, South Africa, 27-21 after extra-time at Twickenham. To reach the final France would have to see off the tournament favourites, New Zealand. This encounter between the northern and southern hemisphere resulted in one of the greatest ever Rugby World Cup final games. The All Blacks led 24-10 at half-time at Twickenham but the French fought back in the second half overturning the 14 points deficit to win the game 43-31 and reach their second Rugby World Cup final (1987). Australia were too strong for France in the final and became the first nation to win the Webb Ellis Cup twice (1991) after beating Les Bleus 35-12.

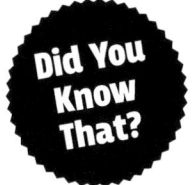

In preparation for their entry into the Six Nations Championship in 2000, Italy played England, France, Ireland, Scotland and Wales in season 1998-99, losing all five matches. Ireland won 39-30 in Dublin on 10 April 1999.

IRELAND RESULTS:
Pool E
Ireland 53 United States of America 8 – Lansdowne Road
Australia 23 Ireland 3 – Lansdowne Road
Ireland 24 Romania 14 – Lansdowne Road
Ireland finished Pool E runners-up to Australia.
Quarter-Final Play-Off Stage
Argentina 28 Ireland 24 – Stade Felix Bollaert

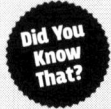

There was a certain irony in Australian captain, John Eales, being presented with the Webb Ellis Cup by the Queen on the very same day Australia had held a referendum on replacing her. The vote was 45.13% in favour with 54.875% against. Incidentally, Australia were coached by Rod Maqueen.

2000s

LOOKING FOR A MARS BAR IN A BUCKET OF S**T

THE RED CARPET INCIDENT

A SECOND GRAND SLAM WIN

'There are many people in the world who have succeeded in climbing the ladder of achievement. Some of these people have persevered throughout their career having met what appeared insurmountable obstacles yet overcame these challenges to keep moving forward.'
Byron Pulsifer

LOOKING FOR A MARS BAR IN A BUCKET OF S**T

'Stringer may as well be looking for a Mars bar in a bucket of s**t.'

Ireland coach Eddie O'Sullivan (2001-08) was watching his players' train. After one play he was angry about how they were protecting rucks and presenting the ball to the scrumhalf (Peter Stringer). O'Sullivan let the pack know exactly what he was thinking.

2000 SIX NATIONS CHAMPIONSHIP – NO COUNTRY FOR OLD MEN

Having finished second from bottom of the table in the previous year's Five Nations Championship, Ireland who were once again coached by Warren Gatland and led by Keith Wood, went into the inaugural Six Nations Championship with high hopes and expectations. Italy, after numerous failed and snubbed applications, finally secured a seat at the big boys' table in the most prestigious northern hemisphere rugby tournament, in 2000.

On Matchday 1, Ireland received a devastating blow to their championship aspirations, losing 50-18 to England at Twickenham. It was a calamitous blow to their hopes, conceding six tries, with Johnny Wilkinson running amok, scoring four conversions and four penalties. Next up were the defending champions, winners of the last ever Five Nations Championship a year earlier, Scotland. The visitors scored 22 points at Lansdowne Road but the men in green doubled that tally to record a 44-22 victory. The team were finally clicking on the pitch and the game marked the debuts of five players who would all go on to become legends in a green jersey and amass a staggering 461 caps between them: Ronan O'Gara 128, John Hayes 105, Peter Stringer 98, Simon Easterby 65 and Shane Horgan 65. Horgan scored a try in the game whilst O'Gara converted two tries and kicked over two penalties. It was a dream start for the 'Famous Five', without Enid Blyton even playing a part in the proceedings, five new internationals and a metamorphosis moment for Irish rugby. The Irish fans were rubbing their eyes in disbelief as they watched an exciting young and remodelled side after having had to endure three previous campaigns without a home win.

Indeed, the team that afternoon threatened to rewrite the record books, by recording Ireland's biggest ever score in the competition, surpassing the 30-17 victory against Wales in 1996, and on course to eclipse the biggest ever Ireland win, 24-0 over France in 1913, until the visitors, who at one point led 10-0, scored two late consolation tries. Mind you, a fortnight earlier the Scots were humiliated after losing 34-20 to Italy in Rome. Wood's try in Ireland's victory was his first as captain in his eleventh outing as their 'General' on the pitch.

To put the game in a song context, the win was a *Rapture* moment on the terraces at Lansdowne Road, celebrating the 1980 song by the band Blondie, entitled *Rapture*.

On 4 March 2000, Ireland welcomed the tournament's virgins to Dublin. In a historical context, Italy, or rather the Roman Empire, made several failed incursions into Ireland (Hibernia) and failed to annex the country into their clutches. And, just as Julius Caesar had failed, so too did Alessandro Troncon, the Italian captain, when his side went down to a heavy defeat in battle on Irish soil, 60-13. O'Gara had slipped into the fly-half role as seamlessly as a master tailor threading the button hole of a bespoke suit, and Ireland had recorded their biggest ever win in the history of the tournament. In their next game Gatland's young newcomers issued a statement to the best sides in the world when they beat France 27-25 in Paris, with Brian O'Driscoll lighting up the City of Light scoring a hat-trick of tries, all converted by O'Gara, with David Humphreys adding two penalties in a famous win.

However, it was a bridge too far for the Ireland side when Wales beat them 23-19 in the Irish capital. They ended the campaign in a disappointing, but given the trust in youth shown to them by their coach, respectable third place finish in the table. Ronan Keating's second No.1 hit in the charts, *Life is a Rollercoaster*, reflected the ups and downs of the team's performances.

In 2000, one of the biggest movies of the year was *Requiem for a Dream*. In the 2000 Six Nations Championship, the Ireland team left their fans dreaming of winning another title.

IRELAND'S SIX NATIONS RECORD				
COUNTRY	PLAYED	WON	DREW	LOST
SCOTLAND	129	64	5	60
ENGLAND	127	52	7	68
WALES	124	51	7	66
FRANCE	94	33	7	54
ITALY	24	23	0	1

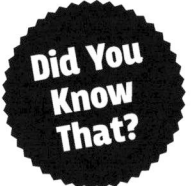

Did You Know That?

On 12 August 1986, the Scottish band, Simple Minds, conquered Paris. The multi-platinum band were in what Jim Kerr, their frontman, has latterly called their 'pomp and circumstance' when they arrived in the French capital to play that night at Le Zénith. And, to ensure the world could hear all about it, the band recorded the two concerts they played. Both were subsequently released as a double album entitled Live In The City Of Light. In 1989, Simple Minds released a single entitled Belfast Child. In the 2000 Six Nations Championship, David Humphreys, a Belfast child born in the city on 10 September 1971, helped Ireland light up the French capital when they beat France in the City of Light in the inaugural edition of the 2000 Six Nations Championship.

> **Did You Know That?** In 2000, the Five Nations became the Six Nations when Italy was welcomed to the top echelon of European rugby. Italy won their first game in the championship with a surprising 34–20 win over Scotland, who had won the previous year's Five Nations on points difference over England, at Stadio Flaminio.

THE BATTLE OF BAYONNE

On 16 August 2007, an Ireland XV played the French club, Aviron Bayonnais (known as – Bayonne), in a warm-up match for the 2007 Rugby World Cup. The match was played at Bayonne's home ground, Stade Jean-Dauger. The game was supposed to be a friendly with France the host nation for the 2007 Rugby World Cup. However, Neil Best, who played for Ireland in the game, described it as: 'The dirtiest game I've ever played'.

In the second-half of the match, Brian O'Driscoll, the Irish captain, was punched in the face by one of the second rows. The initial reports suggested the worst for the men in green, their talisman's cheekbone had been broken. Thankfully, an X-ray revealed less serious damage, a fractured sinus and a deep cut under his right eye. That wasn't going to stop BOD from leading his country in the tournament which was beamed live across the world to a global audience.

The home side played like they wanted to do their nation a massive favour as France and Ireland were both in Pool D at the showpiece event which would begin on 7 September 2007. Looking back on the game, Best thought it was poorly refereed by an inexperienced Wayne Barnes who failed to stamp out the nasty behaviour of some of the home team. And, when he decided it was time to give some back, Best was sent off. That was effectively the end of his Rugby World Cup dreams before the tournament had even started. Ireland won the match 42-6.

Best was only given the last 11 minutes in Ireland's opening game by their coach, Eddie O'Sullivan, a 32-17 win over Namibia: seven minutes in a 14-10 win against Georgia; seven minutes in the 25-3 defeat to France and 18 minutes in a 30-18 loss to Argentina. In total, he was capped by Ireland 18 times and scored 10 points.

Perhaps, O'Driscoll may have summed up the French side perfectly by saying that: 'They were more interested in kicking the shit out of Ireland than trying to put points on the scoreboard'.

But, the most important question has to be: *Why did Ireland agree to play a Rugby World Cup warm-up game against a team whose country were the host nation?* It was senseless, perhaps trying to placate the French fans who attended those games Ireland played against other nations. Stupidity? With hindsight, perhaps.

Wayne Barnes spoke about the game ahead of the 2019 Rugby World Cup in Japan (he officiated as a referee in the 1997 tournament and as an official in 2019) and said: 'It was only about two weeks before the World Cup started. It was quite an interesting appointment when the list came through... you saw Ireland versus Bayonne. I thought... *aren't Ireland playing France in a major game? This is going to be interesting.*'

> **Did You Know That?** The Battle of Bayonne took place on 14 April 1814, which witnessed the French garrison of Bayonne launching an attack on an army of British, Portuguese and Spanish soldiers. It was the last major battle of the Peninsula War, which commenced in 1808, and was fought 10 days after Napoleon abdicated his role as Emperor of France which his troops in Bayonne were unaware of.

In His Own Words

'The heart is willing, the head is willing ... but the body has had enough.'
An emotional Ireland captain, Keith Wood, after playing his final game in the green shirt, a 43-21 loss to France in the quarter-finals of the 2003 Rugby World Cup at Telstra Dome, Melbourne.

WORLD PLAYER OF THE YEAR

The inaugural World Rugby Player of the Year award was presented in 2001 and was won by Ireland's hooker and captain, Keith Wood. At the time the award was known as the IRB International Player of the Year - in 2007 it changed its name to the IRB Player of the Year and in 2014 it changed name again, this time to World Rugby Player of the Year. Two years later, 2016, it became World Rugby Men's 15 Player of the Year. Nominations for this prestigious award have been almost exclusively come from Tier 1 nations - the United States of America's Joe Taufete'e is the only Tier 2 player to receive a nomination. Fly-half is the most successful winning position, with eleven, followed by flanker with five.

When Wood lifted the trophy in 2001, his teammate, Brian O'Driscoll (centre), was one of the five nominees. O'Driscoll was a nominee again in 2002, losing out to the French scrum-half, Fabien Galthié. Other Irish nominations and winners are:

2004: Gordon D'Arcy (centre)	winner, Schalk Burger, flanker, South Africa
2006: Paul O'Connell (lock)	winner, Richie McCaw, flanker, New Zealand
2009: Jamie Heaslip (No.8)	winner, Richie McCaw
2009: Brian O'Driscoll (centre)	
2014: Johnny Sexton (fly-half)	winner, Brodie Retallick, lock, New Zealand
2016: Jamie Heaslip	winner, Beauden Barrett, fly-half, New Zealand
2018: winner Johnny Sexton	
2020: not awarded	
2022: winner Johnny Sexton	
2022: winner Josh van der Flier, flanker	
2023: Bundee Aki (centre)	winner, Ardie Savea, No 8, New Zealand

> **Did You Know That?** Two players have won the award three times: Richie McCaw (2006, 2009 and 2010) and his former All Blacks teammate, fly-half Dan Carter (2005, 2012 and 2015).

SEEING RED

In 2000, the Five Nations became the Six Nations when Italy entered the tournament. Since, Italy's admission there has been a total of 20 red cards dished out, with France on top of the 'Bad Boys League' with six red cards. Scotland are on five whilst Italy have been brandished four red cards. England have had three players sent off. Only two Irish players have been given an early bath, whilst Wales have not lost a single player through a red card since the inaugural Six Nations competition. In 2021, Peter O'Mahony became the first Ireland player to be dismissed in a Six Nations Championship game when he was given his marching orders. On 7 February 2021, Ireland faced Wales at the Millennium Stadium. In the 12th minute of play Ireland won a turnover and during the resulting ruck, the Welsh tighthead prop, Tomas Francis (who was born in York, England), was sitting upright on the ground, trapped by the players standing over him. O'Mahony flung himself into the ruck and made contact with Francis' head. Referee Wayne Barnes had no hesitation in sending the Cork man off. Ireland lost the game 21-16. On 20 March 2021, Bundee Aki was sent off by referee Mathieu Raynal (France) during Ireland's 32-18 victory over England at the Aviva Stadium. The Irish centre was shown the red card in the 64th minute following a high tackle on Billy Vuniploa which resulted in contact with the England No.8's head. It was the second time that Bundee Aki (born in Auckland, New Zealand) had been sent off playing for Ireland, resulting in him being handed a four-week ban by a disciplinary committee.

> **Did You Know That?** On 12 October 2019, Bundee Aki was sent off during Ireland's 47-5 win against Samoa at Fukuoka Hakatanomori Stadium, Fukuoka, Japan in the 2019 Rugby World Cup. Aki, who is of Samoan descent, became the first Irish player to be given a red card in a Rugby World Cup match after he made a dangerous tackle on fly-half Ulupano Seuteni. Mathieu Raynal was due to referee the game but had to withdraw due to illness and was replaced by Wayne Barnes. It was only the third time an Irish player had been shown a red card in the professional era and the first since 11 June 2016, when CJ Stander was given his marching orders playing against his native South Africa (he was born in George, South Africa) in a First Test match versus The Springboks. He was sent off by Raynal for catching the jaw of loose forward Pat Lambie with his hip when he jumped in the air to try and block a kick. Despite being down to 14 men, Ireland recorded a historic first win in South Africa, a 26-20 victory at DHL Newlands, Cape Town.

IRELAND'S TOP APPEARANCE MAKERS IN THE SIX NATIONS

1. Brian O'Driscoll	65 Caps
2. Rory Best	64 Caps
3. Ronan O'Gara	63 Caps
4. Cian Healey	60 Caps
5. Johnny Sexton	60 Caps

In His Own Words

'Listen to me now… I want them standing back thinking what the f**k is going on here. Not for the first five minutes… every f*****g minute of the game… f*****g manic aggression.'
Paul O'Connell, Ireland captain, rallying his teammates before Ireland played France in the 2007 Six Nations Championship. Ireland lost 20-17 to the Les Bleus at Croke Park with France later crowned 2007 Six Nations Champions

2001 SIX NATIONS CHAMPIONSHIP - EVOLUTION

With new blood introduced into the team 12 months earlier, the IRFU opted for a change of coach for the 2001 Six Nations Championship. Out went Warren Gatland and in came Eddie O'Sullivan. Keith Wood retained the captaincy.

IRELAND'S RESULTS
Italy 22-41 Ireland - Stadio Flaminio
Ireland 22-15 France - Lansdowne Road
Scotland 32-10 Ireland - Murrayfield
Wales 6-36 Ireland - Millennium Stadium
Ireland 20-14 England - Lansdowne Road

The tournament was affected by an outbreak of the highly infectious livestock disease foot-and-mouth in Britain. Restrictions on travel were introduced meaning Ireland's three fixtures against their fellow home nations were postponed until September 2001 and October 2001. Ireland's games versus Italy and France away went ahead as planned. On 3 February 2001,

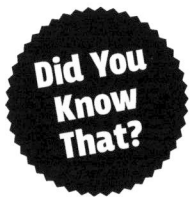

Did You Know That?

Sergio Parisse (Italy) holds the record for most Six Nations appearances with 69 from 2004-19. Alun Wyn Jones (Wales) has made 67 appearances, 2007-23. All of Parisse's caps were won from starting each game, whilst two of the Welsh captain's caps were made from the bench. The Irish trio of O'Driscoll (2000-14), Best (2006-19) and O'Gara (2000-13) occupy third, fourth and fifth place in the all-time appearances list. Healey (2010-23), Sexton (2010-23) and Italy's Marco Castrogiovanni (2003-16) are tied for joint-sixth with 60 caps each.

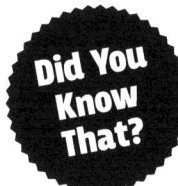

Did You Know That?

In the 2001 Six Nations Championship, England threw away a potential Grand Slam for the third time in three consecutive years. A Celtic hat-trick denied them with Wales stopping them in 1999, Scotland halted their march in 2000, and in 2001, Ireland stopped their runaway train.

Ireland beat Italy 41-22 at Stadio Flaminio thanks to three tries from Rob Henderson and one each from Shane Horgan and Munster's Ronan O'Gara. The Munster kicker added a further 16 points with his boot, two conversions and four penalties. A fortnight later France rolled into Dublin and left the Emerald Isle with their heads bowed as Brian O'Driscoll and O'Gara tore them to shreds, with Ireland winning 22-15. O'Driscoll scored a try which O'Gara converted and Ronan then produced a master class in kicking when he scored all five penalty attempts the French handed him. He was a star in the making. So, two games, two wins, 63 points scored and 37 conceded. Just the start O'Sullivan was hoping for with his young guns.

When the postponed matches were later played, first up for Ireland was a trip to the Scottish capital, Edinburgh. The Ireland team were in buoyant mood although England were the side everyone feared. England were a points-scoring machine having beaten Wales 44-15 in Cardiff, butchered Italy 80-23 at Twickenham followed by two more home wins, 43-3 versus Scotland and 48-19 against France. Ireland were no match for Scotland on the day and lost 32-10 at Murrayfield on 22 September 2001. On 13 October 2001, Ireland were back on track and defeated Wales 36-6 in the Principality with tries from Horgan, O'Driscoll and Denis Hickie. The kicking duties fell to David Humphreys, O'Gara's main rival for the No.10 jersey, and the Ulsterman showed his class by converting all three tries and scoring five penalties.

When England arrived in Dublin on 20 October 2001, they were champions-elect having won all four of their games, scoring 215 points and conceding 60. Ireland had 109 points for and 75 against, meaning they needed a winning margin that a rocket scientist would need to calculate in order for them to win the title. However, Ireland could prevent England from winning the Grand Slam on Irish soil and that was all the motivation they needed winning the match 20-14. Ireland ended the campaign as runners-up to England on points difference.

Evolution was one of the biggest movies of the year and under O'Sullivan it was clear this band of players in green were evolving into a side that would push for a championship win.

THE SIX NATIONS PLAYER OF THE CHAMPIONSHIP

The Six Nations Player of the Championship was first awarded in 2004 with Ireland's Gordon D'Arcy (centre) the inaugural winner. The nominees for the award are shortlisted by a panel made up from former players, rugby commentators and rugby writers from all six participating nations and then shortlisted to put to a public vote, where the player with the most votes is announced the winner. Since D'Arcy's achievement, only four other Irish players have won the award.

2006	Brian O'Driscoll. (He also won in 2007 and 2009)
2010	Tommy Bowe (wing)
2015	Paul O'Connell (lock)
2018	Jacob Stockdale (wing)

 Only Brian O'Driscoll and Antoine Dupont (scrum-half, France in 2020, 2022 and 2023) have won the award three times. O'Driscoll was runner-up on three occasions (2005, 2013 and 2014) whilst Dupont was runner-up in 2021.

In His Own Words

'My opinion on Ireland's Call is it's absolutely necessary. Amhrán na bhFiann is not an anthem for everyone. If you want to be inclusive and want to think of something for the whole island you need a song everyone is capable of singing and has some meaning to it.'
Brian O'Driscoll speaking in the 2018 BT Sport Films documentary
entitled *Shoulder to Shoulder*

THE IRB HALL OF FAME

The Hall of Fame was introduced by the IRB during the 2006 IRB Awards ceremony in Glasgow. There were two inaugural inductees at the 2006 ceremony. William Webb Ellis who is regarded by many rugby commentators to be the Father of Rugby. The second inductee was Rugby School, the school Ellis attended at the time. On 19 November 2014, the IRB rebranded as World Rugby and the Hall of Fame became known as the World Rugby Hall Of Fame. Since 2006, the following Irish players have been inducted:

2008	Jack Kyle
2009	Syd Millar, Tony O'Reilly
2011	Mike Gibson
2013	Ronnie Dawson
2014	Tom Kiernan, Bssil Maclear, Fergus Slattery, Keith Wood
2016	Brian O'Driscoll
2018	Ronan O'Gara

IRELAND'S TOP POINTS SCORERS IN THE FIVE & SIX NATIONS

1. Johnny Sexton 566 points
2. Ronan O'Gara 557 points
3. David Humphreys 270 points
4. Michael Kiernan 207 points
5. Ollie Campbell 182 points

Did You Know That? Sexton and O'Gara are first and second respectively in the all-time list of Six Nations point scorers. England's Johnny Wilkinson (1998-2011) is third with 546 points with his fellow countryman, Owen Farrell (2012-23) sitting fourth in the table with 528 points. Going into the 2023 tournament, Sexton was 26 points behind O'Gara.

2002 SIX NATIONS CHAMPIONSHIP STRIKING THE RIGHT KEY

Eddie O'Sullivan was still the man charged by the IRFU to turn Ireland's fortunes around on the pitch when the 2002 Six Nations Championship came around and the Ireland coach had three captains at his disposal: Mick Galwey, David Humphreys and Keith Wood. Game 1 brought a dragon to Dublin in the shape of Wales and their vast army of fans. All around Lansdowne Road looked like a giant traffic light with the amber middle missing. Ireland got their campaign off to a flier defeating Wales 54-10 in Dublin. Red-green is the most common form of colour blindness but the men in green had no difficulty in picking out their teammates, scoring six tries in the game. Both Humphreys and his young understudy, Ronan O'Gara, played in the game, each trying to outdo one another with the veteran scoring a conversion and six penalties to the young Munster buck's try and two conversions. O'Gara replaced Humphreys during the match which saw a young 21-year-old Munster lock make his debut in a green jersey, Paul O'Connell who scored a try in his first outing for Ireland. After the game O'Sullivan was grinning like a Leeson Street cat knowing that the Irish fly-half position was in safe boots for the foreseeable future. Later in the year, Darius had his first and only No.1 hit which ironically was called *Colourblind*. On 16 February 2002, Ireland met the defending champions, England, at Twickenham. The England side, coached by Clive Woodward and captained by Martin Johnson, were still seething having lost to Ireland in the last game of the 2001 Six Nations Championship which cost them a Grand Slam success. Humphreys and O'Gara scored all of Ireland's points, 11 (O'Gara try and two penalties from Humphreys), but Ireland could not claim successive wins against their old foe as England won 45-11. The wounded lion had roared back into life. In their next game Ireland defeated Scotland 43-22 in Dublin thanks to scores from their gifted attacking trio of Humphreys (16 points), Brian O'Driscoll (15 points) and O'Gara (two points).

Simon Easterby and Shane Horgan also scored a try each. Game 4 brought Italy to the Irish capital with Ireland recording the victory everyone had expected. However, the visitors did not just lie down and left Dublin on the back of a 32-17 loss with O'Gara scoring a conversion and a penalty to the Ulsterman's four successful penalty kicks. Their final game was against France who had won their previous four games and it meant a trip to Paris. The home side were masterful in their Stade de France home and overwhelmed Ireland in every area of the match securing a 44-5 victory that gave them the title and a seventh Grand Slam. In 2002, *The Pianist* was one of the biggest grossing movies. In Humphreys, O'Driscoll and O'Gara, Ireland had three stars who were playing in tune together and who regularly struck the right keys.

WORLD RUGBY COACH OF THE YEAR

The World Rugby Coach of the Year has been awarded by Word Rugby annually each autumn since 2001 when Rod Macqueen (Australia) became the first recipient after leading The Wallabies to the 2001 Tri-Nations title. From 2004 to 2007, the award was called the IRB International Coach of the Year. Only three men who coached Ireland have won the prestigious award.

2009: Declan Kidney
2018: Joe Schmidt
2023: Andy Farrell

In 2009, Kidney led Ireland to the 2009 Six Nations Championship, Triple Crown and Grand Slam. Ireland played nine matches in 2009 and won all of them. Schmidt led Ireland to the 2018 Six Nations Championship, Triple Crown and Grand Slam and Ireland only lost one of the 12 matches they played in 2018.

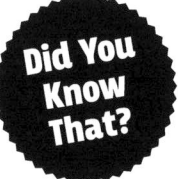

Eddie O'Sullivan was the coach of the United States of America team at the 2011 Rugby World Cup. Ireland, coached by Declan Kidney, defeated the USA Eagles 22-10 in their Pool C game in New Zealand. O'Driscoll and O'Gara played in the game.

Graham Henry (New Zealand) has won the most number of awards, five, winning in 2005, 2006, 2008, 2010 and 2011. He led the All Blacks to glory in the 2011 Rugby World Cup final and five Tri-Nations titles.

2003 SIX NATIONS CHAMPIONSHIP – BRING ME TO LIFE

Eddie O'Sullivan, the Ireland coach, chose a new captain to lead Ireland in the 2003 Six Nations Championship, Leinster's 24-year-old exciting centre, Brian O'Driscoll. The fight to nail down the fly-half position was still an on-going battle closely fought out by O'Gara and Humphreys.

IRELAND'S RESULTS
Scotland 6-36 Ireland - Murrayfield
Italy 13-37 Ireland - Stadio Flaminio
Ireland 15-12 France - Lansdowne Road
Wales 24-25 Ireland - Millennium Stadium
Ireland 6-42 England - Lansdowne Road

Ireland kicked off their tournament with a road trip, an encounter versus Scotland at Murrayfield. Humphreys was O'Sullivan's nominated kicker for the tournament and he would play in all five of Ireland's games whilst his young counterpart had to settle for two appearances as a replacement (against Wales and England). Ireland won the match 36-6 with the Ulster fly-half notching up a try, three conversions and five penalties. O'Gara's time would come, but just not in the 2003 Six Nations Championship.

Game 2 was another road trip, this time to Rome where the visitors beat Italy 37-13 at Stadio Flaminio. The 31-year-old Humphreys was peerless, scoring a try, three conversions and two penalties. O'Driscoll led from the front and scored a try in the victory. Game 3 of Ireland's assault on the championship saw France, the reigning Grand Slam Champions, visit Dublin. It wasn't the cut and thrust of a match that both sets of fans had anticipated and in the end it came down to a kicking game. François Gelez, the SU Agen and French international fly-half, scored four penalties for the visitors. Humphreys matched his rival's tally with Geordan Murphy successfully landing a drop goal attempt to give Ireland a 15-12 win. Three wins from three and Ireland were on a charge. O'Gara, aged 26, could only watch Humphreys, Ireland's premier ballerino, constantly do what he did best on the big stage, score points in a green jersey.

Reconstruction was a popular movie in 2003, and a winning Ireland side was gradually being built by O'Sullivan.

Wales and Ireland played out a toe-to-toe slug fest in their fourth game of the tournament at the Millennium Stadium on 22 March 2003. When Gareth Thomas scored a try, which was converted by Stephen Jones, the home side took a 24-22 lead. The regulation 80 minutes was up, the Welsh fans were ready to cheer their heroes off the pitch and a win was just one kick into touch or a turnover away. Then, enter stage left… O'Gara who came on for Humphreys in the game scored a delightful drop goal two minutes into injury time to break the hearts of every red shirt inside what had been a cauldron of noise up until that point. You could literally hear the ball from O'Gara's pin-point kick land on the other side of the bar with a light thud, but a thud that reverberated around the stands to send shockwaves through the home supporters. O'Driscoll, his teammates, O'Sullivan and the Irish fans were overjoyed with their 25-24 victory. Ireland had a new ballerino and the team were now just one win away from winning the country's first Grand Slam since 1948. It was a morale boosting victory and a match which saw Munster's lock, Donncha O'Callaghan, win the first of his 94 caps for Ireland.

On 30 March 2003, Ireland welcomed England to Dublin for an encounter which would decide the outcome of the championship, the Triple Crown and the Grand Slam. Lansdowne Road looked like it had four Green Monsters surrounding the pitch.

The Green Monster is a popular nickname for the 37-foot-2-inch-high (11.33 m) left field wall at Fenway Park, home to the Boston Red Sox of Major League Baseball which few batters can hit a ball over. England arrived in Dublin in buoyant and confident mood having beaten France (25-17), Italy (40-5) and Scotland (40-9) at home and Wales 26-9 in the Principality. And, if Ireland had two ballerinos to perform for the home fans, England possessed the Rudolf Nureyev of the ballet world, Johnny Wilkinson. The 23-year-old Newcastle Falcons' fly-half was a one-man scoring machine. Going into the game with Ireland he had already scored 62 points in his previous four games of England's total of 132 points. Or, putting things into perspective, in their four games Italy scored 75 points, Wales 77 points and Scotland had only managed to score 48 points. Wilkinson's right boot tortured Ireland and despite O'Driscoll's industry and six points from Humphreys, Ireland were simply no match for an England side that eight months later would become the first northern hemisphere side to win the Rugby World Cup. The visitors, with a rock-solid defence which looked like a White Monster, walked their way, or rather steamrolled their way, to the Grand Slam defeating Ireland 42-6. Wilkinson score a penalty, two drop goals and three conversions to bring his total number of points scored to 77, making him the top scorer in the 2003 Six Nations Championship.

The Ireland versus England game was overshadowed by the infamous 'Red Carpet Incident' when prior to the kick-off the England captain, Martin Johnson, lined his team up on the left facing the tunnel where Ireland always lined-up, meaning the President of Ireland, Mary McAleese had to walk on the grass to greet the Ireland players… as the red carpet came to a finish at the end of the English line of players.

In 2003, Evanescence had a massive No.1 hit in the UK charts with *Bring Me To Life*. O'Driscoll and O'Gara would go on to breathe new life into Ireland in the form of trophy successes.

 **Jonny Wilkinson scored a drop goal in injury time to give England a 20-17 win over the host nation, Australia, in the 2003 Rugby World Cup final.**

In His Own Words

'They say you should never meet your heroes. And they may be right… unless your hero is Moss Keane.'

Mick Galwey, ex-Munster and Ireland, paying tribute to the late Ireland and British and Irish Lions lock, Moss Keane, at his funeral - 7 October 2000

2003 RUGBY WORLD CUP

Australia went into the 2003 Rugby World Cup finals as the defending World champions and looking to become the first nation to win the Webb Ellis Cup back-to-back, which would also make them the first nation to win the trophy three times (1991 & 1999). The Wallabies also had home advantage as the host nation. The Pool stages went according to current form with The Wallabies winning Pool A (Runners-Up, Ireland), France winning Pool B (Runners-Up, Scotland), England winning Pool C (Runners-Up, South Africa) and New Zealand winning Pool D (Runners-Up, Wales).

The first quarter-final saw two southern hemisphere powers, New Zealand (winners in 1991) and South Africa (winners in 1995) do battle at Docklands Stadium, Melbourne, a game the All Blacks won 29-9. The hosts brushed aside Scotland 33-16 at Suncorp Stadium, Brisbane in the second quarter-final whilst France saw off the challenge of Ireland, winning 43-21 at Docklands Stadium. The last quarter-final brought together two old foes, England and Wales. The pair had last met nine months earlier when England beat Wales 26-9 at the Millennium Stadium on their way to winning the 2003 Six Nations Grand Slam. Wales ended up with the wooden spoon having lost all five of their matches. England beat Wales 28-17 at Suncorp Stadium, Brisbane.

The semi-final matches were played at Stadium Australia. First up were the tournament favourites and World champions in 1987, the All Blacks, versus Australia. The great antipodean rivals had met at this stage before when The Wallabies defeated New Zealand 16-6 in the 1991 semi-finals at Lansdowne Road. The southern hemisphere giants have been dominant in the tournament since the inaugural Rugby World Cup finals in 1987 - New Zealand winning the first and runners-up in 1995, whilst Australia were crowned World champs in 1991 and 1999. Indeed, only South Africa in 1995 were able to break their duopoly. New Zealand were favourites to send the partisan fans among the 82,000 in attendance home disappointed, having won both of their 2003 Tri-Nations Series games in the summer (Australia lost 50-21 at Stadium Australia and went down 21-17 at Eden Park, Auckland, New Zealand). The All Blacks also won both of their games versus The Springboks to win their fifth Tri-Nations Series title.

But in the 2003 Rugby World Cup semi-final it was the assured kicking of Elton Flatley who helped The Wallabies win the game 22-10 (he converted Stirling Mortlock's try and scored five penalties). In the second semi-final England won the battle of the northern hemisphere encounter, defeating France 24-7. Jonny Wilkinson scored all of England's points - five penalties and three drop goals, a sign of things to come. The All Blacks regained their form in the Third-Place Pay-Off game, crossing the line 6 times for a try to win 40-13 at Stadium Australia.

So, 12 years after Australia defeated England 12-6 at Twickenham to win the 1991 Rugby World Cup, the two nations met again in the 2003 final. In their Pool, England won all four games scoring 255 points and conceding a meagre 47 (they beat South Africa 25-6). The Wallabies were even more dominant in the Pool stages, winning all four games scoring a total of 273 points and allowing just 32 against (Ireland lost 32-16 to The Wallabies although Australia did set the Rugby World Cup finals record winning margin, which still stands today, beating Namibia 142-0 at the Adelaide Oval; 22 tries and 16 conversions). After having beaten Australia in four successive Tests (22-19, 21-15, 32-31) and a 25-14 win in Melbourne just five months earlier, Clive Woodward's side were red-hot favourites to lift the Webb Ellis Cup. However, buoyed by their surprise semi-final win over the All Blacks, The Wallabies had faith in themselves to make rugby history.

The game ended level, 14-14. Both sides now faced an energy sapping two periods of 10 minutes extra-time. Just two minutes into the first period of extra-time England won a penalty after the referee André Watson blew his whistle when Justin Harrison pulled his man down in a line-out. Wilkinson placed the ball on the kicking tee, did his usual kicking preparations, and fired the ball over the bar to give his side a 17-14 lead. With three minutes of the allotted 100 minutes remaining, England's line-out was as disastrous as it had been throughout the game with hands flapping in the air to grasp the ball. When Lawrence Dallaglio handled the ball on the ground the South African official was left with no other option but to blow his whistle, and much to the delight of the home crowd, award the Wallabies a kickable penalty. With nerves of steel the Wallabies' ice-man, Flatley, made the scores 17-17 to set up a nail-biting finish for the 82,957 fans inside the stadium and the 300 million watching it on TV across the globe. However, heartbreak was soon to follow for the men in gold when, with the clock showing just 26 seconds to go, Wilkinson dropped into the pocket and received a pass from Matt Dawson after having the ball returned to England from a Mat Rogers' kick. Wilkinson dropped the ball to his less-favoured right boot and split the posts to win the 2003 Rugby World Cup final, 20-17, a score which has become the defining moment in Rugby World Cup history. The drop goal was his first success from four drop goal attempts in the game. It was a stunning end to a truly breath-taking final. Martin Johnson, England captain, became the first European to hold aloft the Webb Ellis Cup when the Australian Prime Minister, John Howard, presented him with the trophy.

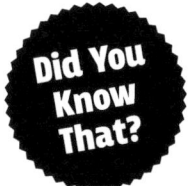

Did You Know That?

During the trophy presentation the flags of St George were out in force with one in particular bearing a message for England's biggest critic, the legendary Australian rugby player, David Campese which read: Campese U woman, Iron my Undies! Swing Low, Sweet Chariot floated across the stadium and after the presentation a number of songs by The Beatles reverberated around the stadium including one which was most appropriate for the England fans, A Hard Day's Night.

Ireland 45 Romania 17 – Central Coast Stadium, Gosford
Ireland 64 Namibia 7 – Aussie Stadium, Brisbane
Argentina 15 Ireland 16 – Adelaide Oval, Adelaide
Australia 17 Ireland 16 – Docklands Stadium, Melbourne
Ireland finished Pool A runners-up to Australia.

KNOCKOUT STAGE

France 43 Ireland 21 – Docklands Stadium, Melbourne

IRELAND'S TOP TRY SCORERS IN THE SIX NATIONS

1. Brian O'Driscoll — 26 Tries
2. Keith Earls — 14 Tries
3. Tommy Bowe — 14 Tries
4. Shane Horgan — 13 Tries
5. Ronan O'Gara, Conor Murray, Jacob Stockdale, James Lowe — 10 Tries

Did You Know That? Brian O'Driscoll is the all-time leading try scorer in Six Nations history. Scotland's Ian Smith (1924-33) is second in the list with 24 tries, whilst George North (Wales 2010-23) sits in third place with 23 tries in the competition.

RTE/IRISH SPORTS COUNCIL HALL OF FAME AWARD

The RTÉ/Irish Sports Council Hall of Fame Award is given annually each December as part of the RTÉ Sports Awards ceremony. It began in 2006, won by Billy Coleman (rallying), with the winner chosen by RTÉ Sport. The award is presented to a sportsperson who has made a significant impact on their sport during their lifetime. Only three Irish Rugby Union players have won the award:

2011	Jack Kyle
2014	Brian O'Driscoll
2016	Anthony Foley

Did You Know That? With the exception of 2012, the award has only ever been won by someone born in Ireland. Jack Charlton (England) was presented with the award in 2012 and during his 10 years in charge of the Republic of Ireland football team (1986-96), he guided Ireland to two FIFA World Cup finals (1990 and 1994), a European Championship finals (1988) and a highest ever FIFA World Ranking place of No.6.

IRELAND'S TOP CONVERSION SCORERS IN THE SIX NATIONS

1	Johnny Sexton 102
2	Ronan O'Gara 81
3	David Humphreys 27
4	Michael Kiernan 21
5	Tom Kiernan 18

Did You Know That? Sexton leads the all-time list for conversions in Six Nations tournaments. In the 2017 edition of the tournament, Ireland's Paddy Jackson successfully completed nine conversions in Ireland's 63-10 win over Italy at Stadio Olimpico. It equalled the single game record set by Johnny Wilkinson in England's 80-23 win over Italy at Twickenham on 17 February 2001. Wilkinson also scored a try and four penalties in the game, his 35 points total remains a record for a Six Nations game, whilst his total of 24 conversions in the 2001 tournament is also a Six Nations record.

RIVALS' NICKNAMES

Along with England and Scotland, Ireland's Rugby Union team does not have a nickname. France are known as Les Bleus, Italy are nicknamed Gil Azzurri, whilst the Welsh national rugby Union side are referred to as The Dragons.

Did You Know That? Argentina are nicknamed Los Pumas (The Pumas). However, the crest on the country's national rugby jersey does not feature a Puma. The animal in their crest is actually a Jaguar.

SOUTH SEAS ADVENTURES

In 2003, Ireland went on a Tour of the South Seas and played three Test Matches. On 7 June 2003, Ireland were well beaten by Australia, The Wallabies racking-up 45 points to the visitors' 16. The Test was played at the Subiaco Oval, Perth, Australia. A week later, Ireland were in Nuku'alofa, the capital city of Tonga where they beat the home nation 40-19 at the Teufaiva Sport Stadium. The final Test took Ireland to Samoa whom they beat Western Samoa 40-14 at Apia Park, Apia which is the island's capital city. Ronan O'Gara was unstoppable against Western Samoa and scored 32 of Ireland points: two tries, two conversions, five penalties and a drop goal. Eric Miller also scored a try which was converted by Paul Burke who replaced O'Gara in the game.

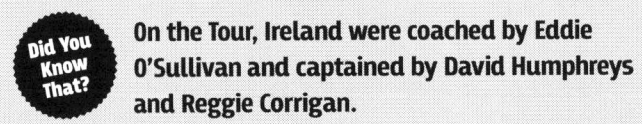

On the Tour, Ireland were coached by Eddie O'Sullivan and captained by David Humphreys and Reggie Corrigan.

2004 SIX NATIONS CHAMPIONSHIP – THE INCREDIBLES

Ireland coach, Eddie O'Sullivan, named the giant Munster lock, Paul O'Connell, as his stand-in captain for Brian O'Driscoll for their opening match of the 2004 Six Nations Championship.

Ireland's campaign got off to the worst possible start, losing 35-17 to France at Stade de France. The two nations had faced one another just two months previously when Les Bleus defeated Ireland 43-21 in the quarter-finals of the 2003 Rugby World Cup in Australia. The game in Melbourne was effectively over after just 20 minutes whilst Ireland failed to score a single point in the first-half. In the French capital Ireland seemed to have learnt their lesson down under and were only trailing France 10-3 at half-time. However, France then slipped into gear after the interval and scored 25 points to Ireland's 14 for a comfortable victory in the end.

Game 2 was an all-Celtic affair, Ireland versus Wales in Dublin. O'Driscoll took the game by the scruff of the neck and scored two of Ireland's six tries, with Ronan O'Gara also helping himself to a try and three conversions. Ireland won the match 36-15. O'Driscoll's second try equalled Denis Hickie's Irish record of 23. Ireland's championship had sparked into life. Next up for Ireland was a visit to the home of English rugby, Twickenham to play England who had not lost a home game since losing 30–16 to New Zealand in a Pool B match during the 1999 Rugby World Cup. Added to the mix was the fact that Ireland had not won at the ground since 1994, a 13-12 victory. Not surprisingly, England, the reigning champions, Grand Slam holders and 2003 Rugby World Cup winners, were the white-hot bookies' short priced favourites to stay on track and win back-to-back Grand Slams having already beaten both Italy (50-9) and Scotland (35-13) away. But the favourite doesn't always win as the Irish horse, Monty's Pass, proved in the previous year's Grand National romping home at 16/1. Ireland were not quite that long in the odds to cause an upset but they shocked everyone by winning the game 19-13. Girvan Dempsey scored a try which O'Gara converted and the Munster fly-half then added four penalties.

In 2004, U2 had their fifth UK No.1 hit single with *Vertigo*. Ireland had hit new heights with their victory over the World champs and had put the smiles back on the Irish faces which were almost as wide as those of the bookies. When Italy arrived in the Irish capital on 20 March 2004, they were expected to be devoured by a hungry Irish pack. However, Ireland barely showed their teeth in the encounter although the conditions were terrible as a wind blew around Lansdowne Road for most of the game. O'Driscoll's try in Ireland's 19-3 win was his 24th for Ireland. The win also meant that Ireland could still win the title although their points scored difference was much inferior to that of both England and France.

A week later, Ireland welcomed Scotland to Dublin whilst France entertained England in the French capital. Ireland ran over five tries against the Scots - surprisingly none of them were scored by O'Driscoll - for a comfortable 37-16 victory. The result meant Ireland won the Triple Crown for a seventh time whilst Scotland collected the wooden spoon after failing to win any of their five matches. In Paris, France defeated England 24-21 to claim their 14th title and an eighth Grand Slam. *The Incredibles* was a huge movie in 2004 at the cinemas which was more than matched by Ireland's incredible performances in the 2004 Six Nations Championship.

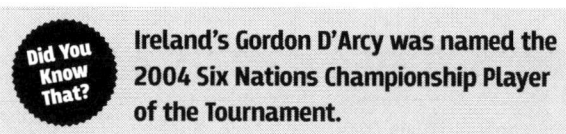

Ireland's Gordon D'Arcy was named the 2004 Six Nations Championship Player of the Tournament.

IRELAND'S TOP PENALTY SCORERS IN THE SIX NATIONS

1	Ronan O'Gara 109
2	Johnny Sexton 106
3	David Humphreys 62
4	Ollie Campbell 48
5	Michael Kiernan 46

O'Gara leads the all-time list for penalties scored in Six Nations tournaments. Leigh Halfpenny (Wales) holds the Six Nations record for scoring the most number of penalties in a single tournament, scoring 19 in 2013.

IRELAND'S CAVE MAN

Darren Cave was born in Holywood, Northern Ireland on 5 April 1987. In 2007, he helped Ireland win the Under 20's Six Nations Championship and in March 2008, signed a professional contract with Ulster. He was included in Ireland's 2009 Six Nations Championship squad and won his first international cap against Canada, a 25-6 win for Ireland on 23 May 2009 in Vancouver. Cave was capped 11 times by Ireland from 2009-15 and scored two tries (against Canada in 2013 and against Wales also in 2013). He also won international honours for Ireland at Under-19, Under-20, Under-21 and Sevens level.

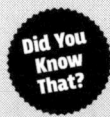

Ireland also won the Under-20s Six Nations Championship in 2010, 2019, 2022 and 2023. England hold the record for the most wins, claiming the title 10 times including the inaugural trophy in 2004, and winners in 2024.

PULLING POWER

The Aviva Stadium is the smallest stadium which plays host to Six Nations Championship game.

Nation	Home stadium	Capacity	City
England	Twickenham Stadium	82,000	London
France	Stade de France	81,338	Paris
Wales	Millennium Stadium	74,500	Cardiff
Italy	Stadio Olimpico	73,261	Rome
Scotland	Murrayfield Stadium	67,144	Edinburgh
Ireland	Aviva Stadium	51,700	Dublin

Did You Know That? Twickenham Stadium is the world's third largest Rugby Union stadium, the second largest stadium in the United Kingdom, behind Wembley, and the fourth biggest stadium in Europe: No.1 – Camp Nou, Barcelona, Spain (99,354 - home to FC Barcelona); No.2 - Wembley Stadium (90,000); No.3 – Croke Park (82,300). When the land upon which Twickenham (first started work building it in 1908) was purchased in 1907 for £5,500, the 10.25-acre site was used to grow cabbages, hence why Twickenham is known as The Cabbage Patch.

IRELAND'S 100TH TEST CAPTAIN

Leo Francis Matthew Cullen was born on 9 January 1978 in Wicklow. He was educated at Willow Park School, Booterstown which is the junior school to Blackrock College which he also attended. In 1995 and 1996, he won a Leinster Schools Cup winners' medal. Upon leaving school he studied Agricultural Science at University College Dublin before graduating in 1999 with a BA in Economics. In 1995, he played for Leinster at schoolboy level and then progressed to the Under-20 side winning seven caps. After making five appearances for the Leinster A team, he made his Leinster debut in season 1998-99 in the interprovincial and Heineken Cup matches. Aged 27, he joined Leicester Tigers in 2005 making 56 appearances for them, 15 of them as club captain. He played for Leicester Tigers from 2005-07 and helped them win the EDF Cup and Guinness Premiership in his final season with the club.

In 2007, he re-joined Leinster and was a member of their squad that won the 2007-08 Celtic League. On 26 August 2008, he was named the captain of Leinster after Brian O'Driscoll stepped down from the role. Cullen led Leinster to victory in their first ever Heineken Cup final in 2009 when they defeated Leicester Tigers 19-16 at Murrayfield. Two years later he skippered the side to a second Heineken Cup win after defeating Northampton Saints 33-

22 at the Millennium Stadium, after trailing 22-6 at half-time. The following year, he became the first player to captain three Heineken Cup winning teams when Leinster beat Ulster 42-14 at Twickenham. After Leinster lifted the 2014 Pro12, Cullen decided it was time to hang-up his boots and retire from playing.

Cullen made his senior debut for Ireland against New Zealand on 22 June 2002, a 40-8 loss at Eden Park, Auckland. On 6 August 2011, he became the 100th player to captain Ireland - a 10-6 defeat to Scotland at Murrayfield. In total he was capped 32 times by his country in a Test match (2002-11).

Although he decided to end his playing career, he was still in love with rugby and remained at Leinster as a forwards coach before being appointed their Head Coach the following year. He guided Leinster to a 15-12 victory over Racing 92 in the 2018 European Rugby Champions Cup final to become the first person to win the top European Rugby trophy as a player and as a coach.

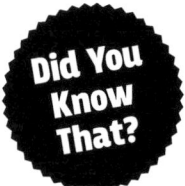

Leo Cullen represented Ireland at all levels, seven caps at schoolboy level; four caps for the Under-19 side (three as captain); he captained the Under-21s 14 times in 16 appearances; played for the Under-25 team and was capped 16 times at 'A' level Irish Wolfhounds (he captained the team in a match versus England).

In His Own Words

'You can't un-ring a bell.'
Eddie O'Sullivan, Ireland Coach 2001-08

2005 SIX NATIONS CHAMPIONSHIP - IRELAND'S LORD OF WAR

Ireland took a major step in getting back to the top of northern hemisphere rugby by winning the Triple Crown in 2004 and just missing out on claiming the Grand Slam after losing in Paris to the eventual Grand Slam winners, France. Eddie O'Sullivan was still in charge of the team and his two trusty Lieutenants on the pitch remained the same, Brian O'Driscoll and Paul O'Connell. And, for the second year in a row, no new caps were awarded by Ireland during the tournament.

IRELAND'S RESULTS
Italy 17-28 Ireland - Stadio Flaminio
Scotland 13-40 Ireland - Murrayfield
Ireland 19-13 England - Lansdowne Road
Ireland 19-26 France - Lansdowne Road
Wales 32-20 Ireland - Millennium Stadium

On the opening weekend of fixtures, the green army visited a sunny Rome and beat their hosts, Italy, 28-17 with Ronan O'Gara kicking 13 points, two conversions and three penalties. The Munster fly-half had firmly established himself as O'Sullivan's preferred No.10 over his closest rival for the position, David Humphreys. O'Gara started all five games in the championship whilst his Ulster counterpart made two replacement appearances, versus Scotland and Wales. Humphreys would retire at the end of the year. O'Gara went on to be a superstar. Game 2 was another road trip with a visit to the Scottish capital, Edinburgh. Ireland and O'Gara were imperious with the men in green jerseys winning the match 40-13. Once again O'Gara scored 13 points in the Irish victory. Ireland maintained their Grand Slam ambitions defeating England 19-13 in Dublin thanks to a try from O'Driscoll and O'Gara who kicked the conversion, two penalties and two delightful drop goals. It was the first time since 1987 that England had lost three games in the tournament. *Lord of War* starring Nicolas Cage was a box office success in 2005. O'Gara was proving to be Ireland's Lord of War. Game 4 was going to be Ireland's toughest test so far in the 2005 Six Nations Championship with an 80 minutes battle against the reigning Grand Slam holders in the Irish capital. If Ireland were to assert themselves as the best side in Europe, then they had to see off the challenge France presented. In their previous game France lost 24-18 at home to a resurgent Wales who were showing glimpses of the form they regularly displayed during their 1970s golden era. Despite O'Gara scoring 14 points (O'Driscoll scored yet another try) Ireland were no match for a very powerful French side who left Dublin with a fully deserved 26-19 win. Alas, Ireland's hopes of winning their first championship since 1985 proved to be out of reach. However, although it was the end of Ireland's dreams of claiming a first Grand Slam since 1948, a win against the unbeaten Welsh team in both nations' final match would see Ireland retain the Triple Crown and spoil a Welsh Grand Slam party. Wales were a totally different side to the team that were wooden spoon winners two years previously and cheered on by a raucous Millennium Stadium crowd they beat Ireland 32-20 to claim the Grand Slam for a ninth time and their first since 1978 when the legendary Phil Bennett captained a side coached by another legend of Welsh rugby, John Dawes. Ireland finished third in the table behind Wales and runners-up France, whilst O'Gara was the leading points scorer in the competition with 60. *Against All Odds* performed by the winner of the 2004 *X Factor* TV series, Steve Brookstein, was the first UK No.1 hit single of 2005. What Wales had achieved in the 2005 Six Nations Championship was most definitely against all odds.

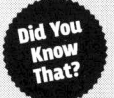

It was the first time since 2000 that Wales had beaten Ireland at home, their first win over Ireland at the Millennium Stadium, their 23rd title and their 18th and first Triple Crown since 1988. Added to this, Wales became the first country to win the Grand Slam having played more games away from home than on their own soil.

WHEN RONAN O'GARA DID NOT SNUB THE QUEEN

Much has been written about the infamous photograph that was taken showing Ronan O'Gara standing in front of the late Queen Elizabeth II with his hands in his pockets. After Ireland had won the 2009 Six Nations Championship, Triple Crown and a first Grand Slam in 61 years, the team were invited to meet the Queen at a civic reception held at Stormont Castle, Belfast. The photograph, which appeared in *The Irish Times* newspaper, shows Brian O'Driscoll, the Ireland captain, accompanying the Queen as she makes her way down a line of players chatting to them and shaking their hand. O'Gara is pictured with his hands in his trouser pockets much to what looked like a shocked O'Driscoll. The media in Northern Ireland had a field day with some journalists saying that the fly-half had snubbed the Queen, the Head of State of Northern Ireland. But O'Gara cleared up the controversy over the incident in 2017 in an interview with Paddy McKenna for the *Be More Frank And Honest* interview series when he was asked about it.

'The situation in terms of the Queen was horrendous. I was in the line to be introduced, my hands were a little bit sweaty. I put them into my pockets to make sure there wasn't a layer of sweat before I shook her hand. But the angle taken, you couldn't have staged it because Brian looks like he's in disbelief with what's going on here. But that's a snapshot, living that live in the seconds, there was no moment for anything,' said O'Gara.

O'Gara said that he never snubbed the Queen and that he did not have any strong beliefs on the monarchy and that he was brought up by his parents to respect older women and women in general. And, when Paddy asked him if he shook hands with the Queen, he said: 'Of course I did. There's a load of photos after the event. It's unbelievable the photo that appeared. I addressed this in my book… but no one read my book.'

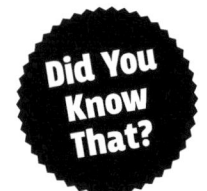

Ronan O'Gara kicked the decisive drop-goal in Ireland's 17-15 win over Wales at the Millennium Stadium to seal the 2009 Grand Slam for Ireland.

IRELAND'S TOP DROP GOAL SCORERS IN THE FIVE/SIX NATIONS

1. Dickie Lloyd 7
2. Ronan O'Gara 6
3. Barry McGann 6
4. Michael Kiernan 5
5. David Humphreys 5

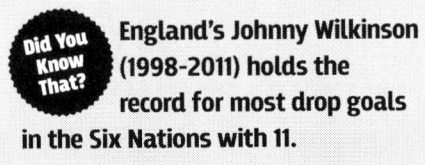

Did You Know That? England's Johnny Wilkinson (1998-2011) holds the record for most drop goals in the Six Nations with 11.

2006 SIX NATIONS CHAMPIONSHIP – THE CURTAIN COMES DOWN

Going into the 2006 Six Nations Championship Ireland were a team on the rise in world rugby. The gloomy 1970's and 1980's, when Ireland had more wooden spoons than the number you would find in a MasterChef kitchen, were well and truly behind them. They were now serious challengers not only to win the competition and the Triple Crown but claim a first Grand Slam since 1948.

Game 1 saw Ireland face off against Italy at Lansdowne Road. Eddie O'Sullivan was still the man in charge of the team and Brian O'Driscoll, a player who could win a tournament on his own, was the Ireland captain. Ireland played like they had a collective hangover and were quite lacklustre in attack. Italy set about Ireland from the first whistle and went in at half-time level with their hosts, 7-7. However, the visitors lacked firepower in their backs and Ireland limped their way to a 26-16 victory. Jerry Flannery and Tommy Bowe scored a try each which Ronan O'Gara converted in addition to the gifted Munster fly-half kicking over four of the five penalties he took.

France, who were slowly becoming Ireland's nemesis, put an end to Ireland's hopes of winning the Grand Slam by defeating Ireland 43-31 at Stade de France. The match was memorable for the 25-year-old O'Gara as he became Ireland's all-time leading points scorer when he converted Andrew Trimble's try. He converted all four tries scored by Ireland, including his own, and kicked over a penalty. The Munster scoring machine had only been playing international rugby for six years and he had another seven in front of him. Eoin Reddan made his Ireland debut in the match and would go on to win 70 more in a green jersey.

In their next game Ireland slipped into the high gear they had shown in the previous year's tournament and battered the reigning Grand Slam holders, Wales, 31-5 in Dublin, the Welsh team's biggest loss to the men in green since 2002, a 54-10 loss in Dublin. It was just the result Ireland needed to make a charge on the title following a scrappy home win over Italy and the loss in Paris.

On 11 March 2006, a chapter of Irish rugby history came to an end because exactly 128 years earlier, 11 March 1878, Ireland played their first international at Lansdowne Road. The 2006 Six Nations Championship match versus Scotland would be the last ever played at the home of Irish rugby in the tournament. O'Gara made the pitch his own stage and would have deserved to play an encore if the fans had cried out for it when he scored all of Ireland's points to give them a 15-9 win. The Irish team brought the curtain down for Six Nations

Championship matches at Lansdowne Road with a victory which kept alive their assault on a first Championship success since 1985. It was Ireland's smallest margin of victory over the Scots since 1988, a 22-18 victory in Dublin.

The Ireland team that celebrated this historic occasion was: Murphy; Horgan, B O'Driscoll (Captain), D'Arcy, Trimble; O'Gara, Stringer; Horan, Flannery, Hayes; O'Connell, O'Kelly; Easterby, Wallace, Leamy. Replacements: R Best, S Best, O'Callaghan, M O'Driscoll, Reddan, Humphreys, Dempsey.

Leona Lewis, winner of the 2006 *X Factor* TV show, had her first UK No.1 hit in 2006 entitled *A Moment Like This*. Alas, for the Irish fans they would no longer enjoy moments such as the wins over Italy, Wales and Scotland in the Six Nations Championship at Lansdowne Road.

So, Ireland headed to London to play England in their final game. The title was still within their grasp as France had also won three of their first four games, they lost 20-16 away to Scotland, and Les Bleus had a tricky away day before them in Cardiff.

On 18 March 2006, Wales versus France kicked off at 3.30pm at the Millennium Stadium in the Principality. The French had won their last three games in the stadium and made it four on the bounce with a 21-16 victory. When England versus Ireland kicked off at 5.30pm a 34-points margin of victory or better for the visitors would see them crowned champions on points difference. France ended their campaign with a +63 points difference whilst Ireland were sitting on +30. Ireland led 11-8 at half-time thanks to a Shane Horgan try and two penalties from O'Gara. The visitors needed to score 31 unanswered points in the second-half and as hard as they tried they just could not break down a resolute England side the number of times they needed to do so. Indeed, a last gasp try from Horgan earned Ireland a dramatic 28-24 win.

The Irish fans were ecstatic, a second Triple Crown in three years helped to ease the disappointment of missing out on winning the title and of course it was a win against the Old Enemy on English soil at the home of English rugby. It was also Ireland's second win in a row over their hosts at Twickenham Stadium. O'Gara scored two of his three conversion attempts, Denis Leamy also scored a try, and O'Gara kicked over three of the five penalties he took to bring his total points tally over the five games played to 72.

In addition to the Triple Crown, Ireland also had a Treble to celebrate. O'Gara finished the top points scorer, Horgan was the tournament's joint top try scorer with three along with Italy's Mirco Bergamasco and O'Driscoll was named Player of the Tournament.

Speaking after the game the Ireland captain said: 'This was the 80-minute performance we have been talking about. To finally get there in the last minute at Twickenham feels good'.

In 2006, *The Departed*, directed by Martin Scorsese and starring Leonardo DiCaprio, Matt Damon, Martin Sheen, Mark Wahlberg and Jack Nicholson, was a massive success at the Box Office. Ireland departed Lansdowne Road.

 **In 2006, Ireland became the first recipients of a new trophy which was introduced by the tournament's sponsors, Royal Bank of Scotland, to be awarded to a side who won the Triple Crown. Prior to this it was a title bestowed on a nation in name only.**

2007 SIX NATIONS CHAMPIONSHIP – O'SULLIVAN'S PACK OF ACES

For the fifth consecutive year the Eddie O'Sullivan and Brian O'Driscoll partnership of coach and captain was in place for Ireland. O'Sullivan was enjoying his seventh year in charge of the team having replaced Warren Gatland after the inaugural Six Nations Championship in 2000. The IRFU felt that consistency was the key to making the team a success on the pitch and, so far, it was reaping dividends.

Ireland were the bookies' favourites to win all five of their games and claim the Grand Slam. Their results in the Autumn 2006 Tests justified this with a 32-15 win over South Africa, a 21-6 victory against Australia and a 61-17 mauling of the Pacific Islanders with all three matches played at Lansdowne Road.

IRELAND'S RESULTS
Wales 9-19 Ireland - Millennium Stadium
Ireland 17-20 France - Croke Park
Ireland 43-13 England - Croke Park
Scotland 18-19 Ireland - Murrayfield
Italy 24-51 Ireland - Stadio Flaminio

In their opening game of the 2007 Six Nations Championship Ireland defeated Wales 19-9 at the Millennium Stadium. Tries from Rory Best, O'Driscoll and Ronan O'Gara along with two conversions by the Munster fly-half sealed the win for the visitors. On 11 February 2007, a new chapter was opened in the history of Irish Rugby. The win over the Pacific Islanders was the last ever rugby union international played at Lansdowne Road which was then demolished to make way for a new home to Ireland, the Aviva Stadium. After having refused any 'Foreign' sports to be played at Croke Park, including cricket, rugby and soccer, the GAA granted the IRFU permission to rent their stadium to play internationals. Not since it opened in 1891, had an oval ball touched the grass at Croke Park, the home of Gaelic sport in Ireland.

France, the reigning champions, were the visitors to Dublin for this landmark occasion. David Skrela became the first player to score a point in a game of rugby at Croke Park when the Stade Francais fly-half kicked over a penalty in the third minute of the game after Munster's Paul O'Connell was penalised for killing the ball. The game was played at a frenetic pace, Ireland roared on by a partisan crowd of 81,000. But France went in at the interval 11-8 ahead. O'Gara scored a try for Ireland in the 31st minute but missed the conversion before adding a penalty to his points tally. The second 40 minutes was as pulsating as the first as both nations had a ding-dong battle for possession and ultimately for points on the scoreboard. With two minutes remaining O'Gara landed his fourth penalty to give Ireland a four-point lead, 17-13, but at the other end the Toulouse winger, Vincent Clerc, ran through the home defence two minutes later for a French try which his club teammate, Lionel Beauxis, converted to give France a 20-17 victory. It was no fairytale start for the men in green at their new temporary home and how Ireland could have done with even a half-fit O'Driscoll in the game which he

IT WAS NO FAIRYTALE START FOR THE MEN IN GREEN AT THEIR NEW TEMPORARY HOME AND HOW IRELAND COULD HAVE DONE WITH EVEN A HALF-FIT O'DRISCOLL IN THE GAME WHICH HE MISSED THROUGH INJURY.

missed through injury.

The Ireland side for this historic occasion was: Dempsey; Murphy, D'Arcy, Horgan, Hickie; O'Gara, Boss; Horan, R Best, Hayes, O'Callaghan, O'Connell, S Easterby, D Wallace, Leamy. Replacements: Flannery, S Best, N Best, M O'Driscoll, Reddan, P Wallace, Trimble.

On 24 February 2007, the old enemy, England rolled into Dublin, to play Ireland in Game 3. England had won their opening two fixtures - 42-20 against Scotland and a 20-7 victory over Italy, with both games played at Twickenham. The English team and fans were sent packing on the back of a majestic Irish performance which saw them win 43-13. It had been an 80 minutes stroll for the men in green who scored four tries, three of which were converted by O'Gara and the other by Paddy Wallace, whilst the Munster kicking machine successfully scored all five penalty attempts. Johnny Wilkinson scored a conversion and two penalties for the visitors but he too could only admire the accuracy and fluency of O'Gara's kicking which was nothing short of perfection. The 30-point margin exceeded Ireland's all-time record winning margin of 22-0 against England set in 1947. It was also the highest points tally conceded by England in a Five or Six Nations Championship game, surpassing a 37-12 loss to France at Stade Colombes in 1972.

During the tournament Take That went to No.1 in the UK charts for the tenth time with the song *Shine*. Ronan O'Gara lit Croke Park up like a Catherine Wheel in a fireworks display.

Game 4 for Ireland took them to the Scottish capital where a win would see Ireland claim back-to-back Triple Crowns. It proved to be a pulsating encounter at Murrayfield with Ireland hobbling over the finish line, 19-18 victors. O'Gara was a 'Man on Fire' scoring all of Ireland's points, a try which he converted and bagging four of the six penalties presented to him. Mind you, his opposite number in blue, Chris Paterson, did his utmost to ignite the home side by scoring all of their points, six from six penalty attempts. It was the ninth time Ireland had won the Triple Crown, their third in four years.

All three matches in week five of the tournament were played on 17 March 2007, and four teams - England, France, Ireland and Italy - all had a chance of winning the tournament: France were narrowly ahead of Ireland on points scored difference, but England and Italy would be crowned Champions if they won by a large margin and the other results went in their favour.

First up was Italy v Ireland at Stadio Flaminio with a 1.30pm kick-off time. The Irish players did their bit in keeping the team on the right track towards the title by beating their hosts 51-24. Ireland were just too classy for their opponents who had won two games in a Six Nations Championship for the first time since entering the tournament in 2000. O'Gara scored a try, four conversions and a penalty to take his individual points score to 82. The France versus Scotland encounter kicked off at 3.30pm at Stade de France with the home side needing to defeat the Scots by 24 points or more to leapfrog Ireland at the top of the championship table. Les Bleus beat the Scots 46-19, a result which condemned Scotland to wooden spoon winners. The trilogy of final day games rounded off with Wales entertaining England in the Principality. If England could beat Wales by 57 points or more, they would be champs. All of France turned on their television sets to watch the game which kicked off at 5.30pm. As it turned out Les Bleus had no cause for concern as the Welsh Dragon managed to slay the English Lion 28-19. It was France's 16th Championship title.

Smokin' Aces was a big hit in the movies in 2007. Eddie O'Sullivan had a squad of 26 Aces in his 2007 Six Nations Championship squad.

 **Ronan O'Gara ended the 2007 Six Nations Championship as the leading points scorer with 82 and finished the joint leading try scorer with four. The Ireland captain, Brian O'Driscoll, scooped the Player of the Tournament award for the second year in a row.**

2007 RUGBY WORLD CUP

The 2007 Rugby World Cup was hosted by France. It was the sixth edition of the quadrennial international rugby union tournament. A total of 20 nations competed for the Webb Ellis Cup which saw 48 matches over 44 days; 42 matches were played in 10 cities throughout France, plus four in Cardiff and two in Edinburgh. The eight quarter-finalists from the 2003 tournament (Australia, England, France, Ireland, New Zealand, Scotland, South Africa and Wales) automatically qualified for the 2007 and the remaining 12 places went to the successful teams in the regional qualifying competitions (Argentina, Canada, Fiji, Georgia, Italy, Japan, Namibia, Romania, Samoa, Tonga, USA and Portugal who were all making their Rugby World Cup debut). South Africa won Pool A (won all four games) with the reigning World champions, England, runners-up; Australia topped Pool B with four wins and Fiji pipped Wales to runners-up position; Pool C went to form with New Zealand winning all four of their games including a 40-0 win over the runners-up, Scotland. Pool D, comprising Argentina, France, Georgia, Ireland and Namibia threw up several surprises with Argentina winning all four of their games and Ireland losing out to France for runners-up spot. In a repeat of the 2003 Rugby World Cup final, England beat Australia 12-10 in the quarter-finals and were joined in the semi-finals by France (beat the All Blacks 20-18), South Africa (defeated Fiji 37-20) and Argentina (beat Scotland 19-13). The first semi-final saw the host nation getting knocked out of the tournament by England (14-9), with South Africa reaching the final after defeating the Pumas 37-13. Argentina won the Bronze Final match by beating France 34-10.

South Africa met England in the final five weeks after beating them 36-0 in their Pool A encounter at Stade de France. But the rematch proved to be a very defensive game as neither side could breach their opponents' stubborn defence. So, it came down to the boots of the kickers and the Springboks led 9-3 at half-time thanks to the reliable kicking of Percy Montgomery. Jonny Wilkinson, the hero of the 2003 Rugby World Cup final replied with a penalty in the first-half in a game of tactical high kicking and little open play. Early into the second-half England went very close to scoring a try through Mark Cueto but following a lengthy deliberation by the TV match official, the England winger was ruled to have been in touch when he crossed over the line in the corner. Wilkinson, who missed two drop goal attempts, made the score 9-6 with his second successful penalty in the 44th minute and seven minutes later Montgomery made it a six points difference once again with his fourth score of the game. South Africa were awarded a penalty in the 62nd minute and Francois Steyn took over the kicking duties and slotted the ball between the uprights from 46 metres out. This was the end of the scoring and South Africa became the second nation to win the Webb Ellis Cup twice following Australia's triumphs in 1991 and 1999. South Africa's captain, John Smit, accepted the famous gold trophy from Nicolas Sarkozy, the President of France. Several Springboks players carried the President of South Africa, Thabo Mbeki, on their shoulders as the beaming President held aloft the Webb Ellis Cup.

IRELAND'S RESULTS:
Pool D
Ireland 32 Namibia 17 – Stade Chaban-Delmas
Georgia 10 Ireland 14 – Stade Chaban-Delmas
France 25 Ireland 3 – Stade de France
Argentina 30 Ireland 15 – Parc des Princes

Ireland finished third in Pool D behind runners-up France and winners, Argentina.

Stade de France became the first stadium to host a FIFA Football World Cup final (1998) and a Rugby World Cup final.

IRELAND'S FANTASTIC FOUR

The Fantastic Four is a team of Superheroes that featured in Marvel Comics. The four characters traditionally associated with the Fantastic Four, who gained superpowers after they were exposed to cosmic rays during a scientific mission to outer space, are: Mister Fantastic (Reed Richards), a scientific genius and the leader of the group, who can stretch his body into incredible lengths and shapes; the Invisible Woman (Susan 'Sue' Storm-Richards), Reed's wife, who can render herself invisible and project powerful invisible force fields and blasts; the Human Torch (Johnny Storm), Sue's younger brother, who can generate flames, surround himself with them and fly; and the enormous Thing (Ben Grimm), their grumpy but benevolent friend, a former college football star, Reed's college roommate and a skilled pilot, who possesses tremendous superhuman strength, durability and endurance due to his stone-like flesh.

In the 2009 Six Nations Championship, Ireland had their own band of superheroes, including their very own *Fantastic Four*. Brian O'Driscoll was their captain, Mister Fantastic, the Player of the Tournament and the joint-leading try scorer: Tommy Bowe was an Invisible Man as he ghosted his way past defenders; Ronan O'Gara was like a Human Torch, his red-hot right boot made the ball fly high over the opponents' goal posts like a meteor and Paul O'Connell was Ireland's Thing, a player of superhuman strength who was a one-man defensive green brick wall.

The Fantastic Four's symbol was a number 4 within a circle. Donncha O'Callaghan was Ireland's No.4 in the 2009 Six Nations Championship, another one of Ireland's rugby Superheroes.

2008 SIX NATIONS CHAMPIONSHIP - DOUBT

Why fix something that is not broken? That is exactly what the selection committee of the IRFU were thinking as they looked out of their office windows staring at a building site as the new home of Irish rugby; the Aviva Stadium, was being constructed in January 2008. The 2008 Six Nations Championship was only a matter of weeks away but there was no need to change the coach, Eddie O'Sullivan, or replace his talismanic captain, Brian O'Driscoll. The pair had delivered three Triple Crown wins in the last four years and in 2008, they were looking to make it three on the bounce. On the first weekend of fixtures Ireland entertained Italy at Croke Park, Dublin. Two years earlier Ireland beat their visitors 25-16 before a crowd of 49,500 at Lansdowne Road on the opening weekend.

When the Italy team ran out of the tunnel at Croke Park to play their first ever game in the stadium, they were greeted with a wall of sound from 75,500 enthusiastic Irish fans. They must have felt like slaves in Ancient Rome having to face a gladiator in a battle to the death in the Coliseum. In the end the game wasn't quite that daunting for the Italian players who made Ireland work very hard to earn a 16-11 victory. When Ronan O'Gara converted a try scored by Girvan Dempsey, it took his career points total in the tournament to 400. On 9 February 2008, Ireland met the reigning champions, France, in Paris. Ireland knew that if they were to win the title then a victory over Les Bleus would be a huge boost to their confidence as they had lost their previous six encounters with France, four in the tournament and two in the Rugby World Cup (2003 and 2007). However, it proved to be a case of Unlucky No.7 for the men in green as the home side won 26-21 at Stade de France. Game 3 brought Scotland to the home of Gaelic sports and Ireland were back to their fluent passing game scoring five tries, three of which O'Gara converted, in an emphatic 34-13 victory. A Grand Slam was off the menu but the Triple Crown was still tantalisingly on offer.

Next up for Ireland was Wales in Dublin. The Welsh Dragon was on fire in the tournament having already defeated England 26-19 away, Scotland 30-15 at home and Italy 47-18 in Cardiff. It was a match that would help decide the outcome of the Triple Crown and the Welsh kept their Grand Slam bandwagon rolling with a slender 16-12 win to claim their 19th Triple Crown. Only France now stood in the path of a Wales side in search of their 10th Grand Slam. In 2008, the movie *Doubt* was released starring Meryl Streep and Philip Seymour Hoffman. The story of the movie centres around a Roman Catholic school principal, played by Streep, who begins to question a Priest's (played by Seymour Hoffman) somewhat ambiguous relationship with a troubled young student. The Irish fans were beginning to doubt that O'Sullivan was still the right man to be in charge of the team. In their final game Ireland went down 33-10 to England at Twickenham which was the first time in five years they had lost to the old enemy. O'Gara captained Ireland in the game as O'Driscoll suffered a hamstring tear in a training session. Wales defeated France 28-12 at the Millennium Stadium to win their 24th title, 19th Triple Crown and 10th Grand Slam. That thing the IRFU had no need to fix was now in the repair shop after Ireland ended the campaign fourth in the table, their worst finish since the competition became the Six Nations Championship in 2000. It was perhaps time to call Bob the Builder away from his duties of building the Aviva Stadium with a view to constructing a new Ireland side. During the 2008 Six Nations Championship Duffy was at No.1 in the UK charts with *Mercy*. After a comfortable seven-year tenure in charge of the national team O'Sullivan now found himself at the mercy of the Ireland selectors.

Eddie O'Sullivan only capped two new players in 2008. On 8 November 2008, Keith Earls won his first international cap scoring a try after only three minutes of play in a 55-0 demolition of Canada at Thomond Park. Two weeks later, 22 November 2008, Donnacha Ryan made his international bow in a 17-3 victory against Argentina at Croke Park.

2009 SIX NATIONS CHAMPIONSHIP - KILLSHOT

On 19 March 2008, four days after Ireland lost 33-10 to England at Twickenham in their final game of the 2008 Six Nations Championship, a result that condemned them to a fourth-place finish in the table, Eddie O'Sullivan tendered his resignation as the coach of the national team. He did not wait to see if the IRFU would be lenient on him and show him a little mercy after having coached Ireland since 2001, guiding them to three Triple Crown wins in 2004, 2006 and 2007. During his tenure Ireland also defeated Australia twice (2002 and 2006) and South Africa twice (2004 and 2006). Ireland defeated England in the Six Nations Championship over four consecutive years (2004–2007) including a record victory (43–13) over their bitter enemies at Croke Park in 2007. O'Sullivan finished with an overall success rate of 64% during his seven years at the helm, helping Ireland reach a highest ever 3rd place ranking in the World Rugby rankings on two occasions in 2003 and 2006.

The first requisite for immortality is death. If the Ireland squad, coached by O'Sullivan's successor, Declan Kidney, and led on the field by the effervescent Brian O'Driscoll, were to become immortals of Irish rugby then they first had to kill all five of their opponents in the 2009 Six Nations Championship. It would be five battles of attrition played over the course of more than 400 minutes of rugby, two battles on home soil and three on foreign territory.

IRELAND'S RESULTS
Ireland 30-21 France - Croke Park
Italy 9-38 Ireland - Stadio Flaminio
Ireland 14-13 England - Croke Park
Scotland 15-22 Ireland - Murrayfield
Wales 15-17 Ireland - Millennium Stadium

'Carry the battle to them. Don't let them bring it to you. Put them on the defensive and don't ever apologise for anything.'
Harry S. Truman, President of the United States of America 1945-53

On 7 February 2009, Ireland walked out of the tunnel at Croke Park to face France. The noise coming from the stands reached such a crescendo that the stadium announcer's voice was drowned out when he called out the names of the players from the two nations. The noise cascading its' way down on to the playing area from Hill 16 was as loud as the roar made by a Fighter Jet flying over the stadium.

In their opening game of the tournament versus France, Ireland heeded Truman's iconic words and carried the battle to Les Bleus. France arrived in Dublin full of pomp and a sprinkling of panache, Six Nations Championship winners in 2007, and future Grand Slam winners in 2010. Ireland and France, previous cohorts against English armies, set aside their historic relationship to see which nation had the game plan to propel them to a winning campaign. Ireland had not won a Grand Slam since 1948, whereas their visitors had won eight of them since the first Golden Era of Irish rugby - 1968, 1971, 1977, 1987, 1997, 1998, 2002 and 2004. Not for a single minute, despite the score of the match, did the 15 men in blue bring their game level over and above the bar set by the home side. Ireland claimed the two points on offer by winning this first battle 30-21of their quest to remove the 61-year-old albatross that hung heavy on their weighted shoulders of expectation.

Game 2 was a trip back in history only in reverse. Ireland throughout its' history had never, unlike England and Italy, invaded or even set out to conquer other countries. Ireland's struggles with England away from an international match regardless of the sport are well documented whilst the Roman Empire failed to conquer the Emerald Isle and make it subservient to them.

But, on 15 February 2009, a day after St Valentine's Day, Ireland brought devastation in the form of match points scored, not Red Roses, to Rome when they defeated Italy 38-9 at Stadio Flaminio. Julius Caesar had been usurped by a Munster fly-half, Ronan O'Gara, who like the legendary Roman Emperor, led his countrymen to a glorious victory on foreign soil by scoring all four conversion attempts he took and the only penalty opportunity he was afforded. Two down, three to go. History recalls the Norman Conquest of England and on 28 February 2009, England's rugby army descended on the Irish capital.

> *'You win battles by knowing the enemy's timing, and using a timing which the enemy does not expect.'*
> **Miyamoto Musashi**

Ireland's first ever international match was against England in 1875. Kidney did not have to recall the 134-year history of the games between the two nations in his pre-match address to his players. Everyone in the home side's dressing-room knew only too well what was at stake. This was a match which would either see Ireland stay on track for the championship and Grand Slam glory or else they would simply just crash and burn like they had done in so many previous campaigns.

Thankfully, Kidney did his homework on the opposition and Ireland beat their biggest enemy 14-13. But, the win by a solitary point, did Ireland an injustice because the men in green were more dominant than their opponents. O'Driscoll scored a try and kicked over a drop goal whilst O'Gara scored two penalties. The Irish duo were the equivalent of Sir Arthur Conan Doyle's Sherlock Holmes and Dr Watson. Under Kidney Ireland's style of play was elementary but highly effective.

> *'No battle was ever won according to plan, but no battle was ever won without one.'*
> **Dwight D. Eisenhower, President of the United States of America 1953-61**

Game 4 for Ireland took them to the capital of Scotland and an encounter at Murrayfield. Hardly a gimme win for a rampant Irish team but a game they had to win regardless of each country's form, Scotland ended the tournament one place above perennial wooden spoon winners, Italy. Ireland defeated their Celtic foes 22-15. A one try, one conversion winning margin. Jamie Heaslip scored the try which O'Gara converted in addition to scoring four of the five penalties he took plus a text book O'Gara drop goal.

> *'Test of Metal: Will of Iron, Nerves of Steel, Heart of Gold, Balls of Brass.'*
> **George Carlin**

On 21 March 2009, Ireland faced their most historic match in 61 years since they beat Wales on the last day of the 1948 Five Nations Championship at Ravenhill to win the coveted Grand Slam for the only time in their history. Once again, they faced Wales as history waited the outcome of 80 minutes of rugby at the Millennium Stadium. The Ireland side that day knew they had a test of metal before them, a will of iron harnessed to nerves of steel to match their pounding hearts was required as well as having big balls, and not the Gilbert sponsored match ball, if they were to etch their names in the annals of Irish rugby history. Wales, the reigning champions and Grand Slam holders, were not going to just roll over for the visitors as a win by 13 points or more would see them retain the title. When the half-time whistle was blown, the hosts went in 6-0 up. But Ireland held their nerve and scored two early second-half tries from O'Driscoll and Tommy Bowe, both of which O'Gara converted. And, after Stephen Jones successfully kicked home his third and fourth penalties followed by a drop goal with only five minutes remaining the Welsh led 15-14. The title was out of the home side's grasp but they had one hand on the Triple Crown trophy having already beaten Scotland 26-13 in Edinburgh and England 23-15 in the Principality. In a sensational climax to the game O'Gara landed a drop goal in the 78th minute to nudge Ireland back into the lead, 17-15. When the match referee, Wayne Barnes (England), awarded Wales a penalty with only 48 seconds left to play the Welsh fans jumped to their feet and exploded into sound like a volcano erupting whilst the green jerseys splattered around the stadium slumped down to their seats. Up stepped Jones to take the 48 metres attempt, the outcome of the game as well as Ireland's hopes and dreams of winning the Grand Slam rested on his right boot. The game clock had turned red when Jones struck the ball which agonisingly for the 15 men in red on the pitch fell just short. Ireland were Grand Slam champions whilst Wales ended up fourth in the table. In 2009, *Killshot* was a popular movie for cinema-goers. O'Gara had delivered a devastating Killshot to Wales. The Munster man had all of the tools in the box at his disposal every time he crossed the white line. With the ball in his hands, he could set fire to the rain and when it came to his kicking game, he could thread a needle with his toes.

'I firmly believe that any man's finest hour, the greatest fulfilment of all that he holds dear, is that moment when he has worked his heart out in a good cause and lies exhausted on the field of battle – victorious.'
Vince Lombardi, Legendary American Football Coach

The Ireland team achieved their finest hour and were victorious in all five battles they fought in the 2009 Six Nations Championship.

O'Driscoll was the joint leading try scorer with four, along with England's Riki Flutey, and the Ireland captain deservedly won the Player of the Tournament award, his third. The Ireland captain not only put his two hands on the Six Nations Championship trophy, he also had two hands on the shirt of the captain of the British and Irish Lions side that would be touring South Africa later in the year. Although he did captain the tourists on the 2009 Tour it was Ireland's Paul O'Connell who led the Lions in the three Tests against The Springboks which they lost 2-1. O'Gara was once again top of the scoring charts in the 2009 Six Nations Championship with 51.

Apart from Queen's rock anthem *We Are The Champions* being belted out in the Ireland dressing-room after the game, it would have been most fitting to dedicate Nickelback's song *Hero* to O'Gara.

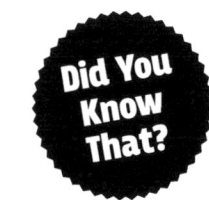

In the autumn of 2009, Eddie O'Sullivan released his autobiography entitled Never Die Wondering.

I am so high. I can hear heaven.
I am so high. I can hear heaven.
No heaven, no heaven don't hear me.

And they say that a hero can save us.
I'm not gonna stand here and wait.
I'll hold onto the wings of the eagles.
Watch as they all fly away.

During the 2009 Six Nations Championship Flo Rida featuring Kesha went to No.1 in the UK charts with the song *Right Round*. Declan Kidney had turned Ireland's fortunes right round in his first year as coach.

GATLAND'S GAFF

Before Ireland played Wales at the Millennium Stadium in the 2009 Six Nations Championship, Warren Gatland, the Welsh coach, had a few words to say about the country he was the coach of from 1998-2001. 'Of all the teams in the Six Nations, the Welsh players dislike the Irish the most and they are all very motivated to be playing on Saturday.'

Gatland's remark backfired on him as Ireland won the game 17-15 to win the Six Nations Championship (their first championship since 1985), the Triple Crown and their first Grand Slam since 1948. The Welsh fans were left wondering why he didn't know that England are Wales' bitterest of rivals.

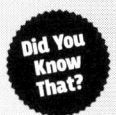

Warren Gatland began his coaching career in Ireland with Galwegians Rugby Football Club, Galway. He was a player/coach with the Irish side and led them to promotion into the All-Ireland League Division 2.

In his own words

'This is all due to the groundwork done by Eddie (O'Sullivan) and all the coaching team, and all that's done in the provinces, and more so in the schools, as they're the ones who enrich the kids. Brian (O'Driscoll) would say this is far from a one-man team - we have 30-odd people who make this team. After 80 minutes, you take what's there. Some days it swings for you, some it doesn't.'
Ireland coach Declan Kidney after Ireland beat Wales 17-15 in Cardiff on 21 March 2009 to win their second Grand Slam (Winners in 1948). It was Kidney's first Six Nations Championship having succeeded Eddie O'Sullivan as coach.

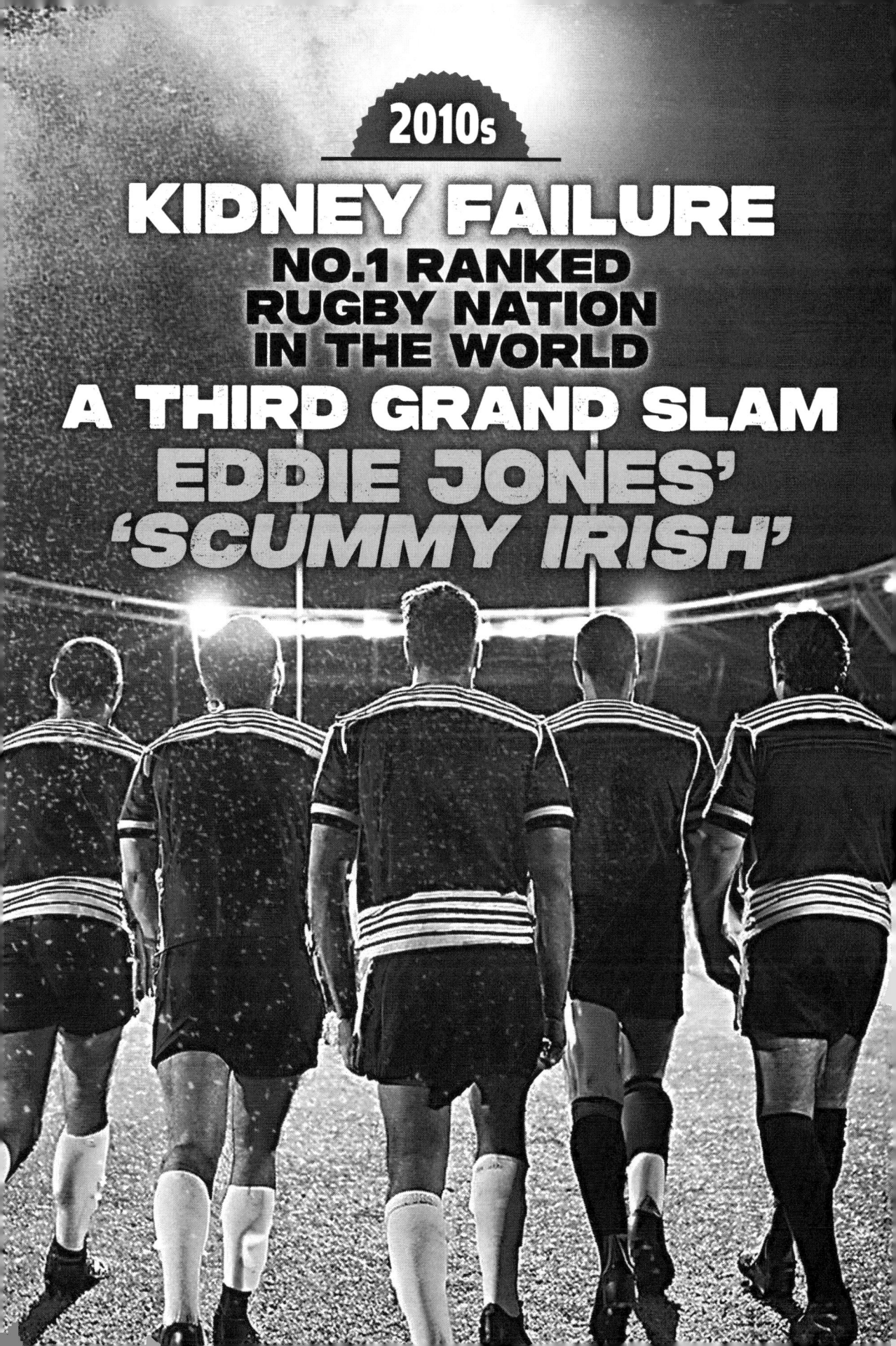

'Nothing in the world can take the place of Persistence. Talent will not; nothing is more common than unsuccessful men with talent. Genius will not; unrewarded genius is almost a proverb. Education will not; the world is full of educated derelicts. Persistence and determination alone are omnipotent. The slogan 'Press On' has solved and always will solve the problems of the human race.'
Calvin Coolidge

KIDNEY FAILURE

In 2013, Ireland toured Canada and the United States of America and played both nations. Prior to the start of the Tour and not long after the 2013 Six Nations Championship had ended, which saw Ireland finish second from bottom, Declan Kidney was sacked as Ireland's coach on 2 April 2013. Joe Schmidt, the coach of Leinster, was named as Kidney's replacement but was unable to lead Ireland on the tour. Kidney's assistant coach, Les Kiss, was appointed interim coach for the tour.

On 8 June 2103, Ireland beat the USA 15-12 at BBVA Compass Stadium, Houston. Fly-half Ian Madigan (Leinster) scored all of Ireland's points, successfully scoring five of the seven penalties he took. Chris Wyles (Saracens) scored all of the USA's points from four penalties and missed one which would have given the Eagles a draw. This match set a record attendance for a rugby match on U.S. soil with a crowd of 20,181. After the game Ireland's captain, Peter O'Mahony, paid tribute to the players who made their debuts for Ireland in the win. 'It is an away from home Test win and I am thrilled to bits for the boys who won their first caps that the rest of the boys got the win on such a special day. I'm thrilled to bits for them, but the overall thing is we got a win away from home, it was a tough game and we expected nothing less.'

A week later Ireland defeated Canada 40-14 at BMO Field, Toronto with Madigan converting three of the six tries scored by Ireland. He missed a conversion whilst his replacement after 61 minutes, Paddy Jackson, scored two from two. Ireland's try scorers were: Andrew Trimble (9 mins), Fergus McFadden (27, 58, 80 mins), Darren Cave (54 mins) and Tommy O'Donnell (67 mins). The match set a record attendance for a rugby match on Canadian soil with 20,396 fans turning out to see the touring side.

In 1991, Canada achieved their best ever result at a Rugby World Cup by reaching the quarter-finals where they lost 29-13 to the All Blacks. Canada was once the dominant power of North American rugby and was the second-best team in the Americas. Before the sport became professional in 1995, Canada were a side who could cause an upset against much stronger nations and beat France, Scotland, Wales and an uncapped England side prior to 2002.

In His Own Words

'They're the best team in world and we had to play the best game of this squad's tenure. The boys showed up everywhere, tackles that shouldn't have been made, plays that shouldn't have been made. It's a big piece of history for us and one we wanted to tick off in Ireland.'

Peter O'Mahony (Man of the Match) after Ireland beat New Zealand (16-9) for the second time in their history, at the Aviva Stadium, Dublin on 17 November 2018

2010 SIX NATIONS CHAMPIONSHIP – HISTORY BECKONS

The question on the lips of all rugby journalists going into the 2010 Six Nations Championship was: 'Who was strong enough to not only wrestle the title from Ireland's grasp, but also prevent the men in green from claiming back-to-back Grand Slams'. In the previous year's tournament Ireland swept all before them. They were an irresistible force who attacked their opponents mercilessly and when they smelt blood, they went in to finish their prey off.

Ireland were still using Croke Park for their home games as the Aviva Stadium, which was built to replace Lansdowne Road, did not open until May 2010. Ireland began the defence of their titles, including the Triple Crown, with a home game against the usual whipping boys in the tournament, Italy, and won 29-11. Next up was a trip to Paris where a very strong France side beat them quite comfortably, 33-10 at Stade de France. Ireland's dream of winning their third Grand Slam had ended at the second hurdle. However, Ireland remained on course to win the Championship and another Triple Crown by defeating England 20-16 at Twickenham on 27 February 2010.

Game 4 brought 81,340 fans to Croke Park for the visit of Wales. Two tries from Keith Earls and a third by Tomas O'Leary helped Ireland secure a 27-12 victory. The final round of games had everything to play for with France on eight points and a home game versus England, whilst Ireland had six points and were at home to face Scotland who had lost three and drawn one of their previous four matches. France beat England to win the Grand Slam whilst Scotland caused a shock by winning 23-20 in Dublin to deny Ireland a Triple Crown.

Did You Know That?

Ireland's Keith Earls and Tommy Bowe shared the title of top try scorers along with the Welsh pair of James Hook and Shane Williams, scoring three tries each. Bowe was named Player of the Tournament pulling almost 50% of the fans' votes.

Ireland finished in second place in the 2010 Six Nations Championship with France winning their 17th title and a 9th Grand Slam.

LUCKY NO.13

Ireland went into the 2015 Six Nations Championship as the reigning champions and after the five rounds of the tournament the Irish held on to the trophy for another year. It was the 121st edition of the competition including all of its previous formats and marked Ireland's 13th triumph, the first time the Irish had retained the title outright since 1949. Ireland won four of their five games, only losing 23-16 to Wales at the Millennium Stadium which denied the men in green both the Triple Crown and the highly prized Grand Slam. Ireland won the Millennium Trophy (their 11th) and the Centenary Quaich (their 13th).

In His Own Words

'I'm massively proud of everyone today. It was a ferocious Test match and words can't describe how we feel having won today. We had to make every moment count and try to build as close to a perfect 80 minutes as we could. We showed what we were made of today.'
Ireland captain, Rory Best, after Ireland beat England 24-15 to win the Grand Slam in 2018

FIRST BATTLE OF THE CELTS ON NEUTRAL TERRITORY

On 22 September 2019, Ireland played Scotland at a neutral venue for the first time in their history. The game was played at the International Stadium, Yokohama, Japan during the 2019 Rugby World Cup. Ireland won their Pool A encounter 27-3.

Did You Know That?

In 2015, Ireland were the first team to be awarded the re-designed RBS Six Nations Championship trophy which was introduced for the 2015 edition of the competition. The new trophy features six sides as opposed to five on the previous one.

Did You Know That? Japan beat Ireland 19-12 at Stadium Ecopa, Fukuroi, Japan a week after the Scotland game to cause a major shock in the tournament. Japan scored four of their six penalties but World Rugby later had to admit that three of the four offside penalties had been incorrectly awarded by the referee. However, the result stood.

In His Own Words

After Ireland's historic 40-29 win over New Zealand on 5 November 2016, played at Soldier Field, Chicago, USA, the coach of Ireland, New Zealand born Joe Schmidt, was asked by a journalist from New Zealand what his mum would say. Schmidt said that he telephoned her after the match and he informed the journalist:

'She thought my apology was false and she was right!'

2011 SIX NATIONS CHAMPIONSHIP – IRELAND GET LUCKY IN THE ETERNAL CITY

Ireland kicked off their 2011 Six Nations Championship in the Eternal City. On 5th February 2011, Ireland beat Italy 13-11 at Stadio Flaminio thanks to a try from Brian O'Driscoll which was converted by Johnny Sexton. Sexton also added a penalty in the 28th minute but with Ireland trailing 11-10 in the 78th minute, a drop goal from Ronan O'Gara sealed victory. Fergus McFadden made his international debut for Ireland in the game.

'It would have been an almighty kick in the balls for us if we'd lost.'
Ronan O'Gara reflecting on Ireland's great escape against Italy

Round 2 of matches welcomed France to Dublin for the first Six Nations game in Ireland's new home, the Aviva Stadium. France, reigning champions and Grand Slam winners the year before, spoilt the day for the Irish fans who saw their team lose 25-22 before 51,000 expectant fans.

Game 3 took Ireland to the Scottish capital to face Scotland at Murrayfield. O'Gara put on a master performance scoring a try which he converted and also made two other successful attempts following tries by Jamie Heaslip and Eoin Reddan. Not surprisingly O'Gara took home the Man of the Match award. Wales soon brought Ireland back down to life by winning 19-13 at the Millennium Stadium on 12 March 2011. Ireland ended their campaign with a convincing 24-18 victory against England in their new Dublin home to send the Green Army away happy.

According to scholars, it was the poet Tibullus who made the first explicit reference of Rome as the Eternal City in the 1st century BC. 'Romulus aeternae nondum formaverat urbis moenia, consorti non habitanda Remo' – Tibullus, from Elegies.
Meaning 'Not yet had Romulus drawn up the Eternal City's walls, where Remus as co-ruler was fated not to live'.

EDDIE JONES' SCUMMY IRISH REMARK

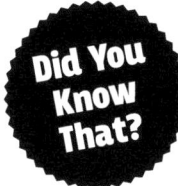

Did You Know That?

Ireland's 2017 victory against England was the fifth time England were denied a Grand Slam in the final game in the Six Nations Championship era (2000, 2001, 2011 and 2013), and the third occasion at the hands of the Irish (2001 and 2011).

In July 2017, Eddie Jones, the England coach, was giving an after-dinner speech on leadership for the Japanese truck manufacturing company Fuso, the sister company of Mitsubishi which sponsored the England team at the time. England won the 2017 Six Nations Championship but Ireland denied them of claiming a Triple Crown and Grand Slam by beating them 13-9 at the Aviva Stadium in the final game. It was Jones' first loss as England coach and he said: 'We've played 23 Tests and we've only lost one Test to the scummy Irish. I'm still dirty about that game, but we'll get that back, don't worry. We've got them next year at home so don't worry, we'll get that back'.

Jones also had a dig at Wales during the dinner. Speaking about Wales with regard to their 125-0 victory against a Japan Under-20s side shortly after he was appointed the coach of Japan in 2012, he said: 'Wales. Who knows Wales? Are there any Welsh people here? So it's this little shit place that has got three million people. Three million!'

Jones' remarks only came to light in March 2018, when a video of the dinner was shown. The RFU acted quickly and a spokeswoman for the organisation said it would be apologising to both the Irish and Welsh rugby unions for the 'inappropriate' remarks, which Jones also himself said he regretted. 'I apologise unreservedly for any offence caused. No excuses and I shouldn't have said what I did.'

As fate would have it, Ireland visited Twickenham for their last game of the 2018 Six Nations Championship. Ireland had already been crowned Six Nations champions with four wins from four games. The match was played on St Patrick's Day and this time England stood in Ireland's way of winning the Triple Crown and a third Grand Slam. Maybe the Irish players had been made aware of Jones' comment because Ireland were magnificent on the day, and beat the home nation 24-15 to ram Jones' words right down his throat.

In His Own Words

'If all the wild horsemen of the apocalypse came around the corner, O'Mahony would charge straight back at them.'
Will Greenwood praising the performances of Ireland's Peter O'Mahony in the 2015 Six Nations Championship

TON-UP FOR BOD

On 13 March 2010, Brian O'Driscoll captained Ireland to a 27-12 victory over Wales at Croke Park in the 2010 Six Nations Championship. It was his 100th cap for his country thereby becoming only the second player to win 100 international caps for Ireland.

> **Did You Know That?** In Ireland's previous game before the win over Wales, John Hayes won his 100th cap for Ireland.

WHEELS FALLING OFF CHARIOTS AND JOLLY GREEN GIANTS

Volkswagen cars were one of the Ireland rugby team's sponsors in 2019, having agreed a deal with the IRFU in 2011. The German car manufacturer caused a bit of a stir in the media before Ireland played England on 2 February 2019, in their opening game of the 2019 Six Nations Championship. The company ran a billboard advertisement mocking England's fall from grace and Ireland's rise to being the No.1 team in the northern hemisphere. Ireland won the Grand Slam in 2018 whilst England could only manage fifth place in the table just one place above the perennial wooden spoon winners, Italy. The billboard depicted a moving image of the wheels falling off a chariot with the strapline: *'Now accepting trade-ins on broken chariots'*. The Irish bookmakers, *Paddy Power*, also cashed in on the act and ran an advertisement referring to England's 800 years rule over Ireland and England losing the last two meetings between the nations – 24-15 in 2018 and 13-9 in 2017 which prevented England from winning the Grand Slam. Paul Grayson, a Rugby World Cup winner with England in 2003, was not impressed saying: 'The best teams are normally the quietest, which is why the VW ad for Ireland is a slightly interesting one'. How true Grayson's comment proved to be because England beat Ireland 32-20 at the Aviva Stadium.

But England fans had previously posted chariot jokes online to vent their anger at their team. When Australia defeated England 33-15 at Twickenham on 3 October 2015 it meant the end of England's 2015 Rugby World Cup campaign. The result meant that England, the host nation of the 2015 Rugby World Cup, could only finish third in Pool A and fail to qualify for the quarter-finals. Australia topped the table with Wales finishing runners-up. One England fan managed to add a new paragraph on Wikipedia's description of a chariot writing: *'Chariots are also often used by the English Rugby Union team to get to World Cup games. However, in 2015, their chariot hit a kangaroo and disintegrated'*.

> **Did You Know That?** During the 2007 Rugby World Cup, Paddy Power managed to persuade the entire Tonga team to dye their hair green prior to their game against England in Paris. Indeed, before the tournament the bookmakers persuaded Tonga's giant centre, Epi Taione (6 feet, 4 inches weighing 18 stones and 2 pounds), to change his name by deed

poll to Paddy Power. This sponsorship deal helped finance the Tongans' 2007 Rugby World Cup preparations. World Rugby did not see the funny side to a bunch of *Jolly Green Giants* taking to the pitch for a Rugby World Cup match and ordered the Tongan team to wash the dye out of their hair and fined Taoine. England won the game 36-20.

In His Own Words

'Every kid grows up dreaming of playing for Ireland. When you do that the next thing you want to do is win something for Ireland. To win something as captain in that special green jersey is what dreams are made of.'

Ireland captain, Rory Best, speaking after Ireland won the Grand Slam in 2018

THE BAA-BAAS HOODOO OVER IRELAND

The Barbarians, nicknamed the *Baa-Baas*, have played Ireland on six occasions and have an impressive record over them, with five victories.

19 May 1996	Won 70-38 at Lansdowne Road
28 May 2000	Won 31-10 at Lansdowne Road
27 May 2008	Lost 39-14 at Kingsholm Stadium, Gloucester, England
4 June 2010	Won 29-23 at Thomond Park
29 May 2012	Won 29-28 at Kingsholm Stadium
28 May 2015	Won 22-21 at Thomond Park

Shane Horgan captained Ireland when they defeated The Barbarians, standing in for Brian O'Driscoll who was attending the funeral of a friend.

THE DRINKS ARE ON US

In September 2014, four Ireland players clubbed together and bought a pub in Ballsbridge, Dublin named '*Bellamy's*'. Jamie Heaslip, brothers Dave and Rob Kearney, and Simon O'Brien refurbished the premises and reopened it under a new name, '*The Bridge 1859*'.

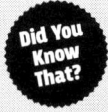

The Barrack Bridge was built over the River Liffey in Dublin in 1859. It was renamed during the 1930's as 'Rory O'Moore Bridge' one of the key figures involved in the plot to capture Dublin as part of the 1641 Irish Rebellion.

A VINTAGE PERFORMANCE FROM THE FRENCH

On 13 August 2011, Ireland played France in a warm-up match for the 2011 Rugby World Cup. The match was played at Stade Chaban-Delmas, Bordeaux, France which the home side won 19-12. Bordeaux is the largest wine growing area in France, but on this occasion it was the French who were raising their glasses in victory after the game ended.

>  Up until 2001, Stade Chaban-Delmas was called Stade du Parc Lescure, named after the fallow lands on which it was built (Lescure is from earlier d'Escure, a transformation of 'des Cures' part of the name of the chapelle Saint-Laurent-des-Cures-lès-Bourdeaus, formerly a prominent feature of the area). But, in 2001, it was renamed Stade Chaban-Delmas in honour of the French resistance fighter and politician, Jacques Chaban-Delmas, who served as Lord Mayor of Bordeaux from 1947-95.

In His Own Words

'It's an incredible achievement for this team. It'll mean so much for them to do it here, to close it out and get over the final hurdle here. There are some world class players in this Irish team. It's very fitting for them to win the Grand Slam.'
Former Ireland wing Denis Hickie after Ireland beat England 24-15 at Twickenham on St Patrick's Day 2018 to win the Grand Slam

WHEN BOD AND ROG CREATED HISTORY IN THE SAME GAME

When Wales beat Ireland 19-13 at the Millennium Stadium on 12 March 2011, the Irish captain, Brian O'Driscoll, scored his 24th try in the tournament which equalled the all-time record of Scotland's Ian Smith who amassed the same number in the Five Nations between 1924 and 1933. O'Driscoll crossed the white line in the second minute of the game and his try was converted by Ronan O'Gara. The two points scored by the Munster fly-half meant he became the fifth player in rugby history to record 1,000 career Test points.

> O'Driscoll scored his 25th try in the tournament in Ireland's next game, a 24-18 victory versus England at the Aviva Stadium on 19 March 2011. Denis Leamy earned his 50th cap for Ireland in the win over England.

2011 RUGBY WORLD CUP

New Zealand played host to the 2011 Rugby World Cup.
The All Blacks went into the 2011 Rugby World Cup final versus France as red hot favourites following impressive performances during the tournament which saw them win five games in

a row including a 37-17 Pool A match victory over France. The men in black looked set to break their 24-year Rugby World Cup bogey, despite having arguably less depth than in previous tournaments and losing one of their best players, Daniel Carter, to injury. They hadn't won the Webb Ellis Cup since 1987, despite being the best team in the world for long periods of time. France were hoping to be crowned Rugby World Cup winners for the first time.

In 1999 and 2007 Les Bleus had spoiled the All Blacks' dreams of glory with dramatic come-from-behind victories whilst this match was a re-enactment of the inaugural Rugby World Cup final in 1987. Both sides were playing in their third Rugby World Cup final (France 1987 and 1999 and New Zealand 1987 and 1995). Simply getting into the final was a great achievement for France who had only shown glimpses of form during the tournament so far. It was difficult to know if this was something to fear or not, given that the All Blacks had been stung twice by France in previous tournaments. The unpredictable nature of France made picking the outcome of the final difficult to choose although the bookmakers made them rank outsiders priced at 7-1 to win the final. New Zealand had played France 50 times since 1906, with 37 wins to the All Blacks, 12 to France and one draw. The teams had met five times previously at the Rugby World Cup, with New Zealand having a 3-2 advantage. Eden Park was a fortress for the All Blacks having not lost on the country's largest ground since 1994 when France scored *'The try from the end of the world'.*

The French advanced on the pre-match haka and seldom took a backward step thereafter. In the final, played in front of a delirious crowd, New Zealand ended 24 years of hurt as they narrowly edged out France 8-7 at Eden Park to win the 2011 Rugby World Cup. France were unrecognisable from the team that had struggled in their Pool games and forced the All Blacks to dig deeper than they had to in earlier games. The collisions were bone-shaking as both fly-halves found out.

At the start of the second-half Dimitri Yachvili had a chance to get France on the board, but like New Zealand's Piri Weepu he dragged his first kick wide of the posts. They were again made to pay when Stephen Donald stepped up to the tee and made it 8-0, with a simple penalty attempt. But France didn't have to wait long to register their first points of the game, great work by Trinh-Duc saw him once again break the line. He got a brilliant offload to Aurélien Rougerie who was held up just a couple of metres from the line. The French then recycled the ball and their inspirational captain, Thierry Dusautoir, crashed through the line to score under the posts. Yachvili added the simple conversion to make the score 8-7. France grew in confidence with each minute that passed and they looked the more confident side. Dusautoir, Julien Bonnaire and Imanol Harinordoquy were superb for Les Bleus really putting their bodies on the line. Dusautoir was again showing the form of 2007 making 20 tackles in the opening 60 minutes. Harinordoquy was ruling the line-out with ease, calling the shots and giving France a real advantage in that area. They had chances to take the lead but Trinh-Duc missed a long-range penalty attempt with 15 minutes to go. The second-half belonged to the visitors, they had all the possession and territory but at crucial times handling errors and penalties cost them the chance to get the victory. To their credit New Zealand just saw out the final few minutes and ended all those years of waiting, it wasn't the prettiest of games but they ground out the win. As one journalist put it: *'The All Black aristocrats survived the French Revolution'.*

THE FRENCH ADVANCED ON THE PRE-MATCH HAKA AND SELDOM TOOK A BACKWARD STEP THEREAFTER. IN THE FINAL, PLAYED IN FRONT OF A DELIRIOUS CROWD, NEW ZEALAND ENDED 24 YEARS OF HURT AS THEY NARROWLY EDGED OUT FRANCE 8-7 AT EDEN PARK TO WIN THE 2011 RUGBY WORLD CUP

Substitute Stephen Donald had been called back from holiday and was visibly not at peak fitness. However, he became an unlikely hero by kicking a wobbly penalty that ultimately secured victory. The real hero of the hour was the All Blacks' captain, Richie McCaw, who played the knockout matches with a broken bone in his foot.

The final was Graham Henry's last as head coach of the All Blacks and a fitting end to his eight year reign in charge which included defeat by France in the quarter-final stages of the 2007 Rugby World Cup finals.

IRELAND'S RESULTS:
Pool C
Ireland 22 United States of America 10 – Stadium Taranaki, New Plymouth
Australia 6 Ireland 15 – Eden Park
Ireland 62 Russia 12 – International Stadium, Rotura
Ireland 36 Italy 6 – Otago Stadium, Dunedin
Ireland won Pool C with Australia finishing runners-up.
Knockout Stage
Ireland 10 Wales 22 – Regional Stadium, Wellington

> **Did You Know That?** In November 2006, the New Zealand government announced that it had decided against building a new stadium on Auckland's waterfront to host the 2011 Rugby World Cup final and opted instead to upgrade Eden Park. The new waterfront stadium was to cost NZ$497 million (£262,417,319) compared to the upgrade of Eden Park which cost NZ$385 million (£203,280,167).

2012 SIX NATIONS CHAMPIONSHIP – THE BOD AND ROG SHOW

The 2012 Six Nations Championship was the 13th edition of the tournament and it became known as the 2012 RBS 6 Nations following a sponsorship deal agreed with the Royal Bank of Scotland.

The first of Ireland's five matches was a home encounter with Wales at the Aviva Stadium. Paul O'Connell captained the side but they lost 23-21 after Leigh Halfpenny scored a penalty in the 79th minute when Wales were trailing 21-20. The Welsh head coach was Warren Gatland, who had previously coached Ireland. In the 76th minute of play, Ronan O'Gara came off the bench to replace Johnny Sexton, winning his 117th cap to draw level with Brian O'Driscoll as Ireland's most capped player. It was also O'Gara's 57th game in the tournament, the most number played by any player. Ireland's Mike Gibson played in 56 Five Nations Championship games from 1964-79.

Ireland's next game was a trip to Paris to face France but the game had to be called off as the pitch at Stade de France was unplayable. It was the first weather-related postponement of a Five/Six Nations Championship game since 1985. On 26 February 2012, Ireland taught Italy a lesson in running the ball by scoring five tries to win the match at the Aviva Stadium, 42-10. Peter O'Mahony made his international debut in the win when he replaced Simon O'Brien after 58 minutes of action, and once again O'Gara came off the bench replacing Gordon D'Arcy in the

69th minute to overtake O'Driscoll as Ireland's most capped player, 118 caps. In their re-arranged fixture, Ireland held France to a 17-17 draw, the first draw between the sides since a 15-15 draw in Dublin in 1985. Ireland then defeated Scotland 32-14 in Dublin and lost their final game 30-9 to England at Twickenham Stadium.

Ireland finished third in the table whilst Tommy Bowe was the leading try scorer with five. Meanwhile, Wales were simply just too good for their opponents, crushing them all, to claim a 25th title, a 20th Triple Crown and an 11th Grand Slam.

> **Did You Know That?** In 2012, Italy continued to play their home matches in Rome, but they moved stadiums from Stadio Flaminio, which they had used since entering the tournament in 2000, to Stadio Olimpico.

BUNDEE AKI JOINS THE RUGBY WORLD CUP'S BAD BOYS

Seventeen countries have seen at least one of their players dismissed at a Rugby World Cup for a total of 33 dismissals– Argentina (2), Australia (1), Canada (4), England (1), Fiji (1), France (1), Ireland (1), Italy (1), Namibia (3), Portugal (1), New Zealand (2), Samoa (4), South Africa (2), Tonga (4), Uruguay (2), USA (1) and Wales (2). The first player to receive a red card was Huw Richards of Wales in the inaugural tournament in 1987. The Welsh lock punched New Zealand lock, Gary Whetton, during his side's 49-6 quarter-final loss and was handed a one-week suspension for his misdemeanor. He missed Wales' final match of the tournament, their Third Place Play-Off versus Australia which they won 22-21. In the latter game, Australian flanker, David Codey, was sent off in the fifth minute, the quickest dismissal in the history of the Rugby World Cup. Codey was given a warning by the referee in the first minute of the game for trampling on an opponent and four minutes later he was given his marching orders after trampling on another Welsh player in a ruck. Three players were dismissed when Canada played South Africa at the 1995 Rugby World Cup – Canada's captain, Gareth Rees, and teammate Rod Snow along with the Springboks' James Dalton. The trio were sent off in the 70th minute of the game which South Africa won 20-0.

Ireland's Bundee Aki was shown the penultimate red card of the 2019 tournament when he was given his marching orders versus Samoa on 12 October 2019.

>  **Did You Know That?** The New Zealand captain, Sam Cane, was sent off in the 2023 Rugby World Cup final, the All Blacks were beaten 12-11 by South Africa.

In His Own Words

'I think I didn't sing it really because I enjoy getting absolutely massacred on social media after the game for not singing it. That's one of the highlights, is refreshing Twitter and people abusing me for not singing the anthem, and playing for Ireland wouldn't be the same without that obviously, that massive encouragement that I get.'

Rory Best speaking to his former Ulster and Ireland teammate, Darren Cave, on an episode of *The Rugby Pod* (2019) explaining why he never sang *Ireland's Call* or *A Soldier's Song* prior to a game.

2013 SIX NATIONS CHAMPIONSHIP – SIMPLY NOT GOOD ENOUGH

Ireland kicked off their 2013 Six Nations Championship campaign by visiting the reigning Grand Slam holders, Wales. However, Wales' form had nosedived since being crowned 2012 Six Nations Champions and went into the tournament with seven consecutive losses, four of which were against Australia. Wales had also lost their head coach, Warren Gatland, who took up his new role as head coach of the British and Irish Lions. The form book didn't change and Ireland made it eight out of eight losses by defeating Wales 30-22 at the Millennium Stadium. It was the first time Wales had suffered five consecutive home defeats.

Game 2 brought England to Dublin and they left the Aviva Stadium with a 12-6 victory. It was a dire game which witnessed six penalties scored, two by Ronan O'Gara and four from Owen Farrell. It was the lowest scoring match since the tournament became the Six Nations Championship in 2000, and England's first away win over Ireland in the competition since winning the Grand Slam in 2003. Ireland suffered back-to-back defeats when Scotland won 12-8 at Murrayfield. Paddy Jackson won his first international cap in the game and incredibly, it was the first time Scotland had won two consecutive games in the tournament since 2001 after beating Italy then Ireland.

France and Ireland drew 13-13 at the Aviva Stadium with the new Ireland captain, Jamie Heaslip, scoring a try which was converted by Jackson who also scored two of the four penalties Ireland were awarded. Eoin Reddan was capped for the 50th time by Ireland whilst Ian Madigan made his international bow. Jackson certainly brought his kicking boots to Rome when Ireland played Italy at Stadio Olimpico, scoring five of the six penalties his side were awarded. But, it wasn't enough to prevent an upset as the home side won the match 22-15. It was the first time Italy had beaten Ireland in a Six Nations Championship match and their first win against Ireland since defeating them 37-22 at Stadio Renato Dall'Arra, Bologna, Italy on 12 December 1997. The loss in Rome also resulted in Ireland dropping down to 9th place in the International Rugby Board's World Rankings since they were first introduced in 2003.

Despite losing their opening game Wales rallied and won their next four matches to retain the title with Ireland finishing fifth, one place above wooden spoon winners, France. It was the first time France finished at the foot of the table since 1999.

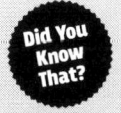 Ireland's draw with France was the first time the two sides had drawn two consecutive matches against each other, the first time this has happened since England and France drew three consecutive matches in 1959 (3-3), 1960 (3-3) and 1961 (5-5).

In His Own Words

'I've been part of a great, great team that can go on and achieve special things.'
Brian O'Driscoll after playing his 133rd and last game for Ireland, a 22-20 victory over France in Paris on 15 March 2014, which won Ireland the 2014 RBS Six Nations Championship

IRELAND'S CLEAN SWEEP OF WORLD RUGBY AWARDS

Ireland ended 2018 by sweeping the board at the annual World Rugby Awards which were held in Monaco on 25 November 2018. The Six Nations Grand Slam winners were named Team of the Year, Joe Schmidt was named Coach of the Year and Johnny Sexton was crowned Men's Player of the Year, the first time in the previous seven years this prestigious individual award was not awarded to a New Zealand player (France's Thierry Dusautoir was the winner in 2011). In his five years in charge of Ireland, Schmidt had guided Ireland from being ranked the eighth best nation in the world to the second best. Sexton, the captain of Leinster, saw off stiff challenges from the other nominees: Rieko Ioane (New Zealand), Faf de Klerk (South Africa), Malcolm Marx (South Africa) and the All Blacks' Beauden Barrett who was looking to claim a hat-trick of consecutive individual awards. It was the first time Ireland had claimed the treble of awards which were introduced by World Rugby in 2001. Ireland suffered just one defeat in 2018, an 18-9 loss in their first Test against Australia in Brisbane in June, a game Sexton was rested for. Sexton returned for the next two Tests and helped Ireland to a first series win in Australia for 39 years. 'If a No 10 wins an award like this it is due to the team around him. We have some of the best coaches in the world and are led superbly,' said the 33-year-old Sexton.

 Ireland's Keith Wood won the inaugural World Rugby Player of the Year award in 2001 and in 2018, Sexton also won the PRO14 and the Champions Cup with Leinster and the Six Nations Championship with Ireland.

2014 SIX NATIONS CHAMPIONSHIP – BOD'S SWAN SONG

Having finished one spot above the Wooden Spoon winners, France, in the 2013 Six Nations Championship, Ireland went into the 2014 tournament more in hope than expectation of success. Brian O'Driscoll, the former captain of Ireland, had decided that he would retire after Ireland's final game versus France (Paul O'Connell was the Irish captain). The 2014 Six Nations

Championship saw the return of a Friday night fixture for the first time in three years.

Ireland got off to a good start, defeating Scotland 28-6 at the Aviva Stadium to reclaim the Centenary Quaich they lost the previous year. Martin Moore won his first Test cap for Ireland whilst O'Driscoll claimed his 129th to overtake Ronan O'Gara as Ireland's most capped player. Meanwhile, Rob Kearney was awarded his 50th cap for Ireland. Back-to-back home games brought Wales to Dublin and once again, Ireland were lethal in attack beating the visitors 26-3 Ireland's defence was rock solid only allowing a 55th minute penalty scored by Leigh Halfpenny. It was Wales' first Six Nations Championship fixture in which they failed to score a try in since their 28–9 loss to France in 2011. The Irish fans made their way home and began to dream of a 12th title, an 11th Triple Crown and a third Grand Slam. Ireland then visited Twickenham knowing that a win would secure the Triple Crown with only the Italians and French to play in pursuit of the Grand Slam. Alas, England beat Ireland 13-10 (they won the Triple Crown in 2014) to retain the Millennium Trophy. Jordi Murphy was handed his first Irish Test cap in the loss but more importantly, O'Driscoll drew level with Australia's George Gregan as the most capped player in international rugby, with 139. It was Brian's 131st cap for his beloved Ireland to add to the eight he won as a British and Irish Lion.

On 8 March 2014, Italy were the visitors to the Aviva Stadium for Ireland's Game 4 encounter. No one gave the Italians a chance of causing an upset in the Irish capital and after the disappointing loss to England, Joe Schmidt, the Ireland coach, produced his favoured A Plan against the Italians and sent out a team to drive forward at every opportunity and not concede silly penalties. In the loss to England, Ireland gave away three penalties, two of which Owen Farrell punished by kicking them over the bar. Italy were hit with an Irish *Tsunami* of aggressive forward play, coupled with a well-drilled back-line, as Ireland crossed the white line seven times to score a try to win the game 46-7. And, the key to the impressive winning score was that Ireland kept their heads and never gave the Welsh referee, Nigel Owens, any opportunity to blow his whistle and give the Italians a penalty. O'Driscoll's participation in the match meant that he became the world's most capped player in international rugby by winning his 140th Test cap. A truly remarkable achievement for a truly remarkable player. And, on the other side, Martin Castrogiovanni became Italy's most capped player.

The fifth and final round of games would decide the outcome of the 2014 Six Nations Championship. The two nations in the frame were England and Ireland who were both on three wins and one loss. France beat England 26-24 in their opening fixture at Stade de France on 1 February 2014. Round 5 meant a trip to Rome for England to face Italy, whereas Ireland had a very difficult game ahead of them against France in Paris. The odds were stacked in England's favour as the French had bounced back from the humiliation of finishing bottom of the table just 12 months earlier. England battered Italy 52-11 at Stadio Olimpico scoring seven tries including one from Farrell who also converted all seven and added a penalty score for good measure.

And, so to O'Driscoll's swan song in one of the most famous cities in the world, his farewell not only to Irish rugby but to the international game to which he had dedicated 15 years of his life to in an Irish international jersey (1999-2014). If Brian could lead the team to victory then the title would be awarded to them. Schmidt's A Plan in previous games, perhaps wishing he had been less defensive in the loss at Twickenham, would reap the dividends it so richly deserved because if the game ended in a draw, or if France won by less than 70 points, England would win the championship. However, if France won the match by 71 points or more, they would win the 2014 Six Nations Championship, and if they won by exactly 70 points, it would be decided on whichever team (France or England) had scored more tries.

On 15 March 2014, Ireland played France at Stade de France. To Schmidt and his players, O'Driscoll in particular, the stadium may well be the iconic arena where France won the 1998 FIFA Football World Cup, but this was not a football match, and besides, both teams had four more players. Pascal Pape, the French captain, led the men in blue into the stadium and BOD (Brian O'Driscoll) walked tall behind his captain, but, history was also calling O'Driscoll's name. Ireland won the game 22-20 meaning they were crowned champions and the statisticians could put away their calculators. Johnny Sexton was imperious, scoring two tries, two of three conversions and one of the two penalty attempts he was presented with. Andrew Trimble was the only other player to score for Ireland, a try in the 25th minute which Johnny converted.

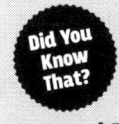
The construction work for Stadio Olimpico began in 1927. During its' early years the stadium was called Stadio dei Cipressi. It was designed and constructed within the larger project of the Foro Mussolini (Mussolini Forum) which was renamed Foro Italico after the Second World War.

In His Own Words

'Once Leo was in the team he was the natural man to captain it. He was knocking on the door during the last Six Nations. I know Leo well and we're fortunate that captaincy sits easily on his shoulders. When there's so much as stake for the players, you don't want to be burdening them with it, but I was delighted to be able to hand it to him.'
Ireland head coach Declan Kidney speaking about Leo Cullen before Cullen won his 30th cap and became the 100th man to captain Ireland on 6 August 2011

2015 SIX NATIONS CHAMPIONSHIP – BACK-TO-BACK TITLES

Ireland were red hot favourites to land back-to-back Six Nations Championships in 2015. If Ireland could retain the title it would be the first time they achieved this feat since the late 1940s. Joe Schmidt was still in charge of Ireland and Paul O'Connell was still the skipper.

Ireland's first match was a trip to Rome to play Italy at Stadio Olimpico. It turned out an easy away day for the Irish winning 26-3. On St Valentine's Day 2015, Ireland faced France at the Aviva Stadium. It was a brutal intense game, very physical and extremely demanding on the body. The French proved to be an immovable object in defence and never allowed the Irish across the white line, leaving Johnny Sexton and Ian Madigan to punish them for their ill-discipline by scoring six penalties, sexton scored five from five and Madigan put the ball over the bar with the single penalty he took. Ireland won the game 18-11.

Consecutive home fixtures brought England to Dublin and they went home with their tails between their legs on the back of a 19-9 loss meaning Ireland won the Millennium Trophy for the first time since 2011. However, Wales, who down the years had proven to be Ireland's curse when it came to Triple Crown aspirations, stopped the Irish bandwagon in their tracks again by winning 23-16 at the Millennium Stadium. Indeed, the Welsh victory meant that no team could win the Grand Slam and none of the Home Nations sides could lift the Triple Crown.

On 21 March 2015, Ireland were in the Scottish capital to play the home nation at Murrayfield. Ireland needed to win the game by 21 points or more to stand a realistic chance of holding on to their title. Thankfully, Ireland's players answered their call and were in majestic form, running over four tries in a 40-10 win; Sexton converted three of the tries (Madigan converted the fourth) and Johnny also slotted over four of the six penalties he took as the Scots were run ragged for the full 80 minutes. Sean O'Brien deservedly won the Man of the Match award and Ireland held on the Centenary Quaich for another year at least. As for the Scots, the drubbing at home meant they would finish-up as wooden spoon winners for the fourth time in the Six Nations Championship era (2000-Present).

The Scotland versus Ireland game was played at 2.30pm, and so practically every household in Ireland, and in many Irish family homes across the globe, tuned in to watch the England versus France match at Twickenham which had a 5.30pm kick-off. Ireland topped the table before England played France and would hold on to their title if France beat England, or if England failed to defeat their opponents by 26 points or more. It was a nerve-wrecking 80 minutes of rugby for the Emerald Isle. At 7.00pm on Saturday 21 March 2015, St Patrick could have been stirred from his grave when the final whistle of the game was blown by Nigel Owens, the Welsh referee. Indeed, Ireland's Patron Saint could have been resurrected from his grave such was the cacophony of sound that reverberated throughout Ireland when England won 55-35, six points short of glory.

Patrick, or Padrig in Welsh, was born around 387 AD and was known as Maewyn (Welsh for devoted friend) Succat (a Pagan term for warlike). He is believed to have come from Bannavem Taburniae, which could be Banwen in Neath Port Talbot, where every year a service is held in his honour. The annual event sees a small collection of residents, historians and school children congregate beside a plaque left in memory of the patron saint of Ireland, before they retire to a community centre for a cup of tea.

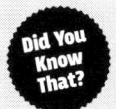

Did You Know That? In the 23-16 defeat to the Welsh, Cian Healy and Johnny Sexton both won their 50th caps whilst O'Connell became a Test Cap centurion, only the fourth Ireland player to win 100 caps.

2015 RUGBY WORLD CUP

England played host to the 2015 Rugby World Cup although some of the games in the tournament were played in the Millennium Stadium.

New Zealand made sporting history at Twickenham Stadium on 31 October 2015 when they became the first team to be crowned Rugby World Cup winners for a second successive time. Tries in each half by wing Nehe Milner-Skudder and centre Ma'a Nonu, followed by a late Beauden Barrett breakaway score, plus 19 points from All Blacks fly-half Dan Carter – including an important late drop-goal – in his 112th and final Test before joining French club Racing 92, saw New Zealand defeat their great trans-Tasman rivals, Australia, 34-17. It extended their record Rugby World Cup winning run to 14 Tests, and meant the Webb Ellis Cup would remain New Zealand's property as they claimed a third world crown since the competition began 28 years earlier in 1987.

But the All Blacks were briefly given a second-half scare as Australia threatened a remarkable fightback from 18 points adrift after 42 minutes as No 8 David Pocock and centre Tevita Kuridrani scored tries, with fly-half Bernard Foley converting both touchdowns that followed an earlier penalty. It proved to be a pulsating final, brilliantly refereed by Nigel Owens, but New Zealand had enough in the tank to guarantee a winning farewell to Test rugby for the likes of Carter, Nonu, Conrad Smith and 148 times-capped Captain Marvel Richie McCaw

'It is my proudest moment. So proud of the way the guys have done it. We played damn good rugby here. We lost a bit of momentum in the second-half but we came back strong which has been the hallmark of this team. I knew the momentum was against us and it was a matter of not panicking and do the simple things right. I still don't want to quit. I want to enjoy the moment,' said Richie McCaw after lifting the Webb Ellis Cup.

The final brought a few tournament firsts: New Zealand were the first side to win back-to-back Rugby World Cups; it was the All Blacks' first Rugby World Cup title outside of New Zealand, with their 1987 and 2011 victories both coming on home soil. The side leading at half-time had now won all eight Rugby World Cup finals; New Zealand's Ma'a Nonu, 33, became the oldest player to score a try in a Rugby World Cup final; this was the highest scoring final in Rugby World Cup history, the tally of five tries was also a record. Dan Carter ended his international career having scored 126 points at Twickenham Stadium, more than any other non-England player and the eighth of anyone.

IRELAND'S RESULTS:
Pool D
Canada 7 Ireland 50 – Millennium Stadium
Ireland 44 Romania 10 – Wembley Stadium
Ireland 16 Italy 9 – Olympic Stadium
France 9 Ireland 24 – Millennium Stadium
Ireland won Pool D with France finishing runners-up.
Knockout Stage
Argentina 43 Ireland 20 – Millennium Stadium

> **Did You Know That?** Dan Carter's 19 points tally in a Rugby World Cup final has only been surpassed by Australia's Matt Burke who scored 25 points when the Wallabies defeated France 35-12 in the 1999 final at the Millennium Stadium, kicking two conversions and scoring seven penalties.

2016 SIX NATIONS CHAMPIONSHIP – IN SEARCH OF A TREBLE

Could Ireland make it a unique hat-trick of consecutive Six Nations Championship title victories in 2016? They almost did it in seasons 1948-50. No country had won three consecutive Five Nations Championship crowns post World War II and the inaugural Six Nations Championship series in 2000. Although, France came within a whisker of it during the four-year period 1986-89, a Golden Era for French rugby. France and Scotland shared the 1986 title, France won the 1987 edition of the tournament and the Grand Slam, France and Wales were co-winners in 1988 and the following year, 1989, France were outright Champions. England were Five Nations Championship winners in 1990 and 1991 (France, 1992), England were double winners again in 1995 and 1996 with the French denying them a Treble in 1997, and Scotland dampened a French parade in 1999 by winning the last ever edition of the Five Nations Championship in a season when France were the reigning Champions.

In the Six Nations Championship era no nation had completed a successive treble: England won the title in 2000 and 2001 (France, 2002), France in 2006 and 2007 (Wales in 2008), Wales won back-to-back titles in 2012 and 2013 before Ireland ended their run in 2014. And, so to the 2016 Six Nations Championship and as far as most rugby pundits were concerned, the outcome of the championship would see a team in green lift the trophy.

Ireland had a new captain for the tournament, Joe Schmidt chose Ulster's Rory Best to lead the side. On 7 February 2016, Wales were the visitors to the Aviva Stadium which had slowly come to be a home fortress for Ireland in international matches. But Wales started the game on the offensive despite conceding two penalties scored by Johnny Sexton in the 4th and 13th minutes of play and a Conor Murray try in the 26th minute which was converted by Sexton. Ireland led 13-10 at half-time, and all was in order for another home win. Warren Gatland, the coach of Wales, must have spiked his players' half-time drink with a powder dust of passion wearing the famous red Welsh jersey, because his team were exceptional in the second-half. Wales were almost exemplary in defence in the second 40 minutes by conceding just a single penalty which Johnny slotted over with ease in the 74th minute of the game. The score at the time was 16-16 as Rhys Priestland scored two second-half penalties (46th and 72nd minute) to add to the penalty he scored in the 31st minute of play (3/3 scored). And, that was the end of the scoring, a 16-16 draw, meaning no Triple Crown and no Grand Slam for either side. CJ Stander made his debut for Ireland in the game and it was the first time Ireland had drawn with Wales since the 21-21 game at the Arms Park in the 1991 Five Nations Championship.

Game 2 saw the Irish green army of fans invade Paris but they lost 10-9 at Stade de France to the home side. Sexton successfully kicked three penalties from three attempts. It was France's first victory over Ireland since their 26–22 win during the 2011 Rugby World Cup warm-up games, 19-12 at Stade Chaban-Delmas. On 27 February 2016, Ireland lost for the second time in a row, this time going down 21-10 to a very strong England team at Twickenham. Ultan Dillane, Stuart McCloskey and Josh van der Flier all made their debuts for Ireland in the game. The Round 4 of games restored a little of the Irish pride with an easy 58-15 win against Italy at the Aviva Stadium. Sean Cronin made his Irish debut in the win. Ireland's final game was another home match, this time Scotland were the visitors to Dublin. Ireland, with Keith Earls in the side winning his 50th cap, won their scrap 35-25 to finish third in the table behind runners-up Wales, and Grand Slam winners for the 13th time, England.

Did You Know That? The nine tries cored by Ireland in their 58-15 annihilation of Italy is the most number of tries scored by Ireland in a Six Nations Championship match.

2017 SIX NATIONS CHAMPIONSHIP – STOPPING THE ENGLAND JUGGERNAUT

England were a juggernaut in the previous tournament winning the title for the 27th time, a 25th Triple Crown and a not so unlucky for them, 13th Grand Slam. Round 1 of matches in the 2017 edition of the tournament meant ferry crossings and short flights for the Irish fans to see their side face Scotland at Murrayfield. The home side won the match 27-22 thanks to a dramatic try scored in the last minute by Greig Laidlaw when the scores were level at 22 each. It was the Scots' first opening day win since 2006 and the first time Ireland lost their opening fixture since 2012. With Scotland winning the Centenary Quaich for the first time since 2013, the last time they had defeated Ireland, it was a bad day all round for Ireland and their green army.

Game 2 was a trip to Rome where Ireland got back on track by demolishing the home side 63-10 at Stadio Olimpico. Ireland scored nine tries to equal their record haul in a Six Nations Championship game, which they did against the same opponents a year earlier. CJ Stander and Craig Gilroy helped themselves to a hat-trick each. Stander became the first forward to score three tries in a Six Nations Championship match. Niall Scannell made his debut for Ireland in the game which is their record winning margin in the competition and by scoring nine tries, Ireland became the first nation to be awarded a bonus try point in the Six Nations Championship.

On 25 February 2017, Les Bleus and their hoard of fans were in Dublin and in good voice, but they quietly made their way back to France following a 19-9 defeat at the Aviva Stadium. Ireland lost their Round 4 game, 22-9 to Wales at the Millennium Stadium. Ireland's last game was against England who had not lost a game in their previous 18 outings. A victory for England in Dublin would not only see them crowned champions, they would also claim back-to-back Grand Slam titles. Andrew Conway was given his Test debut for Ireland whilst the England coach, Eddie Jones, had never before tasted defeat in charge of the national side. The last time

England had been beaten was the 2015 Rugby World Cup when Australia won 33-15. Ireland were in no mood to let England walk all over them and the men in green won a hard fought game 13-9. Despite the defeat, England retained the title they won in 2016. It was the second time in six months that Ireland had beaten a team with 18 straight wins, having also ended New Zealand's winning streak in November 2016.

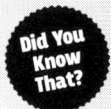 In their 27-22 loss to Scotland, Ireland were awarded a bonus point, which was awarded to a team that lost a game by seven or fewer points. It was the first time a bonus point had been awarded in the tournament.

2018 SIX NATIONS CHAMPIONSHIP – GRAND SLAM WINNERS

Having finished runners-up to England the previous season, Ireland, coached by Joe Schmidt and captained by Ulster's Rory Best, knew they had a squad capable of competing with the best sides in the world. But could they harness the talent they had to aggressive forward play coupled with a tightknit defence. Five games would answer these questions.

Ireland had a tough start to their campaign, France in Paris on 3 February 2018. At the half-time interval a scrappy affair saw Ireland lead 9-3 thanks to three penalties scored by Johnny Sexton. Maxime Machenaud scored a penalty for the home side. Two minutes after the interval, Sexton made it 12-3 followed by a second successful penalty from Machenaud. With 10 minutes remaining, Ireland were in control of the game. Or so it seemed because Teddy Thomas scored a try in the 72nd minute to bring the French within a point of the Irish, trailing 12-11. Machenaud had to leave the field of play in the 67th minute before returning in the 76th minute, leaving Anthony Belleau to attempt the conversion. Belleau's kick was perfect to give France a 13-12 lead before an ecstatic Partizan crowd inside Stade de France. Echoes of the noises that filled the stadium when France won the 1998 Fifa World Cup final in it filled the air in the French capital. Such was the cacophony of sound, the players from both sides could not hear their teammates calling out to them. The horn to announce that the 80 minutes of game play had elapsed could barely be heard but Ireland, in possession of the ball, knew that they just needed their opponents to give away a sixth penalty (Sexton scored 4/5) and victory would be in their grasp.

Total concentration was required with one mistake meaning France would take the win. Three minutes into the added on time Sexton dropped the ball to his left foot and scored a magnificent drop goal which gave Ireland the victory and sent the French crowd home shaking their heads as to how their team could not get over thy winning line. It was the perfect start to the competition for Ireland and gave them the impetus to show they were a team who never gave in and fought to the very end, even if it was three minutes past the customary 80 minutes of match play. Sexton's drop goal sent a message to the other four nations that Ireland were the team to beat, such was the immensity of the way 15 green jerseys hung in and came out the other end triumphant. To use a French word, it was pure *Camaraderie*.

Game 2 was far less dramatic, a 56-19 win over Italy at the Aviva Stadium, a game which marked Jordan Larmour's debut in the green jersey. Next up was a tricky encounter against Wales in Dublin. But, Ireland, now with the momentum of two straight wins behind them, beat the Welsh 37-27. Schmidt's men spoilt a landmark day for the Welsh coach, Warren Gatland, as it was his 100th game in charge of the Dragons. On 10 March 2018, Scotland arrived in Dublin more in hope than expectation. The Scots lost their opening game 34-7 in Wales, beat France 32-26 on Matchday 2 at Murrayfield and England 25-13 at Murrayfield in their third outing. But, they were not good travellers and this proved to be the case in Dublin when they went down 28-8. The win meant Ireland were 2018 Six Nations champions after four games because none of their opponents could match the points they had already amassed. It was their 14th title.

Only England stood in their way of winning their 11th Triple Crown, but more importantly, a third Grand Slam. The game was played at Twickenham on 17 March 2018. England had won 14 games on the bounce on home turf. It was St Patrick's Day and the Irish invaded England just as the Normans had done in 1066. During the Norman Conquest of England in the late 11th century, a famous battle took place at Hastings, England on 14 October 1066. The Normans won the battle and when Ireland crossed the white line at Twickenham, they knew a mighty battle lay ahead before them. The 15 men in green were well up for the fight and won the encounter 24-15 to claim a third Grand Slam, their first since 2009 and their first Triple Crown since 2009. England simply had no answer to Ireland's raw power which saw them earn three bonus points in the win. Garry Ringrose, C.J. Stander and Jacob Stockdale all scored a try, Sexton converted two of them and the third was successfully kicked over the bar by Joseph Carberry, who came on as a substitute in the 67th minute for Ireland's one man kicking machine. It was England's third defeat in the 2018 edition of the tournament, the first time they lost three games since the dark days of the 2006 Six Nations Championship.

It was a monumental day for Irish rugby on several fronts: for Schmidt and his assistants, the players, the fans and the country. It was England's first loss at Twickenham in the Six Nations Championship since 2012 (a run of 15 matches), their first loss at home overall since 2015 (a run of 14 games) and Ireland's first win against England at Twickenham since 2010. Ireland retained the Millennium Trophy for the first time since their three consecutive victories over England between 2009 and 2011. Ireland's victory meant that they became the first team to earn the three points bonus for completing a Grand Slam. Meanwhile, Rory Best and Rob Kearney shared the distinction of being Ireland's only players to have won multiple Grand Slams, having both played in the 2009 Grand Slam winning campaign.

Did You Know That? Ireland's 56-19 victory against Italy was their 300th international victory.

In His Own Words

'I don't really care.'

Wales head coach, Warren Gatland, after a journalist asked him how he felt the match between England and Ireland on 17 March 2018 would pan out. Ireland won 24-15 at Twickenham to claim the Grand Slam for the third time in their history.

2019 SIX NATIONS CHAMPIONSHIP – IN PURSUIT OF BACK-TO-BACK GRAND SLAMS

On 1 January 1987, Starship released a song entitled *Nothing's Gonna Stop Us Now*. It went to No.1 in the UK charts. When the Ireland team ran out of the tunnel at the Aviva Stadium on 2 February 2019, no one in the 51,000 crowd would have batted an eyelid had Starship's song been played along with the Irish national anthem. The match was Ireland's opening game of the 2019 Six Nations Championship, they were the reigning champions and Grand Slam winners the previous year. It was also Rugby World Cup year (Japan) and Joe Schmidt, the Ireland coach, wanted the other five nations in the tournament, along with the southern hemisphere triumvirate of Australia, New Zealand and South Africa, to take notice of just how good a side Ireland was. Who could possibly stop Ireland from doing a clean sweep for the second year in a row?

According to the form book, England did not stand a chance in Dublin having won there just twice in their previous nine trips to the Irish capital (2003, 2013) and failing to score a try in each of their last three visits. Added to this, Ireland had won their last 12 home games in all competitions, their longest winning home sequence of victories in their history. The cards were stacked high against England and the form book rarely lies. But, you write off the underdog at your peril and Ireland kicked off in pursuit of back-to-back Grand Slams with a 32-20 defeat. The game marked several firsts.

Jonny May's try after less than 90 seconds was England's first at the Aviva Stadium since Steve Thompson's in 2011. The Unlucky No.13 curse came to the fore, Ireland suffering their first loss at home since the All Blacks beat them in 2016. It was Schmidt's first home loss as Ireland coach; England recorded their first win against Ireland at the Aviva Stadium since their 12–6 victory in the 2013 Six Nations Championship which was also Ireland's last home Six Nations Championship loss bringing an end to a run of 12 games unbeaten in front of a Dublin crowd. And, England's victory meant that they won back the Millennium Trophy for the first time since 2016.

In the Round 2 of matches, Ireland restored a little pride by beating Scotland 22-13 at Murrayfield. The men in green could not win the Grand Slam or retain the Triple Crown but the outcome of the 2019 Six Nations Championship was still within their grasp.

'We have a lot of belief. That was a really tough game. But we asked for a physical reaction and by and large we got that. Maybe it was not the most especially attractive game but it was two teams who went hard and we are very grateful to win.'

Rory Best, Ireland captain speaking after the win over Scotland

It was Scotland's first loss at Murrayfield Stadium in the Six Nations Championship since the opening round of the 2016 tournament when they lost 15-9 to England, bringing an end to a run of seven consecutive home wins in the competition, their longest run of home wins in the Six Nations Championship era. The nine-point margin of defeat was Scotland's biggest defeat in any international match at Murrayfield Stadium since Ireland won 40–10 on the final day of the 2015 Six Nations Championship. Ireland's 22-13 victory meant that they retained the Centenary Quaich. Next up for Ireland was a trip to Rome and a head-to-head versus Italy. Ireland recorded their fourth away win in a row in the competition with a 26-16 victory at Stadio Olimpico. Jack Carty made his debut for Ireland in the game. Matchday 4 brought France to the Aviva Stadium and a rejuvenated Irish side beat their opponents 26-14. Ireland's half-time lead of 19–0 is their largest ever interval lead against France. Schmidt's side now had to go to Cardiff to take-on the Grand Slam chasing Wales in the final round of games, trailing the Welsh by just two points in the table. Four points were awarded for a win, two points were awarded for a draw and a bonus point was awarded to a team that scored four or more tries in a match or loses a match by seven points or fewer. If a team scored four tries in a match and lost by seven points or fewer, they were awarded both bonus points.

On 16 March 2019, Wales and Ireland went toe-to-toe at the Millennium Stadium with the outcome of the championship on the line. It proved to be a bridge too far for Ireland, trailing 16-0 at the interval, and going on to lose 25-7 to a superb Welsh side It was Wales' biggest winning margin over Ireland since 1976, a 34-9 win at Lansdowne Road in the Five Nations Championship. The win meant Wales lifted their 12th Grand Slam and had won 14 Tests in a row, extending their own national record, with a loss to Ireland in last year's Six Nations Championship their most recent defeat. This was the first time Ireland lost an away Six Nations Championship game since 2017, when Wales beat them 22-9 at the same venue. It was Wales' fourth Grand Slam in the Six Nations Championship era, breaking a tie with France on three for the most by any country. The game was Warren Gatland's and Schmidt's last Six Nations Championship encounter as the head coach of each country, having both announced prior to the 2019 tournament their resignations following the 2019 Rugby World Cup. Gatland bid farewell to the tournament by becoming the first coach to land three Grand Slams (2008 and 2012) whilst Schmidt bowed out having never won a Six Nations Championship game in the Principality.

In His Own Words

'I thought our boys showed that they can deliver in the big moments on a number of occasions today. They worked incredibly hard and merited the win. We showed a little bit of class where we opened them up and at the other end of the pitch it was pure courage.'

Joe Schmidt, Ireland coach, after Ireland beat England 24-15 to win the Grand Slam in 2018

 **Ireland completed the Grand Slam in 2018, but no side had managed to achieve this in consecutive seasons in the Six Nations Championship era, with France the last side to do it in the Five Nations Championship (1997-98).**

2019 RUGBY WORLD CUP

Japan hosted the 2019 Rugby World Cup.

The All Blacks were red hot favourites to win their third successive world crown and when they defeated South Africa 23-13 in their opening game, the bookmakers shortened their odds of victory that much that it was pointless laying a bet on New Zealand to win the coveted Webb Ellis Cup. Ireland were in Pool A along with the host nation, Russia, Samoa and familiar foes Scotland.

New Zealand topped Pool B with South Africa runners-up. Ireland defeated Scotland in their opening match but were then surprisingly beaten by Japan, a match which proved to be controversial for some of the refereeing decisions made by Angus Gardner (Australia). Ireland managed to put their Cherry Blossoms upset behind them to whitewash Russia and see off the challenge of a good Samoa side to finish runners-up in Pool A to the host nation. Ireland's loss to Japan was their first loss to a Tier 2 nation since losing 40–25 to Samoa in 1996 and Japan's first victory against Ireland. Ian Henderson won his 50th cap for Ireland in the game. And amazingly, it was the first time that Ireland failed to score any points in the second half of a match since their 10-9 loss to France in the 2016 Six Nations Championship at Stade de France.

Ireland faced New Zealand in the knockout Stage/Quarter-Finals with their encounter played at Tokyo Stadium, Chofu. The All Blacks were in devastating form having scored 157 points to top Pool B and conceding only 22, securing two Bonus Points. Ireland were no match for the onslaught that the All Blacks brought upon them running over seven tries to Ireland's solitary try scored by Robbie Henshaw. The favourites to win the competition ran out comfortable 46-14 winners. To rub salt into gaping Irish wounds the 32 points victory margin was Ireland's largest defeat in a Rugby World Cup match surpassing their 43–19 defeat to New Zealand in 1995.

In the other quarter-final games, England battered Australia 40-16, Wales eked past France with a single point margin of a win scoring 20 points to the 19 France posted and Japan's fairy tale run came to an end when the Springboks taught them a lesson, winning 26-3 at Tokyo Stadium. South Africa were now the team to fear and despite finishing runners-up to the All Blacks in their Pool, they outscored them by notching-up 185 points and conceded 36 to give them a +149 Points For compared to New Zealand's +135. The Springboks also scored one Bonus Point more than the All Blacks.

The draw for the semi-finals pitched England against New Zealand and South Africa versus Wales. No one outside the England camp gave them a chance of beating the tournament favourites but they caused a huge upset by beating the All Blacks 19-7. South Africa squeezed their way into the final with a 19-16 win over Wales. In the 76th minute of the South Africa versus Wales scrap, the Welsh were penalised for collapsing a maul with the scores level at 16-16. Up stepped Handre Pollard, who had already converted Damian de Allende's 57th minute try and successfully kicked his three previous penalties in the match (15th, 20th and 35th minute), to attempt a kick which if it went between the posts, would book South Africa a spot in the final. His kick was Robin Hood-esque as it arrowed its' way over the bar. The 2019 Rugby World

Cup final was a rematch of the 2007 final when South Africa defeated England 15-6 at Stade de France. The Springboks beat England 32-12 at the International Stadium Yokohama to claim their third Webb Ellis Cup, following their previous triumphs on home soil in 1995 and in France in 2007.

IRELAND'S RESULTS:
Pool A
Ireland 27 Scotland 3 – International Stadium Yokohama, Yokahama
Ireland 12 Japan 19 – Shizuoka Stadium Ecopa, Fukuroi
Ireland 35 Russia 0 – Kobe Misaki Stadium, Kobe
Ireland 47 Samoa 5 – Fukuoka Hakatanomori Stadium, Fukuoka
Ireland finished runners-up to Japan in Pool A.
Knockout Stage/Quarter-Finals
Ireland 14 New Zealand 46 – Tokyo Stadium, Chofu

In His Own Words

'I don't need to come off.' **(as he wiped the blood from his face)** Johnny Sexton speaking to referee Angus Gardner in the 28th minute of Ireland's historic 25-14 victory against England at Twickenham on 17 March 2018 which gave Ireland the Grand Slam. However, the medics eventually dragged him off the pitch to receive medical attention.

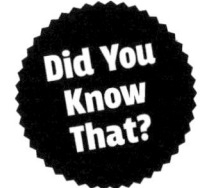

Did You Know That?

The 2019 Rugby World Cup final was the most watched television programme in the United Kingdom in 2019, with a peak audience of 12.8 million people tuning in to the broadcast which was shown by ITV.

2020s

GRAND SLAM WINNERS FOR A FOURTH TIME

THE BEST TEAM IN THE WORLD

A TEST SERIES VICTORY IN NEW ZEALAND

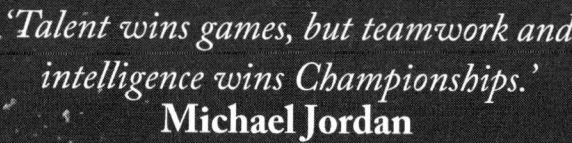

'Talent wins games, but teamwork and intelligence wins Championships.'
Michael Jordan

THE BEST TEAM IN THE WORLD

Going into the 2023 Rugby World Cup, Ireland were the No.1 ranked team in World Rugby.

1.	Ireland	91.82 points
2.	France	90.47 points
3.	New Zealand	88.98 points
4.	South Africa	88.97 points
5.	Scotland	82.77 points
6.	England	82.12 points
7.	Australia	81.80 points
8.	Argentina	80.72 points
9.	Wales	78.08 points
10.	Japan	77.39 points

A points system is used, with each nation awarded points on the basis of their results in international matches sanctioned by World Rugby. The rankings are based on the country's performance, with more recent results and more significant matches being more heavily weighted to help reflect the current competitive state of a team. The men's ranking system was introduced the month before the 2003 Rugby World Cup and at the time were called the *'International Rugby Board Rankings'.*

When Ireland beat Wales 19-10 at the Aviva Stadium on 7 September 2019 in a warm-up match for the 2019 Rugby World Cup, Ireland were installed as the No.1 ranked team in the world for the first time in their history. Since the rankings began, the winners of the Rugby World Cup have held the No.1 spot at the end of each tournament. New Zealand have been the most consistently ranked No.1 team having been on top of Rugby Union's perch for 75% of the time since 2003, South Africa 20% whilst Ireland, England, Wales and France make up the remaining 5%.

After winning the 2023 Rugby World Cup, South Africa became the new No.1 ranked team in the world, Ireland are second.

 Ireland's lowest ever ranking is No.9 which occurred in 2013. England's lowest ranking is No.8, France No.10, Wales No.10 and Scotland No.12.

IRELAND'S GRAND SLAM WINNING CAPTAINS

1948 – Karl Mullen
2009 – Brian O'Driscoll
2018 – Rory Best
2023 – Johnny Sexton

In His Own Words

'This is a special group. This is probably the toughest thing to do in World Rugby. We said it was going to be the start of our World Cup (2023) year but, I don't know, it's probably a little bit bigger than that.'

Andy Farrell, Ireland coach, after Ireland beat New Zealand 32-22 at Sky Stadium, Wellington, New Zealand on 16 July 2022. It was the first time Ireland won a Test Series (2-1) in New Zealand in their history.

THE 2020 SIX NATIONS CHAMPIONSHIP – BAD TRAVELLERS

Coached by Andy Farrell, and captained by Johnny Sexton, Ireland could only manage three victories in the 2020 Six Nations Championship, all at home. They beat Scotland 19-12 at the Aviva Stadium, Wales 24-14 and battered Italy 50-17. England defeated Ireland 24-12 at Twickenham Stadium and they lost 35-27 to France at Stade de France.

The tournament began on 1 February 2020, and was scheduled to end on 14 March 2020. However, as a direct result of the COVID-19 pandemic, Ireland's final two matches were postponed. It was the first time a Six Nations Championship game had been postponed since 2012 when the France versus Ireland match at Stade de France on 11 February 2012 was called off due to an unplayable pitch, the first weather-related postponement of a Five/Six Nations Championship match since 1985. The 2020 tournament also marked the first time more than one game had to be postponed since the outbreak of foot and mouth disease in 2001.

The last four games in the tournament took place in October 2020, with Ireland playing in two of them. On 24 October 2020, Ireland beat Italy and on 31 October 2020, Ireland lost to France. England became the first team to win the title despite losing their first game (24-17 away to France) since Wales did so in 2013 (30-22 to Ireland in Cardiff) It was England's 39th title overall (including shared titles) and their 26th Triple Crown, drawing them level with the record Wales set the previous year, and extended their record of 29 outright titles.

SCOTLAND MATCH

Caelan Doris and Ronan Kelleher made their international debuts for Ireland. Ireland retained the Centenary Quaich.

WALES MATCH
Max Deegan made his international debut for Ireland.
ENGLAND MATCH
England retained the Millennium Trophy.
ITALY MATCH
Ed Byrne, Will Connors, Jamison Gibson-Park and Hugo Keenan made their international debuts for Ireland. Italy won the wooden spoon for the fifth year in a row, their 15th since joining the Six Nations Championship in 2000.
FRANCE MATCH
Cian Healy became the sixth player to win 100 Test caps for Ireland.

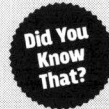 **If France had beaten Ireland by 28 points, they would have won the Championship whilst Ireland too could have won the title but they needed a bonus-point win or a margin of seven points (or six if they scored at least one try).**

PRESIDENT BIDEN, THE ALL BLACKS AND THE BLACK AND TANS

On 13 April 2023, President Joe Biden was in the Windsor Pub, Dundalk, on the first day of his three-day visit to Ireland. Biden was paying tribute to Rob Kearney who won 95 caps, scoring 82 points for Ireland from 2007-19, who is a distant fifth cousin of the U.S. President. Kearney was born in Cooley Peninsula, County Louth near Dundalk and after Ireland famously defeated the All Blacks 40-29 at Soldier Field, Chicago, on 5 November 2016, Kearney presented Biden with a tie with a shamrock on it Biden recalled the occasion by referring to the tie he was wearing with Kearney watching on but he mixed up the All Blacks with the Black and Tans who are notoriously famous for the brutality they dished out to Irish Republicans and the shameful atrocities they committed on innocent Irish citizens during the Irish War of Independence in 1920. The name 'Black and Tans' reflected the colour of their uniforms.

'This was given to me by one of these guys, right here. He was a hell of a rugby player. He beat the hell out of the Black and Tans,' said Biden. Kearney played in Ireland's victory in Chicago, their first against the giants of southern hemisphere rugby in history.

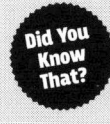 **A short time after President Biden's innocent gaffe, the Wikipedia entry for 'Black and Tans' was amended to jokingly declare their 'defeat' by the Irish rugby star (Rob Kearney) 'ending their reign of terror'.**

SOVIET BOYCOTT

Ireland have met and defeated Russia three times in an international match.
21 September 2002 – Rugby World Cup Qualifier:
Russia 3 Ireland 35 - Central Stadium, Krasnoyarsk, Russia
15 September 2011 – Rugby World Cup Pool C:
Ireland 62 Russia 12 - International Stadium, Rotorua, New Zealand
3 October 2019 – Rugby World Cup Pool A: **Ireland 35 Russia 0** – Noevir Stadium, Kobe, Japan
A total of 16 nations competed in the inaugural Rugby World Cup in 1987. Seven of the 16 places were automatic choices as they were all members of the International Rugby Football Board (IRFB) – Australia, England, France, Ireland, New Zealand, Scotland and Wales. The remaining nine slots were offered to Argentina, Canada, Fiji, Italy, Japan, Romania, Tonga, USA and Zimbabwe. The Soviet Union declined an invitation to participate in the inaugural Rugby World Cup on political grounds, allegedly due to the continued IRB membership of South Africa. At the time Georgia and Russia were part of the Soviet Union and both of these nations qualified for the 2019 tournament. Argentina, Canada, Fiji, Italy, Japan, Romania, Tonga, USA and Zimbabwe were all made IRFB members post the 1987 tournament.

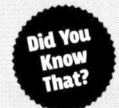 **The most popular sports in Georgia are basketball, football, judo, rugby union, weightlifting and wrestling.**

THE 2021 SIX NATIONS CHAMPIONSHIP BEHIND CLOSED DOORS

For the first time in the history of the competition, the 22nd Six Nations Championship and the 127th edition of the competition overall, all 10 games were played behind closed doors. No spectators were permitted into the stadiums because of the COVID-19 pandemic. Ireland lost 21-16 to Wales at the Millennium Stadium in their opening fixture and were then defeated 15-13 at the Aviva Stadium by France. Round 3 finally brought a win, 48-10 over Italy at Stadio Olimpico. On 14 March 2021, Scotland lost 27-24 to Ireland at Murrayfield and in their final match, Ireland defeated England 32-18 in Dublin. Wales won their 28th title and their 22nd Triple Crown. The Welsh were denied the Grand Slam after conceding a try in the last minute of their game versus France in Paris, losing 32-30.

WALES MATCH
Peter O'Mahony became the first Irish player to be shown a red card in a Six Nations Championship match.
FRANCE MATCH
This was the 100th meeting between the two nations, and the first time Ireland had lost their

opening two games in a Six Nations Championship campaign. Iain Henderson captained Ireland for the first time.

ITALY MATCH

Robbie Henshaw won his 50th Test cap for Ireland. Ryan Baird and Craig Casey made their international debuts for Ireland. The Ireland coach, Andy Farrell, selected an all-Leinster starting backline, the first time this had occurred since 1931 and the third time in history.

SCOTLAND MATCH

CJ Stander won his 50th Test cap for Ireland. Ireland retained the Centenary Quaich. It was also the 138th time the two sides had met, Ireland 67 wins, Scotland 66 wins and 5 draws. It was Ireland's sixth consecutive win over the Scots and 17 wins in their last 20 meetings in the Six Nations Championship.

ENGLAND MATCH

Bundee Aki was sent off in the 64th minute for a dangerous tackle on Billy Vunipola. Ireland reclaimed the Millennium Trophy. It was the first time since 1976, England lost to all three home nations.

> **Did You Know That?** Johnny Sexton, the Ireland captain, was the tournament's leading points scorer with 65.

WORLD RUGBY MEN'S 15S – DREAM TEAM OF THE YEAR 2023

Five Ireland players were named in the World Rugby Men's 15s Dream Team of the Year for 2023: Dan Sheehan, Tadgh Furlong, Caelan Doris, Bundee Aki and Garry Ringrose.

Only three players from the 2022 dream team made it into the 2023 side, Antoine Dupont (France), Will Jordan (New Zealand) and Furlong. Indeed, it was the third year in a row the famous trio were selected.

Andy Farrell was named World Rugby Coach of the Year.

> **Did You Know That?** Andy Farrell was on the list of nominees for the 2022 World Rugby Coach of the year but missed out on the award to Wayne Smith, the New Zealand Black Ferns' World Cup-winning head coach. In 2021, Smith led the Black Ferns to their sixth Rugby World Cup success (1998, 2002, 2006, 2010, 2017 and 2021). Smith became the first coach to win both the men's and the women's Rugby World Cup having been an assistant coach of the All Blacks team which won the Webb Ellis Cup in 2011 and 2015.

GEORGIA ON MY MIND

Ireland have played Georgia five times in an international match and have a 100% winning record against their eastern European opponents.

14 November 1998 – Rugby World Cup Qualifier: **Ireland 70 Georgia 0** - Lansdowne Road
28 September 2002 – Rugby World Cup Qualifier: **Ireland 63 Georgia 14** - Lansdowne Road
15 September 2007 – Rugby World Cup Pool D: **Ireland 14 Georgia 10** - Stade Chaban Delmas, Bordeaux
16 November 2004 – Guinness Series: **Ireland 49 Georgia 7** - Aviva Stadium
29 November 2020 – Autumn Nations Cup, Group A: **Ireland 23 Georgia 10** – Aviva Stadium

Georgia have played in six Rugby World Cups (2003, 2007, 2011, 2015, 2019 and 2023). Their best ever finish was 12th in 2015 and they recorded their first ever World Cup win in 2007 when they defeated Namibia 30-0.

 In 1930, Hoagy Carmichael and Stuart Gorrell wrote the song Georgia on My Mind and in 1979, the State of Georgia, USA designated it the official state song.

RUCK ME, WHAT A FLANKER!

In January 2022, Rugby Dome published who they considered to be the five best blindside or open-side flankers to play for Ireland.

Sean O'Brien
Fergus Slattery
David Wallace
Stephen Ferris
Gordon Hamilton

Gordon Hamilton played for North of Ireland Football Club, Howe of Fife (Scotland), Ballymena and Ulster, winning 10 caps for Ireland from 1991-92 He only scored one try for Ireland but it almost put Ireland into the semi-finals of the Rugby World Cup. On 20 October 1991, Ireland faced Australia at Lansdowne Road in the quarter-finals of the 1991 Rugby World Cup. With only a few minutes remaining, Hamilton scored a try, converted by Ralph Keyes, which gave Ireland the lead, 18-12. But Michael Lynagh broke the hearts of the 54,000 Irish fans inside the stadium when he scored a try down the other end and made the conversion to give the Wallabies a 19-18 victory.

SEA EAGLES NOT SOARING SO HIGH

Ireland have played Tonga in three international matches and won them all. Their first encounter was in the 1991 Rugby World Cup when Ireland won the game 32-9 at Ballymore, Brisbane, Australia. On 15 June 2003, Ireland beat Tonga 40-19 in Nuku'alofa during their Summer Tour of the Southern Hemisphere. They last met in a Pool B match during the 2023 Rugby World Cup in France which Ireland won 59-16.

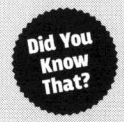

Did You Know That? Since the inaugural Rugby World Cup in 1987, Tonga have only missed out on qualification once, in 1991.

RUGBY IN IRELAND

On the island of Ireland (Northern Ireland and the Republic of Ireland) 23 clubs are affiliated to the Connacht Branch of the Irish Rugby Football Union, 71 clubs are affiliated to the Leinster Branch, 59 clubs are affiliated to the Munster Branch and 56 clubs are affiliated to the Ulster Branch. In addition, there are 246 Schools playing rugby, Connacht (23), Leinster (75), Munster (41) and Ulster (107). There is a National League of 50 senior clubs.

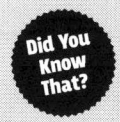

Did You Know That? Founded in 1879, the IRFU is the third-oldest rugby union in the world after England (1871) and Scotland (1873), and was formed two years before the Welsh Rugby Union.

THE GREEN AND THE BLACK – KIWIS AND SHAMROCKS

In 1905, Ireland played New Zealand for the first time The All Blacks were on their 1905-06 Tour of Europe and North America, and beat Ireland 15-0 at Lansdowne Road on 25 November 1905 in front of 12,000 home fans. Since then the two power houses of International Rugby Union have met in 36 more Test Matches with the All Blacks dominating their Head-to-Heads winning 31, Ireland won five and one game ended in a 10-10 draw (20 January 1975 at the home of Irish rugby, Lansdowne Road). The two nations last faced one another in at the Stade de France in the quarter-finals of the 2023 Rugby World Cup with New Zealand winning 28-24.

IRELAND'S WINS

5 November 2016
Soldier Field, Chicago, United States of America
Ireland 40 (25) New Zealand 29 (8)
Attendance: 62,300
Tries: Murphy (9), Stander (16), Murray (33), Zebo (47), Henshaw (75)
Cons: Sexton (10, 34), Carbery (76)
Pens: Sexton (3, 23), Murray (58)
Memorable for:
This was Ireland's first ever victory over New Zealand in 28 attempts since 1905.
Joey Carbery made his international debut.

This was the most points (40) and tries (5) New Zealand conceded in a single Test Match since Steve Hansen became head coach of the All Blacks in 2012, surpassing the 38 points England scored against New Zealand in December 2012 and the four tries South Africa scored in the final match of the 2013 Rugby Championship.

17 November 2018
Aviva Stadium
Ireland 16 (9) New Zealand 9 (6)
Attendance: 51,000
Tries: Stockdale (48)
Cons: Sexton (50)
Pens: Sexton (11, 27, 39)
Memorable for:
This was Ireland's first home victory over The All Blacks.

13 November 2021
Aviva Stadium
Attendance: 51,000
Ireland 29 (5) New Zealand 20 (10)
Tries: Lowe (14), Kelleher (43), Doris (50)
Cons: Sexton (51)
Pens: Sexton (55), Carbery (64, 73, 79)
Memorable for:
This was Ireland's seventh consecutive win in all Tests.

9 July 2022
Forsyth Barr Stadium, Dunedin, New Zealand
Attendance: 28,191
New Zealand 12 (7) Ireland 23 (10)
Tries: Porter (3, 48)
Cons: Sexton (4, 49)
Pens: Sexton (14, 56, 68)
Memorable for:
This was Ireland's first ever victory over The All Blacks on New Zealand soil.

16 July 2022
Sky Stadium, Wellington, New Zealand
Attendance: 30,748
New Zealand 22 (3) Ireland 32 (22)
Tries: Van der Flier (3), Keenan (27), Henshaw (36), Herring (64)
Cons: Sexton (28, 37, 65)
Pens: Sexton (31, 55)

Memorable for:
This was the first time since 1998 that New Zealand lost back-to-back home Test Matches.
This was the first time that Ireland won back-to-back matches against New Zealand.
It was the first time Ireland won a Test Series (2-1) in New Zealand in their history.
It was the first time since 1994, and just the fifth occasion in their history, that the All Blacks lost a home Test Series – South Africa (1937), Australia (1949 and 1986), British & Irish Lions (1971) and France (1994).
By defeating the All Blacks in the third Test Match of the Series, Ireland went to No.1 spot in World Rugby rankings for the first time since 2019.

> **Did You Know That?** The name All Blacks was first coined when the New Zealand Rugby Union team toured the British Isles, France and the United States of America in 1905-06. There are two stories as to how the New Zealand team became known as the All Blacks. The first is that a newspaper misprinted 'all backs' as 'all blacks', when describing the team's style of play with the entire team being capable of kicking and passing the ball with the same skill as backs. The other story is that they were named after their all-black playing outfit of jersey, shorts and socks. Whatever, the correct version is the name stood.

In His Own Words

'I watched a game of beach volleyball between the Lions and four local girls, two of whom had represented Australia at the London Olympics. With Paulie involved, it became ridiculously competitive. He was up front with Geoff Parling and nearly killed one of the poor girls with a spike.'

Johnny Sexton recalling the time during the British and Irish Lions 2013 tour of Australia when he went to the beach with Paul O'Connell and England lock, Geoff Parling – from Johnny's autobiography Becoming A Lion.

THE 2022 SIX NATIONS CHAMPIONSHIP – LONG RUNS THE FOX

Ireland got their campaign off to the best possible start, defeating the reigning champions, and Triple Crown holders, Wales, 29-7 at the Aviva Stadium. Johnny Sexton, the Ireland captain, was ruled out of round 2 of matches and James Ryan stood in for him against France. Ireland went down 30-24 to France at Stade de France. Coach Andy Farrell then made Peter O'Mahony captain for the home game versus Italy which Ireland won comfortably, 57-6. Round 4 of matches took Ireland on the road and a visit to bitter rivals, England, at Twickenham. The home side were no match for the visitors who marched through their defence scoring four tries to earn a bonus point. Sexton was back for this game and made his presence known as he bossed the show from the first whistle until he was replaced in the last minute of the game by Joey Carbery. Sexton was applauded off the pitch by the invading Irish Army of fans inside the stadium having made three of the four conversions from Ireland's tries scored and he successfully kicked two from two penalty kicks. But, Farrell was also making a statement to his former employers, and more importantly to England coach Eddie Jones.

On 28 June 2012, Farrell joined England on a three and a half year contract as their Defensive Coach under their Head Coach, Stuart Lancaster. Then on 15 December 2015, after Lancaster resigned (11 November 2015), Eddie Jones succeeded him and sacked Farrell and the rest of the coaching team. *Long Runs The Fox* as the saying goes and Farrell most definitely outfoxed Jones. England failed to get behind the Irish Wall of a backline and all of their points came from Marcus Smith who kicked over five of the six penalties he attempted. Owen Farrell, Andy's son, was originally named in the England squad as captain ahead of the 2022 Six Nations Championship, but was later ruled out due to injury.

Matchday 5 brought the Scots and their tartan clad fans to Dublin which saw 51,000 fans packed into the Aviva Stadium, but the visitors to the Irish capital should have stayed at home and watched their team crumble before their eyes on television instead of in person, losing 26-5.

Before the England game Eddie Jones had a history of making comments about Ireland which ranged from concern about Johnny Sexton's injury profile, to Ireland being a 'Kick and Clap' side. The Aussie coach of England even had a dig about the 'United Nations' make-up of the Ireland squad. But Farrell, who worked under Jones at Saracens, didn't take the bait when he was asked if he thought Jones' comments were part of his 'Mind Games' ahead of their encounter and said: 'I don't know what it is. I don't know what it is and I don't care to be fair. No, I love Eddie's comments. I love reading them. I think it's great for the game. I love his character and charisma, I've learned a lot off him. I've worked under him. I've been a captain of a side for him. I've been in his company etc, but in answer to your question, I don't see the need. I don't see the need. I don't get it sometimes but I like reading it. I think it's intriguing.'

WALES MATCH
Mack Hansen made his international debut for Ireland.

FRANCE MATCH
France's victory helped them win the Grand Slam in 2022.

ITALY MATCH
Michael Lowry made his international debut for Ireland.

ENGLAND MATCH
Ireland retained the Millennium Trophy. The victory was Ireland's biggest win over England at Twickenham Stadium since 1964, surpassing the 13-point winning margin in 1964, an 18-5 win on 8 February 1964 (Ireland won the wooden spoon).

SCOTLAND MATCH
Ireland won the Triple Crown for the first time since 2018, and the first time they did so on home soil since 2004. They also retained the Centenary Quaich.

> **Did You Know That?** Italy went into the 2022 Six Nations Championship, having tasted defeat in their previous 36 outings in the tournament. On 28 February 2015, Italy beat Scotland 22-19 at Murrayfield. Trailing 21-15 with less than two minutes remaining in their final game against Wales at the Millennium Stadium in the 2022 edition of the tournament, Edoardo Padovani, scored a try to win the match for Italy, 22-21. It was Italy's first victory against Wales since 10 March 2007, 23-20 at Stadio Flaminio, Rome, and their first international win in Wales. It was also the Italians' first success against a Tier 1 nation since they defeated South Africa 20-18 at Stadio Artemio Franchi, Florence, Italy on 19 November 2016. The two Nations have met 16 times, with the Springboks winning the other 15 matches.

ALWAYS AT THE BIG SHOW

Since the inaugural Rugby World Cup in 1987, only 11 countries have contested every tournament: Argentina, Australia, England, France, Ireland, Italy, Japan, New Zealand, Romania, Scotland and Wales. South Africa were banned from participating in the 1987 and 1991 Rugby World Cups because of the country's apartheid system. Canada played in every Rugby World Cup from 1987 to 2019, but failed to qualify for the 2023 tournament after losing a two-leg qualifying tie to Chile 54-46 on aggregate. Canada beat Chile 22-21 in the first leg at Starlight Stadium, Langford, British Colombia but were beaten 33-24 at Estadio Elías Figueroa Brander, Valparaíso, Chile in the second leg.

> **Did You Know That?** It was Chile's first ever victory over Canada and they qualified for the 2023 tournament, their first Rugby World Cup, after defeating the USA 52-51 over two legs in the Round 5, Americas Qualifier. Ireland has never played Chile in an international match.

WHEN IRISH EYES WERE NOT SMILING

Three Rugby Unions submitted bids to World Rugby to play host to the 2023 Rugby World Cup, namely France, Ireland and South Africa. Italy was also in the fray to host the tournament but without their government promising any financial support, they lost their bid. The World Rugby Board recommended South Africa's bid taking into consideration the vision, tournament scheduling, and organising process, infrastructure, venues for the tournament and financial commitments presented by the three countries. South Africa ranked the highest with 78.97 per cent, with France on 75.88 per cent and Ireland 72.25 per cent. On the day of the voting process, 15 November 2017, Ireland had a shocking day as they were eliminated in the first round with just eight votes compared to France and South Africa who had 18 and 13 respectively. In the second round, France gained 24 votes as compared to South Africa's 15 to win the rights for hosting the showpiece event in 2023. The 2023 Rugby World Cup was the third time France hosted the tournament (1991 and 2007).

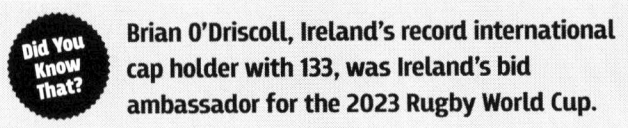

Did You Know That? Brian O'Driscoll, Ireland's record international cap holder with 133, was Ireland's bid ambassador for the 2023 Rugby World Cup.

GROUNDS WHERE IRELAND CLINCHED THE GRAND SLAM

1948	Ravenhill – Ireland beat Wales 6-3
2009	Millennium Stadium – Ireland beat Wales 17-15
2018	Twickenham Stadium – Ireland beat England 25-14
2023	Aviva Stadium – Ireland beat England 29-16

2023 SIX NATIONS CHAMPIONSHIP – THERE IS NO 'I' IN TEAM

'It is amazing what you can accomplish if you do not care who gets the credit.'
Harry Truman, the 33rd President of the United States of America.

Ireland's 37-man squad for the 2023 Six Nations Championship was assembled by coach Andy Farrell with two things in mind, teamwork and success. Despite winning the Triple Crown a year earlier (their 12th), Ireland fell short of winning the 2022 Six Nations Championship and a Grand Slam with it by losing 30-24 to France at Stade de France on Matchday 2. Ireland scored more tries than France in the game, 3-2, but it was needless and senseless penalties that eventually cost Ireland victory in the French capital. The France Head Coach, Fabien Galthie and his assistant coach, Raphael Ibanez, had built a very tight knit squad of players whose camaraderie and attention to detail propelled them to the title and a tenth Grand Slam. In Galthie they had a former scrum half who made 64 appearances for Les Bleus, scoring 49 points (1991-2003). But, in Ibanez they possessed a gem, a hooker who drove his team forward and who was the bedrock of their defence during his 98 international matches for his country, 1995-2007, scoring 40 points. Ibanez knew what it took to win, claiming two successive Grand Slams in 1997 and 1998 and led them to the 1999 Rugby World Cup final where they were defeated 35-12 by Australia at the Millennium Stadium. But more importantly the leadership qualities he gained during his career at the top of the sport, he captained France on 41 occasions, were seamlessly transferred to the French squad, and in particular to their talismanic playmaker and captain in 2023, Antoine Dupont.

In the minds of Ireland fans, 'The Foreigner', Farrell, had more than proved his managerial qualities since being appointed the coach of Ireland in 2020, but in the 2023 Six Nations Championship he had to somehow get his mix of youth and experience to gel together in order to outwit the two wily foxes who were the French management team. France had Dupont, aged 26 with 42 caps under his belt, but Farrell had a 37-year-old Johnny Sexton as his leader who had a world of experience over his young French adversary. Sexton had already accumulated 113 caps in the green jersey as well as six caps for the British and Irish Lions. It was a throwback to two teams competing in the BBC TV show called *It's A Knockout*, which was aired from 1966-82. Eddie Waring, a British Rugby League football coach, commentator and television presenter, was one of the judges on the show. The winning team in each event scored three points, the second-place finisher scored two points and the third-place team scored one point. Each competing nation was given a Joker Card, which they could play before any one event to double the points they scored for it. In the 2023 Six Nations Championship, Farrell and Galthie produced their Joker Cards, their 'Get Out Of Jail Free' Monopoly cards in the form of their respective team captains.

Yes, Dupont had the air of 'Je ne sais quoi,' about him, a quality that cannot be easily described, an ability capable of inspiring his teammates to victory, which was never in doubt, but Sexton was capable of winning games on his own. The French fans knew the danger Sexton brought across the white line with him only too well as the Leinster fly-half scored a magnificent 45-metre drop goal with the very last kick of the game, and after 41 phases, to beat France at Stade de France 15-13 in 2018. When the ball sailed over the bar in the 83rd minute of play, the French players on the pitch, and on the bench including Dupont, held their heads in dismay whilst one lay flat out on his back with blood pouring from his right eye and right knee. Sexton had delivered a death knell blow to France which broke the hearts of a nation. It was each nation's opening game of the 2018 Six Nations Championship and proved to be the winning start, a springboard which Ireland used to win their next four games in the tournament to win the country's third Grand Slam.

On 4 February 2023, Ireland got their assault on the 2023 Six Nations Championship underway with a 34-10 victory against Wales in Cardiff. Ireland were awarded a bonus point having scored five tries whilst Johnny was just Johnny, scoring 3/3 penalties and kicking 2/2 conversions. It was Ireland's first victory in a Six Nations Championship match at the Millennium Stadium since 2013 Next up on their path to reclaiming the title they last won in 2018, was France, the reigning champions and Grand Slam holders, and a team who would not give up their Crown Jewels to any ordinary thief. There is a saying that 'Possession is 9/10 of the Law'. If Ireland really wanted what France had then the Irish players would need to take control of the game by dominating time in possession of the ball, but more importantly they had to keep their discipline by not falling foul of the Rules of the game by conceding unnecessary penalties.

Three Rugby World Players of the Year took to the field of play at the Aviva Stadium, Sexton the winner in 2018, Dupont the winner in 2021 and Johnny's Leinster comrade, flanker Josh van der Flier, the incumbent holder of the crown having been named 2022 Rugby World Player of the Year just three months before the 2023 Six Nations Championship kicked-off. The France side were vastly experienced and unlocking their defence was not going to be an easy task with players such as Gael Fickou (Aged 28, Centre, 74 caps) Uini Antonio (Aged 32, Tighthead Prop, 47 caps) Cyril Bailie (Aged 29, Loose Head Prop, 38 caps) and Charles Ollivon (Aged 29, Back Row, 28 caps) in their starting XV. Mind you, Ireland were not exactly lacking a wealth of experience in their starting XV: Andrew Porter and James Ryan were making their 50th appearance for Ireland whilst Peter O'Mahony, Tadgh Furlong, Connor Murray and Garry

Ringrose had more than 300 international caps between them.

This was not only going to be a battle of 'Mind Games' between Sexton and Dupont but a titanic struggle to determine who would be the 'Masters of Rugby' in the northern hemisphere. Ireland had recently been named the No.1 team in the world in the International Rugby Board rankings system whilst France were No.2. It was the first time the two top ranked nations in World Rugby had faced one another in a Six Nations Championship match. If the game could not be built up any higher in terms of importance than it already had by the sports journalists who had the hottest ticket in town to see the game, or in this case the hottest ticket in the city as Dublin played host to these two rugby giants, Ireland had won their previous 12 home games and France were on an unbeaten 14 match run dating back to November 2021. Something had to give unless both teams played a game of chess with each Grand Master, Sexton and Dupont, negating one another's influence to force a draw. It was France who got off to a flying start forcing a penalty after just four minutes of play when Porter went searching for a turnover when his teammate, Tadgh Beirne, smothered the ball with his body. It may have been some 40 metres from goal but Thomas Ramos slotted the ball over the Irish bar to give the visitors a 3-0 lead. Clearly the Irish pair had forgotten about not giving away senseless penalties. Echoes of Paris a year earlier were on the minds of many Ireland fans. The game was being played at a frenetic pace and Hugo Keenan scored a try four minutes later, converted by Sexton. But, France hit back in the 17th minute when Damian Penaud penetrated the Ireland back line to score a try which Ramos coolly converted. Ireland's defensive game plan went out the window conceding two further penalties in the first half which Ramos gladly devoured. Thankfully for Farrell, his forwards took the game to France and scored two more tries through Lowe (20 mins) and the half-centurion Porter (26 mins). Johnny hit one of the two conversions sweetly, slotting the ball over the bar following Lowe's try, but fell short of converting Porter's. Ireland were dominating the proceedings and led 22-16 at the interval.

Farrell's half-time team talk worked a trick as Ireland rarely put a foot wrong in the second 40 minutes of a bruising but totally pulsating encounter. The mistakes which cost Ireland the penalties in the first-half were but a distant memory as they kept their discipline and more importantly, kept the French attack at bay. The barn door had firmly been shut to stop the horse from bolting although Ramos did add a drop goal to France's total score in the 61st minute two minutes after Ross Byrne scored a penalty for Ireland. But, Ireland rammed home their advantage and scored again through Ringrose (try, 71 mins) and Byrne hammered the final nail in the French coffin which left Dublin by converting Ringrose's try. The final whistle couldn't come sooner for Les Bleus who lost 32-19. Dave Kilcoyne won his 50th cap for Ireland when he came on as a replacement in the 69th minute for Porter.

Ireland had exorcised their loss in Paris twelve months earlier and set out to take down England, Italy and Scotland in their remaining three matches, which they did.

ITALY 20 V IRELAND 34 - STADIO OLIMPICO

SCOTLAND 7 V IRELAND 22 - MURRAYFIELD

Garry Ringrose won his 50th cap in the match. Johnny Sexton drew level with Ronan O'Gara's record as the leading points scorer in the history of the Six Nations Championship, 557. Ireland retained the Centenary Quaich and became the first team to notch-up 80 wins in the Six Nations Championship.

IRELAND 29 V ENGLAND 16 - AVIVA STADIUM

Josh van der Flier was awarded his 50th cap. Ireland retained the Millennium Trophy. It was the 15th time Ireland had been crowned champions in the tournament, the first time they won it on home soil since 1985. Ireland became the first team to win back-to-back Triple Crowns since they achieved the same feat in 2006 and 2007. It was a fourth Grand Slam victory for Ireland and their first on home soil since their inaugural Grand Slam win in 1948. Johnny Sexton scored 9 points in the game to move up to 566 points overall in the competition thereby surpassing Ronan O'Gara's record number of points.

> **Did You Know That?** Ireland became the first nation to see their senior men's side and their Under-20s side win the Grand Slam in the same year.

IRELAND COACHES RECORDS IN THE PROFESSIONAL ERA

COACH	YEAR(S)	GAMES	WON	DREW	LOST	WIN %
Murray Kidd	1995-97	9	3	0	6	33.33%
Brian Ashton	1997-98	8	2	0	6	25.00%
Warren Gatland	1998-2001	38	18	1	19	47.40%
Eddie O'Sullivan	2001-08	78	50	0	28	64.10%
Michael Bradley	2008	2	0	0	2	0.00%
Declan Kidney	2008-13	53	28	3	22	52.80%
Less Kiss	2013	2	2	0	0	100.00%
Joe Schmidt	2013-19	76	55	1	20	72.40%
Andy Farrell	2019-	50	40	0	10	80.00%

Notes (includes Ireland's 2024 Tour of South Africa):
1. Eddie O'Sullivan won the Triple Crown in 2004, 2006 & 2007.
2. Michael Bradley was an Interim Coach.
3. Declan Kidney won the 2009 Six Nations Championship and Grand Slam. Named World Rugby Coach of the Year in 2009.
4. Les Kiss was an Interim Coach.
5. Joe Schmidt won the Six Nations Championship in 2014, 2015 and 2018 (Grand Slam winners), Ireland were named World Rugby Team of the Year in 2018 and Schmidt was named World Rugby Coach of the Year in 2018. In 2019, Ireland were ranked the o.1 side in the world for the first time.
6. Andy Farrell won the Triple Crown in 2022 and Ireland went to No.1 in the world rankings in July 2022. Ireland won the Six Nations Championship in 2023 (Grand Slam winners) and the Six Nations Championship in 2024.

> **Did You Know That?** The World Rugby Team of the Year was first awarded in 2001 and went to Australia.

ALWAYS THERE

The winners of the Five/Six Nations Championship have never failed to reach at least the quarter-final stages of the Rugby World Cup.

YEAR	FIVE/SIX NATIONS WINNERS	RUGBY WORLD CUP FINISH
1987	France	Runners-up
1991	England	Runners-up
1995	England	Semi-finals
1999	Scotland	Quarter-finals
2003	England	Winners
2007	France	Semi-finals
2011	England	Quarter-finals
2015	Ireland	Quarter-finals
2019	Wales	Semi-finals
2023	Ireland	Quarter-finals

2023 RUGBY WORLD CUP

France hosted the 2023 Rugby World Cup. Ireland kicked-off their 2023 Rugby World Cup campaign against Romania in Bordeaux.

Ireland 82-8 Romania
Pool B
9 September 2023
Noveau Stade de Bordeaux, Bordeaux

The previous evening France lit up Paris to mirror its' nickname of being the City of Light with a scintillating 27-13 victory over New Zealand in the opening game of the tournament. Now it was Ireland's turn to show just why they were the No.1 ranked nation in the world since topping the world rankings after the previous year's Test Series win against New Zealand, and the firm favourites to win the famous Webb Ellis Cup for the first time.

The temperature in the stadium, and on the pitch, was stifling and the Romanians were on the scoreboard before most of the fans attending the game had even taken their seats. Gabriel Rupanu scored a try inside three minutes but the Timosoara Saracens' scrum-half missed the conversion attempt.

Johnny Sexton, who had not played for Ireland since their win over England in the Six Nations Championship on 18 March 2023 because of a slight injury and suspension, rallied the Irish players just like a great captain can. He missed all three of Ireland's warm-up matches, wins against Italy, England and Samoa, through suspension following 'confrontational and aggressive' behaviour towards referee Jaco Peyper (South Africa). The incident that landed Johnny in hot water with World Rugby happened following Leinster's 27-26 Champions Cup final defeat to La Rochelle at the Aviva Stadium on 20 May 2023, when Sexton, who was not playing in the final due to injury, confronted the match officials after the final whistle.

Sexton was playing in his fourth Rugby World Cup campaign (2011, 2015 and 2019) and making his 114th appearance for Ireland. He became the first 38-year old (38 years and 60 days) to win an international cap for Ireland when he led the side out to face the 19th ranked nation in World Rugby. When it came to winning a game from going behind Sexton was a master at it having starred in the movie, had the t-shirt and adorned the front cover of the match programme. If he had been an actor and not a fly-half his performances for Ireland merited Oscar status.

Ireland were magnificent in the game and blitzed their opponents 82-8 scoring 12 tries: Gibson-Park, Keenan, Beirne 2, Aki 2, Sexton 2, Herring, O'Mahony 2, McCarthy. Johnny converted seven of the tries with Jack Crowley kicking home another four after he came on as a replacement for the Ireland captain with 16 minutes remaining. Sexton received a standing ovation when he walked off the pitch to the sound of *The Fields of Athenry* being sung by thousands of Irish fans. Meanwhile, his personal tally of 24 points moved him past the Munster legend, Ronan O'Gara's, previous record of 93 points as Ireland's leading points scorer at the Rugby World Cup with 102. Johnny had already eclipsed O'Gara's Six Nations Championship record earlier in the year and was now just nine points adrift of the Munster man's Ireland Test record of 1,083 points. Bordeaux is the undisputed wine capital of the world and Bordeaux wines are often amongst the most expensive in the world thanks to the famous terroir. The entire Ireland squad deserved an exquisite bottle of the famous red wine courtesy of their coach, Andy Farrell, when they returned to their hotel to relax and enjoy an evening meal.

Ireland were totally ruthless against their eastern European opponents and played on after the 80 minute hooter was sounded rather than end the match at 77-8, to score Ireland's twelfth try of the game in the third minute of added on time. *Wicked Game* is a song by American rock musician Chris Isaak, released from his third album entitled *Heart Shaped World*. Sexton and Ireland played a wicked game against Romania and won the hearts of the Irish travelling army which resembled a sea of green in the stands.

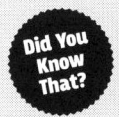 **The 74 points winning margin surpassed Ireland's previous record winning margin at a Rugby World Cup, 57, when they beat Namibia 64-7 at Aussie Stadium, Sydney in the 2003 Rugby World Cup. It was also Ireland's second biggest ever victory behind the 83-3 win over the United States of America on 10 June 2000 in Manchester, New Hampshire, USA.**

Ireland 59-16 Tonga
Pool B
16 September 2023
Stade de la Beaujoire, Nantes

This was the first match between Ireland and Tonga at a Rugby World Cup since the inaugural tournament in 1987, when the two nations met in a Pool 2 game which Ireland won 32-9 at Ballymore, Brisbane.

Ireland didn't so much as ease to an impressive 43 points victory over Tonga, scoring eight tries, more a case of a luxury cruise ship slowly making its' way into port so as those watching on could admire the splendour before them. Johnny Sexton was making his 115th appearance for his country and had his mind on more than helping his side to a win. The fly-half was nine points short of Ronan O'Gara's all-time points scoring record for Ireland of 1,083 (scored in 128 Test Matches).

Sexton was already an Ireland rugby great but he paved his way to becoming a legend by just doing his stuff. He opened the scoring in the game with a penalty and then pulled his luxury liner alongside O'Gara's when he converted tries scored by Tadhg Beirne, Caelan Doris and Mack Hansen. In the 38th minute the 38-year old Dublin man broke the Munster man's record when he ran in between the posts to score a try to make it a personal total of 1,088 points for him. Johnny then converted his try (1,090 points). Peter O'Mahony was sin-binned in added on time at the end of the first half which allowed the No.15 ranked team in the world to score a try which they converted. Ireland led 31-13 at the interval.

Sexton was given the second 40 minutes off by Andy Farrell who wanted to rest his inspirational General for Ireland's next match, an encounter against the reigning World Champions, South Africa. Ross Byrne replaced him. Ireland added four more tries in the second-half from Bundee Aki (2), James Lowe and Rob Herring, all four were converted by Byrne.

The game ended 59-16 with Ireland going top of Pool B. Ireland had now scored 20 tries in their opening two fixtures.

Nantes is named after a tribe of Gaul, the Namnetes, who established a settlement between the end of the second century and the beginning of the first century BC on the north bank of the Loire River. The origin of the name *Namnetes* is uncertain, but it is believed to derive from the Gaulish root *nant* meaning river or from *Amnites*, another tribal name possibly meaning '*Men of the River*'. Johnny Sexton left Nantes a Leviathan.

 The Tonga Rugby Football Union was founded in 1923. On 24 November 2012, Tonga defeated Scotland 21-15 at Pittodrie Stadium, Aberdeen, Scotland (the home of Aberdeen Football Club) to give The Sea Eagles their first ever victory over a traditional rugby power on a European pitch.

Ireland 13-8 South Africa
Pool B
23 September 2023
Stade de France

Going into this mammoth game, the reigning Rugby World Cup holders versus the 2023 Grand Slam Champions and No.1 ranked nation in the world, the two Giants of the sport had met each other on 27 previous occasions. Seventeen of their encounters took place in Dublin with Ireland winning 7, The Springboks 9 and an 8-8 draw at Lansdowne Road on 8 January 1970. Of the remaining 10 fixtures, all were played in South Africa, and the home nation won 9 and were only beaten once, a 26-20 loss in Cape Town on 11 June 2016. This was the first game the pair played at a neutral venue and their first ever match-up at a Rugby World Cup.

The stadium was a sea of green, the home colour of both sides, but it was the green worn by the fans from the Emerald Isle that dominated the stands. Paris had been invaded by an Irish Army and the city had not seen as many green shirts on the streets since AS Saint Etienne (their home jersey is green) beat Stade de Reims 2-1 in the 1977 Coupe de France (the French equivalent to the English FA Cup) at Parc des Princes.

The match was a slugfest, a scrappy affair, an arm wrestle between two Titans of World Rugby. South Africa's Maine Libbok's penalty edged South Africa ahead in the first-half before Mack Hansen's try, converted by Johnny Sexton, put Ireland 7-3 in front at half-time.

Ireland had major line-out issues early on, winning none of their first four, but the players stabilised and it was a line-out won by Ireland that helped set up Hansen's try. Cheslin Kolbe hit back for the Springboks from a dominant scrum which came right after four replacement forwards - the so-called 'Bomb Squad' - had been introduced. However, Libbock missed the conversion attempt making the score 8-7 to South Africa. The miss took the momentum away from South Africa and gave Ireland a huge lift at a time they needed it most. A Johnny Sexton penalty put Ireland 10-8 ahead and in a nail-biting finish, Ireland's defence absorbed pressure before Jack Crowley's penalty sealed an epic 13-8 victory for the Boys in Green.

It was an intense encounter that was always going to come down to fine margins and ultimately missed penalties by Libbock and Faf de Klerk cost the Springboks' dearly. Ireland's victory over the reigning Champions delivered a Statement which the other competing nations paid attention to.

'THE STADIUM WAS A SEA OF GREEN, THE HOME COLOUR OF BOTH SIDES, BUT IT WAS THE GREEN WORN BY THE FANS FROM THE EMERALD ISLE THAT DOMINATED THE STANDS. PARIS HAD BEEN INVADED BY AN IRISH ARMY AND THE CITY HAD NOT SEEN AS MANY GREEN SHIRTS ON THE STREETS SINCE AS SAINT ETIENNE (THEIR HOME JERSEY IS GREEN) BEAT STADE DE REIMS 2-1 IN THE 1977 COUPE DE FRANCE AT PARC DES PRINCES.'

Bundee Aki, won his 50th cap for Ireland and was named Man of the Match.

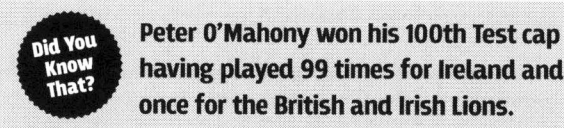

Did You Know That? Peter O'Mahony won his 100th Test cap having played 99 times for Ireland and once for the British and Irish Lions.

Ireland 36-14 Scotland
Pool B
7 October 2023
Stade de France

Peter O'Mahony won his 100th cap for Ireland in this match which was all but over inside 67 seconds when James Lowe scored a diving try in the corner after receiving a pass from Garry Ringrose who made his way through the Scotland defence like a hot knife sliding through butter. Johnny Sexton missed the conversion but Ireland just slipped seamlessly into top gear scoring at will and were nothing short of imperious throughout the contest. Scotland spent a fair amount of time in the Ireland half in the first 40 minutes but it was more a case of huffing and puffing than causing a tornado. The Scots went in at the interval 26-0 down as Hugo Keenan scored two tries with Iain Henderson adding a fourth to give Ireland a Pool B bonus point. Sexton converted all three conversion attempts.

If this had been a World Heavyweight Championship boxing match, the Scotland coach would have thrown the white towel into the ring at the interval to save his fighter from further embarrassment.

Scotland had lost their previous eight outings against Ireland and despite their best efforts in the second-half they were not going to bring this run to an end against an Irish side who were just far too clinical in every aspect of their play. For those watching, including their forthcoming quarter-final opponents, New Zealand, they were in awe of an Ireland side who created scoring opportunity after scoring opportunity and just as they had done a week earlier against South Africa, they simply just overwhelmed their opponents. The men in green were everywhere on the pitch and the Scotland coach Gregor Townsend must have felt as though Ireland had 17 men on the pitch such was their superiority with the ball and winning it back. Ireland managed to find gaps and expose them at will whilst at the same time suffocating the Scotland forwards.

In the second-half Ireland added 12 more points to make it 36-0 thanks to tries from Dan Sheehan and Ringrose, with Scotland scoring two consolation tries which were both converted, to make the final score a little more respectable, 36-14.

Ireland didn't just win Pool B, they ripped it apart recording 19 points from their four games, all victories, their highest tally of points in a Pool Stage of a Rugby World Cup. Added to this they scored 26 tries in those games, more than they scored at any previous Rugby World Cup, and racked up 190 points on the pitch to eclipse their previous best of 141 in 2003.

The Springboks finished runners-up in Pool B (to play Pool A winners France) whilst the Scots exited the Pool Stages for the third time in the past four Rugby World Cup tournaments.

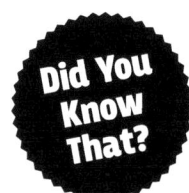

Did You Know That?

The victory over Scotland was Ireland's 17th win in a row and their 29th victory in 31 Test Matches.

The Ireland fans were in every stand inside the stadium which resembled a cauldron of green jerseys who were making a cacophony of noise in support of their heroes. They had travelled to the French capital by air, land and sea. Sexton paid tribute to the Irish fans saying: 'They give us the best days of our lives and we give them something similar, I'm sure'.

Next up for Ireland would be the All Blacks, runners-up in Pool A, who defeated Ireland in the quarter-final stages in Japan four years earlier. But a lot had changed in world rugby during that time with Ireland no longer looking to be invited to the top table to sit with the French, the Springboks and New Zealand. Ireland were rightfully the No.1 side in the world and the others could only sit back and admire their remarkable achievements which made Ireland the most feared of all opponents in world rugby at the 2023 tournament. Prior to Ireland's game versus Scotland, both The Springboks coach, Rassie Erasmus, and Ian Foster, the coach of the All Blacks tried to unsettle Ireland by engaging in some trash talk. There were even rumours that Ireland and Scotland had conspired and decided what the score of their game would be which would mean them both progressing to the quarter-final stages at the expense of South Africa. Andy Farrell's side gave their answer in emphatic style with a performance that all nations could only hope to reach the level of. Ireland knew that they had to treat their encounter with New Zealand with the utmost respect but would not fear them. Ireland won their previous two games against the All Blacks, won three of the last four and five out of the last eight battles with their Southern Hemisphere foes.

Ireland 24-28 New Zealand
Quarter-Finals
Saturday 14 October 2023
Stade de France

Prior to the kick-off New Zealand performed their traditional Haka, drowned out by the Irish fans singing *The Fields of Athenry*, as the Ireland players watched on in the shape of a number eight, two circles made up from all 23 of Ireland's playing squad standing facing the All Blacks arrow shaped formation. The men in green were paying tribute to their former player Anthony Foley by forming a figure of eight, his number during his playing career. Foley passed away in his sleep in a hotel in Paris on 16 October 2016, aged just 42. He was a hugely popular player winning 62 caps between 1995-2005 and a highly respected coach. Ireland did the same thing at Soldier Field, Chicago in 2016 prior to recording their first ever victory over New Zealand.

Ireland's hopes of winning the 2023 Rugby World Cup were ended by a side who were now on course to win their fourth Webb Ellis Cup. There is a saying in rugby that there isn't a bad New Zealand side and having lost the opening game of this tournament to the host nation, France, questions were being asked in the *Land of the Long White Cloud* if their team were good enough to win the trophy. Let's not forget that four years ago in Japan, South Africa lost their opening game, ironically to the All Blacks, and yet went on to win the 2019 Rugby World Cup. As for Ireland, not even the fervent passion of their fans, or several renditions of *The Fields of Athenry*, was enough to see them across the finishing line in the Stade de France. A black New Zealand cloud had blanketed them.

Ireland did what they do best in games and went for the jugular of their opponents from the moment the first whistle was blown. But the All Blacks are an ever evolving team and coached by the High Priest of New Zealand rugby, Ian Foster, and assisted by Joe Schmidt who brought so much success to Ireland during his six years in charge of the national team, they upped their game from their work rate against France and put on a world class performance scoring three tries to defeat Ireland 28-24. It was the first time in 17 games the No.1 ranked side in the world had experienced the bitter taste of defeat.

IRELAND'S 17 GAME UNBEATEN RUN

Saturday, July 9: **New Zealand 12-23 Ireland**	Forsyth Barr Stadium, Dunedin, New Zealand
Saturday, July 16: **New Zealand 22-32 Ireland**	Sky Stadium, Wellington, New Zealand
Saturday, November 5: **Ireland 19-16 South Africa**	Aviva Stadium
Saturday, November 12: **Ireland 35-17 Fiji**	Aviva Stadium
Saturday, November 19: **Ireland 13-10 Australia**	Aviva Stadium
Saturday, February 4: **Wales 10-34 Ireland**	Millennium Stadium
Saturday, February 11: **Ireland 32-19 France**	Aviva Stadium
Saturday, February 25: **Italy 20-34 Ireland**	Stadio Olimpico
Sunday, March 12: **Scotland 7-22 Ireland**	Murrayfield
Saturday, March 18: **Ireland 29-16 England**	Aviva Stadium
Saturday, August 5: **Ireland 33-17 Italy**	Aviva Stadium
Saturday, August 19: **Ireland 29-10 England**	Aviva Stadium
Saturday, August 26: **Ireland 17-13 Samoa**	Stade Jean Dauger, Bayonne, France
Saturday, September 9: **Ireland 82-8 Romania**	Matmut Atlantique, Bordeaux, France
Saturday, September 16: **Ireland 59-16 Tonga**	Stade de la Beaujoire, Nantes, France
Saturday, September 23: **South Africa 8-13 Ireland**	Stade de France
Saturday, October 7: **Ireland 36-14 Scotland**	Stade de France

It was a pulsating quarter-final battle between arguably the two best sides in the world regardless of World Rugby's rankings and its' outcome hung in the balance until the final whistle was blown to end the dreams of the men in green, and their army of fans in green who were supporting them inside the stadium, the fans back home in Ireland and around the globe. Indeed, Ireland could have snatched victory. Needing a try to win the game, they launched a late attack comprising 37 phases with the players from both sides completely out on their feet before the giant All Blacks' veteran lock, Sam Whitelock (151 caps) won a penalty to send his side into a semi-final clash with Argentina who defeated Wales 29-17 earlier in the day.

However, despite not choking on the big scene, Andy Farrell's side did not feel sorry for themselves and nor did they take any level of comfort from the Herculean effort they put into the game. Their Parisian party was just gate crashed by an unwelcome guest. And, Ireland's jinx at being the only team to host a game at a Rugby World Cup final tournament and not reach the semi-final stages continued.

After the heartbreak of missing out on yet another semi-final, Johnny Sexton led the team on a lap of honour to pay tribute to the fans whose unwavering support was priceless to the players throughout the tournament. The stadium announcer played Gloria Gaynor's song, *I Will Survive*, as the players walked with heavy legs, wiping tears from their eyes around the perimeter of the pitch. Many Irish fans were left wondering if Johnny, aged 38, would survive and do a U-turn on his decision to bring the curtain down on his glittering 14-year career when Ireland's participation in the 2023 Rugby World Cup came to an end. He made 119 appearances for his country and scored 1,108 points, the highest number of points by an Irish player.

IRELAND
Tries: Aki 27, Gibson-Park 39, Penalty 64
Cons: Sexton 29, 40
Pens: Sexton 22

NEW ZEALAND
Tries: Fainga'anuku 19, Savea 33, Jordan 54
Cons: Mo'unga 21, J Barrett 55
Pens: Mo'unga 8, J Barrett 14, 69

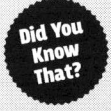

The television cameras covering the game captured Johnny after the game ended applauding the Irish fans and holding his hand on his heart with his son, Luca, walking alongside him. Although the microphones around the pitch did not capture it, Luca looked up at his father, clearly sensing his disappointment, and summed Johnny up for every Ireland fan when he said to his father: 'You're still the best, Dad'. These five words melted hearts everywhere and had tens of thousands of fans around the world reaching for a handkerchief.

2024 SIX NATIONS CHAMPIONSHIP - TRIPLE BACK-TO-BACK WINS

The 2024 Six Nations Championship was the 130th edition of the competition under all of its' previous names - Home Nations Championship and Five Nations Championship. This was the 25th edition of the competition as the Six Nations Championship and a chance for Ireland to bounce back from their 2023 Rugby World Cup experience.

Round 1
France 17-38 Ireland

Ireland were the reigning champions having won their fourth Grand Slam a year earlier and began the defence of their title away to France. It was their first competitive game since their 2023 Rugby World Cup disappointment. On 2 February 2024, Andy Farrell sent out his team at Stade Vélodrome, Marseille to face France in a Friday night game. Peter O'Mahony was the new Ireland captain following the retirement of Johnny Sexton after the 2023 Rugby World Cup. France were using the stadium, home to the French Ligue 1 football side Olympique de Marseille, as their normal home, Stade de France, was being worked on in preparation for Paris hosting the 2024 Summer Olympic Games. Stade Vélodrome is also known as the Orange Vélodrome for sponsorship purposes dating back to 2016.

On this particular evening it looked more like the Green Vélodrome given the vast number of Irish green jerseys amongst the 65,000 sellout crowd in attendance. It was a mild evening in the Provence-Alpes-Côte d'Azur region of Southern France. The motto of Marseille is 'The city of Marseille shines from its great achievements'. But, it was the visitors who came away with five points, four points for a win and one bonus point for scoring four or more tries, after achieving a comfortable 38-17 win over Les Bleus. Ireland ran over five tries from Jamison Gibson-Park, Tadgh Beirne, Calvin Nash, Dan Sheehan and substitute Ronan Kelleher. Munster's fly-half, Jack Crowley, was faultless in his conversion attempts as all five sailed between the posts and over the bar. He also scored and missed a penalty. The French Lock, Paul Willemse, was sent to the Sin Bin in the 7th minute and then shown a red card in the 30th minute. O'Mahony was sent to the Sin Bin in the 53rd minute.

It was Ireland's biggest ever away victory over France in terms of both the margin of victory and total points scored. For France, it was their heaviest home defeat in the competition in 110 years when England beat them 39-13 in the 1914 Five Nations Championship at Parc de Princes, Paris.

Round 2
Ireland 36-0 Italy

Next up for the men in green were Italy in Dublin. On 11 February 2024, Ireland were in a destructive mood and swept aside their visitors like a lion bathing in the shadow of a tree from the baking midday sun swatting an irritating mosquito with his huge tail. The *Gli Azzurri* (The Blues) left the Aviva Stadium with their tails firmly tucked between their legs after a 36-0 whitewashing. Another five points for Ireland were firmly in the bag with tries from Sheehan (2), Crowley, Jack Conan, James Lowe and Nash. Crowley scored 2/5 conversion attempts with Harry Byrne also converting one. Caelan Doris captained Ireland in the match. It was the first time Ireland managed to keep a clean sheet in the Six Nations era dating back to the inaugural competition in 2000, and it was the first time Italy had failed to score a point against Ireland. In the 1987 Five Nations Championship Ireland defeated England 17-0 at Lansdowne Road.

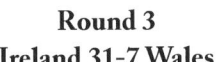

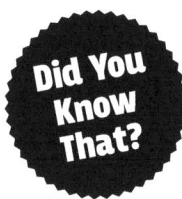

Ireland won back-to-back titles for the second time in the Six Nations era after consecutive triumphs in 2014 and 2015, and back-to-back titles for the third time overall following their triumphs in 1948 (Grand Slam winners) and 1949.

Round 3
Ireland 31-7 Wales

Successive home games came Ireland's way in Round 3 on 24 February 2024. Once again the Irish secured five points after racking-up four tries in their 31-7 victory: Sheehan, Lowe, Ciarán Frawley and Beirne. Crowley was imperious slotting over all four conversion attempts and the only penalty awarded in the game. The Munster prop, Oli Jager, made his debut for Ireland whilst Andrea Piardi became the first Italian to referee a Six Nations Championship match The win saw Ireland equal England's record of eleven consecutive victories in the competition which they set from 2015-17.

Round 4
England 23-22 Ireland

On 9 March 2024, an army of Irish fans poured into Twickenham with their team sitting on top of the table with maximum points, 15, from their opening three contests. Winning back-to-back Grand Slams was within Ireland's grasp. But, Ireland lost a pulsating game by a single point when leading 22-20 and the game clock showing the regulation 80 minutes were up, conceded a drop goal scored by Marcus Smith in the 81st minute. Lowe scored two tries and Crowley hit 4/4 penalty kicks. England reclaimed the Millennium Trophy for the first time since 2020, when they defeated Ireland 24-12 at Twickenham Stadium.

Failing is not falling. Staying down is.

Round 5
Ireland 17-13 Scotland

Going into the final game the championship was Ireland's to lose if Scotland beat them and then England won by a big enough margin over France in Paris a few hours later. It was a tense game but Ireland finally hauled themselves over the winning line to see of the challenge from Scotland winning 17-13 thanks to two tries scored by Sheehan and Andrew Porter with Crowley dipping over two conversions and a penalty. Tadgh Beirne was awarded his 50th Ireland cap in the game.

Ireland retained their Six Nations Championship crown. Ireland's comeback journey to once more becoming the No.1 ranked team in the world begins now.

IRELAND AND A JOURNEY TO THE TOP OF THE WORLD

Ireland played two Tests against South Africa in the summer of 2024, their first head-to-head Test Series since 2016 and their seventh Tour of the country. The Springboks were the No.1 ranked nation in the world having leapfrogged Ireland to top spot following their 12-11 victory over New Zealand in the 2023 Rugby World Cup final. Ireland moved back one place to No.2 post the tournament hosted by France. This would be Andy Farrell's last Test Series before taking a year's sabbatical to coach the British and Irish Lions on their Tour of Australia in 2025.

FIRST TEST - 6 JULY 2024
Loftus Versfeld Stadium, Pretoria
South Africa 27-20 Ireland
Attendance: 50,066

This was the first meeting between these two giants of world rugby since Ireland defeated the Springboks 13-8 in their Pool B game at the 2023 Rugby World Cup and was played at Loftus Versfeld Stadium which is the second biggest stadium in the Rainbow Nation behind Ellis Park, Johannesburg. Post the retirement of Johnny Sexton there was only one obvious choice for Andy Farrell to succeed the Leinster Legend as his on field General, Peter O'Mahony. South Africa had not beaten Ireland since 2016, a 19-13 win at Nelson Mandela Bay Stadium, Port Elizabeth in the Third Test of a three match Series, a victory that gave the home side a 2-1 Test Series success. Ireland's win in 2016 was their first and only victory over the Springboks in South Africa where they had never won a Test Series.

Going into the game Ireland had won the pair's three previous encounters and five of the last seven. Leinster full-back Jamie Osborne made his debut for Ireland in the game which saw the Springboks field no less than twelve of their fifteen which started the 2023 Rugby World Cup final. It turned out to be a niggly game played before a partisan crowd and for most of the 80 minutes contested it did not resemble a game that was being contested by the two highest ranked teams in the sport. At times The Springboks were sublime but also guilty of poor ball handling at the same time. The home side went in at the half-time interval 13-8 in front and in the 49th minute Rassie Erasmus sent on his 'Bomb Squad', of Vincent Koch, Malcolm Marx, Salmaan Moerat, RG Snyman and Marco Van Staden. They didn't exactly set off any explosive devices after their entrance but they did help South Africa to a 27-20 victory to put them 1-0 up in the Castle Lager Incoming Series.

Ireland scorers: Tries: Jamie Osborne, Conor Murray, Ryan Baird. Conversion: Jack Crowley. Penalty goal: Crowley.

SECOND TEST - 13 JULY 2024
Kings Park Stadium, Durban
South Africa 24-25 Ireland
Attendance: 52,000

During the week leading-up to the Second Test O'Farrell gathered his players together for 'an open and honest discussion' about how the team had collectively performed in the First Test. The Bomb Squad were not in attendance at the Ireland team meeting which was explosive after O'Mahony was dropped to the bench with Caelan Doris taking over as captain, James Ryan was moved to lock and Tadgh Beirne was switched to flanker. Dan Sheehan (knee injury) and halfback Craig Casey (concussion) had already been ruled out after being hurt in the First Test. Farrell faced the press and admitted that his decision to drop his captain had not gone down well with the Munster Legend but praised O'Mahony for how he took the decision saying: 'You don't expect those conversations to be easy and don't get me wrong, he's not accepting and he's not happy obviously but he does the right thing for the team. That's at the forefront of his mind constantly, and that's proper leadership. He understands that we want to have a look in this direction to see how it goes.'

The South African XV which took to the pitch at Kings Park Stadium was the most experienced side in the country's international history with 990 caps between them. This was their second meeting in Durban following South Africa's 12-10 victory on 6 June 1981. Their encounter 43 years previously saw South Africa take to the field of play with a collective 122 caps. Fast forward to 13 July 2024, and Eben Etzebeth was making his 122nd appearance for his country on a ground the giant Lock knew well as he played his club rugby for the Sharks.

There is a sign greeting the players when they leave the tunnel reminding them of just how high the stadium is above sea level to let them know how energy sapping playing there can be. The Springboks had not lost in Durban in eight years but Ireland were up for the fight in Durban from the moment the referee blew his whistle to let battle commence. Farrell had admitted that his players were passive in Pretoria but in a stadium nicknamed 'The Shark Tank', they fronted-up, showed their teeth and had fifteen green killer sharks who as soon as they smelled Springbok blood went in for the kill. At half-time Ireland deservedly led by 10 points, 16-6. When Doris was sin-binned in the 48th minute for a croc roll the atmosphere inside the stadium changed as the home fans roared for their team to lift their game and show the world just why they were back-to-back World Champions.

And The Springboks responded to roar back to lead 24-19 with eleven minutes left on the game clock. Handre Pollard was the player who did all the damage to the men in green kicking 8/8 penalties scoring all of his nation's points. But Irish pride was at stake as they had not lost consecutive matches since 2021 and Ciarán Frawley, who had replaced Jack Crowley (4/4 penalties) after 59 minutes, scored a superbly taken long range drop goal to reduce the deficit to just two points. It was a score of tremendous bravery and composure as Frawley, who was winning his sixth international cap, had experienced the heartbreak of missing a drop goal in Leinster's 2024 Champions Cup final defeat to Toulouse two months earlier which if he had scored would have won the game for his side. When his shot dragged agonisingly wide it meant three successive Champions Cup final defeats for Leinster.

With 90 seconds remaining at Kings Park Stadium Ireland won a scrum on their own 22-metre line. It was 'Bomb Squad' time, just diffuse the situation, hold Ireland back, let the clock turn red and see the game out, a 2-0 Test Series win in the bag. After all, Ireland had struggled with the scrum throughout the game. But game plans don't always follow the predicted script and this game highlighted this with devastating effect. Doris showed his leadership qualities and substantiated Farrell's selection choice when he rallied his troops in the scrum and told them to just keep believing as there was still time to turn the result around. The closing stages of the game were pure drama that not even a Hollywood scriptwriter could have penned. Ireland won the scrum and Frawley booted it deep into Springbok territory with the on-rushing Ireland pack bundling the Stormers' full-back Sacha Feinberg-Mngomezulu over the white line and into touch. Ireland needed to win the line-out to keep the game alive as the clock edged into added-on time. And they did. When the ball was passed to O'Mahony (a 56th minute replacement for James Ryan) the Tour captain tossed a pass back to Frawley who sent the ball high into the night sky which sailed between the posts. Toulouse was long forgotten… it was Johnny Wilkinson time and Game Over! The Test Series ended 1-1.

And, with the 2027 Rugby World Cup in Australia to look forward to, the question now is can Ireland stay on top of the summit of World Rugby after regaining the No.1 ranking from South Africa on 21 September 2024, following the Springboks' 29-28 away loss to Argentina.

WHEN IRISH EYES WERE SMILING AGAIN

On 21 September 2024, Ireland reclaimed their place as World Rugby's No.1 ranked team. Ireland returned to the summit of World Rugby following South Africa's 29-28 loss to Argentina in the penultimate round of the 2024 Rugby Championship. The Pumas defeated the reigning World Champions at Estadio Único Madre de Ciudades, Santiago del Estero, Argentina. The loss not only cost the Springboks their No.1 world ranking but the Pumas' victory also stopped them from winning the 2024 Rugby Championship title with a game to spare. The defeat was their first in five games since losing 25-24 to Ireland at Kings Park Stadium, Durban on 13 July 2024, and it cost them 1.81 points meaning their new rating of 91.77 leaves them 0.35 points adrift of Andy Farrell's team. Ireland are the No.1 team again for the first time since October 2023 when the Springboks replaced them after winning the 2023 Rugby World Cup.

MEN'S RANKINGS – OCTOBER 2024

1.	Ireland	92.12
2.	South Africa	91.77
3.	New Zealand	88.70
4.	France	86.96
5.	England	85.40
6.	Argentina	84.30
7.	Scotland	82.82
8.	Italy	79.98
9.	Fiji	79.64
10.	Australia	79.32

THE HISTORY BOOKS 1874-1947

THE BIRTH OF THE IRFU COUNT DRACULA

A WIMBLEDON TENNIS CHAMPION

WORLD WAR I HEROES

THE 1966 EASTER RISING

THE TOURING ALL BLACKS

'The direction you choose to face determines whether you're standing at the end or the beginning of a road.'
Richelle E. Goodrich

THE BIRTH OF THE IRISH RUGBY FOOTBALL UNION

In December 1874, the Irish Football Union (IFU) was formed in the south of Ireland and they were responsible for the rugby clubs in Leinster, Munster and some parts of Ulster (Connacht were not represented at the time) and in the north of the country, the Northern Football Union (NFU) was formed in January 1875, and they were responsible for the clubs in the Belfast area. On 2 November 1878, a historic meeting was held at No.9 Trinity College during which the IFU and the NFU, decided to amalgamate and become the Football Union of Ireland (FUI). However, the FUI never came to fruition and 23 days later, 25 November 1878, the IFU held a meeting at No.9 Trinity College, Dublin to discuss a proposal put forward by the NFU seeking to set up one governing body for the sport in Ireland. Then, on 11 January 1879, the IFU met again and at this meeting the proposal for an all-Ireland Rugby Union was duly accepted by both parties. The newspapers recorded the event by claiming that the Irish Rugby Football Union (IRFU) had been formed. However, the IRFU was not officially formed until 1879 and held its' first meeting at 12.00 noon on 5 February 1880 at 63 Grafton Street, Dublin. The Connacht Branch was not formed until 1900.

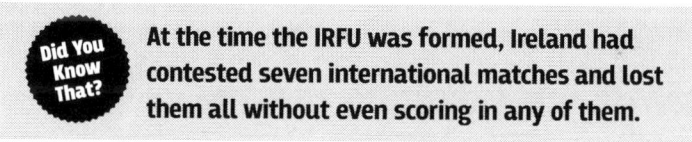

At the time the IRFU was formed, Ireland had contested seven international matches and lost them all without even scoring in any of them.

IRISH CAPTAINS

'The greatest leader is not necessarily the one who does the greatest things. He is the one that gets the people to do the greatest things.'
Ronald Reagan, President of the United States of America, 20 January 1981 – 20 January 1989

Leading your country is a unique position which is bestowed on the few who are charged with leading the many, whether their leader is a member of a political party or their captain on the field of play in a sport. On 15 February 1875, George Stack became the first player to lead Ireland in an international match. Ireland lost their inaugural international by two goals to nil. A points scoring system was not used in rugby at the time.

On 11 February 2024, Caelan Doris became the last different player to captain Ireland when they defeated Italy 36-0 in Dublin in the 2024 Six Nations Championship. He made his debut on 1 February 2020, when he started at number 8 in Ireland's opening fixture of the 2020 Six Nations Championship. However, his international bow only lasted five minutes as he had to leave the game with a concussion. Ireland won the encounter 19-12 at the Aviva Stadium. Doris was selected by his fellow players as the Irish Men's Players' Player of the Year 2023 at the Rugby Players Ireland awards.

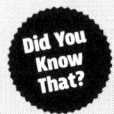 Tadgh Furlong has won 77 caps for Ireland, scoring 25 points, and also played Gaelic football and hurling for St Augustine's and Our Lady of Good Counsel College, County Wexford.

In His Own Words

'The best time I had personally on the whole tour was in Ireland. The Dublin people gave us a grand reception.'
William 'Billy' Joseph Wallace, Utility Back, New Zealand speaking about the All Blacks' 15-0 win over Ireland at Lansdowne Road on their 1905 Tour of the British Isles, France and the United States of America. It was the first time the All Blacks had embarked on a Tour outside Australasia. He played 51 matches for the All Blacks (1903-08), including 11 internationals, scoring 50 points.

THE BISHOP OF CASHEL WHO WAS GOOD WITH A BAT AND A BALL

Thomas Arnold Harvey made his debut for Ireland on 17 March 1900 in a 3-0 defeat to Wales at the Balmoral Showgrounds, Belfast in the 1900 Home Nations Championship. He impressed the Irish selectors with his displays in the green jersey during Ireland's Tour of Canada, October to November 1899. However, none of the touring party were awarded caps for any of the 11 games the team played. Harvey was an all-round sportsman, a good hurdler and a decent cricketer. A right-handed batsman and right-arm medium pace bowler, he made his Ireland cricket debut in June 1901 versus South Africa. It was an inauspicious start to his international cricket career, bowled out for just one run and no wickets taken when he was bowling. His cricket claim to fame is that when playing in a match at College Park (Trinity College) in Dublin for Dublin University against a London County XI in 1903, he caught and bowled the legendary English cricketer, W.G. Grace, for a duck. He played three times for Ireland, scoring 115 runs and took two wickets.

In total, he made 8 appearances for the Ireland rugby team from 1900-03. In 1904, he was ordained a clergyman in the Church of Ireland (Anglican) and was a curate at St Stephen's Church, Dublin. Four years later, 1908, he was appointed Rector at Lissadell, Sligo and went on to serve parishes in Portrush, County Antrim and Booterstown, County Dublin. Between 1929-35, Harvey was Professor of Pastoral Theology at Trinity College Dublin and from 1933 to 1935 he was the Dean of St Patrick's Cathedral, Dublin before being appointed Bishop of Cashel and Waterford in 1935, a position he held until 1958.

> **Did You Know That?** Two of Thomas' brothers, George Alfred Duncan and Frederick Maurice Watson, also played rugby union for Ireland, winning five and two caps respectively. Thomas' son, Brian, also a clergyman, played for Leinster. During World War I, Lieutenant Frederick Harvey was awarded the Victoria Cross, the Military Cross and the Croix de Guerre (a military decoration of France) for most conspicuous bravery and devotion to duty. He was later awarded a CBE. His Victoria Cross is on display at the Museum of the Regiments and is the only Victoria Cross currently on display in the world that shows both sides of the medal.

ON TOUR FOR THE FIRST TIME

In October 1899, some 24 years after Ireland's first ever international match, the team went on a Tour of Canada. It was the first ever Tour that Ireland had embarked on and the first ever Tour by any of the Home Nations. The IRFU Selection Committee picked a squad of 17 players, 6 were from from Dublin University, Lansdowne (5) and North of Ireland FC (4). The remaining two were from City of Derry (James Myles) and Dungannon (H. Stevenson). However, none of the 17 would be awarded a Test cap playing on the Tour as many of them had never represented the country before and after the Tour, a large number of them never pulled on an Irish jersey again. Ireland were Home Nations Champions and Triple Crown winners in 1899, but the vast majority of that side declined an invitation from the IRFU to go on the Tour because they simply could not afford to take the time off work. James Franks (Dublin University), who won his first cap for Ireland the previous year, a 9-6 win over England at Richmond, London on 5 February 1898, captained the touring side. Meanwhile, the only member of the squad who had played in the 1899 Triple Crown victory was Ian Davidson, who had played on the wing against England in a 6-0 win at Lansdowne Road and then went on to win eight more caps (1898-1902) plus one for Great Britain in 1903 when they toured South Africa. Franks won three caps for Ireland.

In some of the games, Ireland had to play with 14 men due to injuries in the squad. Ireland played 11 games, winning 10 and losing just one, their third game of the Tour when a Halifax XV beat Ireland 5-0 at Wanderers Ground, Halifax, Nova Scotia. The Halifax XV was a combined team picked from seven cruisers of the British Atlantic Fleet and the province of Nova Scotia. On their Tour, Ireland scored 150 points and only conceded 51. It was not until 1932 that the Canadians entered the international arena, although the game has been played there since 1864. The first visit by a Canadian team to Ireland was in 1903 when a Canadian representative side played 23 matches, won 8, drew 2 and lost 13. On that Tour the Canadians made their first visit to Dublin and played against Dublin University in College Park. Trinity beat the visitors by two tries and a dropped goal to nil. All in all the 1899 visit to Canada proved to be a very successful Tour for Ireland who played matches in Brockville, Halifax, Hamilton, Montreal, Ottawa, Peterborough, Quebec and Toronto. It was financed by Duke Collins from Toronto, an Irish Canadian who came from Dublin before immigrating to Canada.

> **Did You Know That?** James Myles was one of the players who got injured on the Tour. He broke his leg and had to remain in Canada until December 1899 by which time his teammates had already been home a month. During the First World War he served in the British Army with the Royal Inniskilling Fusiliers and the Royal Engineers. He won the Military Cross and achieved the rank of Major. In 1923, Myles was elected as an Independent Teachta Dala (TD) of East Donegal at his first attempt and was re-elected six times.

THE HORTICULTURIST WHO BECAME A KNIGHT

Frederick William Moore made his debut for Ireland versus Wales at the National Stadium, Cardiff on 12 April 1884 in the Home Nations Championship. Ireland lost the game by one goal to nil. Moore, a forward who played for Wanderers, was capped four times by his country from 1884-86: against Wales (1884), England (1885), and versus Scotland (1885 and 1886). Two of his brothers also played for Ireland in forward positions: D. Frank Moore, who won four caps (1883–84) playing against England (1883 and 1884), Scotland (1883) and Wales (1884), and C. Malcolm Moore, who was capped three times (1887–88), versus Scotland (1887 and 1888) and against Wales (1887). When Frederick made his debut he played in the same team as his brother, Frank, who was the captain of the Ireland team. C. Malcolm Moore was a member of the first Irish side to beat Wales, a two goals to nil victory at Lansdowne Road on 3 March 1888.

Away from rugby, Frederick Moore was a keen horticulturist and was in charge at the Royal Botanic Gardens, Glasnevin, Dublin for 43 years. In 1911, he received a knighthood from King George V, Sir Frederick William Moore.

> **Did You Know That?** Frederick Moore was the first Wanderers player to become the President of the Irish Rugby Football Union (1889-90) and during the time the four Home Nations were disputing the regulations of the game, he proposed establishing an International Board which became a reality in 1886 and became the ruling authority for rugby union.

IRELAND WIN THE TRIPLE CROWN FOR THE FIRST TIME

In 1894, Ireland won the Home Nations Championship for the first time in their history and also claimed their first Triple Crown. Ireland beat England 7-5 at Rectory Field, Blackheath,

England followed by a 5-0 victory over Scotland at Lansdowne Road and then defeated Wales 3-0 at the Ormeau Cricket Ground, Belfast.

It was the fourth time in a row that the Triple Crown had been won and on each occasion it was won by a different nation. Scotland won their first Triple Crown in 1891, England claimed their third in 1892 and Wales won their inaugural Triple Crown in 1893. Scotland achieved the feat again in 1895.

> **Did You Know That?** Lucius Gwynn was a member of Ireland's Triple Crown wining side but had played cricket for Ireland before he made his rugby debut for his country. He made his cricket debut for Ireland on 1 July 1892 versus I Zingara, an English amateur side, and went on to make 13 appearances for his country. He played his last match for Ireland in May 1902 against Marylebone Cricket Club, London whilst two of his appearances attracted First-Class status. Gwynn made his rugby debut for Ireland on 17 February 1883, a 1-0 loss to Scotland played at Ormeau Cricket Ground. He played in all three of Ireland's victories in the 1894 Home Nations Championship, making a total of 7 appearances between 1893 and 1898.

THE IRISH PLAYER WHO BECAME A WIMBLEDON TENNIS CHAMPION AND HIS LINK TO COUNT DRACULA

Francis 'Frank' Owen Stoker was born in Dublin on 29 May 1867, the youngest of five sons of Alexander and Henrietta Stoker. His father was a doctor and one of the most distinguished of Irish anatomists and was distantly related to Sir Thomley Stoker, President of the Royal College of Surgeons in Ireland, and his brother, the novelist, Abraham 'Bram' Stoker who is famous for writing his 1897 Gothic horror novel *Dracula*.

Aged 16, Frank began his rugby career in 1883 in the Second XV of Wanderers FC in the city of his birth. In 1885, he played for Irish Schools at their annual meeting with English Schools and for Dublin United Hospitals the following year when he was a medical student at Jervis Street Hospital, Dublin. He broke into Wanderers' First XV side in 1886 and on 20 February 1886, he won the first of his five caps for Ireland in a 4-0 loss to Scotland at Inverleith Sports Ground, Edinburgh in the 1886 Home International Championship. His second cap came in the 1888 Home International Championship, a 1-0 loss to Scotland at Inverleith. That same year he played against Wales (1888 Home International Championship) and a New Zealand touring side. During the 1888 Home International Championship, he played alongside his brother Ernest who also played for Wanderers His final cap came against Scotland in the 1889 Home International Championship, a 1-0 loss at Ravenhill, Belfast on 16 February 1889.

Frank was a very keen sportsman and played golf and lawn tennis. Along with his brother, Ernest, they played as a doubles' team in several Irish tennis tournaments of the mid-1880s and in 1886 were successful in a doubles semi-final at the Greystones Tournament in Bray, County Wicklow. In 1890, Frank had a new tennis partner, Joshua Pim, a fellow member of

Did You Know That?

After Frank Stoker's rugby and tennis careers came to an end, he took up golf and competed in the 1907 Irish Open Amateur Championship. He and his wife had five daughters, of whom Monica, Joan and Norma survived to adulthood. Like her father, Norma was an excellent tennis player and won the Irish Girls' Lawn Tennis Championship in 1922 (aged 17) and lost in the singles' final of the Irish Open in 1931 and 1933. Norma was also an excellent badminton player, winning the Irish Singles' title four consecutive times, 1934-37, and the Womens' Doubles title at the Irish Open in 1937 and again in 1938.

Dublin's Lansdowne Tennis Club. Pim was born in Bray on 20 May 1869, and the pair were hugely successful winning the Men's Irish Doubles Championship five times between 1890 and 1895. They also won the Doubles' title at the Northern Championships in England in 1890, 1892, 1893 and 1894.

The pair reached the pinnacle of their tennis career by winning the All England Men's Doubles Championship at Wimbledon in 1890 and 1893. They were considered by many at the time to be 'the finest combination the world had ever seen'. Pim was an outstanding player and was runner-up in the All England Men's Singles Championship in 1891 and 1892, losing to Wilfred Baddeley on both occasions. However, he was crowned Wimbledon Men's Champion in 1893 and 1894 defeating Baddeley in the final on each occasion.

He remains the only rugby international to win a Wimbledon title.

In His Own Words

'There is no football game to match rugby. If all our young men played rugby not only would we beat England and Wales, but France and the whole lot of them together.'

Éamonn de Valera who served as Taoiseach on three different occasions: from 1937 to 1948, from 1951 to 1954, and finally from 1957 to 1959. He also served as President of Ireland from 1959 to 1973, two full terms in office.

THE INTRODUCTION OF THE HOME INTERNATIONAL CHAMPIONSHIP

The first Home International Championship began in 1883, and was won by England who also claimed the Calcutta Cup and the Triple Crown. England and Scotland both played three games whereas Ireland and Wales only played twice. Ireland's first ever game in the competition was played on 5 February 1883, a 1-0 loss to England at Whalley Range, Manchester, England. Scotland defeated Ireland 1-0 at Ravenhill on 17 February 1883, meaning that despite Lansdowne Road being the spiritual and undisputed home of Irish rugby, Ireland's first ever game in the Home International Championship took place 100 miles away from Dublin.

Although Ireland's game against England was the

first meeting between the old rivals in the Home Nations Championship, it was the ninth time they had faced each other in an international rugby union game, and the ninth failure by the Irish side to beat England. However, Ireland played most of the game with only 14 men, after R.W. Hughes (North of Ireland Football Club) withdrew from the game after suffering sea-sickness on a rough ferry crossing across the Irish Sea. The match also saw the debuts of four players who were one cap internationals for Ireland; W. W. Fletcher (Kingstown), A. J. Forrest (Wanderers), A. Millar (Kingstown) and J. P. Warren (Kingstown).

The game against Scotland, again the first ever meeting between the Celtic rivals in the history of the competition, was played on what can only be described as a quagmire and despite being the home team, at one point Ireland were playing with only 10 fit players on the pitch due to injuries. No substitutes were permitted at the time. Had it not been for the valiant efforts of the Irish back line, the visitors would have ran out comfortable winners. Scotland continued their practice of awarding debuts to promising Schoolboys and included, Marshall Reid, an 18-year-old from Loretto School, Musselburgh, East Lothian.

IRISH RUGBY'S FIRST WORLD WAR HEROES

Six Irish international rugby players lost their lives during the Great War, 1914-18.

Jasper Brett: 1 cap - suicide.

Robert Burgess: 1 cap - he died after he was hit by a shell while cycling down the Rue de Dunkerque in Armentières, France.

Ernest Deane MC: 1 cap - during the Great War he served as Medical Officer in the Leicestershire Regiment on the Western Front. A Military Cross recipient for his bravery during the hostilities in the Battle of Loos, France, Deane, who was born in Limerick on 4 May 1887, risked his life to rescue men who had been caught up in German barbed wire, and whilst attempting to rescue his comrades, he was killed instantly by a gunshot to the head.

William Victor Edwards: 1 cap – when the war broke out he joined the Royal Irish Fusiliers and was gazetted 2nd Lieutenant on 22 September 1914. In December 1914, he was promoted

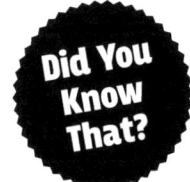

England were the inaugural winners of the Home International Championship in 1883, and in beating the other three nations became the first winners of the Triple Crown, although the phrase was not in use at the time.

In His Own Words

'Rugby is a good occasion for keeping 30 bullies far from the centre of the city.'
Oscar Wilde

to Lieutenant followed by Captain in April 1915 Edwards served in France and Flanders, Belgium and saw much action before being badly wounded in the head at the Battle of Ginchy, France in September 1916. After a period of recuperation in Ireland, he was transferred to the Royal Dublin Fusiliers and served in Salonica, Greece and Palestine, Israel. He took part in the Third Battle of Gaza (1-7 November 1917) and the capture of Jerusalem on 9 December 1917. On 26 December 1917, he was given command of 'D' Company, 7th Battalion, Royal Dublin Fusiliers but had little time to enjoy his promotion. Three days later he was killed in action near Deir Ibzia, Palestine. His body was initially buried 700 yards from the south-east corner of the village of Deir Ibzia, Palestine but was subsequently re-buried east of the village of Deis Ibsis, close to Mount Horeb at the Jerusalem War Cemetery in 1918.

Basil Maclear: 11 caps – he served as a captain with the Royal Dublin Fusiliers and was killed during the Second Battle of Ypres, Belgium. His remains were not recovered from the battlefield and his name is recorded on the Menin Gate Memorial to the Missing, located near Ypres. The Memorial is dedicated to the British and Commonwealth soldiers who were killed in the Ypres Salient of the First World War.

Vincent McNamara: 3 caps – he served in the Royal Engineers and died from gas poisoning in the trenches in Suvla Bay, Gallipoli (modern day Turkey).

Roberston Smyth: 3 caps – in 1904 he joined the Royal Army Medical Corps and served in India until the outbreak of the First World War in 1914. Smyth served on the Western Front but was sent home, invalided due to exposure to gas. He died a few months after returning home. In 1903, Roberston Smyth was also capped three times by Great Britain.

Albert Stewart DSO: 2 caps – Stewart served with the Royal Irish Rifles before being transferred to the 22nd Machine Gun Company serving as a temporary Captain then Major. He fought in the Battle of the Somme, France (1 July 1916-18 November 1916) and was killed in the Battle of Broodseinde during the Battle of Passchendaele, Belgium (part of the Third Battle of Ypres). On 1 January 1918, Stewart was posthumously awarded the Distinguished Service Order (DSO) the 'for distinguished service in the field'.

Albert Squire Taylor: 4 caps – he served in the Royal Army Medical Corps and died in the Third Battle of Ypres.

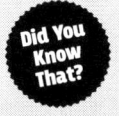

The Irish National War Memorial Gardens *(Gairdíní Náisiúnta Cuimhneacháin Cogaidh na hÉireann)* **is situated on Island Bridge, Dublin and is dedicated 'to the memory of the 49,400 Irish soldiers who gave their lives in World War I (1914-18), from a total of 206,000 Irishmen who served in the British forces during the conflict'.**

FROM A ZENITH YEAR TO A NADIR YEAR

In 1899, Ireland were an unstoppable force winning the Home Nations Championship after defeating England, Scotland and Wales. The betting man looked no further than Ireland retaining the title and Triple Crown in 1900, but as everyone knows the favourite doesn't always come good. Ireland played three, lost two, drew one, scored four points and conceded 18 to finish the campaign rooted to the foot of the table. The Champs had become Chumps, losing 15-4 against England at Richmond and 3-0 to Wales (Belfast) with a 0-0 draw versus Scotland (Dublin) sandwiched between both games. Hardly an inspiring start to the 20th Century for Irish rugby.

Did You Know That? In 1900, Wales won their second Championship title and their second Triple Crown.

SCHOOLBOY MAKES IRELAND RUGBY HISTORY

Royal School Dungannon pupil, George McAllan, made Irish rugby history on 15 February 1896 when he became the first schoolboy to play for Ireland. McAllan was 18 years and two months old when he played in Ireland's 0-0 draw versus Scotland at Lansdowne Road in the 1896 Home Nations Championship.

Did You Know That? Edinburgh Academy pupils Ninian Jamieson Finlay (1858-1936) and Charles Reid (1864-1909) were both 17 years and 36 days old when they played for Scotland against England in 1875 and 1881 respectively.

THE SICK MAN OF RUGBY

During the period from the turn of the 20th Century, up until the outbreak of the First World War in 1914, Ireland were simply awful, by far the Sick Man of Rugby in the Northern Hemisphere. Ireland failed to win a Home Nations Championship outright whilst Wales claimed 6, Scotland won 4 and England notched-up three. However, Ireland did finish joint-winners with Wales in 1906 and shared the title again in 1912, this time with England.

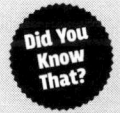

Did You Know That? Ireland played 54 international matches from 1900-14, winning 21, drawing two and losing 31: 6 wins against England, 6 versus France, 6 victories over Scotland and just the three triumphs against Wales. The two draws were against Scotland in 1900 and England in 1910.

STAND MADE FROM BEER BARRELS

When Ireland played England at Mardyke, Cork on 11 February 1905, the ground was not big enough to accommodate the demand for match tickets. But, the local brewery came to the rescue when Beamish and Crawford and J.J. Murphy loaned the IRFU hundreds of empty barrels, large and small to build a stand. The barrels were bound together with strong thick wire and incredibly the temporary Stand passed the safety test which was conducted by official engineers the day before the big clash. A crowd of 12,000, paying record gate receipts for an Ireland international match, watched Ireland beat England 17-3 in their 1905 Home Nations Championship encounter.

 The Mardyke ground was part of the site of the 1902 Cork International Exhibition. When the exhibition closed in 1903, the ground was handed over to Cork County and Cork Constitution as joint-tenants.

NO PLACE LIKE HOME

Lansdowne Road is the traditional, and spiritual, home of Irish rugby. Today it is known as the Aviva Stadium, with the naming rights of it sold to the insurance company, Aviva, after the ground was rebuilt from 2007-10. On 11 March 1878, Lansdowne Road played host to its' first ever rugby Test when Ireland played England (the first representative rugby match had taken place prior to the Test, a game between Ulster and Leinster). Ireland lost by 2 goals to nil in the 1877-78 Home Nations Rugby Championship which was contested by England, Scotland and Ireland. A goal was awarded for a successful conversion after a try was scored, for a dropped goal or for a goal from mark. If a game was drawn during this points scoring system, any unconverted tries were tallied to give a winner. If there was still no clear winner, the match was declared a draw.

In the summer of 2006, Lansdowne Road had a maximum capacity of 49,000. After it was demolished the new stadium had a capacity of 51,700 and it was opened in May 2010. In the final Test at the stadium before it was rebuilt, Ireland defeated Pacific Islands 61-17 on 26 November 2006. It was the first time the two sides had ever met.

In 2007, the GAA permitted Ireland to play their Test matches at Croke Park, Dublin which had a capacity of 82,500, until the new Lansdowne Road was fully constructed. Rugby had never been played on the hallowed turf of Croke Park before which is the spiritual home of Gaelic football and hurling. On 11 February 2007, the Irish team ran out at Croke Park for their first home game in the 2007 Six Nations Championship.

France were the visitors for this historic occasion and memorable international match in the history of Irish rugby and Les Bleus christened Ireland's temporary new home by inflicting a 20-17 defeat on them. Ronan O'Gara scored all 17 of Ireland's points thereby becoming the first Irishman to score a try and a penalty (he scored 4) in a game of rugby on the Croke Park pitch. France were crowned Six Nations Champions with Ireland runners-up, but Ireland won the Triple Crown for the second year in a row and for the third time in four years.

On 20 March 2010, Ireland played their last ever Six Nations game at Croke Park, a decider for the Triple Crown as France were Champions (their 17th title). Ireland's opponents were Scotland who inflicted a surprise 23-20 win against the Irish team, a result which saw Scotland avoid winning the unwanted "Wooden Spoon" for the third time since 2004. Declan Kidney, Ireland's coach, described the loss as: *"Not our greatest day."*

Ireland took to the new Lansdowne Road (Aviva Stadium) pitch for the first time on 6 November 2010, against the reigning Rugby World Cup holders, South Africa. The Springboks won 23-21 and prior to the historic clash they had decided to wear their white away kit and permit Ireland to wear their traditional green home jerseys. South Africa recognised the historic significance of the game and announced they would wear white even though the home team change their colours in the event of a clash.

On 18 March 2023, Ireland beat England 29-16 at the Aviva Stadium in their final game of the 2023 Six Nations Championship. The win meant Ireland had won their 15th Home Nations/Five Nations/Six Nations title, a 13th Triple Crown and their fourth Grand Slam title (their first Home Grand Slam since 1948 and Home Championship since 1985). It was a historic tournament for Ireland as they became the first team to win the Triple Crown in consecutive seasons since they achieved the same feat in 2006 and 2007. Ireland also became the first country to have their Senior Men's side and their Under-20's side achieve the coveted Grand Slam in the same year.

IRELAND HELP COIN THE PHRASE 'SPRINGBOKS'

Ireland first played South Africa on 24 November 1906 and lost their inaugural Test match 15-12 against The Springboks. The game was played in Belfast at the Balmoral Showgrounds in the south of the city before a crowd of 15,000 fans. South Africa were on a 1906-07 Tour of Europe, played 29 matches, winning 26, drawing one and losing two. Their matches also included Tests against England (drew 3-3 at Crystal Palace, London), France (won 55-6 at Parc des Princes, Paris), Scotland (lost 6-0 at Hampden Park, Glasgow) and Wales (won 13-0 at St Helen's, Swansea). The only other team to beat them was Cardiff who won 17-0 at the Arms Park in the Principality, their penultimate game of the Tour (France was their final encounter). The Springboks' victory over Wales was their most unexpected victory and resulted in the end of several of the Welsh side's international careers.

This was the inaugural Tour for South Africa and is recognised as the event that coined the phrase *Springboks* as a nickname for the South African Rugby Union team. In 1906, the sports-themed novelty song, *The Springboks' Waltz* was released to commemorate the tour.

Did You Know That?

The original Lansdowne Road ground was constructed in 1872 and was founded in 1879. The venue continues to hold the distinction of being the oldest stadium still in use for international rugby.

Did You Know That?

The 1906 Springboks were the first national team to adopt the 3–4–1 formation in a scrum.

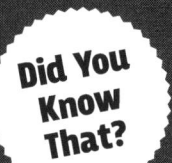

Did You Know That?

Crowds flocked to grounds to watch New Zealand play and demand for a ticket to the Ireland game at Lansdowne Road on 25 November 1905, was so high that the IRFU had to make it an all-ticket affair, the first of its' kind for an international rugby match.

SHOW BIZ APPEAL

The first touring All Blacks side came to Britain in 1905 as a very much unknown quantity. Captained by an Irishman, Dave Gallaher, they played a total of 33 games on their Tour including matches against England, Ireland, Scotland and Wales. They won 32 of the games, scored 976 points and conceded just 59. A total of 24 teams failed to score against them with their only defeat being against Wales, a 3-0 reversal at the Arms Park on 16 December 1905 in Game No.28. They beat England 15-0, Ireland 15-0 and Scotland 12-7. They also defeated France 38-8 in Paris in their final game. Gallaher was born in Ramelton, County Donegal and before returning home from the Tour, he co-wrote the classic rugby book: *The Complete Rugby Footballer* with his vice-captain Billy Stead.

In His Own Words

'Having relationships with the likes of Doc (David Irwin) and knowing Willie John (McBride) and even being able to attend an Orange Parade, because they are Irish rugby fans, counted when it came to being accepted into their environment.'
Brian O'Driscoll in an interview with *The Irish Times* speaking about a visit to Northern Ireland

THE IRISH SPRINGBOK

John Harvey Gage played for Queen's University and was capped four times by Ireland between 1926 and 1927. He holds the distinction of also being capped once by South Africa, a 17-3 victory over Australia at Newlands Stadium, Cape Town, South Africa on 8 July 1933.

 During the Second World War, Gage served as a Major in the British Army's Raiding Support Unit. He was awarded the Military Cross in 1944.

PLAYING WITH BAT AND BALL

Fourteen men have represented Ireland at international level in cricket and rugby union.

NAME	FIRST CLASS CRICKET CAPS	RUGBY UNION TEST CAPS
Robert Alexander	1	11
Robert Barnes	8	1
Harry Corley	4	8
Michael Dargan	1	2
Arthur Douglas	7	5
Jim Ganly	14	12
Lucius Gwynn	2	7
Arnold Harvey	2	8
Raymond Hunter	11	10
Finlay Jackson	3	1
Ham Lambert	9	2
Dickie Lloyd	2	19
Gerry Quinn	1	0
Kevin Quinn	3	5

Did You Know That? Richard Averill 'Dickie' Lloyd won 19 caps for the Ireland rugby team, scoring 72 points (under the current scoring system) comprising 2 tries, 16 conversions, seven drop goals and three penalties and he was widely considered to be one of the best goal kickers of his generation. He was a right-handed batsman and a right-arm medium pace bowler. Dickie went to Portora Royal School, Enniskillen, County Fermanagh and along with Samuel Beckett and Oscar Wilde, he is regarded as one of their most famous pupils. After his playing career ended, he became an international rugby referee.

In His Own Words

'What always attracted me (about rugby) was the thrill – some would say the sheer brown-trouser terror – of running out knowing nothing about your opponents. Humiliation or glory, pain or ecstasy, lie ahead. But which will it be?'

Terence Alan 'Spike' Milligan, actor, comedian, writer, musician, poet and playwright. During World War II, Spike, whose mother was English and his father Irish, played rugby with the 56th Heavy Regiment, which he described as full of 'mad hard-drinking Welshmen'.

HERE COME THE MEN IN BLACK

The New Zealand Rugby Union Test side was not always referred to as the All Blacks. When they played their first ever Test, a 22-3 win over Australia in Sydney, Australia on 15 August 1903, they were known as 'Maorilanders' or the 'Colonials'. It is claimed that they were given the tag of 'All Blacks' during their famous 1905 Tour of the British Isles, Canada and France. However, some reports suggest that the New Zealand team were referred to as 'The Blacks' in newspaper articles before 1905 as it was customary for sports journalists to refer to teams by the colour of their jerseys. In 1893, an Auckland newspaper wrote about New Zealand's forthcoming tour of New South Wales, Australia with one sports writer saying: '*I expect to see the all blacks come out on top*,' and in 1904, a sports journalist for the Wellington's *Evening Post* wrote: '*I think the chances favour the 'all blacks*'. Even their early kit colours were not black. When the New Zealand Rugby Union was formed in 1892, the team's colours were a black jersey with a silver fern leaf on the left breast, a black cap with a silver monogram, white knickerbockers and black stockings. Prior to 1892, various New Zealand representative teams had worn a variety of colours including a dark blue jersey with a gold fern leaf over the left breast. On the 1905 Tour the shorts were changed to black ones. *The Express and Echo*, a Devon-based newspaper, covered the first game of the 1905 Tour, a 55-4 win by the tourists over Devon RFC on 16 September 1905 at the County Ground, Exeter and wrote: '*The All Blacks, as they are styled by reason of their sable and unrelieved costume…*'

Did You Know That?

When a London sports news agency received The Express and Echo's match report of New Zealand's 55-4 victory, a sub-editor did not believe it and was of the opinion that an error had occurred in transmission. He then reversed the score claiming that Devon had beaten New Zealand 55-4.

WHITE KID GLOVES AND A KHAKI PUTTEE

When Ireland defeated Wales 11-6 at Ravenhill on 10 March 1906, it meant that Ireland would share the 1906 Home Rugby Championship with England who also won two games and lost one. However, had Scotland defeated England at home a week after the win over the Welsh on Saint Patrick's Day, Ireland would have been championship and Triple Crown winners. England won their encounter against Scotland at Inverleith, 9-3 In the win over Wales, Ireland's Basil Maclear, wore his customary white kid gloves and khaki puttee. A puttee (also

spelled puttie, adapted from the Hindi paṭṭī, meaning 'bandage') is a covering for the lower part of the leg from the ankle to the knee, in other words a protective leg wrap.

> **Did You Know That?** Basil Maclear finished the tournament's top scorer with eight points.

A RECORD EARLY DEFEAT

When Ireland lost 38-0 to South Africa at Lansdowne Road on 30 November 1912, it was a record loss for the nation. Since then the 38 points deficit has been equalled twice and surpassed six times.

> **Did You Know That?** New Zealand totally humiliated Ireland almost 100 years after their 1912 debacle when they beat them at Waikato Stadium, Hamilton, New Zealand on 23 June 2012. On this occasion the All Blacks ran out 60-0 winners, Ireland's record defeat.

A SECOND HOME NATIONS CHAMPIONSHIP FOR IRELAND

Two years after winning their first Home Nations Championship in 1894, Ireland were crowned Champions again in 1896. Ireland won two games and drew the other to top the table with five points from a possible six. In their opening fixture Ireland beat England 10-4 at Meanwood, Leeds and then drew 0-0 with Scotland at Lansdowne Road. Ireland needed a victory over Wales in Dublin to secure the title and the players duly delivered, winning the game 8-4 at Lansdowne Road.

> **Did You Know That?** James Sealy scored a try in their win over England. He was capped nine times by Ireland and four times by the British Isles (British Lions) during their tour of South Africa in 1896. Sealy also played hockey at international level for Ireland and in 1928 he was appointed the President of the IRFU.

WAR BRINGS A HALT TO GAMES

In September 1914, the First World War broke out across Europe resulting in the IRFU meeting and making the decision that all club games and international/representative matches would be suspended for the duration of the hostilities. Only school matches and interprovincial matches were permitted.

> **Did You Know That?** Jasper Thomas Brett was the last player to make his international debut for Ireland before the First World War. On 14 March 1914, Ireland lost 11-3 to Wales at Balmoral Showgrounds in the 1914 Five Nations Championship. During the war he served in the British Army as Second Lieutenant in the 7th Battalion of the Royal Dublin Fusiliers. He suffered shell shock and took his own life by shooting himself in February 1917, aged just 21, two days before he was due to return to active service in the frontline. He won just a single cap for Ireland.

STEPHENSON'S ROCKET

Stephenson's *Rocket* is an early steam locomotive train designed and built by Robert Stephenson in October 1829.

George Vaughan Stephenson was awarded his first international cap for Ireland in the 1920 Five Nations Championship. On 3 April 1920, he donned the green jersey for the first time in a 15-7 defeat at the hands, and the boots, of France. It was a remarkable rise to international recognition for the 19-year-old from Dromore, County Down who started the 1920-21 season in Queen's University's third XV. Stephenson knew only too well when he faced France that this was his big chance to show his full potential, his *'One Moment In Time'*, when it was all down to him to show the IRFU's selection committee why they decided to give him a chance to display his talents. Stephenson did not disappoint the selectors and played well enough to ensure that his name was one of the first written down on the Irish team sheet up until his final appearance for his country on 8 March 1930. For almost a decade Stephenson played in every Ireland international, 42, with 41 of them played consecutively. The game that ended his consecutive appearances run was played on 23 February 1929, a 16-7 loss to Scotland at Lansdowne Road in the 1929 Five Nations Championship. He missed the game through injury. He made his final appearance for Ireland on 8 March 1930, Wales winning the game 12-7 in Swansea. When he bowed out of the international scene, his haul of 42 Test caps and 89 points scored, made him the leading cap-winner and points-scorer in international history at the time of his retirement. He played at wing and centre for Ireland and broke the Irish caps record held by George Hamlet, 30 Test (27 in the Five Nations Championship) caps from 1902-11.

His father was a Church of Ireland clergyman. George played club rugby for Queen's University, North of Ireland, Middlesex, the London Hospital, Haileybury College, London Irish and Barbarians. His older brother, Henry William Vaughan, also represented Ireland, 14 caps from 1922-28.

> *'He possessed quickness of foot, swiftness and grace, and the beauty of a deceptive swerve, he played for his fellows, he made openings and gave his passes with the accuracy and judgment of a master. He was a lovely kicker and was magnificent in defence. In many a game he was a rock against which the waves of attack broke in vain.'*
>
> Welsh writer Townsend Collins speaking about George Vaughan Stephenson

> **Did You Know That?** Stephenson's 14 tries remained an Irish record until Brendan Mullin broke it on 16 March 1991 in a 28-25 defeat to Scotland at Murrayfield in the 1991 Five Nations Championship. His Test match records stood for many years: he was the leading points scorer in all international rugby until overtaken by France's Jean Prat in 1952 and his Test caps record was unsurpassed until Ken Jones won his 43rd cap in 1957. Jack Kyle took his Irish appearances record a year later, and the points record lasted until Tom Kiernan reached 90 points for Ireland in 1968.

TRUTH OR FICTION

History tells us that in 1823, William Webb Ellis, a pupil at Rugby School took a fine disregard for the rules of football and took the ball in his arms and ran with it, originating the game of rugby football. However, others think he was merely playing caid (a word used by people in some parts of Ireland to refer to modern Gaelic football). William's father, James, served as a comet in the 7th and 3rd Dragoon Guards and it is claimed that during his early life William's father was stationed in Ireland where William played caid with his friends. Although the story of William inventing rugby has become firmly entrenched in the sport's folklore, most rugby historians discount it as an origin myth.

> **Did You Know That?** Shane Horgan had a background in Gaelic football, a Meath minor (Under-18 level) who played for Bellewstown GAA Club before becoming an Irish international, winning 65 Test caps between 2000-09, scoring 105 points.

IRELAND'S FAT CUPID

Lawrence 'Larry' Quinlivan Bulger won the 1896 Home Nations Championship with Ireland, their second success in the tournament. However, he could have won a second Triple Crown for Ireland had he scored a penalty in the 0-0 draw with Scotland after they had beaten England and defeated Wales in their final game. Although nicknamed 'Fat Cupid', he was an outstanding athlete who was an Irish 220-yard sprint champion, and because of his connection with athletics, Bulger was a representative at the meeting held in the Sorbonne Building (University of Paris) on 23 June 1894, when Baron Pierre de Coubertin first suggested the creation of a modern-day Olympic Games.

On 6 February 1897, he became the first player in history to score a goal from mark in a 13-9 victory against England at Lansdowne Road. He represented the British Isles team on their 1896 Tour of South Africa, winning four caps and scoring three points. Bulger, played in all four Test matches, scoring a try in the first test at Port Elizabeth and set a tour record of 19 tries in the 21 games played.

After his international career came to an end, Bulger continued playing rugby in England. Along with his brother, Michael, he formed a medical practice in London and the two brothers were founder members of the exiles team, London Irish, in 1898. Larry and Michael turned out for London Irish on many occasions.

Both of Larry's older brothers, Daniel and Michael, were notable athletes with Michael winning five British Amateur Athletics Association Championships. Michael also won a single cap for Ireland, representing his country versus the New Zealand Natives team at Lansdowne Road on 1 December 1888, a match they lost by 4 goals to one

> **Did You Know That?** Dr Michael Bulger was one of the umpires who helped Italy's Dorando Pietri across the finishing line in the Marathon at the 1908 Olympic Games hosted by London. Pietri was dead on his feet having ran 25 miles and with only 1.2 miles to go to the Finish Line, Pietri began to feel the effects of extreme fatigue and total dehydration. There were no water points or feeding stations for Marathon runners at the Olympiad. When Pietri entered the White City Stadium, Shepherd's Bush, he took the wrong route and when the umpires redirected him, he fell down for the first time. But, with their help, he got back on his feet much to the delight of the 75,000 spectators in attendance. Pietri fell down on the track four more times, and each time the umpires had to help him up. In the end, and totally exhausted, he managed to finish the race in first place. He completed the race distance of 26 miles, 385 yards in 2 hours, 54 minutes and 46 seconds, but a full 10 minutes were needed for the final 380 yards inside the stadium. Johnny Haynes (USA) finished in second place in a time of 2 hours, 55 minutes and 18 seconds. The USA team lodged a formal complaint against the help Pietri received from Dr Michael Bulger and his fellow umpires resulting in the diminutive Italian runner being disqualified and removed from the list of finishers in the event.

A RIGHT ROYAL FAMILY OCCASION

On 8 March 1924, Frank Hewitt became the youngest man to play for Ireland. Aged 17, he helped his country beat Wales 13-10 at the Arms Park in front of two future kings - the Prince of Wales (later King Edward VIII) and the Duke of York (later King George VI). The first Labour Prime Minister, Ramsey MacDonald, was also at the game. It was a great family day out for the Hewitt's as his older brother, Thomas, also made his debut in the 1924 Five Nations Championship game against Wales and the brothers scored Ireland's tries.

> **Did You Know That?** In the 1924 Five Nations Championship, the England winger, Carston Catcheside, became the first player to score a try against each one of the other teams in the history of the tournament (Five Nations Championship).

FIRST FATHER AND SON TO TOUR WITH THE BRITISH LIONS

Andrew Daniel 'Coo' Clinch played for Dublin University and Leinster and was capped 10 times by Ireland from 1892-97 and four times by the British Lions when they toured South Africa in 1896. He made his debut for Ireland on 20 February 1892 in a 2-0 loss to Scotland at Raeburn Place, Edinburgh in the 1892 Home Nations Championship. He was a doctor and his son James Daniel 'Jammie' Clinch won 30 caps for Ireland between 1923 and 1931. James toured South Africa with the British Lions in 1924 but was not selected for any of the four Tests played. The Clinch's became the first father and son to tour with the Lions.

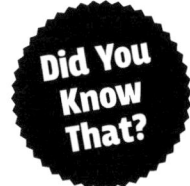

Andrew's grandfather, James Clinch, was a jeweller and made Claddagh rings in Galway in the early 1800s.

BARGAIN OF THE CENTURY

In 1923, the IRFU purchased a new ground to stage home international matches along with Lansdowne Road. They paid £2,300 for Ravenhill, a ground in south Belfast.

 **The first international played at Ravenhill was a 1924 Five Nations Championship game. Ireland lost 14-3 to England on 9 February 1924.**

DRAWING A BLANK

In the 753 Test Matches Ireland played (up to the end of the 2024 Tour of South Africa), they have only ever failed to defeat three of the sides they have played, recording at least one win over all of the others. In season 1888-89, the New Zealand Natives rugby union squad toured Britain, Ireland, Australia and New Zealand. They were a team comprising of players mainly from Māori ancestry. On 1 December 1888, they faced Ireland at Lansdowne Road in what was their first ever match against a nation. Despite trailing 3-0 at half-time, the visitors won the game 14-13. Ireland toured Namibia in 1991 and were embarrassed by their hosts who beat them in both Test Matches played. The only other team Ireland has never beaten is a President's XV selected by the Rugby Football Union.

Ireland has recorded more Test match victories against Scotland, 69, than against any other nation.

IRISH RUGBY AND THE 1916 EASTER RISING

Francis Henry Browning was born on 23 June 1868 in Kingstown (Dun Laoghaire), County Dublin. He came from an old Anglo-Irish family of County Limerick, descendants of a Cromwellian officer. The young Francis enjoyed playing cricket although his distant cousin, TB Reeves, played for Ireland's rugby union side Aged 18 he went to Dublin University where he was a regular in the Starting XI from 1888 to 1893, described as: 'A short and stockily built man with powerful forearms. An excellent wicket keeper and an effective bat with a pretty style'. He was a right-handed batsman and a wicket-keeper. In August 1888, he made his debut for Ireland's cricket team against Scotland, and went on to play for his country a further 37 times, his last game coming against Philadelphia (USA) in September 1909. Eleven of his 38 appearances (13 as captain of the side) for Ireland were given first-class status (the sport's highest ranking). When he didn't have a bat in his hand or gloves on, he was a barrister-at-law and in 1912, was appointed the President of the IRFU.

On the outbreak of The Great War (World War I) on 28 July 1914, Browning formed the Volunteer Corps, and many of his recruits joined the Royal Dublin Fusiliers to form a '*Pals Battalion*' made up of rugby players from across Ireland to fight against Germany and her partners (Austria-Hungary and the Ottoman Empire). On 26 April 1916, he was killed in the Easter Rising of 1916, serving with the part-time Volunteer Training Corps that he had formed (VTC: a form of Home Guard). On Easter Monday 1916, his VTC unit were on an exercise in the Dublin mountainside when they received news of the outbreak of the Easter Rising in Dublin (24-29 April 1916). The unit decided to return to Beggar's Bush Barracks, Dublin and the route led them across the narrow Mount Street Bridge (Conyngham Bridge) where the men of the 1 (Dublin) battalion VTC in civilian clothes with arm-bands and carrying rifles but not ammunition, came under fire from an Irish Volunteer position which was situated at Boland's Mills in the city led by Commandant Éamon de Valera. Seven of Browning's men were wounded, four of them, including Browning, fatally with a shot to the head. He was taken to Beggars Bush Barracks, Dublin and then transferred to Baggot Street Hospital, Dublin where he died two days later, aged just 47.

Days after his death, members of the IRFU Volunteer Corp wrote that Browning's work would have a 'lasting benefit on his country and his memory will always be revered by members of the corps'. The inscription on his gravestone, erected by the IRFU in Deans Grange Cemetery, Dublin includes the wording: *He will live in the memory of all as an honourable comrade and distinguished sportsman*. Francis Henry Browning was the only first-class cricketer to die in the 1916 Easter Rising.

The seven members of Irish Republican Brotherhood (IRB) Military Council who planned the 1916 Easter Rising were Eamonn Ceannt, Thomas Clarke, James Connolly, Thomas MacDonagh, Sean MacDermott, Patrick Pearse and Joseph Plunkett. All seven were executed in Kilmanhaim Gaol after the Rising. The IRB was subsequently superseded by the Irish Republican Army (IRA).

REARRANGING THE NUMBERS TO MAKE IRISH RUGBY UNION HISTORY

In 1894, Ireland were crowned Home Nations Champions for the first time. Fifty-four years later, and a re-arrangement of the numbers in that historic date, Ireland won the coveted Grand Slam for the first time in 1948.

HARRY CORLEY – DUAL SPORTSMAN AND IRELAND CAPTAIN

Harry Cecil Corley played both rugby union and cricket at international level. He played club rugby for Dublin University and Wanderers. On 8 February 1902, he made his debut for Ireland in the Home Nations Championship, a 6-3 loss to England at Welford Road, Leicester (home to the Leicester Tigers). Corley impressed the Irish selectors in his debut and was chosen for the next two games in the competition which saw Ireland defeat Scotland 5-3 at Ravenhill and lose 15-0 to Wales at Lansdowne Road. He scored in the win over Scotland by converting a try scored by Gerry Doran. One of the first

Did You Know That? When Harry retired from playing he became a rugby referee.

Irish players to specialise as a fly-half he was described in the press as a brilliant attacking player and a superb drop-kicker. In total he was capped 8 times and scored four points. He captained the team versus England on 14 February 1903, a 6-0 win in Dublin in the 1903 Home Nations Championship.

A right-handed batsman, he made his debut for Ireland's cricket team in June 1904 versus South Africa. He played nine times for his country with four of the games at First-Class status.

HORSEY BROWNE

On 14 February 1925, William Fraser Browne made his debut for Ireland in a 6-6 draw with England at Twickenham in the 1925 Five Nations Championship. Browne, nicknamed 'Horsey' played for Devonport Services Rugby Football Club and United

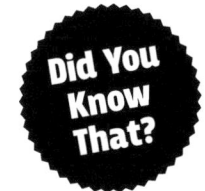

Did You Know That? In 1948, the body of W. B. Yeats was re-buried at Drumcliffe, County Sligo, "Under bare Ben Bulben's head." In 1948, the points awarded for a drop goal was reduced from 4 to 3.

Services Rugby Football Club and was capped 12 times by Ireland.

Did You Know That? He only started playing rugby when he was serving as a Lieutenant in the Duke of Wellington's Regiment.

NO WOODEN SPOONS FOR THE IRISH

A 'Wooden Spoon' is an award that is given to an individual or team that has come last in a competition and ranges from the academic to sport. In most cases it is simply a colloquial term for finishing in last position and there is no actual award presented to the unlucky 'winner'.

Since the inaugural Six Nations Championship in 2000, only Ireland and England have never finished bottom of the table and awarded the infamous and much unwanted Wooden Spoon.

NATION	WOODEN SPOONS	YEARS AWARDED
Italy	10	2000, 2001, 2002, 2005, 2006, 2008, 2009, 2010, 2011, 2014, 2016, 2017, 2018, 2019, 2020, 2021, 2002, 2023
Scotland	4	2004, 2007, 2012, 2015
Wales	1	2003, 2024
France	1	2013

However, if you go back to the start of the Home Nations Championship in 1883 then the Wooden Spoon table is as follows:

NATION	WOODEN SPOONS	LAST WOODEN SPOON
Ireland	25	1998
Scotland	24	2015
Italy	18	2023
Wales	18	2024
England	17	1987
France	13	2013

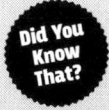 The first wooden spoon was presented at the University of Cambridge, England by the students to their fellow student who received the lowest exam marks but still scored enough marks to earn a Third-Class Degree in the Mathematical Tripos. It soon became quite famous as a booby prize:

> And while he lives, he wields the boasted prize
> Whose value all can feel, the weak, the wise
> Displays in triumph his distinguish'd boon
> The solid honours of the Wooden Spoon

The custom dates back to the late 18th century and continued until 1909. However, in 1910, the University published the exam results in alphabetical order rather than score order, and so it was impossible to identify who came last.

RUGBY'S UNOFFICIAL HIGH JUMP WORLD CHAMPION

Edward J 'Ned' Walsh was born in 1861 in Graiguenahown, Abbeyleix, County Laois and was the first former student from Blackrock College to win an Irish rugby union international cap. In season 1884-85 he joined Lansdowne Rugby Football Club and won the Leinster Cup with them in 1891. When he left Lansdowne RFC at the end of the 1892-93 season, he had also played at interprovincial level for Leinster (1886–93), making five appearances for his province. Walsh was awarded the first of his seven Ireland caps versus England at Lansdowne Road on 5 February 1887. Ireland won the 1887 Home Nations Championship game 2-0 and he went on to play in the other two matches of that year's competition, a 2-0 loss against Scotland at Ravenhill and a 1-0 loss versus Wales at Birkenhead Park, Birkenhead, England. Injury ruled him out of action until he played in all three of Ireland's games in the 1892 Home Nations Championship. His last appearance in a green shirt was a 4-0 loss to England on 4 February 1893, in a Home International Championship game played at Lansdowne Road.

 Edward Walsh was a civil servant by profession, he rose to the position of accountant general of the supreme court of Ireland before his retirement.

Ned Walsh was also an outstanding athlete. In 1885, he was the joint-holder of the Irish Amateur Athletic Association (IAAA) high jump title and that same year he won an 'unofficial' World Championship title when he beat the American high jump champion, William Fordan. The Irish Athletic team were touring the United States of America. He won the IAAA 120 yards hurdles title in 1885 and in 1886.

IRELAND INTRODUCE NUMBERED SHIRTS

When the Irish team ran out of the tunnel at Lansdowne Road on 13 February 1926, to play

England they wore numbers on the back of their jerseys for the first time. Ireland won the 1926 Five Nations Championship match 19-15. The Wales versus England game at the Arms Park on 21 January 1922, was the first time players wore numbers in the Five Nations Championship. Wales beat England 28-6.

> Shirt numbering in rugby union matches began in the 1890s and were first worn by Australia and New Zealand. At the time match programmes were in high demand which led to a lot of counterfeit ones being printed to sell to the fans going into the grounds. However, to encourage the fans to purchase the official match programme the respective Rugby Unions assigned players numbers and sold the official matchday programme inside the ground. When the Welsh Rugby Union introduced numbering they chose not to field a number 13 and also had lettered, rather than numbered, shirts. It was not until 1967 that numbering became standardised.

POOR LIGHT HINDERS PLAY

Dolway Bell Walkington was born in Belfast on 25 January 1867. Rugby union was in his family as his brother, Robert, had played for Ireland before him. Dolway made his debut in the green jersey on 5 February 1887, a 2 goals to nil win against England at Lansdowne Road in the 1887 Home Nations Championship. It was a historic occasion for Ireland as it was the first time they had beaten England following 12 previous unsuccessful attempts. In 1891, Dolway was made captain of the Ireland team, an honour he held twice in the eight games he played for his country (scored three points).

Dolway Walkington was described as one of the best full-backs produced by Ireland before the turn of the century, but as one reporter at the time noted: '*Only in bright conditions*'. Indeed, his eyesight was so poor that when the light faded during a game, he wore a monocle but removed it before he made a tackle.

> Dolway never played in the same Ireland team as his brother. Dolway won his caps between 1887 and 1891 whilst Robert represented Ireland from 1875-81. Robert Walkington became the President of the IRFU after he retired from playing.

IN THE BEGINNING

On 24 October 1874, Trinity Football Club held its' Annual General Meeting at Trinity College, Dublin. An Executive Committee was formed with the remit of arranging a rugby union match for an Ireland team to play England during the 1874-75 season. The rugby club at Trinity is the second oldest in the world having been formed in 1854, Guy's Hospital Football Club holds the distinction of being the oldest having been formed in 1843.

On 12 February 1875, Ireland's selected team of 20 players set off for London to play in the country's inaugural international match. The team and officials stayed in the Golden Cross Hotel. The game was played on Monday 15 February 1875, and Ireland lost by two goals and a try to nil in front of 3,000 spectators.

The Ireland team comprised players from the following five clubs:

Trinity	9
North of Ireland Football Club	6
Wanderers	3
Methodist College, Belfast	1
Windsor	1

When the 20 players took to the pitch at the Oval, Kennington, London they wore green and white hooped jerseys, white knickerbockers and green and white hooped stockings.

> **Did You Know That?** Rugby is believed to have first been played in England in the seventh and eighth centuries. It then spread to Ireland before the sport was banned by Royal Proclamation in 1365.

WHEN 20 BECAME 15

When Ireland played in their third international match, 5 February 1877, the number of players on each side had been reduced from 20 to 15. Ireland lost to England for the third time in succession, losing on this occasion by two goals and two tries to nil at The Oval.

> **Did You Know That?** The Oval is built on part of the former Kennington Common and was used for cricket matches from the early 18th century with the first recorded game there being played in June 1724, London versus Dartford. However, because the Common was also used for public executions of individuals convicted of serious crimes at the Surrey Assizes, London, cricket matches were then moved to the Artillery Ground, Finsbury, London during the 1740s.

LANSDOWNE ROAD NOT GOOD ENOUGH TO HOST A TEST MATCH

On 13 December 1875, the first rugby international match to be played in Ireland took place in Dublin. The IFU invited England over to play them and then decided upon a venue. Trinity's College Park Ground was deemed unsuitable to host the game as the IFU anticipated a bumper crowd. The *'Nine Acres'* at Phoenix Park, Dublin was then discussed but following due consideration, it was rejected. Henry Wallace Doveton Dunlop, the Honorary Secretary of the Irish Champion

Athletic Club offered the IFU a ground he was renting from the Earl of Pembroke. The ground was Lansdowne Road. However, the IFU declined his offer stating that the ground was: 'quite inadequate for an international rugby match'. In the end, the honour of hosting the inaugural international rugby match on Irish soil fell to the Leinster Cricket Club (LCC) and their ground at Rathmines, Dublin. The IFU paid the LCC the princely sum of £10.00 to rent their ground. England won the match by one goal and one try to nil.

> **Did You Know That?** Ireland wore white jerseys with a shamrock on the chest, navy blue knickerbockers and blue stockings. England also wore white jerseys but somehow the players were able to distinguish their teammates from their opponents.

IRELAND'S FIRST TRY SCORER

On 2 February 1880, John Loftus Cuppaidge who played for Trinity, became the first Irish player to score a try for his country. Ireland were beaten by England at Lansdowne Road in the 1880 Home Rugby Nations Cup. The score was Ireland one try, England one try and one goal. He was born on 25 December 1856 and was capped three times by Ireland, 1879-80.

IRFU ADOPT THE SHAMROCK AS THEIR EMBLEM

At the Annual General Meeting of the IRFU in 1885, the organisation decided that a shamrock would appear on the chest of the Irish jersey for all future international matches.

> **Did You Know That?** It is believed that the Patron Saint of Ireland, Saint Patrick, used the shamrock as a metaphor for the Holy Trinity of God the Father, God the Son and God the Holy Spirit.

> **Did You Know That?** After his playing career ended, John Loftus Cuppaidge immigrated to Australia and worked as a doctor. During the First World War he played a key role in setting up a medical facility in Queensland to deal with casualties of the war for which he received national recognition.

A FIRST VICTORY FOR IRELAND

On 19 February 1881, Ireland welcomed Scotland to Ormeau Cricket Ground for an 1881 Home Rugby Nations Cup game. The matches for this season were decided on goals scored. A goal was awarded for a successful conversion after a try was scored, for a dropped goal or for a goal from a mark. If a match ended in a draw then any tries that had not been converted were added up to give a winner. However, in the event that there was still no clear winner, the game was declared a draw.

Ireland had never won a Test match before but on this occasion they finally removed the albatross from around their neck by beating the Scots 1-0; Ireland scored a drop goal to the visitors' try. John Bagot scored the drop goal.

Ireland's only other game in the 1881 tournament was a 2-0 loss to England at Whalley Range whilst Wales competed in the competition for the first time and were humiliated by England, losing 8-0 at Richardson's Field, Blackheath, England.

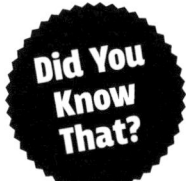

John Bagot scored Ireland's drop goal in his last international. The match also saw Scotland play a three man three-quarter line, the first time this style of play had been adopted in an international match.

THE PRESIDENT PLAYING CAPTAIN

When Ireland competed in the 1883 Home Rugby Nations Cup games, George Scriven was not only the captain of the Ireland team, but he was also the President of the IRFU.

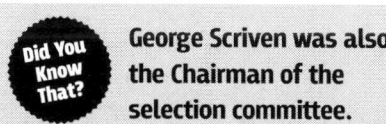

George Scriven was also the Chairman of the selection committee.

A FIRST MEETING WITH WALES

On 28 January 1882, Ireland met Wales in an international match for the first time. Ten of the Irish XV were Test match debutants as 10 of the original side selected withdrew from the game. Ireland were down to 14 men when Kennedy had to leave the field of play through injury and JR Atkinson suffered a serious nose injury. Fights broke out between the players at Lansdowne Road throughout the game which Wales won by four tries to Ireland's two goals. Not even the Irish referee, W

J Goulding could prevent the numerous on-field battles which unfolded around him. It was Wales' first ever victory against an international side.

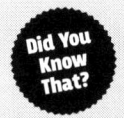 **Thomas St George McCarthy (Dublin University) played in the match for Ireland. Two years later he became a founder member of the GAA when he attended their inaugural meeting at Hayes' Hotel, Thurles, County Tipperary on 1 November 1884.**

TWO WELSH PLAYERS CAPPED BY IRELAND

When Ireland played Wales on 12 April 1884 at the Arms Park in the 1884 Home Nations Championship, Ireland were two players short as Ernest Greene and Robert Gibson Warren never made the trip to the Principality. Ireland played two uncapped Welsh players in order to be able to field a starting XV.

No definitive information exists to verify who the two Welsh players were but it is believed they were Charles Jordan and Harry McDaniel, both Newport Rugby Football Club players. Wales won the game by two tries and a drop goal to nil. Neither Jordan nor McDaniel were ever capped by Wales.

 **Charles Jordan's brother, Martyn, played in the same Newport RFC team as him and Martyn was capped three times by Wales: versus England and Scotland in 1885 and against Scotland in 1889.**

FLYING THE FLAG

In 1925, the IRFU had its' own flag designed. The flag incorporated the arms of the four Provinces in Ireland and was the only flag the IRFU permitted to be flown at home international matches.

 **It was not until 1932, when the IRFU permitted the Irish tricolour to be flown alongside the IRFU flag at home international games following a meeting held by the organisation on 5 February 1932. This occurred for the first time on 13 February 1932, Ireland lost 11-8 to England at Lansdowne Road in the 1932 Home Nations Championship.**

CONNACHT'S FIRST CAPPED PLAYER

Henry John Anderson was born in Cape Town, South Africa on 17 March 1882. On 14 February 1903, Anderson became the first Connacht player to be capped by Ireland when they beat England 6-0 Lansdowne Road in the 1903 Home Nations Championship. He went on to be one of the founders of Galwegians Rugby Football Club in Connacht in 1922.

In 1945, Anderson became the first Connacht Branch representative to serve as President of the IRFU. His tenure in office lasted just one year.

IRELAND VERSUS WALLABIES CANCELLED BECAUSE OF THE WAR

On 21 July 1939, the Australian Rugby Union team set sail from Freemantle, Australia onboard RMS Mooltan for their planned Tour of Britain and Ireland during which they would play 28 matches. On 1 September 1939, when the squad and officials were still at sea, Britain declared war on Nazi Germany. The following day they arrived in Plymouth, England to learn the news that their Tour was cancelled because of the war. However, they did not return home immediately and stayed two weeks in Torquay where they spent a lot of their time filling sandbags. The team met King George VI and Queen Elizabeth and were taken on a tour of Twickenham. Before travelling home, they were given a cocktail party at The Savoy Hotel, London hosted by the British Sportsman's Club. But, not all of the players went home, some stayed behind to join the British Army and Royal Air Force to fight in the war.

The Wallabies were due to play England, Ireland, Scotland and Wales. The IRFU had to pay their agreed share of the Tourists' expenses, £1,050.

DES O'BRIEN – IRELAND'S RUGBY, SQUASH AND TENNIS STAR

Desmond Joseph O'Brien was born in Dublin on 22 May 1919, and was a member of Ireland's 1948 Grand Slam winning team. He won two Leinster Senior Cup titles with Old Belvedere in 1940 and 1941 before winning his first cap for Ireland when he was 28 years old. He wore the green jersey for the first time on 14 February 1948, an 11-10 victory over England at Twickenham in the 1948 Five Nations Championship when he was playing his club rugby for London Irish.

His selection at No 8 against England saw him play alongside James McCarthy and James McKay in a back row that became renowned as one of the best in world rugby at the time. 'The

Three Musketeers' were that good they are considered to be the finest ever back row fielded by Ireland. In total the famous trio played 14 games together from 1948 and 1952, with Ireland winning 10, drawing one and only tasting defeat three times in these matches. He captained Ireland on their 1952 Tour of Argentina where they won six, lost one and drew two of their nine games. O'Brien won the Five Nations Championship with Ireland again in 1949 (Triple Crown winners) and 1951 and claimed a total of 20 caps for his country, one of the greatest back-row forwards of his generation. In 1966, he managed the British and Irish Lions on their Tour of Australia and New Zealand, defeating the Wallabies 2-0 but losing 4-0 to the mighty All Blacks.

> **Did You Know That?** O'Brien also represented Ireland 14 times in international squash matches and was a Welsh hockey international and Welsh tennis reserve.

IRELAND'S 500TH TEST CAP

On 11 March 1933, Charles Beamish had the honour of becoming the 500th player to be capped in an international match by Ireland. Wales were the opponents, losing 10-5 to Ireland at Ravenhill in the 1933 Home Nations Championship. Beamish was capped 12 times by Ireland, scored three points, and also represented the British Isles (later named, British and Irish Lions) on their 1936 Tour of Argentina.

> **Did You Know That?** He was one of the four Beamish brothers, his elder brother George also played for Ireland and captained the side when Charles made his debut. During the Second World War, Charles served as an RAF pilot and his two other brothers, Cecil and Victor, were also accomplished sportsmen whilst all three also served in the RAF.

THE BRITISH AND IRISH LIONS

'It's not the size of the dog in the fight, it's the size of the fight in the dog.'
Mark Twain

IRELAND'S LION KINGS

In 1888, the British & Irish Lions began their touring tradition when a party of 22 players from England, Ireland, Scotland and Wales, captained by Robert Lionel 'Bob' Seddon (England), one of only four capped players in the squad, embarked on a Tour of Australia and New Zealand that lasted 249 days. The first British & Irish Lions Tour was the brainchild of three England cricketers at the time, James Lillywhite, Arthur Shrewsbury and Alfred Shaw, who famously bowled the first ever ball in Test cricket in 1876-77. England provided the majority of the players for the inaugural Lions' Tour, although it also included Richie Thomas (Wales), three Scottish players (Robert and William Burnet and Alex Laing) and an Irishman, Arthur Paul, who was born in Belfast on 24 July 1864. However, Paul never played a rugby union international for Ireland, but he did represent Lancashire as a first-class cricketer.

Since Robert Seddon, only 12 Irish players have been afforded the unique honour of captaining a British & Irish Lions touring side.

1896	Tom Crean (Lion No.53, Ireland) v South Africa
1910	Tommy Smyth (Lion No.183, Ireland) v South Africa
1938	Sam Walker (Lion No.311, Ireland) v South Africa
1950	Karl Mullen (Lion No.333, Ireland) v Australia & New Zealand
1955	Robin Thompson (Lion No.367, Ireland) v South Africa
1959	Ronnie Dawson (Lion No.388, Ireland) v New Zealand and Australia
1968	Tom Kiernan (Lion No.428, Ireland) v South Africa
1974	Willie John McBride (Lion No.433, Ireland) v South Africa
1983	Ciaran Fitzgerald (Lion No.579, Ireland) v New Zealand
2005	Brian O'Driscoll (Lion No.697, Ireland) v New Zealand
2009	Paul O'Connell (Lion No.738, Ireland) v South Africa
2017	Peter O'Mahony (Lion No.832, Ireland) v New Zealand

Did You Know That? The inaugural British & Irish Lions Tour was a hugely successful one. They played 35 games in New Zealand and Australia, winning 27, drawing six and losing only two. However, the 1888 Tour was tinged with tragedy, when Bob Seddon, who had won three caps for England in 1887, drowned in Australia after a sculling accident on the Hunter River in New South Wales, halfway through the Tour. He was just 27 years old. In 2013, Sneddon and his teammates from the 1888 Tour were honoured with induction into the International Rugby Board Hall of Fame.

SPEAR TACKLE TAKES O'DRISCOLL OUT

In 2005, the British & Irish Lions toured New Zealand, playing 11 games which included three Test matches against the All Blacks. The first Test was played on 25 June 2005, at Lancaster Park, Christchurch and will forever be remembered for one of the ugliest incidents that has ever happened in a game of international rugby. Brian O'Driscoll was the Lions' captain, their talisman and unquestionably one of the best players in the world. He was key to a Test Series win over the All Blacks and they knew it. Less than two minutes into the game Tana Umaga, the New Zealand captain, and Kevin Mealumu carried out a dangerous tackle on O'Driscoll. At a ruck, the pair each grabbed one of O'Driscoll's legs and drove him into the ground. To protect his head from hitting the hard surface first, he twisted his body meaning that his shoulder took the full force of the landing. His shoulder was instantly dislocated, his tour was over. Clive Woodward, the Lions' coach, was enraged and adamant that it was a spear tackle but the All Blacks' pair walked away from the incident unpunished by the French referee, Joel Jutge. Woodard referred the incident to the International Rugby Board's citing commissioner, William Venter. Incredibly, Venter decided that based on the video footage available, not to refer the matter to a disciplinary tribunal.

Jutge admitted in 2017 that he should have shown at least one red card to Umaga and Mealamu for the tackle. Too little, too late, the Lions lost the game 21-3 and lost the Series 3-0.

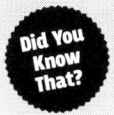 **New Zealand were so incensed by the Lions' outraged response that when they won the second Test a week later, 48-18 at Wellington Regional Stadium, Wellington, Umaga screamed expletives into the camera as he walked off the pitch.**

ANDY FARRELL'S WAR CRY TO THE BRITISH & IRISH LIONS

During the 2013 British and Irish Lions Tour of Australia, Andy Farrell delivered a speech that Al Pacino's character, Tony D'Amato the Head Coach of the Miami Sharks American football team, would have been proud of following D'Amato's own captivating speech to his players in the 1999 movie *Any Given Sunday*.

In the first Test against The Wallabies in 2013, the Lions, coached by Warren Gatland, beat them 23-21 at Suncorp Stadium, Brisbane. The Lions should have wrapped up the three Test series with victory in the second Test but narrowly lost the game 16-15 in the Etihad Stadium, Melbourne. The Lions led the game 15-9 with 18 minutes remaining thanks to five penalties from Leigh Halfpenny (Wales). In the 74th minute Adam Ashley-Cooper scored a try which was converted by Christian Leali'ifano, 16-15 to the Wallabies. Halfpenny had a chance to seal Test Series glory for the Lions in the last minute of play with a penalty but his kick fell short of the posts.

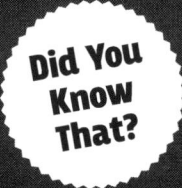

Did You Know That?

Before their 2013 Tour of Australia, the Lions played the Barbarians on 1 June 2013 in Hong Kong, to celebrate the 125th anniversary of the first Lions tour. They won the game 59-18 at Hong Kong Stadium with Ireland's Paul O'Connell scoring a try in the win and Johnny Sexton converting two of five conversion attempts.

Prior to the Third and final Test, Andy Farrell, who was an Assistant Defence Coach on the Tour stood up in front of the players in their briefing room and delivered the following speech.

'Last weekend, good effort, good effort as far as D's concerned. A lot of pressure coming on us, especially on our own line. They kept pounding away and pounding away and it was a gallant effort boys. That's what I would say to you if I was your club coach or your international coach, but I'm not. We're your Lions coaches. And a good defence, or good spirit ain't enough at this level. On D, we cannot allow our emotional energy to dip whatsoever. You know why?... Because there is no tomorrow... there is no tomorrow. We are taking them boys to the hurt arena this weekend. Because our mentality is going to be a different mentality to what the British Lions teams have had over the last 16 years. Right, a different mentality. Because the last 16 years, it's been about failure. You shock yourself by taking yourself to another level. Because that's what being a Lion is about. It ain't about anything other than that. It ain't about taking part, it ain't about being here, it's about winning.'

It was all the motivation the Lions players needed when they crossed the white line at the ANZ Stadium, Sydney on 6 July 2013 in the third Test. The tourists eased to a comfortable 41-16 victory to take the series 2-1. Halfpenny found his shooting boots again and scored five from five penalties and made three of his four conversion attempts. Johnny Sexton scored a try in the win and three of his fellow Irish teammates also played: Tommy Bowe and Sean O'Brien with Conor Murray coming on in the 51st minute.

The 2013 Test series against Australia attracted a record sporting attendance figure to each stadium used. The first test saw 52,499 at Suncorp Stadium, the second test drew 56,771 fans to the Etihad Stadium and a mammoth crowd of 83,704 attended the deciding Test at the ANZ Stadium.

LEADER OF THE PACK

Ireland's Willie John McBride has been capped more times by the British & Irish Lions than any other player since they first toured the southern hemisphere in 1888. The Ulsterman won 17 Lions' caps in five Tours from 1962-74. Dickie Jeeps (England) is second with 13 caps (1955-62) whilst three men share joint-third place with 12 caps each – Mike Gibson (Ireland, 1966-71), Graham Price (Wales, 1977-83) and Alun Wyn Jones (Wales, 2009-21).

> 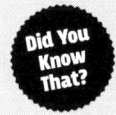 Syd Millar, who played for Ireland (1958-70), and who was Ireland's coach from 1955-59, was capped nine times by the Lions. He passed away on 10 December 2023 aged 89.

MOST POINTS BY AN IRISH LION

Tom Kiernan has scored more Test points for the British and Irish Lions than any other Irish player. The Cork-born Kiernan (7 January 1933) is seventh in the all-time points table having scored 25 points in his five Lions Tests from 1962-68, captaining the Tour of South Africa in 1968 and played in all four Tests. Kiernan won 54 caps for Ireland as a full-back between 1960 and 1973, and when he hung up his boots he was Ireland's most capped international, Ireland's most experienced captain and his country's record scorer with 158 points to his name. On 21 October 1978, he famously coached Munster to a historic 12-0 victory over a touring New Zealand side at Thomond Park. It was the first time any Irish side, including the international team, had defeated the all-conquering All Blacks.

Kiernan played for Ireland against the All Blacks in 1963 and 1973 and his Munster side were not expected to win but on the day, the Irish side dominated the game and were roared on to victory in front of a partisan 12,000 crowd. After the game, the All Blacks' winger, Stu Wilson, said that they were lucky to get nil and it seemed like they were playing in front of a crowd of 100,000 such was the noise inside the ground. Donal Canniffe captained Munster. It was the only defeat on their 1978 Tour of Britain and Ireland, winning all 17 of their other games including Test wins over England (16-6), Ireland (10-6), Scotland (18-9) and Wales (13-12) plus an 18-16 victory in their final game against the Barbarians at the Arms Park. It remained the All Blacks' only defeat by any Irish team until they lost to Ireland in 2016 with the victory inspiring a stage play entitled *Alone it Stands*.

Kiernan went on to become a highly influential administrator, serving as the President at the IRFU and Director of the 1999 Rugby World Cup. He served as the Chairman of the Five Nations Championship and was an influential figure in the formation of the European Rugby Cup in 1995, serving as its first Chairman for four years. In 2001, Kiernan received the International Rugby Board Distinguished Service Award. His nephew, Mike Kiernan, also played for Ireland and the Lions. Tom Kiernan died on 3 February 2022, aged 83.

>  However, Tom Kiernan is a long way off the all-time Lions points scorer, Scotland's Gavin Hastings who notched up 69 points in 7 Tests from 1986-93.

THE IRISH COMMANDO

James William 'Bill' McKay served as a commando in the British Army during the Second World War. He was a member of 'The Chindits', a special Operations Unit of the British and Indian Armies which saw action in 1943-44 during the Burma Campaign. The special unit as formed by British Army Brigadier Orde Wingate with their priority being long-range penetration missions, attacking Japanese troop facilities and lines of communication deep behind the Japanese lines.

'He was with the Chindits in the war, and General Orde Wingate was the madman who didn't give any thought to his own life or those of his soldiers. They had outstanding victories. Bill went behind Japanese lines into Burma and I think that out of something like a hundred men only six came back. He was through it. I had him with me on the British and Irish Lions Tour to New Zealand in 1950 when I was the captain and he was a terrific help to me. It was a bit daunting I can tell you because I was given 29 players and we got on a boat at Liverpool that went out through the Panama Canal and back through the Suez and it took us nearly seven months to do New Zealand and Australia.'

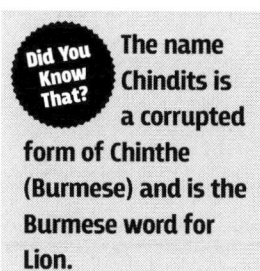
Did You Know That? The name Chindits is a corrupted form of Chinthe (Burmese) and is the Burmese word for Lion.

Karl Mullen speaking in 2003 about his fellow 1948 Grand Slam winning teammate, Bill McKay

Mullen was an intern in Jervis Street Hospital, Dublin at the time. 'You took time off without pay. We got £2.50 allowance and it paid for the stamps to send letters home. But you didn't have to buy anything then, because you couldn't cope with the presents from the locals. You were brought to factories every week and you got dresses for the girls at home and all the apparel you could possibly take,' added Mullen.

WHEN THE LION KING GAVE WORDS OF WISDOM TO THE CUBS

Prior to the British & Irish Lions first Test against Australia in 2001, the former Legendary Ireland British and Irish Lions captain, Willie John McBride, was asked by the Lions' Tour Manager, Donal Lenihan (52 caps for Ireland 1981-92, scoring four points), to make a speech to the squad at their traditional ceremony of awarding a Lions' shirt to a previously uncapped player. McBride is the 'Greatest Ever Lion' and his inspirational speech would have brought the dead back to life.

'Thanks, ah, Don. I don't want to sort of stand. I want to sit with you. Men, I think it is a great privilege to be asked to come along here today, and just be part of this. I'm sure you are excited. Biggest day in your rugby lives for most of you. Biggest day in your rugby lives. I was never a professional rugby player. Many changes over the last number of years, but at this stage some things never change. Like the pain in the gut, the agony and the worry. That should be there. Today, here, you are representing four countries. Today is putting another layer of Lions' history on the table. There are times in this game today where you've got to reach into the inner depths of your inner being, to pick it up and go again. That's what it's about. And finally it's about winning. That's the only thing that's acceptable at this stage. Worth it, it's worth all that pain. All that agony. You'll never forget it for the rest of your life. Good luck, and you make your own luck in this game.'

The Lions, coached by Graham Henry, won the first Test 29-13 at Brisbane Cricket Ground.

The stadium is nicknamed *The Gabba*, which derives from the suburb of Woolloongabba, in which it is located. But, the Lions lost the Test Series 2-1 following a 35-14 loss at Colonial Stadium, Melbourne and a 29-23 defeat at Stadium Australia, Sydney. The Lions were so close to victory in the final Test, with the scores standing at 23-23 after 68 minutes. Matt Burke then kicked two penalties to give Australia a 29-23 advantage, but the Lions created one final chance to score a try and make the conversion they needed to win with a lineout in the Wallabies' 22. Keith Wood (Ireland) threw to his captain, Martin Johnson (England), but the Australian lock, Justin Harrison, pulled off the steal of the Series to take possession which secured victory for the home nation.

THE LIONS' RECORD TRY SCORER

Ireland's Anthony Francis O'Reilly's place in the history of the British & Irish Lions is assured. Born in Dublin on 7 May 1936, the winger scored a record six Test tries for the Lions winning 10 caps for the Touring side from 1955-59. The legendary J.J. Williams (Wales) scored five Test tries for the Lions from his seven caps (1974-77) also from the wing. O'Reilly made his Ireland debut on 22 January 1955 in a 5-3 loss to France at Lansdowne Road in the 1955 Five Nations Championship. He was just 18 years old at the time and went on to make a further 28 appearances for Ireland, scoring four tries: versus France on 28 January 1956, versus Scotland on 25 February 1956, versus Wales on 14 March 1959 and versus France on 26 January 1963. His final game in the green jersey was against England on 14 February 1970, a 9-3 loss at Twickenham Stadium in the 1970 Five Nations Championship, following a six year hiatus from international rugby union.

O'Reilly went on two tours with the Lions, 1955 to South Africa and 1959 to Australia and New Zealand. He made his debut for the Lions on 29 June 1955, scoring two tries in a 32-6 win against a Northern Universities team at Ellis Park, Johannesburg. In total, he played 15 times on the Tour including all four Tests against the Springboks, scoring a total of 16 tries. His first Lions' cap came on 6 August 1955, playing on the wing before 95,000 fans at Ellis Park, scoring a try in a close game which the Lions won 23-22. He scored another try in the fourth

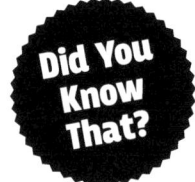

Graham Henry (born in New Zealand, and the coach of Wales at the time) was the first coach of the British & Irish Lions who was born outside the British Isles. Martin Johnson was the first player to captain two Lions' Tours having captained the 2007 Tour of South Africa which they won 2-1 in a three Test Match Series.

Test, a 22-8 defeat at Crusaders Ground, Port Elizabeth. The series ended in a 2-2 draw.

On the 1959 tour, he played in 23 of the 33 games and scored 22 tries, including a hat-trick versus King County/Counties in a 25-5 win at Taumarunui, New Zealand on 19 August 1959. O'Reilly played in all six Tests of the Tour, two versus the Wallabies and four against the All Blacks, scoring tries in the two Test wins against Australia and in the first and fourth Tests against New Zealand. His total of 38 tries for the Lions on two tours remains a record.

Between 1955 and 1963, Tony also guested for the Barbarians, making 30 appearances and scoring 38 tries and remains the Baa-Baas record appearance maker and record try scorer.

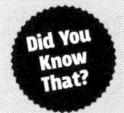

Did You Know That? When he made his final appearance in an Irish jersey he did so as an 11th hour replacement for Frank O'Driscoll, father of the legendary Brian O'Driscoll, to deny Frank the opportunity of winning a Test cap.

WHEN THE LIONS CLIMBED MOUNT EVEREST

'It is not the mountain we conquer, but ourselves.'
Inspirational words from Sir Edmund Hilary who on 29 May 1953, along with a Sherpa mountaineer, Tenzing Norgay, became the first climbers confirmed to have reached the summit of Mount Everest, the highest mountain on earth.

In 1997, the British & Irish Lions were on Tour in South Africa. Ian McGeehan was the Lions' head coach but alongside him he had a fellow Scot, Jim Telfer, as his assistant/forwards coach. Telfer was born in Pathhead, Midlothian on 17 March 1940, and won 22 caps for his country at No 8 between his debut against France in 1964 and 1970, captaining his country on most of his appearances. He was selected for two British & Irish Lions tours, the first to New Zealand in 1966, then to South Africa two years later. He also toured New Zealand with Scotland in 1967. Following his retirement from playing Telfer went on to coach the 1984 Five Nations Championship Grand Slam winning Scotland side. Telfer coached Scotland from 1980-84, 1988-93 as an Assistant Coach, 1993-95, was Scotland's Director of Rugby from 1995-98, Scotland coach again 1998-99 and then assistant coach on the national team from 1999-2003. He was also an assistant coach of the British and Irish Lions in 1983.

Telfer was made of granite despite the fact that he wasn't born in Aberdeen, the *Granite City*, but his motivational speeches to his teammates and to the players he coached is legendary. Prior to the Lions' first Test Match versus the Springboks on 21 June 1997, Telfer who himself was capped six times by the Lions from 1966-68 (23 games in Australia and New Zealand in 1966 and 11 games in South Africa in 1968), sat the players down and spoke to them about what it meant to represent the Lions.

'This is your f***ing Everest, boys. Very few ever get a chance in rugby terms to get for the top of Everest. You have the chance today.

Being picked is the easy bit. To win for the Lions in a Test match is the ultimate, but you'll not do it unless you put your bodies on the line. Every one jack of you for 80 minutes. Defeat doesn't worry me. I've had it often and so have you. It's performance that matters. If you put in the performance, you'll get what you deserve. No luck attached to it. If you don't put it in, then we're second-raters.

They don't respect you. They don't rate you. The only way to be rated is to stick one on them, to get right up in their faces and turn them back, knock them back. Outdo what they do. Outjump them, out scrum them, out ruck them, outdrive them, out tackle them, until they're f***ing sick of you.

Remember the pledges you made. Remember how you depend on each other at every phase, teams within teams, scrums, lineouts, ruck ball, tackles.

They are better than you've played against so far. They are better individually or they wouldn't be there. So it's an awesome task you have and it will only be done if everybody commits them self now.

You are privileged. You are the chosen few. Many are considered but few are chosen. They don't think f*** all of us. Nothing. We're here just to make up the f***ing numbers. No one's going to do it for you. You have to find your own solace - your own drive, your ambition, your own inner strength, because the moment's arrived for the greatest game of your f***ing life.'

The Lions won the first Test 25-16 at Newlands Stadium, Cape Town. Three Irish players played in the game: Jeremy Davidson, Paul Wallace and Keith Wood. They then won the second Test 18-15 at King's Park, Durban with Ireland's Davidson, Wallace and Wood starting again and Eric Miller coming on as a substitute. The Springboks won the Third Test but lost the Series 2-1. Only Davidson and Wallace featured in the game. Wallace replaced his injured Ireland teammate, Peter Clohessy, before the start of the Tour.

Telfer's Everest Speech helped the Lions conquer their Everest in South Africa by defeating the reigning Rugby World Cup holders. It was the last occasion on which the Lions returned victorious from a tour until their victorious tour of Australia in 2013.

FIRST TEST MATCH SUBSTITUTE

Ireland's Mike Gibson became the first substitute in a Test Match when he came on for Barry John during the British and Irish Lions Tour of South Africa in 1968. The Welsh fly-half started the game at Loftus Versfeld, Pretoria on 8 June 1968, but broke his collar bone 15 minutes into it. When John was lying on the pitch injured, Gibson was sitting in the stands wearing his tour blazer as substitutes could not change into their kit until a doctor had authorised the need for a replacement.

In March 1968, the IRB announced that substitutions would be permitted to replace an injured player in official trial games and international representative matches. Ireland's Barry Bresnihan became the sport's first replacement when he came on for an injured Mike Gibson during the British and Irish Lions opening game of their 1968 Tour of South Africa. Ireland's fly-half got injured in the 20-12 win over Western Transvaal in Potchefstroom.

EPILOGUE

'Sport has the power to overcome old divisions and create the bond of common aspirations.'
Nelson Mandela

Every time an Ireland player takes to the pitch at the Aviva Stadium, Dublin he is taking one step across the white chalk line to represent the green jersey of his country, but at the same time, he is crossing over a line on to a green area that is hallowed ground steeped in history, Irish Rugby history. For the grass laden turf at the home of Irish rugby since 2010, it was built on the same site that Ireland's former home of Lansdowne Road hosted Ireland international matches from 1878 to 2006, sends echoes of the past rushing through the veins of every Ireland player who makes an appearance there.

'The ground that a good man treads is hallowed.'
Johann Wolfgang von Goethe

The Aviva Stadium is a multi-purpose venue which also hosts the Republic of Ireland's home international football matches, just as Lansdowne Road did before it. On 1 September 2012, the stadium hosted an American College Football game billed as the *Emerald Isle Classic*, with the Notre Dame Fighting Irish defeating the Navy Midshipmen 50-10. Some 40,000 American visitors descended on the Irish capital such was the attraction of the game, many of them just wanting to say they visited the homeland of their parents, grandparents or great grandparents. In other words, bragging rights for those 4th July American Independence celebrations.

The Stadium has also been a concert venue for some of the world's leading artists and bands including Neil Diamond, Madonna, Robbie Williams, Rhianna, Billy Joel, AC/DC, Phil Collins, Eagles and the mega Irish bands, Westlife, The Script. But, ask any Ireland fan who has watched his team play at Lansdowne Road or at the Aviva Stadium, if he or she would have swapped their match ticket to go and listen to any of the very popular musicians who graced a stage at the venue, and the reply is a 100% unequivocal "*No.*" There is nothing quite like watching Ireland play in Dublin.

To paraphrase the late Legendary Dublin singer, Sinead O'Connor, *nothing really compares to it*. It does not even come down to a flip of a coin unless of course, you are an Ireland rugby fan in possession of a doubled headed coin.

And, for a player representing Ireland in a Test Match, a cap is more important to him than a ticket stub from a concert. At the concert you know you will hear songs like *Sweet Caroline, Like A Virgin, Millennium* (nothing whatsoever to do with the home of Welsh rugby), *We Found Love* (parts of the video were filmed in a Belfast Chip Shop), *Uptown Girl, You Shook Me All Night Long, In The Air Tonight, Hotel California, You Raise Me Up* or *Hall of Fame.* However, before the concert all of these great songs could quite easily be downloaded on your phone weeks, if not months, before the artist strutted out on to the stage at Lansdowne Road or at the Aviva Stadium. Irish Rugby fans knew where their loyalties lay and purchased a ticket to watch their heroes in green play, and before the game they listened to these very same songs of their favourite artists on the radio in the car, or on the coach, or on the train on their way to the match. The more gadget friendly Irish fans just downloaded the songs to their mobile phones.

You know what to expect from the concert, the artist's impressive back catalogue of hits belted out one after another. Totally entertaining. It was as stated on the tin! However, at Lansdowne Road, or at the Aviva Stadium, you were on virgin territory because you never knew what to expect when you watched Ireland play at home. That script has not been written in advance, the fans just want to be shook from top to bottom with the excitement of watching Ireland play, hoping to go home with a broad smile following a win.

'Losses are the building blocks of a stronger foundation. Resilience is the art of bouncing back after a loss. The pain of loss is temporary; the glory of victory is eternal. You will use your setbacks as fuel for your comeback. The stronger you come back, the harder you'll be to beat. Losing is not an option; you are coming back stronger.'

A quote from the Diary For Life

And, going back to a player crossing the white chalk line to represent the green jersey of Ireland, it was as if he was stepping on peat clad ground, only to find the ancient past alive on the terraces, a silent but soon to become a boisterous welcome. Playing on the pitch for any player must be like going on a trip through history. It was as though the Ireland players could hear the echoes of past glories from the men in green played out on Irish soil, but memories are the key not to the past, but to the future, and now it was their turn to make new memories and create a page in the history book of the players who famously wore the green jersey of Ireland.

'But in a larger sense, we cannot dedicate, we cannot consecrate, we cannot hallow this ground. The brave men, living and dead, who struggled here, have consecrated it, far above our poor power to add or to detract. The world will little note, nor long remember what we say here, but it can never forget what they did here.'

Abraham Lincoln, 16th President of the United States of America, 1861-65
– Lincoln delivered this speech during the American Civil War, on Thursday 19 November 1863, at the dedication of the Soldier's National Cemetery in Gettysburg, Pennsylvania.

What does it mean to a player to wear the famous green jersey of Ireland? Is it just a trophy for him to hang on the wall his living room, a trinket, a sweaty shirt with grass stains splattered over it as it is encased in a picture frame to show off to his friends and family as if to say, 'I did my bit for my country against an opposing nation'. Many players have worn the green jersey for the first time in their careers. Too many wannabee Ireland legends, to use the words of Tom Cruise in *Top Gun* (1986), crashed and burned on their debut. Just being given your international debut for Ireland is not in my opinion an embodiment of you being an Irish international rugby union player. For me, I want an Irish player who is willing to put his life on the line in the service of his country.

If I was a member of the backroom staff of Andy Farrell's side, I would remind the players what it meant to the fans to play for Ireland. With Andy's permission, and I do not think that he would have objected, I would have gathered the players in the dressing-room before a game and pinched the inspirational speech Tony D'Amato (played in the movie by Al Pacino), the coach of the Miami Sharks gave to his players in the 1999 movie, *Any Given Sunday*. I don't know about you, but if I was an Ireland player and I heard these impassioned words before I pulled on my green jersey, I would have ran through brick walls for my teammates. And, to echo the iconic line from D'Amato…

'That's a team, gentlemen, and either, we heal, now, as a team, or we will die as individuals. That's football guys, that's all it is. Now, what are you gonna do?'

John D. T. White
(Ireland caps 0, Appearances in front of the TV 275, Points scored 0, TV's smashed in the corner of the living room 10)

BIBLIOGRAPHY

https://www.lionsrugby.com/history/

https://punditarena.com/rugby/thepateam/the-all-time-greatest-lions-xv/

https://www.independent.co.uk/sport/rugby/rugby-union/international/the-boys-of-48-winning-the-grand-slam-for-ireland-1649372.html

https://www.newsletter.co.uk/sport/rugby-union/six-nations-remembering-irelands-inaugural-grand-slam-in-1948-4070667

https://www.world.rugby/tournaments/rankings/mru

https://www.irishexaminer.com/sport/rugby/arid-20325368.html

https://www.theguardian.com/sport/2009/mar/20/ireland-grand-slam-1948-six-nations

https://www.dib.ie/biography/strathdee-ernest-ernie-a8353

https://www.independent.ie/sport/rugby/its-a-different-world-since-it-all-began-in-1987-26767940.html

https://en.wikipedia.org/wiki/History_of_rugby_union_matches_between_Ireland_and_New_Zealand

https://www.irishtimes.com/sport/rugby/time-to-recognise-uncapped-irish-internationals-who-tackled-the-pumas-1.3692549

https://www.newsletter.co.uk/sport/rugby-league/ulster-great-willie-anderson-recalls-jailtime-in-argentina-over-flag-gaffe-3411984

https://web.archive.org/web/20070401091640/http://sport.independent.co.uk/rugby_union/article2248715.ece

https://web.archive.org/web/20071121112651/http://www.irishrugby.ie/6855_2821.php

https://www.independent.ie/sport/rugby/wheres-your-fking-pride-the-day-fitzie-rallied-nation/31024412.html

http://rugbyfootballhistory.com/timeline1950s.html

https://www.newsletter.co.uk/sport/rugby-union/past-great-noel-henderson-made-an-unforgettable-mark-for-ireland-in-famous-win-over-australia-3923703

https://www.newsletter.co.uk/sport/rugby-league/ulster-great-willie-anderson-recalls-jailtime-in-argentina-over-flag-gaffe-3411984

https://www.sportsjoe.ie/rugby/willie-anderson-flag-argentina-236275

https://www.irishtimes.com/sport/rugby/international/on-a-cold-december-day-ireland-s-15-victims-almost-slayed-the-all-blacks-1.3695547

https://www.independent.ie/sport/obituary-willie-duggan/36094755.html

https://www.theguardian.com/observer/osm/story/0,,1229715,00.html

https://www.irishtimes.com/life-and-style/people/willie-duggan-a-ferocious-ruthless-rugby-great-1.3205244

https://www.lionsrugby.com/2022/02/11/lions-legend-fergus-slattery/

https://www.independent.ie/sport/rugby/where-are-they-now/29839304.html

https://www.espn.co.uk/rugby/story/_/id/15333501/mike-gibson-most-complete-footballer-ever-saw

https://www.rugbyworld.com/rugby-positions/fly-halves/jack-kyle-65412

https://www.bbc.co.uk/news/uk-northern-ireland-25875102

https://www.irishtimes.com/sport/rugby/international/lions-memories-jack-kyle-s-major-impact-in-new-zealand-in-1950-1.3131107

https://www.irishtimes.com/sport/rugby/jack-kyle-irish-rugby-legend-who-led-a-life-less-ordinary-1.2019372

https://www.uafc.co.uk/viewtopic.php?t=17708&start=15

https://www.irishrugby.ie/2015/04/21/jim-mccarthy-a-rugby-life-in-quotes/

https://www.belfasttelegraph.co.uk/sport/rugby/there-was-only-one-jack-kyle-he-was-phenomenal-we-will-never-see-the-likes-of-this-great-rugby-player-again/30783834.html

https://www.bbc.co.uk/sport/rugby-union/35530075

https://www.irishtimes.com/sport/rugby/international/how-ucd-helped-brian-o-driscoll-s-change-of-direction-1.1726172

https://www.sixnationsrugby.com/2020/08/28/greatest-xv-profile-keith-wood/

https://www.independent.ie/sport/rugby/john-hayes-i-couldnt-face-that-again-i-was-gone-from-rugby-body-and-soul/26898635.html

https://www.independent.ie/sport/rugby/six-nations/odriscoll-you-knew-how-important-the-england-game-was-when-that-freak-john-hayes-was-crying/31022724.html

https://www.dailymail.co.uk/sport/rugbyunion/article-1253371/SIX-NATIONS-2010-Ireland-prop-John-Hayes-milk-cows-celebrate-100th-cap.html

https://www.sportsjoe.ie/rugby/john-hayes-ireland-202989

https://www.irishrugby.ie/2011/12/26/shannon-rfc-pay-tribute-to-bull-hayes/#:~:text=He%20epitomises%20humility%20and%20dedication,praise%20is%20sincere%20and%20heartfelt.

https://www.irishrugby.ie/2009/02/05/kidney-pays-tribute-as-hayes-hits-90/

https://www.limerickleader.ie/news/home/509757/dying-limerick-man-thanks-rugby-legend-john-hayes-for-gift-which-means-the-world.html

https://www.independent.ie/sport/rugby/six-nations/from-the-archives-when-paul-oconnell-took-a-not-so-subtle-dig-at-prince-william/34438721.html

https://www.irishcentral.com/sports/john-hayes-set-to-make-irish-rugby-history-with-100-caps-85336272-237686001

https://www.independent.ie/irish-news/triple-crown-rugby-legend-fitzgerald-recalls-snubbing-haughey-by-mistake/41364394.html

https://www.nytimes.com/1986/03/23/world/irish-rugby-the-attention-is-undivided.html

https://magill.ie/archive/ollie-campbell-and-fruit-machine

http://that1980ssportsblog.blogspot.com/2017/06/1983-british-and-irish-lions-warm-up-matches.html

https://www.balls.ie/rugby/donncha-ocallaghans-beautiful-quote-on-munster-is-the-antidote-to-cynicism-307337

https://www.belfasttelegraph.co.uk/sport/rugby/donncha-ocallaghans-last-laugh-on-rivals/28696734.html

https://alastaircampbell.org/2009/06/the-day-lions-skipper-paul-oconnell-took-my-trousers-down/

http://en.espn.co.uk/ireland/rugby/story/174947.html

https://www.lionsrugby.com/2021/03/04/lions-legend-ollie-campbell/

https://www.sportsjoe.ie/rugby/pic-ollie-campbell-did-the-nicest-thing-in-the-world-for-two-ireland-rugby-fans-3101

https://www.sporting-heroes.net/rugby/ireland-rugby/ollie-campbell-3802/international-rugby-union-caps_a02589/

https://www.irishexaminer.com/sport/rugby/arid-41087221.html

https://www.therugbypaper.co.uk/features/my-life-in-rugby/24039/my-life-in-rugby-ollie-campbell-former-ireland-and-lions-fly-half/

https://www.independent.ie/regionals/dublin/fingal/ollie-campbell-is-a-legend-in-life/27783053.html

https://thecircular.org/an-interview-with-ollie-campbell/

https://www.irishrugby.ie/video/ollie-campbell-park-home-of-old-belvedere/

https://www.rugbyfootballhistory.com/lansdowne.html

https://comeheretome.com/2015/02/03/45-years-ago-the-controversial-visit-of-the-springbok-team-to-dublin/

https://www.marxists.org/history/erol/ireland/springboks.pdf

https://www.irishexaminer.com/sport/rugby/arid-20148644.html

BOOKS

A Miscellany of Rugby's World Cup by John White – Pitch Publishing

The Story of Irish Rugby by Edmund Van Esbeck – Stanley Paul & Co. Ltd

Crossing the Line by Brendan Fanning - Reach Sports

Behind The Green Jersey, Playing Rugby for Ireland by Tom English – Arena Sport

Reggie Corrigan – Leinster In The Beginning by Reggie Corrigan – Hero Books, Dublin

Joking Apart, My Autobiography by Donncha O'Callaghan – Penguin Books

POEMS

The Sperrin Mountains by Aine MacAodha

Printed in Great Britain
by Amazon

f006f394-1b8c-4eb2-b146-698b2d4ed919R01